About the Editor

Michael J. Rosen has been called the unofficial organizer of the National Humor Writer's Union, a would-be organization that offers no benefits whatsoever to its struggling members (currently 450+). He has been called other things as well, like in third grade, and then in seventh grade especially, by certain older kids known as "hoods," who made his life miserable, specifically during gym class, lunch period, and after school, walking home. Later, much later, the *Washington Post* called him a "fidosopher" because of his extensive publications on dogs, dog training, and dog-besotted people. The *New York Times* called him an example of creative philanthropy in their special "Giving" section for persuading "writers, artists, photographers and illustrators to contribute their time and talent . . . to books" that benefit animal-welfare efforts and Share Our Strength's fight to end hunger. (Yes, he has published *Cooking from the Heart* and *Baking from the Heart,* two cookbooks with some 150 chefs to aid their cause.) As an author of a couple dozen books for children, he's been called—okay, enough with the calling business.

For nearly twenty years, he served as literary director at the Thurber House, a cultural center in the restored home of James Thurber. Garrison Keillor, bless his heart, called it (sorry), "the capital of American humor." While there, Rosen helped to create the Thurber Prize for American Humor, a national book award for humor writing, and edited four anthologies of Thurber's previously unpublished and uncollected work, most recently *The Dog Department: James Thurber on Hounds, Scotties, and Talking Poodles,* happily published by HarperCollins as well.

In his capacity as editor for this biennial, Rosen reads manuscripts year-round, beseeching and beleaguering the nation's most renowned and well-published authors, and fending off the rants and screeds from folks who've discovered the ease of self-publishing on the Web. Rosen also edited a lovely book, *101 Damnations: The Humorists' Tour of Personal Hells*; while some critics (all right, one rather outspoken friend) considered this a book of complaints, Rosen has argued that humor, like voting and protesting and returning an appliance that "worked" all of four months before requiring a repair that costs more than the purchase price—humor is about the desire for change. It's responding to the way things are when compared to the way you'd like them to be. And it's a much more convivial response than pouting or cornering unsuspecting guests at dinner parties.

For more information about Michael J. Rosen and his umpteen books, there is his ever-under-construction Web site (www.fidosopher.com), and for more information about this biennial anthology, there is www.mirth-of-a-nation.com. You can also e-mail him from either Web site, unless you plan on behaving like a hood, in which case he will ignore you, despite the fact that he knows this is an ineffectual ploy, as it has always been, ever since his mom and dad and Miss Mahoney the guidance counselor suggested it way back in seventh grade.

List of Works
(as of press time)
Joyce Carol Oates

I'm a Zombie
Guy Crazy
We Were the Bugzonics
Where Was I?
Foxfart
I'm Stuck in the Cupboard
Puddles (Poems)
Because I Wrote It and It Is There
Effluzia
Do Me If You Will
On Boxes: Observations
Under Boxers
Wonderbra (Odes)
Thems (Fictions)
Processed Words
Coming to a Bookstore Near You
I Just Wrote Another One
Hold On, I Just Got Out of the Shower (and Other Essays)
I'll Get It to You Thursday
With Shuddering Frequency
I'm Another Zombie
Untitled Novel
I Wrote It Anyway
Fast Opinions
A Quick History of the American Civil War (12 Volumes)
Stuck in Traffic (Poems)
I Thought You Said "Civil War," Sorry (and Other Essays)
Waiting in the Dentist's Office (and Other Poems)
The Prolix Saga (4 Volumes)

Dictions (Fictions)
The Pendletons of Puddlesfield
The Puddlesfields of Pendleton
Well F**k Me Sideways
I Like That Brad Pitt (and Other Observations)
Whodathunkit (I Did)
On Being Black (Essays)
Monica's Diary
I Am Kennedy (Eat Me)
Yalees Spit (and Other Plays)
Lint in My Pocket (Poems)
Penny Arcadia (Ephemera)
O.J. Simpson Is My Suitcase
James Joyce Carol Oates (Dreams)
Mike Tyson Electric Vaudeville
The Complicated Saga (5 Volumes)
Dental Cleavage: Thoughts on Lookism
Lisa Gotthead Is 13 Years Old Tomorrow
I Think I Stepped in Something (No, It's You)
Princess Diana's Last Buttered Moments (10-Play Cycle)
Correspondence (12 Volumes)
Selected Telephone Calls
Collected Menus
The Diary of Otto Frank (withdrawn)
Fiction Affected
Afflicted Affections
I Can't Stop Thinking About That Ben Affleck (and Other Observations)
(sic) (Thoughts)
Hitler's Panties (Poems)
Cleopatra's Penis (Lyrics)
Churchill's Titties (Libretto)
Contractual Obligation Novel
Is That the Time? (Stories)
I'm Thinking of Remodeling the Kitchen (and Other Observations)
I'm a Believer: Musings on the Monkees

I'm a Zombie Again
On Wrestling
On Baseball
On Knitting
On Sleeping
On Onanism
On or About June 24th
Tracy Bickle's First Orgasm
John Updike's Stutter (An Appreciation)
Pantaloons (Sudden Fictions)
Gas Station Attendants Is My Weakness (Stories)
Celluloid Cellulite: Older Women in the Movies
Whorehol (Art Criticism)
Moz/Art (Music/Art Criticism)
Danny Kaye Was Pretty Talented, You Gotta Admit
(Appreciation)
DVD/DDT: On Poisonous Popular Culture
Roach Motels (Travel Essays)
Popular Mechanics (Friends in Suburbia)
No, I Ordered the Chicken Marsala (Thoughts on Dining)
On a Roll (Restaurant Reviews)
I Think I'm Allergic to Peas (Musings on Food)
Bedpans: Hospital Experiences
On the Mend: Observations on Getting Well
Why Haven't You Called Me Lately? (and Other Whines)
Married to My Work
Tome (Novel)
I'm a Different Zombie, Completely Unlike the Other Ones
A Catholic Girlhood
On Being Jewish
Muslim Weekends
Buddhist Mistress
WASPism
The Norton Book of Knitting (Editor)
Remembering 'Nam (Sam I Am)
Presidential Platform
Winning Is the Only Thing (Essays)

Losing Is No Disgrace (Poems)
Hubert H. Humphrey: A Biography (3 Volumes)
The Life of Humbert Humbert (6 Volumes)
I'm Writing as Fast as I Can (Lyrics)
French Agricultural Systems of the 16th Century:
An Introduction
Selected Double Acrostics
Woody Allen Broke My Carburetor (A Gothic Romance)
Look for This Space (Selected Criticism)
The Oates Book of Eye Design
The Extremely Long Saga (6 Volumes)
Faster Than Stephen King (7 Novellas)
Dress Patterns
Interstate Maps (Editor)
This Just In . . .
Shrill Screeds
Collected Leaflets (1964–86)
The Oxford Book of Dog Grooming (Editor)
Boswell's Life of Johnson's Life of Boswell (Essays)
Internest
The Complete E-Mails (3 Volumes)
The Oates Bran Muffin Cookbook
Blistered Fingers (Memoir)
Harvard Schmarvard (Collected Graduation Speeches)
Remainder Bin (Essays 1968–1998)

—J. B. Miller

may CONTAIN nuts

A Very Loose Canon of American Humor

Edited by

Michael J. Rosen

Perennial Currents

An Imprint of HarperCollins*Publishers*

FIRST EDITION

Designed by Sparkomatic Studios

Library of Congress Cataloging-in-Publication Data
May contain nuts: a very loose canon of American humor / edited by Michael J. Rosen.—1 st ed.
   p. cm
ISBN 0-06-051626-7
1. American wit and humor. I. Rosen, Michael J., 1954– .
PN6165.M36 2004
817'.608—dc22
2004040899

04 05 06 07 08 ❖/RRD 10 9 8 7 6 5 4 3 2 1

Instructions for Reaching the Bridge to the Twenty-first Century

Okay, first thing you have to do is get on the boulevard of American dreams and stay on that until you reach the street of raised hopes. You can't miss it, it's after the road of heightened expectations, the avenue of very appealing visions and the alley of discarded notions and disproved theories. You take a hard right at the street of raised hopes and stay in the left-hand lane. You'll pass by the streets of recalcitrance, remorse, resentment, and reticence.

About one-half mile after reticence, raised hopes ends, right at this construction site of no particular significance. You're in tranquillity park now. Where the lake of forgotten purpose is? You also got the zoo of the perpetual second childhood there, the ballpark of the self-proclaimed champion, the soccer field of the unconvincingly youthful, and the statue of the unsigned artist. The hotel of unexpressed longing will be on your right and across the street are the borrowed trust building, the blinding ambition building, and the bank of universal value. That's the bank that has that new modern sculpture dedicated to the spirit of ceaselessly compounding interest installed in its plaza. That's also right where the street of raised hopes seems to end. Actually what it does though is it does like a little zigzag number and turns into the road of subtle misgivings.

Now you stay on the road of subtle misgivings, passing the avenue of honorable endeavor, the avenue of rewarding work, and the avenue of sublimated vocation. Immediately after that, you'll see the parking garage of wide-open possibilities. All fifteen stories. It's on your right. Pull in there and park. You're going to have to hoof it the rest of the way.

Take the footpath of security past the porch of happiness, the household of harmony, and the stoop of understanding and keep on walking until you reach the mountains of the new millennium. You'll see the tower of knowledge off a ways as well as the library of conventional wisdom, the school of kindness and civility, the church of human endeavor, the used-car lot of human folly, the mall of innumerable passions, and the grocery store of well-stocked plenty.

Behind the grocery store, back by the Dumpster of rotted desire, you'll need to slide down the bank of the stream of lost causes, wade through the water of dampened spirits, ford the river of unfulfilled promise, dash across the field of fallow abilities, and trudge through the swamp of good deeds left undone. The quicksand pit of tempting solutions should be avoided at all costs.

You used to have to climb the mountains of the new millennium, now you can just ride the escalator to tomorrow right up to the first summit. From there what you're looking for is the ladder of opportunity. There are lots of ladders around, but the one you want is beside the fire hydrant of gut feelings and the newspaper vending machine of all that is sad and lonely.

Climb the ladder of opportunity up to the steppe of joyful yet oddly sorrowful prospects. The stairway to really big ideas is close by, carved directly into the cliff face of sheer arrogance. When you get to the top of the stairs, go through the doorway of newly discovered options and down the hallway of somewhat distracting choices. You could normally take the roller coaster of life here, but it's closed for routine maintenance during the off-season. So instead what you have to do is you have to ride the moving sidewalk of carefree living down the concourse of lassitude past the snack bar of bittersweet memories and the delicatessen of foggy recollections. Swing across the pit of iniquity on the knotted rope of the very last chance, and the bridge to the twenty-first century is right there, right on the other side. You can't miss it.

—**Paul Maliszewski**

How to Contact Us

Should you, despite our best efforts, accidentally find our telephone number, we welcome all calls to our 24-hour service center. In order to reduce wait time on our phone lines we have made changes in our voice mail system. You may want to keep this as a handy reference should you call.

NOTE: The following options have changed. Drastically!
- 1 is the former 8. Press 1 to repeat these options
- 2 has been changed to 6. This also applies to your bank statements. Please note the change for future reference.
- 3 is now 13. No, you can't press 1 and then 3. You may press 9 and 4 to get the former three. You may also press 8 and 5. Please don't press 7 and 6 as that is a hard one for the voice mail to remember.
- 4 remains 4—questions about your account. However, we will no longer answer any personal questions. Press 4 only if you have general questions like, "What is an account?" or "Where do accounts come from?"
- 5 is what used to be 1. Press 5 to get recorded information of no pertinence to your immediate concerns.
- 6 becomes 9. This is accomplished by turning the phone upside down or standing on your head. If you have a rotary phone, stand on your head and remain on the line.
- Remember 7? Remember how you used to be so frustrated by the time you got to 7? You were annoyed that your area of concern had not been mentioned and you wondered whether you should press "0" and assume

you'd get an operator, but you weren't certain because on some systems the star button got you to the operator and that "0" might simply say "Not a valid entry" and make you start all over again? Well, go ahead. Try it. Just ask yourself, "Do I feel lucky?"

- 8 is now 3—technical questions. You will hear a series of clicks followed by a long pause when you will wonder whether you have been cut off or not. When you hear a busy signal you will know that you have been.
- 9 has changed to 5—the company directory. Press the first three letters of the person's last name. Please note, the letters of the alphabet have been changed so listen to the whole alphabet before making your selection. A is now G . . .
- 0 is nothing and always will be.

If you wish to reach an operator you may dial ∏ at any time. Your wait time is approximately. . . . 24 . . . hours. That's why it's called a . . . 24 . . . hour service center.

You may find it easier to access us through the Internet. If you don't have access to the Internet you can run a mouse over the following with the same result:

Click *here* to be taken *there* and end up who knows *where* because although you simply want to contact us we've got some very enticing *links* to distract you like *porno*graphy and *gambling* and *shopping* and *games* that will keep your mind from ever finding us.

If you have a suggestion or complaint please select from the following areas:

front cover (prettypicture@mirth.com)
back cover (blahblahblah@mirth.com)
spine (afraidtotell@mirth.com)
font (curlycues@mirth.com)
stickiness (pulp@mirth.com)
opacity (flimsiness@mirth.com)

pagination (Bob32451@mirth.com)
humor (nobodyhere@mirth.com)

Click *here* for the fun of clicking
Click *here* to see an image of a hand with its index finger pointing
Click *here* 100 times for carpal tunnel syndrome
Click *here* 1,000 times really fast to sound like a cricket
Click *here* if you want to donate a cup of rice to a poor child
Click *here* for the poor child's address and a map so you can find your way to the poor child's house and give him/her their cup of rice
Click *here* if you'll be bringing a salad or side dish

Send inquiries to leaveusalone@mirth.com/html. Html stands for Hate Mail. We hate mail. And we also hate vowels. That's why we leave them out of html. If you wish to write to us through the postal service and are willing to forgo vowels we will reply /prmptl (y is a vowel, dammit).

—**Marc Jaffe**

Contents

D I R E C

TORY

—**Stephanie Brooks**

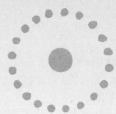

Contents

Throughout the pages of this volume, Ironic Times creators **Matt Neuman**, **Lane Sarasohn**, and **Larry Arnstein** have supplied a timeless, rather than up-to-the-minute, newscrawl, which appears across the bottom of the pages at irregular intervals.

A LIST OF CHARTS

—Andrew Marlatt

Special Interest Tables of Contents

Under increasing pressure to be all things to all people, Mirth of a Nation is providing customized tables of contents so that each reader may home in on those pieces most likely to suit his or her individual needs.

TV GUIDANCE

We know that, in their spare time, many of our readers watch television. What you might not know is that many of our *writers*, in *their* spare time, *write* for television. (Also, you might not know that italics is *far* underutilized—and takes up *less space!*) In an effort to compete in the marketplace where everything is vying for your attention and dollars, we are providing a sort of *TV Guide* to this volume of *Mirth of a Nation*. Readers can now *multitask*, spending the "prime time" of their lives reading/watching a book/the television. Or, you may think of this as our friends at amazon.com do so nicely, "if you liked [fill-in], then you'll like [fill-in]." In other words, if you enjoyed this television program, surely you'll enjoy another piece of writing by its creative genius or part-time staff writer.

You don't even need to check your local listings for times. An asterisk denotes stardom and the fact that the *May Contain Nuts* contributor is *acting in*, rather than writing for, a given program.

[1] *Mr. Altes plays Brad Pitt's stand-in; there are, according to the author, women in this country for whom this fact is an aphrodisiac.*

[2] *Mr. Altes is the one who shot Charlie Sheen.*

[3] *Mr. Altes is the one who saved Martin Sheen from being shot.*

[4] *Mr. Altes notes that this has paid more bills than humor writing ever will.*

THE GOURMAND'S TABLE OF CONTENTS

Convinced by the media that chefs are the new rock stars (which must mean that chef "whites" are the new black . . . and that dry cleaners will become the new wealth), we have hand-selected for the most discriminating readers those choice items in this volume of Mirth of a Nation that "really cook," as the rock stars would say. Here is a table of contents designed for those foodies who are the new roadies, those culinarians who know that "stressed tsuj" spelled backward is "just desserts," those insatiable souls always on the lookout for an authentic recipe for "eye candy." (A recipe for rock candy appears on page 379) While other pages in the present collection may also feature chefs, dining experiences, or edible items, here is your stocked pantry, arranged by key ingredient.

Additionally, because we are equally committed to truth in advertising, here is a favorite nut recipe especially created in our test kitchens for this third volume, *May Contain Nuts.*

Nut Case Brittle

A bold, buttery batch of nutty brittle. Do you need more entice-ment? They're a cross between the peanut brittle the lady next door brings over at Christmas to make you feel guilty that you don't shovel her walk and those spicy, pralined nuts that, with a few beers, you could consider a complete meal.

Makes about 1 pound (or one substantial, albeit regrettable, dinner)

> 4 tablespoons (1/2 stick) unsalted butter
> 1/2 cup packed light brown sugar
> 2 tablespoons light corn syrup
> 1/2 teaspoon ground cayenne pepper, or to taste
> 2 cups cashew pieces
> 1 cup pine nuts

1. Line a jellyroll pan with aluminum foil and butter the surface.
2. Place the butter, brown sugar, corn syrup and cayenne pepper in a medium-size, heavy-gauge saucepan over medium heat.
3. Stir everything together. Once the butter has incorporated the sugar and syrup, add the nuts. Continue to stir and raise the heat to medium-high. The nuts will become toasty brown in color and the mixture will begin to thicken and turn amber; this should take 5 minutes.
4. Dump the mixture into the pan and smooth the surface with the back of a spoon. Create as thin a layer as possible.
5. Once the brittle has cooled, break it into pieces, peeling away any clinging foil. Store in an airtight container.

FOR THOSE WHO FEEL ENTIRELY BUSHED

Another table of contents for those readers who are celebrating/ruing the recent elections. While the editors at Mirth have selected all pieces for a certain timelessness and temerity, it might be helpful to remember that all of the works appearing here were prepared for publication in the summer of 2003. In other words, we could not ask our contributors to prognosticate. Any gloating or hint of "sour grapes" is purely coincidental.

BELLE LITERATURE AND BEAUX ART

A survey course, if you will, of those pieces that refer to canonical figures in arts and letters. GED or equivalent suggested.

POPULAR GOOGLE SEARCH WORDS

A table of contents centered around topics frequently Googled, or added here for comic, narrative effect. (Readers might enjoy knowing that "google" did not come from the words "giggled" and "ogled," but rather, "googol," the word that designates the number 1 followed by 100 zeros.) We are indebted to Stephanie Brooks for the inspiration for this table of contents; her own "hit" piece appears on page 49. For the record, these are actual Google hits recorded at 2:30 p.m., EST, October 19, 2003, and arranged as if (!) to show how statistics lie.

Search Phrase	# of Google Hits	Page
kittens	1,710,000	253
puppies	2,630,000	172
lost cat	14,600	192
sex kitten(s)	48,200	70
babes	20,600,000	71
babies	23,300,000	291
Bible	21,600,000	74
celebrities	28,300,000	37
sex	29,000,000	294
rock star	503,000	209
centerfold	881,000	228
XXX	31,500,000	305
Xmas	3,300,000	26
"may contain nuts"	6,570	82
Michael Ian Black	7,000	40
John Edward	26,600	106

Search Phrase	# of Google Hits	Page
Orson Welles	201,000	332
Jerry Springer	266,000	93
Dale Earnhardt	450,000	50
Celine Dion	1,220,000	123
Arnold Schwarzenegger	2,030,000	297
Coca-Cola	2,100,000	78
nuts	5,100,000	91
just nuts	7,330	180
totally nuts	28,200	xxviii
George W. Bush	6,770,000	140
president	103,000,000	389
doctor	38,900,000	149
lawyer	11,100,000	350
Indian chief	80,600	213
chief	61,300,000	200
superchef	3,460	188
supermodel	442,000	301
superstar	798,000	83
porn star	1,680,000	93
star	65,800,000	328
astronaut	2,030,000	303
Harry Potter	7,220,000	261
God	60,600,000	102
death	43,000,000	56
life	388,000,000	17
afterlife	1,080,000	106
the	1,440,000,000	your choice

Letters to HQ

Being a selection of the letters, e-mails, and correspondence-like ephemera that has crossed our desk in the intervening years between volumes.

Dear Mirth HQ,

Enclosed is my exchange with Beck's publicist regarding his client's participation (or lack thereof) in January's *More Mirth* reading. Again, I am terribly sorry if you feel I somehow misled you regarding the musician's appearance; as I'm sure you can ascertain from the below exchange, I had every reason to feel confident that he would, indeed, show up.

Sincerely,
Jay Ruttenberg
Music Writer, *Time Out* (New York)

P.S. I suppose I should also take this time to apologize for what some have deemed my "excessive" profanity during the reading.

Dear D——,

In addition to working here at *Time Out*, I write humor pieces, mostly of the non-funny variety. I have a couple things in *More Mirth of a Nation: The Best Contemporary Humor*, a book recently published by HarperCollins. Most of the people in it are much more important than me—Steve Martin, Rick Moranis, Russell Crowe, etc. . . . Anyway, one of the pieces I wrote is about Beck. Or, more precisely, a kid trying to arrange for Beck to perform at his Bar Mitzvah party. On January 27, there is a New York reading with many of the book's contributors. I wanted to see if Beck might be interested in reading the piece, in part so I do not have to do it myself. I realize that this is something of a long shot—particularly as I do not believe Beck lives in New York?—but it seemed to be in the spirit of things to at least ask. It could be really funny, and my father says he will pay for Beck's plane ticket using his considerable stash of frequent flyer miles, aka "the pride of suburban Chicago."

Thank you,
Jay Ruttenberg

Dear D——,

I wrote you a couple weeks ago about a comedy reading for this book, *More Mirth of a Nation: The Best Contemporary Humor*, to see if I could invite Beck to read a humor piece about a Bar Mitzvah. Weird that you didn't respond! It's going to be quite a festive night, with readings by people who write for the *New York Times, The New Yorker* and even Bill Clinton (what? you thought he wrote all those funny speeches himself?). There are off-the-record rumors of a Rick Moranis appearance—and where Rick Moranis goes, Steve Martin follows. Even I know that. I'm assuming from your silence that Beck is not interested, but I wanted to contact you once more to see if he possibly *would* be interested in simply sending a tape of himself reading the piece. I think it would be awfully funny; my father says he will foot any postage bills that Beck accrues through this endeavor. (He has a special "contact" at FedEx.)

Thank you in advance for any consideration.
All the best,
Jay

hi jay,

beck is really backed up with press requests right now, and i doubt we will find time to do this, unfortunately.

don't remember your first e-mail, but i was on vacation for three weeks, so please accept my apology for not getting back to you. might have been accidentally deleted.

d——

Dear D——,

Must I be the one to remind you that your client has not released a decent album in nearly seven years? In pop time, seven years is . . . I believe it is death, actually. The Beatles released their whole oeuvre in seven years. Bob Dylan reinvented popular music in seven years. But Beck? Nothing but dreck!

I'm not going to be the one to tell you how to run your artist's life—though the fact that you allowed him to publicly date Winona Ryder, a NOTORIOUS career-killer, absolutely astounds me—but I certainly *do* think it would be in his best interests to make the reading. As mentioned in previous letters, the swinging shindig will feature writers from the *New York Times*, Bill Clinton's staff and also Rick Moranis. I wonder what Beck's fans might think if the *New York Times* were to describe him as a Republican who doesn't like *Ghostbusters*?

Sincerely,

Jay

Dear Editor(s):

In light of recent tragic events and an ever-increasing cultural sensitivity toward humor that is hurtful or offensive, you and your staff (if you have a staff) must be hard-pressed to find pieces that will not trigger boycotts, burnings-in-effigy, or Internet slander campaigns.

Allow me to offer my assistance in this matter. I have gathered a team of professional humor consultants, who have tested over 100,000 topics in focus groups across the nation. Following are subjects that are unequivocally acceptable for lampooning in your upcoming volume:

Hangnails; mild allergy symptoms (no peanut, antibiotic, or sperm allergies); long lines at the DMV (if attributed to enthusiasm); cute things babies do; unlikely performances of "Rapper's Delight" (especially by elderly women, animals, or Sir Ian McKellen); compact disc packaging (difficulty removing); American evening wear fashions of the late 1890s;

Zen Buddhism (offensive but violent backlash unlikely); irrational numbers (excluding pi); the Hawley-Smoot tariff; confusion related to Daylight Savings Time (avoid blaming farmers); lines from *Caddyshack* or *Monty Python and the Holy Grail* (if recited verbatim); the Muncie, Indiana, Council on Wastewater and Sewage Disposal (by special agreement); certain brands of fabric softener (write for approved list); any president between Van Buren and Cleveland (excluding Lincoln and Garfield); the decline and fall of *Scooby Doo* in the post-Scrappy era; constant use of the phrase "You go, girl!" (may be used as comedy or as target of comedy); golf (but not golf club policies); Mundane, Abstract Concepts and Categories, Capitalized Ironically; and early, impractical prototypes of the combine harvester.

Also, *Infinite Jest* (difficulty completing); Guy Fawkes Day; the length of German nouns (avoid terms coined between 1919 and 1945); moons of planets beyond Neptune; the Macarena (for use in analogies and metaphors only; do not trivialize Macarenian culture); pretentious color names used in catalogs (except Mahogany, Albino, and Herpetic Discharge); states of mind relating to relative position in the work week (cf. popular mimeographed Snoopy poster); the Periodic Table of the Elements (excluding actinide series); Madonna (but not *the* Madonna); and the relative sizes of major bodies of water (if located in nonhostile nations).

Finally, airline food (only if airplanes, airports, or air travel are not discussed or referenced); bad habits of males (excluding rape, murder); Thomas Pynchon (difficulty locating); Lamarckian evolution; minor complaints of aging baby boomers (permission expires in 2006); your own sexual proclivities, in graphic detail; dogs vs. cats (do not compare flavor); lawn gnomes; and Christians.

Sincerely,
Justin Warner
New York City

Editor's note: Mr. Warner graciously also enclosed the following article in his letter.

Gender Differences in Spontaneous Pseudo-Athletic Behavior
An Empirical Study by Justin Warner

Athletic and pseudo-athletic competition has remained primarily a male preoccupation since long before the first Olympics. For example, evidence suggests that male clans of the early hominid Australopithecus africanus developed a complex, cricket-like game involving heavy stone disks, a wooden paddle, and the ashes of their deceased ancestors. In ancient Egypt, slaves who were sealed in tombs with their masters were said to compete to be the first to die, by such means as self-asphyxiation and repeatedly slamming one's head in the lid of the sarcophagus. Indeed, impromptu competition among males has been documented even outside the human species: male red-tailed deer, for example, have been observed not only attempting to outrun each other for no apparent reason, but also taunting their opponents with elaborately choreographed "end zone" dances when successful.

Is the tendency to create competitive quasi-sports specifically endemic to the male gender? We set out to answer this question by isolating small, single-sex groups in windowless rooms equipped with hidden cameras and a few randomly selected objects. Their behaviors are summarized in the following table.

EXAMPLES OF OBJECT USE BY MALE AND FEMALE GROUPS

Objects in Room	Usage by Female Group	Usage by Male Group
6 frozen trout filets GE microwave oven 2 sticks butter Thyme	Dinner.	Using trout filets as bats, attempted to knock butter sticks into open microwave oven from 5-yard distance. Bonus points were awarded for knocking oven door closed. Thyme sprigs used for scorekeeping.
2 folding chairs Set of 8 coasters 2 umbrellas	Sat in chairs, reminisced about parents' cocktail parties, discussed Gene Kelly movies.	Two teams attempted to toss coasters into upside-down umbrellas. Umbrellas guarded by goalies who used folding chairs to block opposing team's throws. Use of hands by goalie penalized by repeated spankings with collapsed umbrella.
Large, empty cardboard box Pickle fork	Using pickle fork, broke down cardboard box, stacked pieces neatly in corner.	Using pickle fork, players attempted to flip cardboard box from one end of the room to the other. Fewest number of flips won the match. Players frequently stabbed one another's buttocks with pickle fork (reasons unclear).
64-oz. Listerine® The *Bhagavad-Gita*	Spiritual enlightenment, oral hygiene verses.	Players took turns reading aloud. For every mention of the word "Krishna," other players drank a shot of Listerine. Last man standing declared winner.
Duct tape Sony PlayStation™ Former Canadian prime minister Brian Mulroney	Duct-taped over drafty A/C vent; tinkered with PlayStation but lost interest; thoughtfully analyzed Quebeçois secessionist movement.	Competed to see who could run 100 times around the perimeter of the room most quickly while duct-taped to PM Mulroney. Winner awarded Sony PlayStation.

If, as this study suggests, the male instinct to compete is indeed innate, it may be possible to rechannel its more destructive manifestations, such as the nuclear arms race, into relatively harmless, controlled competitions like those described above. We call on the world's leaders to do so, and note that at the time of this writing, Mr. Mulroney is still available at a reasonable hourly rate.

July 22, 2003
Dear Editors,

I received your piquant flush letter, the one that said "to publish your piece would violate a pact Mirth of a Nation has with its readers—namely that its contents will be, in fact, mirthful."

In light of your rejoinder, I have reviewed my essay and found it to be side-splittingly hysterical. Perhaps my rejection stems from a more sinister reason. I believe you are discriminating against me because, as the subject matter of my submission indicates, I am a male model. You assume that because I model, I cannot be funny.

Now I admit there may be some inverse correlation between beauty and humor (humor as an evolutionary compensation for the aesthetically challenged), but please keep an open mind. Models can be funny too! I remember a particularly amusing anecdote Tyra Banks told on *The Tonight Show*. Something about a limousine being late to pick her up to go jewelry shopping while she was vacationing on Ibiza (service is so spotty in the Balearic Islands!).

Do reconsider my article (and your prejudices). Must humor be borne of parental neglect, schoolyard trauma, and chronic romantic rejection? Can't it rise from adoration, flattery, and pampering? Must my comedy career be hamstrung by my high cheekbones? I ask you, are cheekbones destiny?

Steve Altes
Humorist, first; Hot Male Model, second

August 14, 2003

Dear Editors,

I see you've passed on a second round of my of submissions. I think you're being short-sighted. Mirth needs me because, unless *Advertising Age* has been lying to us all these years, Sex Sells. Having a model as a contributor would give Mirth sex appeal.

Anna Kournikova's career owes more to her backside than her backhand. Even staid old CNN promoted Paula Zahn as "just a little sexy" over the sound of a zipper opening!

Picture this: *"Mirth of a Nation . . . Now with Humorist Centerfolds!"*

Writing humor is like being naked anyway—baring your soul, exposing your vulnerabilities. Why not take it all the way? Nude humorists! Who among us doesn't harbor a secret desire to see Sarah Vowell in the raw? I know I do. Rick Moranis sprawled languidly on a bear-skin rug (caption: "Honey, I Shrunk My Gonads"). David—no, wait . . . *Amy* Sedaris in a bed of rose petals.

Enthusiastically,
Steve Altes

P.S. I'm nude right now!

September 1, 2003

Dear Editors,

Evidently you found my online portfolio. Hooray for Google. Yes, I am a *hand* model. And yes, hand modeling is a *real* form of modeling. I don't tell you that humor isn't a *real* form of literature (even though, ahem, my bookstore sandwiches *Mirth of a Nation* between *The Duct Tape Book* and *The Tenth Garfield Treasury*, not with Twain and Thurber).

It was good of you not to make the obligatory "did you see the *Seinfeld* episode where George Costanza was a hand model" remark. You rise in my esteem as a result.

Anyway, pursuant to my previous letter, I enclose a photo of myself, on the job as a hand model—your inaugural humorist centerfold!

Persistently,
Steve Altes

Editor's note: We are pleased to publish a "work" of Mr. Altes on pages 228–29.

Dear Mirth,

I'm sure your readers travel as much as I do, so I thought your book would be the right place to send this letter. If it's not, maybe you can just write back and tell me I'm not out of my mind.

I'm waiting to board my flight to San Diego when the gate attendant begins her litany of the anointed travelers deemed worthy to board the aircraft before the rest of the unwashed masses. (Understand, I am among the worthy by virtue of my Premium Mileage Membership.) But this announcement makes no sense to me. Airlines preboard old people traveling without their children, young people traveling without their parents, parents with babies. (First Class may, of course, board at their leisure, but if they were truly "at their leisure" they wouldn't be in an airport, carrying their laptops and cell phones.)

They then call on frequent fliers, a group that, according to each airline includes Gold Members, Elite Members, 100K Mileage Members, Premium Fliers, One-Pass Members and the more showy Aviators, World Perks Members and Rapid Rewards Members. They may as well include the infirm, the injured, the depraved, the indecisive, the condescending, the annoying, the sarcastic, the jet-lagged, and then wrap it up with my personal favorite, the "Anyone needing a little extra time to board."

Who the hell is that? Someone who wants to try out the seats? Someone who wants to chat with the attendant about the shortage of honey-roasted peanuts these days? I swear, one time in the Ottawa airport, the attendant finished her preboarding process and two guys and I were left in the gate area.

Here's the part I really don't get. As a frequent flier, the very last thing you want to do is spend even more time on a plane. The people who need the time provided during preboarding are the *In*frequent Fliers: the folks seated on the aisle who buckle and unbuckle—twice—before their row is full. They can't quite grasp that "ABC" is on the right and "DEF" is on the left. They need to look around, get comfortable, and read the card in the seat pocket in front of them.

As it stands, the airlines can make whatever announcement they like but all we hear is this: "Thanks for flying with us week after week after week and for knowing the Starbucks guy by name near Gate C32 at O'Hare and thanks for continuing to fly into Minneapolis even though you have to walk six miles to your rental car. Thanks for trusting us with your life as you leave behind family, friends and accumulating e-mails in your in-box. Thanks for being grateful for the child-size portions of "grilled" chicken. Thanks again for your continued loyalty. Welcome aboard!"

We, the Too-Frequent Fliers, we get it! We absolutely get it! We know about limiting our carry-on bags. We exercise caution when opening the overhead bins. We've read *Skymall* over and over and in a moment of recirculated air delirium, have come within seconds of actually ordering the martini mister.

So why "reward" us by having us spend the most amount of time in our seats? Frequent Fliers should be allowed to virtually jump into their seats as the jetway is firing up to leave the plane. Honor us with the following announcement: "Attention, Frequent Fliers: your flight is departing in T-minus 3 minutes." Or better yet, come tap me on the shoulder while I'm sipping my latte and cracking the cover of the new Dean Koontz, and say, "Run for it."

Sincerely,
Renee A. James
Allentown, PA

To: MARIAM SESE-SEKO
Widow of the former Minister of Petroleum Resources
Nigeria
Subject: Urgent Business Proposal

It is with my profound dignity that I write to you in Nigeria with this very important and highly confidential letter. First, I must solicit your strictest secrecy in this transaction. I am Dick Cheney of the United States of America, and I have an URGENT and CONFIDENTIAL business proposal for you.

Due to the arcane and reactionary "insider-trader" laws of the democratic country of the United States of America of which I am Vice-President, certain money that I have obtained in a completely respectable fashion is now in dispute. I assure you that said money was obtained in honorable transactions during my time as Chief Executive Officer of an American oil company and as a result of my secret business partnership and torrid love affair with Martha Stewart, of whom I am sure you are familiar.

We have acquired a huge reserve of money from our recent business transactions. However, by virtue of my high-ranking position in our government and a frivolous legal investigation against my colleague, we cannot acquire this money in our name. I was therefore delegated as a matter of urgency by my colleague to look for an overseas partner into whose account we would transfer the sum of 2,711,900,000.00 Nigerian Naira (equivalent to US $21,320,000.00).

I have acquired your name from a mutual contact who assures me of your discretion and prior experience at transactions of this nature. I noticed on the Internet that you had been able to transfer the money of your late husband out of your country using a similar business model, and I hope, God willing, that you can use your considerable expertise to assist us in our dire time of need.

I guarantee that this proposal is 100% risk-free, provided that you treat it with utmost secrecy and confidentiality. For your dutiful assistance in allowing this money to be deposited into your bank account, we would be happy to share some of the proceeds with you. For the temporary use of your bank account, we would be willing to offer to you 1,000,000.00 (ONE MILLION) Nigerian Naira, as well as a lifetime subscription to *Martha Stewart Living*, which this month has a lovely cover feature on how to make homemade caramel-covered apples for Halloween. As one who has personally tasted Martha's caramel-covered apples many times, I know that you will not want to miss out.

Your urgent response will be highly appreciated to enable us to transfer the funds during this present quarter of the year 2002. Please use my Hotmail account listed below to contact me, as other methods of contact may not be secure. I thank you for listening to my plea, and, if you are able to assist us, I implore upon you to contact me as soon as possible.

Thank you and God Bless.

Yours faithfully,
Dick Cheney
prezofvice46@hotmail.com

—Joe Lavin

Dear Chile Pepper,

Here is a picture of my daughter on Halloween. Love your magazine!

Robert Orsini
Morgantown, PA

Dear Robert,

We want you to know that we share your pain; two years ago, our Peruvian ajis became infested with babies (*Rattus carpita*). We were very lucky to have discovered them early, and a quick application of sulfur saved about half of our yield.

Your case seems much more advanced. Sadly, once the larvae are in the fruit (as is obviously the case here), practical control is impossible. You've probably lost most of your crop to premature drop by this point. To avoid the possibility of the pest wintering to haunt you next year, you should burn all your crop residue, including noninfested chiles, as well as other members of the nightshade family such as potato, eggplant, and tomato.

Several companies manufacture a product known as "Baby Powder," but we have been very disappointed with it effectiveness as a repellant.

—David K. Gibson

April 17, 2003
Dear Editors,

I am submitting these seven essays for your consideration for Mirth of a Nation in a last, desperate attempt to secure a position playing guitar in the Rock Bottom Remainders, Dave Barry's rock band.

This may sound like a silly, naïve ambition. After all, who *wouldn't* want to join a legendary band, and perform with rock-and-roll superstars? But I assure you, I'm not just some silly, wide-eyed kid.

Of course, like perhaps many people of my age, early exposure to RBR had a definite giddy effect on me. My first experience hearing the band galvanized me into abandoning my studies in medical school and joining the many "Remaindroids" who followed the band from book conference to book conference.

But unlike my peers, I had the drive and audacity to emulate my heroes and, like them, dedicate my life to music. I threw myself body and soul into my guitar playing and singing, neglecting my health and personal hygiene. I learned the entire RBR oeuvre—the songs that are now synonymous with the band—like "Wild Thing," "Proud Mary," "Midnight

Hour," "Smoke on the Water" and "Closer to Home (I'm Your Captain)."

For a time, I performed with one of the many Rock Bottom Remainder tribute bands. Ours was known as Torn Covers— quite a clever name, I thought, considering we were a "cover" band (ha!) "ripping off" RBR. We actually enjoyed some success for a time, but broke up over artistic differences (chiefly, whether it was enough to cover RBR songs, or whether we should exactly replicate their performances. I was in the latter camp. I didn't spend endless hours learning the nuances of each guitar lick only to have my bandmates ruin it with their pathetic "improvising.")

Once Torn Covers broke up, it became clear to me that my destiny lay not in emulating RBR but in actually being a part of it. Unfortunately, my increasingly desperate requests for an audition were answered only with auto-signed glossies of the band and a form letter suggesting I join their fan club.

Then, I discovered something. Something that led directly to this letter to you, and my desire to be published in Mirth of a Nation. As you are probably well aware (but, believe me, not so the vast majority of RBR fans), the Rock Bottom Remainders insist that all their band members be published authors! I had thought it odd that they performed primarily at book-related venues, but I was totally unprepared for this seemingly frivo- lous employment requirement.

Still, if they weren't eccentric, we wouldn't love them so much, right? I mean, you've gotta love a band that in a single set can convincingly jump from "Purple Haze" to "These Boots Were Made for Walkin'."

In any case, I have thrown myself into writing with the same fervor I threw myself into learning Amy Tan's dance steps. I hope you will find at least one of the enclosed essays worthy of inclusion in your next book. I have chosen Mirth of a Nation because RBR guitarist Dave Barry himself has published work with you. I'm hoping a piece from me in your pages will not escape his attention.

Thank you for your kind consideration. I look forward to

hearing from you soon. And if you happen to speak with Dave Barry, please tell him that I can play the lead solo to "Born to Be Wild" with my teeth.

Sincerely,
Bob Hirshon

Editor's note: We are pleased to publish a work by Mr. Hirshon on page 123. We have yet to learn anything regarding his status as a member of the aforementioned band.

May
CONTAIN
nuts

Business Tips of the Dead

HENRY ALFORD

The dead, as we are reminded every time we see Keith Richards or Carol Channing, can exhibit a power from beyond the grave. But who knew that this power could take the form of management strategies and tips on leadership? Recent books have flouted the business savvy of various erstwhile luminaries—Jesus, Moses, Elizabeth I, Machiavelli, Shakespeare, W. C. Fields, Goldilocks, the Road Runner, and the *Star Trek* crew. Who's next? We can only imagine.

FROM *PIECE OF MY HEART: THE JANIS JOPLIN GUIDE TO MANAGEMENT*

Joplin knew that if you started drinking after you'd taken a few hits of speed, you ran the risk of becoming messy and vague; but if you got drunk and *then* took the speed, you could prolong the drunk, you could power the drunk.

Power your drunk. Take a bold step toward prioritizing your company's future by implementing that growth-centered, results-driven, Big Picture Thinking change *after* you've already scored a victory with a smaller, easier change. The second change can coast in the first one's jetstream.

You'll see the change. Your company's future will be a better place. *Then* you can look at your spreadsheet and be confident you won't wake up with a blinding headache on the first day of your next quarter; *then* you can lie in a hotel bed and take heroin with a reporter from *Rolling Stone*.

FROM *CALL ME COCO: SWINGIN' DEALS WITH COCO CHANEL*

Most people do not realize that fashion legend Coco Chanel was born Cocoa Chanel, but dropped the *a* following the advice of a consultant. The consultant explained that, in terms of establishing a brand, too narrow a focus could hurt the Chanel brand. "Cocoa is very specifically either the powder made from cacoa seeds, or the refreshing, hot beverage made from that powder," the consultant told Chanel. "But Coco . . . Coco could be coconut or *coq au vin*, or cocktail-cocktail, or company-company, or cost effective–cost ineffective, or commission basis–commission yield, or coaxial cable–coaxial cable storage unit, or cold welding–cold welding helmet, or Co-Chair of the Cote d'Azur Congress for Constant Coconut Oil-Enhanced Copulation."

Lesson #37: Leave your options open.

FROM *VLAD TO BE HERE: VLAD THE IMPALER MEANS BUSINESS*

One summer day in 1463, one of Vlad's sentries told him the whereabouts of Vlad's archrival, Brad the Extruder. Vlad quickly tracked Brad down in a field in a remote Transylvanian town; then Vlad lunged at his archrival, gored him with a pike, carried him to a steep-faced mountain, removed him from the pike and dragged him to the mountain's summit, then dropped him off a cliff such that he fell directly onto the up-pointed pike's sharp tip, now white-hot from a roaring blaze built at the pike's base.

Vlad's paradigm is one we can all learn from. Vlad was successful not because he had insider information, but because he *strategically implemented* this insider information. The implementation was brilliantly simple. 1) Find archrival. 2) Kabob him.

FROM *LASSIE, CEO*

While her competitors were all too happy to meet the low
demands of others' expectations of them—by licking all stains
on the kitchen floor in an attempt to locate a beverage source,
or by issuing stalactites of drool while watching others eat—
Lassie incentivized herself. Lassie found her niche. Lassie
found the brand that was Lassie: she made herself the dog who
alerts her master of others' imminent death. Your company can
benefit from hiring a similarly incentivized individual, an outside consultant who tours your premises and tells you not to ask
Tom in H.R. to send that fax for you, because Tom is minutes
away from the massive coronary seizure that will finally fell
him; someone who'll encourage you to start grooming a succes-
sor for Noreen in Accounting because research suggests she is
130 years old. In short, you need a Lassie. You need to get help.

... Smart bombs destroy Mensa headquarters ... Yacht club
evicts boat people ... Pie in the sky just that, says Air Force ...
Man drinks eight glasses of water in one day ...

The Ultimate B&B?

HENRY ALFORD

*Each sentence of the following reconstituted "brochure" is taken
verbatim from an actual guidebook or from a Web site for one of 55
bed-and-breakfasts nationwide. Only the names have been
changed to protect the innocent.*

The Ravenscroft is a truly unique inn amid the country's
largest concentration of furniture showrooms. Hosts Vann
and Linda Bartle are likely to welcome guests wearing turn-of-
the-century costumes. Their 13-year-old daughter, Naomi, frequently delights guests with her classical piano pieces. *Artist in
residence!*

The Ravenscroft can sleep six people (it helps if you are
very good friends). Our claim to fame is the unique customized
stenciling in each room and our "early attic" décor. But it's the
bric-a-brac that sets the tone. The cozy sitting room and dining
area in the main house contain trophy birds and mammals,
many of which Linda has stuffed.

In each bedchamber, you will find a Victorian nightgown
and an old-fashioned sleep-shirt laid out for a lullaby night. The
bed and table linens are hand-pressed and smell as if they've
been dried on a line in the Alps.

In every way your hosts try to transport guests back 100
years to a gentler era where people cared about each other.
Authentic Civil War music playing in the background brings
this historic time to life. Guests will be involved in hands-on
demonstrations involving cannons, muskets, and uniforms on a
daily rotation.

Restoration, of course, is constant. The second renovation

stage has resulted in a two-level addition, decorated with the assistance of an artist who has "an idea a minute." You can actually observe creek life through a glass coffee table in the sitting room. Though few of us today would want to live day to day with the rigors of pioneer life, we can still savor a sample of it, thanks to the Bartles.

The front yard has been landscaped in a manner so no maintenance is required. Although the Bartles no longer keep pigs, horses, or chickens, you'll be entertained by several friendly cats and a herd of visiting javelinas (sticks are provided to keep these somewhat stinky wild pigs from poking their noses into your business). Joy reigns. Observe your being relax and expand. Our dogs will greet you.

Guests staying on the upper floors might be startled by the sight of "Chili Bean," a star bovine on the rodeo circuit who died of natural causes.

Here's good news for guests: Some of what you see is for sale. Linda gives a fascinating tour, which can last as long as two hours (can last much longer).

ROOMS

The Egyptian Room is designed to make a couple feel like Antony and Cleopatra camping out in the desert. Guests remove shoes upon entering. The bathroom door is a life-size statue of King Tut, opened by tugging his beard, and the bathroom itself resembles the inside of a pyramid. The innkeepers try to maintain a romantic atmosphere that is not suitable for young children.

Aunt Myrtle's Bedroom was originally the dining room. You will enjoy the same hospitality experienced by thousands of guests, including Lady Bird Johnson, Alex Haley, George Bush's staff, congressmen, senators, and Fabio.

Uncle Frank's Room, found on the first floor, has easy access to the dining room and invites you to get to know Uncle Frank through pictures and memorabilia.

The Harley Room is decorated with motorcycle memorabilia. Its tin roof and rain make a great combination. Just like Nature, this room holds its own little wonders.

The Athena-Wise Artisan is a carpeted room that says, "I'm glad you're here. I've created a relaxing place just for you."

The Paint Brush Room, at $65 per night, is an experience, not just a room.

In the neighboring yellow three-story 1864 mansion, mere whimsy gives way to flat-out fantasy. The three guest rooms are named the Carousel (merry-go-round appointments), Reflections (mirrors), and Iowa State (masculine). The slate-floor tavern beyond the dining room has a working fireplace and is reputedly where James Michener wrote the outline for *Chesapeake*.

The hot tub is in a wonderful historic setting, with an eclectic monogrammed towel collection. Don't forget to check out the framed hatchet hanging on the kitchen wall. It was found in a closet during a 1948 renovation; police have determined it was not the murder weapon.

Breakfast is where the magic happens. Enjoy Vann's "mouth-watering" breakfast that has a touch of gourmet (sometimes there is a little brandy or orange liqueur in the product). You may then look forward to Linda's breakfast, each one an edible adventure! "Our own sausage." Everything is garnished.

. . . Idle gossip plagues rumor mill . . . Edible clothing, wearable food vie for "next big thing" . . . Masochists strike for lower pay, worse conditions . . . Comics' protest turns into laugh riot . . .

Olive Fab: The War Diaries of an Embedded Fashion Journalist

HENRY ALFORD

07:00 In Iraq, fashion meets its greatest challenge: this is a country bereft of alcohol and colorful homosexuals. *Women's Wear Daily* has sent me here to try to answer the questions, "Is there style in war?" and "War: In or Out?" The answer to these two questions, my brief exposure to the troops leads me to believe, are "No" and "Out": everyone here, it seems, has fallen prey to the unimaginative, unstructured look of camouflage. Camo, camo, camo—Jean Paul Gaultier and Marc Jacobs sent this stuff down their runways *two years ago*. *Talk* about derivative! These people aren't referencing a look, they're color-Xeroxing it. I mean, hello.

Out on the tennis court of the Kuwait Hilton, one of the officers who's giving me and the other journalist "embeds" our training hands me *my* camos and then asks me, "What's your name, son?"

"Bruce Plushton."

"What publication you with, Bruce?"

"*W.W.D.*," I mumble, hoping the abbreviation sounds butch, and possibly related to wrestling.

"You don't look too thrilled about the uniform."

"Well, I don't love-it-love-it-love-it," I confess, fingering the dun-colored mass, and imagining it in another fabric, like shantung or shirred georgette. Every garment tells a story, and the story these are telling is, I Know No Dry Cleaners.

"This gonna be a problem?" the officer asks.

"No, sir," I say. "I will Iraquiesce."

I don the fatigues; but not before accessorizing with black

Armani underwear, a Hugo Boss belt, and Prada boots. You say olive drab, I say olive fab.

13:00 Oh, Style, where are you? (*Oh, la mode, où êtes-vous?*) One of the biggest improvements in combat gear in recent years, I'm told, is our soldiers' night-vision equipment. I'm shown an illustration of the PVS-14 night-vision goggle, which mounts on a Kevlar helmet, and greatly intensifies ambient light. The illustration is not without promise (*c'est pas sans promise*). Indeed, it occurs to me that maybe night-vision goggles are the little black dress of warfare—they take you from day *into* evening. But suddenly I need to see the goggles on a soldier, so I jump in a Jeep, drive for an hour (idea for fragrance: Sandstorm. "Sandstorm . . . The future is unseeable.") and find the 101st Airborne Division on the outskirts of Baghdad. I gaze diagnostically at a recruit and his goggles. Are they stylish? No, they are insectoid. Are they *très à la mode*? Only if your mode is house flies.

Another stirring example of *"Plus ça change."*

16:35 I scurry amidst the 101st, who are skirmishing with the Republican Guard, and ask various recruits if they think it's possible to be stylish during warfare. They seem distracted, unwilling to talk. One becomes quite irritated by my presence, so I get huffy right back at him. He gets more irritated, I get huffier. Finally, he asks me to leave, causing me to snap, "A little Botox would do wonders for all those screw-toppy frown lines on your brow, darling! Maybe then they wouldn't call you a jarhead!"

21:34 The assignment is taking its toll on me. I have become bitchier than normal, and no one thought that was possible. I need Evian, sushi, track lighting. I walk into the canteen and fall into conversation with a corporal who is appalled by my assignment, not to mention my glibness. He thinks I am belittling the extremely noble and generous efforts of my country's servicemen. He tells me an emotionally harrowing story about a marine who died in combat and suddenly I'm sobbing. It's true: I'm a big bitch. I'm shallow as glass. I feel awful.

I apologize to the corporal. I plead mea culpa. His response surprises me: "To tell you the truth, I'm of the opinion that embedding and the constant broadcasting of war make war banal. It trivializes it." I nod my head. He continues, "But *you're* not a trivializer, Bruce. You're just someone who needs to have a licensed professional sit him down and tell him all about lithium."

"Thank you, sir," I say, moved. "You're very generous."

"Anything for my country."

HARMON LEON'S OFFICE PRANKS
BIBLICAL OFFICE PLAGUE

things needed
- thousands of locusts
- an altered Bible
- large garbage bags

Come into the office one day, reading the Bible, paying close attention to biblical plagues. Like Nostradamus, show direct correlation to biblical plagues to events that have occurred recently in the office. Perk coworkers' interest in the sections that talk about locusts, claiming your office will be infested with this vermin due to a prophecy written thousands of years ago—and there's nothing anyone can do about it! Most likely coworkers will scoff, claiming that you are dribbling the ranting of a madman. Drop the subject. Later in the day, release thousands of locusts, which you have hidden in garbage bags under your desk. Say to everyone, "See, I told you so!" Treat yourself to a coffee break.

Summer Recipes

HENRY ALFORD

"Seasonal cooking is anyway better suited to those who live in sunnier climates. The rest of us need to make the most of what warmth is offered, and much of the time this has to emanate from the kitchen rather than from the skies outside. Summer, then, is an idea, a memory, a hopeful projection."
—Nigella Lawson, *Forever Summer*

SUN-DRIED TOMATOES
8 tomatoes
6 c. olive oil

Unscrew a 100-watt lightbulb while it is still gorgeously warm. With a rubbing motion, thrill the skins of the tomatoes until they start to pucker and tumesce. Uncork the oil; drizzle onto tomatoes until lubricious.

SKINNY-DIPPING AT NIGHT
2 qt. water
25 lbs. cocoa

Store the water in a cool place, allowing it to bio-ripen for a period lasting months or even years. Meanwhile, fill your largest roasting pan with cocoa. Roll in cocoa.

GONE FISHIN'
1 telephone
1 couch

Unplug the telephone and assume a position on your couch that suggests an odalisque or any late-career Ingres portrait. Should people or problems present themselves, bite into a nougatty chocolate and say teasingly, "I can't help you. I'm very Ingres-y with you." Let the slipcovers puddle around you like a light vinaigrette.

SUMMERY CHINESE TOBOGGAN SALAD

  1 can bamboo shoots
  1/2 c. sesame oil
  4 stalks celery, chopped
  Juice and zest of 3 lemons
  1 wooden toboggan

Put the toboggan in a food processor and pulse for ten seconds on Eviscerate. Remove the splinters from the processor and toss with other ingredients. Arrange on a plate with your bare hands, letting your fingers burrow into the mixture as they do when encountering the rich loam of the earth. Strike your gong.

SUMMER ROMANCE

  2 c. high-quality vinegar
  10 toffee caramels

Unsheath the caramels laughingly, unconcerned of outcome. Fork-prick to soften. Using the soft pads of your thumb and index finger to palpate the caramels, and the moist cavern of your mouth to remove their protective shell, tease them into the vinegar, saying, "Mummy knows what's best." Put the whole concoction away someplace cool and dark. Have a glass of Prosecco with a friend, displaying blitheness and a tendency, when food has been dropped onto the floor, to plop it back onto your plate with an expression that is soulful and plump-lipped. Can you leave the vinegar alone for a period lasting between three days and three weeks? Try to, darling—what you're doing here is tempering yourself as well as the candy. Enjoy this. Because when you return to the vinegar, the caramels will be gone.

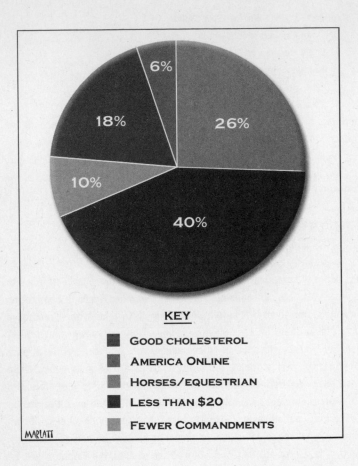

KEY

- Good cholesterol
- America Online
- Horses/equestrian
- Less than $20
- Fewer Commandments

MARLATT

Romeo and Juliet Versus Mrs. Jackson's Seventh-Grade English Class

ETHAN ANDERSON

Why do they teach Romeo and Juliet *in seventh grade? When boys turn 13? When Romeo and Juliet are medieval seventh-graders? When they make love once and kill themselves? What are they thinking?*

THE AVERAGE BOY SITTING BEHIND SUZY WARNER
IN MRS. JACKSON'S CLASS

One, Suzy Warner is incredibly hot.
Two, no one is hotter than Suzy Warner.
Three, I'm hungry.
Four, last year I was a kickball superstar.
Five, this year I am a virgin.
Six, Suzy Warner is incredibly hot.
Seven, there's a muffled noise coming from the front of
the room.
Eight, the muffled noise is Mrs. Jackson, trying to teach.
Nine, Mrs. Jackson is incredibly hot.
Ten, Suzy Warner beats Juliet
any century, any day of the week.
Eleven, how hot would Suzy Warner look in the 14th century?
Twelve, the correct answer is crazy 14th-century hot.
Thirteen, let's say I'm Romeo
and Suzy Warner not only does it with me,
but then she tells me she wants to do it AGAIN the next day.

Fourteen, gaphphnuggungh, my brain has imploded.
Fifteen, I didn't think it was possible to be this hungry.
Sixteen, according to Shakespeare,
the day after I do it with Suzy Warner,
I'm across town lying dead in a crypt.
Seventeen, NO WAY that happens in real life, okay?

Because One, if I'm Romeo,
that means I'm not a virgin anymore,
WHICH IS AWESOME.
And because Two, if Suzy Warner's in bed with me,
no way I'm leaving bed, EVER.
I would never get out of bed.
There is no upside to leaving bed.
Skittles, skateboarding, food and water—
things of the past, my friend.
Let's assume for some totally unbelievable hypothetical reason
that I leave Suzy Warner in bed.
Let's suppose later that day,
one of Suzy Warner's relatives
kills my best friend Mercutio.
On one hand, I hate that dude.
On the other hand,
I know Suzy Warner
WANTS IT AGAIN, FROM ME, TONIGHT.

So let's review.
Either I avenge my best friend, who is tragically dead.
Or I sleep with Suzy Warner, who is totally hot.
Door number one,
avenge friend's death, return to kickball.
Door number two,
SUZY WARNER.
In conclusion, Shakespeare, total idiot.
Class dismissed.
And if I don't get Cheetos in the next five minutes,
I will pass out and die.

SUZY WARNER

One, Mrs. Jackson is my favorite teacher and
Romeo and Juliet is not just a great play,
it is also an incredible movie.
Two, in the movie Leonardo DiCaprio played Romeo
and he is an amazing actor.
Three, the only movie I have seen more times than
Romeo and Juliet is *Titanic*,
starring Leonardo DiCaprio.
Four, you should be allowed to drink Diet Coke in English
class.
Five, Leonardo DiCaprio is so amazing in *Titanic*
that I almost forget the ending every time. I swear.
Six, my other favorite movie
behind *Titanic* and *Romeo and Juliet*
is *The Beach*, starring Leonardo DiCaprio.
Seven, I haven't seen *What's Eating Gilbert Grape* yet,
but I want to.
It stars Leonardo DiCaprio and Johnny Depp,
who is also an amazing actor.
Eight, I could not believe how incredibly much
Johnny Depp loved Winona Ryder
in *Edward Scissorhands*. They were like unicorns.
Nine, if I were Juliet,
that would mean I would be married to Leonardo DiCaprio.
Ten, if I were married to Leonardo DiCaprio
we would have houses in Hollywood and Europe and Florida
that my friends could visit any time
and I would have my own successful business
and I would still write in my journal
when Leonardo is out making movies
and I would decorate one of the houses entirely in kelly green,
which is an amazing color.
Eleven, if I were married to Leonardo DiCaprio
and he was Romeo,
and I woke up and I saw that he had killed himself

unicorns

because he thought I was dead even though I wasn't,
I would definitely do what Juliet did,
which is incredibly sad, but I definitely would.
Twelve, I would definitely NOT EVER do what Juliet did
for any boy in my class.
NOT IN A BILLION YEARS.
Thirteen, I know Leonardo is fat now, but I don't care.

In conclusion, Shakespeare is an amazing writer,
and it makes me sad that there are no boys in my class
who are anything like Leonardo DiCaprio.

MRS. JACKSON

One, if Suzy Warner calls Romeo "Leonardo" one more time,
I will kill her and lose my pension.
Two, you should be allowed to drink Diet Coke in English class.
And three, what's that boy behind Suzy thinking?
He's not even in this class.

Reality Check

SARA HOPE ANDERSON

Age	Perfect Life	Real Life
15	Be a champion in at least one sport, have absolutely flat tummy, be continually mistaken for a college freshman, and get outstanding results on the PSAT while being scouted by a senior editor at *Seventeen* magazine.	Avoid all organized sports and join the rock-climbing club because the teacher, though missing two teeth, looks great in flannel, and knows how to drive a stick-shift van. Have absolutely flat tummy that no one knows about because you mostly wear oversized oxford shirts and sweaters and never appear in a bathing suit without a long T-shirt. Be continually mistaken for a college freshman by boys your own age. Do well on the PSAT, but overhear your parents talk about how it's really only "practice." Hate *Seventeen* magazine after a quiz you took labeled you "A Wet Blanket." Start smoking.
16	Obtain driver's license after two tries (failing once because it's charming). Drive cute Volkswagen convertible and always have a mix-tape of the Go-Go's or Go-Go's equivalent on hand. One week after receiving license, get in minor fender-bender with kind college professor who stays in touch as an invaluable college admissions advisor.	Obtain driver's license after four humiliating attempts. Successfully beg to take out parents' Oldsmobile and celebrate wildly until you realize that the radio dial is permanently stuck on AM All News station. Then, while being mauled by boyfriend and listening to the Chicago Mercantile Exchange wrapup, discover a mix-tape of the Go-Go's or Go-Go's equivalent under backseat along with four pieces of Good & Plenty

Age	Perfect Life	Real Life
		and some mulch. One week after receiving license, total Oldsmobile while parallel parking. Make mental note that your mother will never let you forget that you were wearing pajama bottoms and flip-flops while driving.
	Become favorite babysitter for adorable fraternal twins whose father and mother are influential artists/politicos/attorneys/researchers who would be solid references for summer internships/college applications.	Become favorite babysitter for hyperactive children of influential artist/politico/attorney/researcher neighbors, but see hopes for promising summer internship/college application references dashed when husband's sexual advances send you sprinting out the door without collecting babysitting cash. Land summer job at local candy store, "Oh Fudge." Gain 20 pounds.
18	Attend first or second choice college (disappointments leave you stronger and may merit a new outfit or expensive dress-up dinner). Begin with several AP credits, get first pick of dorm, and refuse to attend a "Drink 'Til You Sink" party until your sophomore year.	Attend college you've never visited after acceptance letter is used as a coaster for your sister's chocolate Dunkachino. Begin first semester without any AP credits because your high school advisor never completed the proper paperwork. Live off-campus in a four-bedroom "Dumplex."
21	Recognize a definitive career path and have practical goals you actually realize, thanks to full funding from corporate grants, Fulbright scholarships, and notes from your state senator. Be buoyed by the steady stream of cards, gifts, and Mylar balloons from family, friends, and chance acquaintances encouraging you to reach for the stars.	Admit you have no clue what you want to do for a living, but convince yourself that as long as you don't have to sell anything or scold anyone, you'll be fine. Believe you can always be a librarian or go to law school if nothing else works out. Become horribly depressed and angry that everyone in all of your classes cheats all the time.

Age	Perfect Life	Real Life
25	Have serious boyfriend who is attractive, ambitious, and infinitely desirable, and knows he will never do better than you.	Have serious boyfriend who is attractive, ambitious, and infinitely desirable, yet doesn't know you are The One.
	Obtain choice job with travel opportunities and an incredibly talented assistant from a Seven Sisters school who always catches typos and tells you when your tag is exposed on your casual-Friday sweater.	Obtain job you are absurdly overqualified for, which requires you to report to a Seven Sisters graduate who always catches typos and tells you when your tag is exposed on your casual-Friday sweater.
26	Experience savage breakup with boyfriend that leaves you more confident and able to spend more time reading, working out, and constructing impressive strategy summaries for senior management. Find out later your ex has substance abuse problem and repeatedly requests that you visit him at the sanatorium in Marin. Remain good friends and truly appreciate it when he mentions you specifically as his muse during subsequent Grammy speeches.	Experience savage breakup with boyfriend that leaves you wallowing and alienated from your friends who knew it was coming and just couldn't tell you. Be on road to recovery until lapse when you discover that he's just gotten married to a Danish film star and the wedding was, according to your invited friends, "the event of the year."
27	Meet the man you will marry while buying Christmas tree, changing tire, or humming the same Ella Fitzgerald tune on the Amtrak platform. Toy with him for six months until he is absolutely perfect, and then, under a weeping willow tree and starry sky, tearfully accept his proposal and the wonking four-carat ring his great grandmother wore that's been tastefully reset into a contemporary platinum with the express permission of all key women in the family.	Meet the man you will marry while arguing with the pharmacist over the $10 co-pay on your birth control pills (for your complexion). Tentatively date him for six months, all the time waiting for the other shoe to drop, and then when it doesn't, while in line together at Home Depot, realize you want to be married right away in anticipation of never having to worry about another busted fuse you have to fix in the dark standing in water all by yourself. Propose on the spot.

Age	Perfect Life	Real Life
28	Be a major player in your industry, quoted heavily in respected trade publications and occasionally appear on *The NewsHour with Jim Lehrer.* Seem confident, professional, and brilliant the day before you are the calm, glowing bride in simple yet elegant gown during playful yet traditional wedding ceremony and reception documented in *Town & Country.*	Read about your college room-mate, who is now a major player in your industry, quoted heavily in respected trade publications and occasionally appears on *The NewsHour with Jim Lehrer.* Wonder how she transformed from the pothead bulimic who diluted your shampoo into this confident professional who never RSVPs to your Save the Date announcements, which you had printed on costly rice paper that everyone assumed was coffee filters.
29	Buy first home, a "fixer-upper" with original moldings intact in "transi-tioning" area, further amplifying your hip (yet responsible) I-am-not-a-lemming profile—all while garnering a below-market price and exceptional financing. Decorate with marvelous "finds" from honeymoon in Venice (Venizia!).	Have all offers for first home, dilapidated pits in Superfund neighborhoods, brutally rejected by snitty realtor who drives a low-level Mercedes. Continue to pay exploitive rent to live in building with downstairs neighbor who leaves threatening notes in mail box accusing you of taking her Poland Spring water.
	Give birth to healthy, joyous baby with no complications and exceptional birth announcements.	Find out you are pregnant and wonder if you inadvertently threw up your birth control pill when you ate a chili dog at that carni-val last month. Give birth during nor'easter and wonder if a snow day at the office actually counts as a part of your allotted mater-nity leave.
30	Take time to enjoy being new mother while remaining within inner circle of professional peers. Get body back in shape quickly. Avoid diaper bags that look like diaper bags, keep up with daily news, refrain from cutting hair short in attempt to look like Meg Ryan.	Live in fear of something going wrong with your child and fret over all stories people tell you about dry cleaning bags, bal-loons, gummy bears, etc. Return to work after a month. Try to get body back in shape quickly but

Age	Perfect Life	Real Life
		be destroyed when mother says, "You look beautiful. Have you lost any weight since having the baby?" Try to look streamlined and cute with baby, but realize you never have what you need (sippy cup, diaper, wipes, change of clothes, pacifier, etc.), requiring you to continually purchase duplicate items. Be exhausted. Cut hair short in misguided attempt to look like Meg Ryan.
31 & 32	Maintain rigorous work schedule, enjoy laughter-filled, late-night chats with caring nanny from upper-class British background, plan for indulgent getaway to Pacific Rim with husband to celebrate a marriage in which you both Really Listen and have equal housekeeping responsibilities that include dual oversight on the under-budget completion of the new kitchen, guest bathroom, and deck.	Maintain rigorous work schedule.
33	Twins! Delivered early without painkillers or stitches! Embossed birth announcements look terrific in lower-case Palatino designed by your best friend since college who is staying with you and doing laundry, scrubbing the tub, making meals and not sleeping with your still-very-sexy and-increasingly-wealthy husband. Sister who was homecoming queen but never amounted to anything and drinks is also a big help.	After enduring ridiculously painful fertility procedures, briefly consider snatching cute little Brittany from the playground across the street from your gym. Think about when you were nearly voted homecoming queen. Drink.
34 to 40	Write insightful work of historical fiction that allows you to take time off from hugely successful career and eventually lands you a multi-picture deal that is negotiated by a husband who doesn't let you interface with	Rethink career because everyone around you is doing better than you are. Wonder why your assistant just purchased beautiful condo on water with marble fireplace and is thinking of buying a

Age	Perfect Life	Real Life
	the ugly money-grubbers and agents.	Mini. Write desperate and insipid work of historical fiction that takes all your free time and over-hear your son tell his kinder-garten teacher that "Mommy is often by herself writhing."
40 to 50	Publish string of successes regarded as seminal achievements and required reading for grad students coast to coast, bringing you awards and honorary degrees. Take full advantage of the transfers provided by your husband's burgeoning business and move to Paris, Athens, and London. Find yourself financially prepared when that dream beach house is for sale, the one you dis-covered in your twenties when walking your dog in Dr. Scholl's and Nantucket reds.	Maintain rigorous work schedule.
50 to 70	Retire to dream beach house, listening to Chet Baker, teaching autistic children watercolor, and taking Elderhostel trips to learn new culinary techniques. Look forward to multiple grandchildren and annual reunions in which everyone gets very involved in high-spirited game of capture the flag but no one gets sunburned or drinks too much.	Maintain rigorous work schedule.
Death	Loose mortal coil warm in the know-ledge you will be mentioned as closing segment on network news, with photographers respecting family privacy, and knowing your estate planning is perfect—generous and uncontested, with several charitable interests discussing expansions in your honor. Have ashes dropped into the sea while soprano soloist be-friended on QE2 sings tribute in front	Die in a hospital bed with tubes going in and out of everywhere and reading the Senate subcom-mittee testimony of the CEO of your life insurance company. Expire as you finish reading that the CEO said "Yes, *technically*, I'd guess we'd have to say all of our policies are pretty much worthless at this point." Have ashes dropped into sea as

Age	Perfect Life	Real Life
	of dazzling photo of you at Nobel ceremonies looking beautifully wrinkled with soft gray hair and sparkling eyes conveying undeniable *joie de vivre*—still a perfect size 8 in Michael Kors.	planned. Realize the sea is cold and dark.
Afterlife	Watch family and still terribly bereaved husband and dog from on high. Note that though surveillance opportunities are constant and clear you never witness children having sex or your husband mildly flirting with the young thing at the copy center. Secretly visit grandchildren before they walk down the aisle, appearing each time in a backlit vision of kind wisdom and grace. Dwell in infinite peace, knowing that no one will ever sell anything of yours at yard sale on the "All things under $5" card table.	Watch family and still terribly bereaved husband and dog from on high. Note that you always seem to catch your child having sex and your husband in the bathroom. Secretly visit grandchild before he walks down the aisle, but attempted backlit vision of inspiring love and kindness on your part just turns out creepy and leaves everyone teary-eyed and in need of medication. Witness everything you've ever owned on an "All things under $5" card table at a yard sale.
	Spend eternity in very pleasant company of excellent Mah Jongg players and delightful conversationalists— Gandhi, Audrey Hepburn, Joey Ramone, Frederick Douglass, Samuel Johnson, Billie Holiday, Andy Warhol, Anne Boleyn, and your great uncle Jack who may have been a Communist, though not in a mean way.	Spend eternity bitching relentlessly to/with Richard Nixon, Joan of Arc, River Phoenix, and your Uncle Jack, who continually calls you a Communist in a mean way.

Developmental Valley School District Lunch Menus for This Week

PHIL AUSTIN

PLAIZMENTARY SCHOOL
MON: Paper Stack; Boneless Burrito; Paste; Kitten on a Stick; Milkaroni

TUE: White Bread on Toast; Glass of Sugar; See-Through Lettuce; Liquid Milk

WED: Sponge; Sugar Sandwich; Butter Plate; Cloth Pudding; Milk

THURS: Simple Pie; Banana Splat; Sugar Mound; Blanched Cookie; Milk

FRI: Diaper Surprise; Clear Peaches; Steamed Cereal Boxes; Sugar; Milk

MYSTERY ISLAND SCHOOL FOR GIRLS
MON: Soft Eggs on a Mirror; Hard-boiled Hollow Birds; Handful of Tacos; Milk

TUE: Rack of Clever Hans; Whisked Apple Fly; Coronation Ham; Nylon Bunnies; Big Carton

WED: Mystery Potato; Curd; Slippery Tart; Milk Pie; Leg Salad Sandwich; Clear Liquid

THURS: Oysters Frightened by Chickens; Liver Mounds; Nest of Interesting Spiders; Mai Tai; Pack of Camels

FRI: Breast of Clam à la "Eddie"; Wieners in a Basket under a Blanket; Teacher's Surprise; Milk

EARNEST BOYS ACADEMY
MON: Beef Throats; Smoked Leg; Hind Quarters; Gros Livers; Old-Fashioned Milk; Cigars

TUE: Flat Motor Pies; Fisherman's Regret; Loin of Fat; Stunned Ducks in Alcohol Sauce; Milk

WED: Tart Bottoms; Slick Fritters; Breasts of Toast; Sweetbreads in Hand; Cuckoo Punch; Cigars; Milk

THURS: Roast Puffins; Revenge Pudding; Pancakes in Water; Baked Salad; Ring of Fire; Milk

FRI: Ducklings à la Moron; Smothered Rodents; Closet Pie; Turbo Skeletons; Champagne; Brandies; Cigars; Milk

WILLY LOMAN PUBLIC HIGH SCHOOL

MON: Horse Butter Sandwiches; Hot Jello Salad; French Kisses; Curb Cake; Milk

TUE: Toads in Blanket in a Hole; Complicated Salad; Ice Bread; Lomax Pie; Milk Cocktail

WED: Hat with Cheese; Insurance Salad; V6 Bread; Field Surprise; Milk

THURS: Battered Vegetables; Wax Wrappers; Wallet and Raisin Salad; Adult Milkshake

FRI: Fried Chuck; Paper Salad; Responsibility Pie; White Dessert; Retirement Milk

ALTERNATE CURRENT MAGNET SCHOOL

MON: Eco-Veggie Bar; Rainbow Krazy Krunch; Twig Sticks; Turkey Straws; Cow Milk

TUE: Helpless Nuggets with Sour Sauce; Gator Tots; Trial Mix; White Milk

WED: False Rabbit Wedges; Farm Dip; Sloppy Joans; French Acid; Goat Milk

THURS: Meatless Hot Creatures; Sweetened Cherries; Meltdown on a Bun; Squares; Mother's Milk

FRI: Refried Fries; Early Dismissal Cup; Hemp Wheels; Party on a Bun; Dip; Sheep Milk

X Is for Christmas:
A Tale of the Old Detective

PHIL AUSTIN

It's a mystery, Christmas, that's what it is," the Old Detective grumbled. "I mean Christmas in Hollywood. There's no mystery to Chanukah in Hollywood, for instance. It's a celebration tailor-made for creatures of the desert, it's about victory and oil and counting, and Jews, for all their intelligence, are not a basically ironic people, but Christmas in the desert of Hollywood is a kind of puzzle, you've got to admit, especially for someone from a more northern climate. Irony is kind of built in, if you see what I mean."

The old man and I were sitting in a little bar on Hollywood Boulevard, one he'd liked to frequent in older, more violent days, when dolls and sharpies ruled the Boulevard. It was the day before the day that even down here in the chaparral we like to call Christmas. The bar was called the Blue Mechanism, for reasons I couldn't begin to imagine, and it was frankly run-down, a dive, in fact. I had to agree with his remarks about the holiday, however, much as I disliked his choice of hangouts. Through the dark thick blue glass of the windows I could make out Swedish tourists toppling in the December heat wave. Wilted palm trees were festooned with jolly melting plastic Santas. Garlands drooped sadly. We sat as close as we could to a dangerous old fan that vainly tried to stir up the turgid air. My friend was talking, however, and that was good news for me. In fact, he seemed swept up in an odd wave of nostalgia on this searing winter afternoon that needed some cheer to it, given the imminence of the Big Day itself.

"You see," he said, tapping the battered fedora back on his

grizzled head, "I never, in the old days, had any visions of sugar fairies and reindeers and guys named Frosty, because all I knew was the seamy world of the police blotter, the run-down underside of what we called life, back then. Back in those days, if I saw some socks dangling from a mantel, I'd start looking for the rest of the body, see what I mean? There were no smiling faces upturned in their big woolly mufflers asking me for a free turkey."

I told him his days as a detective had certainly hardened him.

"Now I'm as soft as soft-water taffy," he said. "But in those days, I was hard, all right. I was as hard as a big rock candy mountain, until one Christmas, years ago . . ."

I found my notebook and searched for my pen, the one I hoped wouldn't leak onto my shirt. We were drinking shots of Black Label in the late afternoon and smoking cigarettes just for fun.

"You see," said the Old Detective, lighting up another with his old brass lighter, "I took on a case one Christmas for a guy named Kringle, an old guy with a white Santa Claus beard and an annoying twinkle in his eyes who beat the elevator up to my office one crisp December day when the new smog hung from the eaves in frozen stillness and the crunch of actual snow could be heard on half the soundstages around town. Kringle was an enthusiastic bird, full of fizz and he poured out a story as old as Time itself. It was all the usual stuff: flying fantasies, chimneys, large ungulates, whips, something about a red nose and implications about Sears Roebuck that couldn't be proved. I'd been down that street before."

"What street?" I asked. It was a stupid question, but I already had misgivings about the old man's tale.

"In those days, Sears had a store over on Santa Monica Boulevard. You know what I mean."

"Do I?"

"I'm feelin' good today, I'm feelin' frisky. Are you getting this down?"

I told him I was getting it down. Actually, I wasn't. The min-

ute he'd mentioned "Kringle" and "Christmas" in the same sentence, I'd merely written the word "Xmas" on my notepad and
was now idly tracing over and over the *x*. I began to draw a
snowman.

"Now, on that day of cheer and goodwill—you getting this
all down?—there was a Christmas party goin' on across the hall
from my office. This was when I had magazines in nice magazine racks in the outside office and a great-lookin' secretary
named Ruby who used to sit out there with her legs crossed."

I asked him if the correct word wasn't "gams."

"If I'd meant gams, I'd have said gams. Ruby had legs a mile
and a half long and a mother who couldn't remember her name,
she was so far gone on hooch. That's 'hooch,' h-double-o-c-h."

I pretended to write. Actually, I'd now drawn a reindeer on
its back, legs straight up, two *x*'s for eyes, but the Old Detective
seemed satisfied and continued on.

"After awhile, mostly because of Ruby, the party spilled over
across the hall to my place. The usual crazies from the Five
Star/Hopeless Talent Agency were around. You remember the
name Paul Bunyan?"

"The giant lumberjack?"

"Yeah. Well, he was there."

I asked him how that could be, since I remembered Paul
Bunyan as mythical at best and imaginary at worst.

"You're too young, you wouldn't remember," he replied,
puffing smoke. "By that time in his career, he was good for
occasional guest shots on the *Gary Moore Show* and such. He
was getting bookings, is what I mean. Now Miss Mysterioso,
Mistress of Mystery? Played the organ? Everybody remembers
her. Well, she was there with some potato salad that was really
good, as I recall, and she had on a green-and-red sequined
number that showed the two or three things about her that
were no damn mystery at all."

I said I understood him to mean that Miss Mysterioso, the
Mistress of Mystery, was a looker.

"You got that right, son." He smiled. "Curves up ahead or
whatever the road sign says, if you subscribe to my meaning."

I asked him if perhaps she had great gams.

"If I'd meant she'd had gams, I woulda mentioned it," he said stiffly. "That Argentine guy who had the trained bears showed up with some fruitcake that had candied mushrooms in it, and the girls from downstairs at Henrietta's House of Hair came upstairs and put on some Chet Baker records and started dancin' with each other real slow. There was a big ol' traditional roast albatross with that sage and treacle dressing. After awhile even old Kringle had a few shots of toddy and pretty soon he was doin' the stroll or whatever they called it in those days. At one point, even the bears were doin' it. The party got pretty wild and I lost track of Kringle. You see, I'd forgotten to tell Ruby to sweep my rod off the top of my desk."

I asked if it was common practice in those days for a detective to leave a loaded weapon out on his desk. Was this Kringle so intimidating?

"I wasn't intimidated by anything in those days," he said roughly. "But you never know. I was as hard as the big rock candy mountains and thought that Christmas was just a fancy way of spelling burglary. I was on alert, lemme put it that way."

"Fine," I said and pretended to cross something out and write something in.

"Now, I was leanin' in on Miss Mysterioso pretty good—and believe me, there was a lot to lean over—when we heard the shot."

"A gunshot?"

"That's what everyone figured."

"Kringle shot himself?"

"Did I say that? Of course, that's the first thing an amateur like you would think."

I suggested that he tell me, then, what actually happened.

"It was the crack of a tree splitting. Seems this Bunyan guy was outside choppin' down a magnolia tree. He wanted a magnolia blossom to give to Miss Mysterioso, because he was so in love with her. Sometimes a guy like that will just go crazy over a woman."

I replied that, of course, I'd been down that street before.

"Nearly everyone in this town has been down Santa Monica Boulevard, sometimes twice a day. You ain't heard the half of it, kid."

"Well, the half I've heard isn't exactly worth writing down," I snapped back. He stared at me for a long moment.

"Should I be getting royalties for these stories about me?" He looked serious.

"No," I lied. "Because I don't get any."

"Good," he said. "Royalty is a mistaken idea anyway, much like Christmas, or at least that's what Kringle found out."

I said, he was certainly aware—wasn't he?—that there had been a famous old black-and-white movie made about a guy named Kringle who looked just like Santa Claus.

"This wasn't the same guy," he said defensively. "This guy's name was Ferdinand Kringle. Ferdinand L. Kringle. I can see the name on the file folder to this day."

I told him he certainly had a good memory. I looked around in vain for the bartender, who I suspected was lying on the floor behind the bar gasping for air.

"No," he muttered. "I had the file out last night because I'm thinkin' of writing up some of my adventures myself. Cut out the middleman, so to speak."

"You mean me?"

"Do I? You be the judge. You getting this down?"

I started to write. "Yes," I said grimly, "I'm getting this down."

"Good. There was a shot later on, by the way, so if you were on a computer, you could save the word "shot" onto a file someplace and have it ready to reinsert when I get to the shot part."

I said thanks and when was he going to get to the shot part?

"When I'm good and ready," he snarled. "We better think about modernizing some. I think you ought to buy a computer and then you could get online and do some networking and maybe we could make some money off of these stories about me."

I replied that I had every hope that in the future there might be some money from these stories, and of course, some of that money might be his and in the meantime I might see my way clear to advancing him a little something.

"Aha," he said. "That's the Christmas spirit. Now we're talking. You write and I'll talk. I'm thinkin' of getting a hot tub, you know? I'll soak and reminisce and you'll get it all down on the mainframe. Now, Christmas was all humbug to me, remember? You've already got that down, right?"

"Right."

"So, that night, when the boys in blue found Kringle under the Hollywood Christmas Tree of Light, strangled with those awful twisted green and red double wires they used to have, and bearing strange marks on his body, they normally wouldn't have come looking for me. Unfortunately, he had my card in his pocket."

I asked him if they thought he'd killed Kringle. He looked pensive and faraway for a minute.

"Well, they were hoping I'd done *something*. I didn't have too many friends down at Hollywood Division in those days. I'd embarrassed those boys one too many times. They hauled me down to headquarters in a black-and-white and set me up under that one bare lightbulb they were so proud of and they all sat back in the shadows and started firing questions at me that I couldn't answer. Most of them seemed to be about a drunk reindeer and Sears. I didn't think much of it had to do with Christmas, frankly."

I gritted my teeth and asked him if, by any chance, we were somehow talking about "Rudolph, the Red-nosed Reindeer," a Christmas ditty that was originally composed, as I understood it, by a man in Chicago who worked for Sears.

"No," he said firmly. "Wrong again. There was no singing on this one. This turned out to be only about a hard-drinking reindeer who may or may not have had a red nose. It's immaterial whether it was red or not. Seems like he'd been letting himself out of those cages where he hung out with his buddies on top of that real estate office on Crenshaw. They had reindeer cages and white Christmas trees. I think they sprayed the reindeers white. Anyway, this one had been breaking into Sears and stealing power tools to take back to Alaska and sell for big bucks. It was logical. Kringle worked as a Santa at the same place, waving to cars. He must have caught on. The forensic boys noticed that the marks on Kringle exactly matched the dado head on a Craftsman table saw, lucky for me. After twenty-four hours of questioning, they had to let me go."

"That's it?" I asked.

"Here's the heart of the story," he smiled. "When I got back to the office, the party was still goin' on. I managed to find Miss Mysterioso. Paul Bunyan had her backed up against a moonlit brick wall covered with variegated ivy and was telling her a lot of lies. I said 'Is this guy bothering you?' and she said, lookin' up at me through half-closed eyes, 'You bother me, big boy. This guy is just plain annoying.' I took a deep breath and told Bunyan to take a hike and he launched off into the same story he'd already told on the *Merv Griffin Show* about some hike he took once with a Blue Ox and I pretended to look interested—same as Merv had—and after awhile he got so wrapped up in laughing at his own jokes that I just walked her away into the moonlight and the rest is history."

"Where," I asked, looking up from my notes, "is this history written?"

"In the newspapers. The print boys loved it: 'Ripsaw Rudolphs Mortis Santa!' You get the picture. But the real story went right to the hearts of mankind," the Old Detective answered, seriously enough. "You see, she was very, very good to me. Kinda changed my mind about Xmas, after all. She had a pair of gams on her that would melt the heart of Black Peter himself."

So there was some justice to the season after all in those long-gone days. I like to think there was, anyway, back when Santa had a tan and Mrs. Santa was named Monica and wore a bikini and sunglasses and high heels and after the parade down Hollywood Boulevard they'd get together a bunch of their friends and they'd all pile into the big old turquoise convertible and bomb out to Palm Springs for Christmas because it was the kind of place where the Prince of Peace himself might feel right at home, out there among the road-runners and the cactuses and the Joshua trees, with the stars out at night—so many you couldn't hope to imagine them all—and the natural evils of the human spirit damped down for once and calmed, on this one night of all nights in our mysterious town.

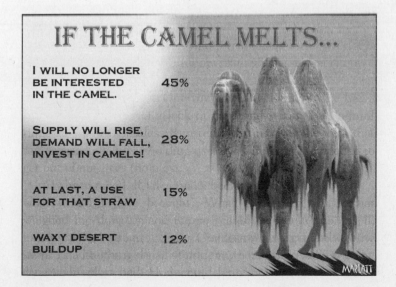

Nursery News

ANDREW BARLOW

School has barely begun and already so much has happened. Thank you to everyone for an eventful and challenging year so far.

MUSIC HELPS THE HEART GROW

The theme that your children selected for this month's enrichment unit is "Music All Around Us." (The title was actually chosen by Miss Paula, who adapted it from the students' suggestion, "Pokémon.") Maybe you've noticed some of the unusual sounds emanating from our activities room. Your kids are acquiring fresh appreciation for "sounding off" on pots and pans and the wood part of our piano. Our morning sing-alongs have shown that music can reach even the shyest youngster, Bernard. We are requesting the following materials for the program: shoe boxes, macaroni, empty baby-food jars, earplugs—whatever you can spare.

THANK YOU

Thank you to the moms who brought us newspapers and pasta shells for last term's Mother's Day art project. The results, as many of you suggested, were mixed. Likewise, thank you, Mrs. Ventura, for replenishing our first-aid kit. You have no idea how much this means to us and the kids, especially William.

ANIMAL FRIENDS

After the death of Mr. Furry last week, we have been keeping a watchful eye on Sparkles, the school's other pet bunny rabbit. We are unsure about what caused the disappearance and then the grossly unacceptable reappearance of Mr. Furry on Wednesday, but any parent with special knowledge of foul play should report to us.

IN THE CLASSROOM

Here's what the children are working on:
Shark Group (ages four and five): "Folks in Our Community." What does a police officer do? What do firefighters do? What does a firefighter wear? Why did the Fire Department have to come last week? Why is it important to let Miss Nadine be in charge of the candles on Cupcake Day?
Pokémon Group (ages two and three): Funeral services for Mr. Furry.

GOOD-BYE, MRS. PILSTON

Dorothy Pilston, our nurse at the school for nine years, is missing. We began to worry when she didn't come to work for three days last week and was unreachable at home. Miss Jenny's four-year-olds formed a search party to find Mrs. Pilston, but the effort was unsuccessful and their methods not systematic. Many of you may not know that it was Dorothy who instituted our annual Invertebrates Gala. Dottie, bon voyage.

PARENT-TEACHER MEETINGS

To spare ourselves such meeting-time outcries as "Is everybody O.K.?" and "What do you mean, 'hostages'?" we will establish a priority list for mishaps, to be addressed at parent-teacher meetings. List No. 1: Hazing. Students fighting during last week's fire. Excessive taunting during "The Cheese Stands Alone." Attempts to form juntas. Please join us on October 15th and find out who's doing what: names will be named.

ODDS AND ENDS

This newsletter will be seeing some changes. The "Kids Say the Nuttiest Things" and "That's Toddlers for Ya!" sections have been discontinued. Two new features, "Naptime Observations" and "Police Blotter," will replace them, beginning next month. We will also be opening our reconstructed rumpus room.

Already, it's been a difficult year, and more excitement is planned. Our field trip to the juvenile-detention center is still on for next week. Thank you for your promptness in returning permission slips for that event.

Treasure these days.

━ ━ ∙ ━ ━ ∙ ━ ━ ∙ ━ ∙ ━ ∙ ━ ∙ ━ ∙ ━ ∙ ━ ∙ ━ ∙ ━ ∙ ━

. . . Lumberjacks, Smucker's in logjam . . . PBS admits "viewers like you" not at all like you . . . NASA: Jupiter moon may have had casinos . . . Universe, economy flat, say unemployed astronomers . . .

The Complete Idiot's Guide to Meeting People More Famous Than You

MICHAEL IAN BLACK

A scenario: you are gamboling along the promenade when you spot your favorite celebrity enjoying a gelato. You stop in your tracks, jaw agape. You have often felt that you and this celebrity would become fast friends were you ever to meet; now, finally, is your opportunity.

What to do? How best to approach? Casually? With vigor? Should you "accidentally" spill your Big Gulp on his sweater? Discreetly cup his buttocks? Sweat begins to pool in your unmentionables. You are as frozen as that gelato your favorite celebrity passionately licks, as you yourself would like to be licked. What the hell are you supposed to do?

Don't worry. I am going to help you.

As a celebrity myself (very famous), I have often heard other celebrities talk about "giving back to the community," and that's great for them. I'm told volunteering for stuff is a terrific way to get laid. And while I have no interest in donating time or money to "causes," I would like to give something back to the little people who have made me so very popular on basic cable.

It is in that spirit that I offer these simple tips for approaching tremendous stars like myself:

First of all, relax. Famous people are just like you. Yes, we have more money. Yes, we are invited to parties so fabulous your head would explode were you ever to get past the velvet ropes. But after the flashbulbs have stopped popping and we roll out of bed around noon, we have people who put our pants on us one leg at a time.

Approach a celebrity the way you would an old friend. An old friend who doesn't remember you. Just walk up, extend your hand, and give a hearty, "Ahoy!" Everybody enjoys a familiar naval greeting, especially stars. If you have the time to doff naval dress whites, all the better.

Next, have a plan in mind. Many people are so happy just to be in the presence of the famous that they become tongue-tied and flummoxed once they've achieved this goal. Not you. You will know what you want to say and you will say it. For example, when approaching John Travolta, you might say, "Ahoy, John. I'm a big fan. Is it true you're gay?" Then, the two of you can have a long and meaningful discussion about his sexuality. The next thing you know, he's jetting you off to meet Kelly and the kids in his private 747 while whispering the secrets to getting past the infamous Xemu's Wall of Fire level in your Scientology training. All because you had a plan.

Maybe you want an autograph. Most stars are happy to oblige. A word to the wise, however: have your pen at the ready. Nothing is more awkward than spending long minutes fishing through your purse trying to find something to write with, only to emerge with a melty lipstick. It's awkward and it makes you look cheap. If you don't have a pen, remember that God gave you natural ink—your own blood.

Pay that person a compliment, but don't kiss their ass. For example, one time I saw Cameron Diaz at a party and told her I thought she was pretty funny for a girl. She was very flattered because she understood that I respected her enough to not insult her intelligence by saying she was as funny as a man. Long story short: I banged her.

Also, don't be afraid to offer money. Think about all the enjoyment that person has given you over the years. Would it kill you to approach with a twenty-dollar bill in hand? Some celebs will take checks. Personally, I walk around with one of those slidy doodads for imprinting credit cards. Sure it's heavy, but I do it. Why? Because I care about the fans.

Finally, know how to make a graceful exit. You've met that big star, gotten an autograph. Maybe the two of you made out a little. Great. Now it's time to go. Yes, there will be tears. Some hurtful words might be exchanged, but that's just because love can be so painful. Causing a scene will only make it harder for both of you to let go. A quick hug, and then it's back to your separate lives. You, to your humdrum workaday world, the star back to his gated community, opulent lifestyle, and prescription narcotics.

It doesn't seem fair, does it? Of course not. And yet, that's just the natural order of things. Some people are famous and some are not. It doesn't mean one person is better than the other.

I'm just kidding. That's exactly what it means.

—— · —— · —— · —— · —— · —— · —— · —— · —— · —— · ——

. . . Hackers hack Hackensack hacky sack site, say hacks . . . Think tank explodes . . . Survey: pre-owned vehicles more reliable than used cars . . . Life imitates art, is sued . . .

VH1 Hate Mail

MICHAEL IAN BLACK

Some people just don't like me. I know this is hard to believe, especially when you consider the following:

I am a celebrity (very famous).
I give sixty percent of my income to "Jerry's Kids."
I hardly ever kick my dog.

Two of these things are true, and shouldn't that be enough to ensure me a large measure of goodwill from my fellow man? After all, I harbor no ill will toward anybody (except for that motherfucker Paul Newman—he knows why).

This is why it was so surprising for me to learn that there are people out there, people I have never even met, who do not like me.

I first became aware of this after appearing on the VH1 television program *I Love the '70s*. You may have seen this show. According to the VH1 press release, it's a "fun-filled ride through the music, movies, TV shows, products, fashions, fads, trends, and major events that defined pop culture each year of the decade." Whatever. They paid me two grand.

For people who feel the need to share their thoughts about television shows with complete strangers, VH1 maintains an Internet message board. It was while perusing these boards that I first encountered several dispiriting posts under topics like, "Michael Ian Black sucks," "Michael Ian Black—DIE!" and perhaps most painful of all, "Michael Ian Black is not that cute."

Needless to say, I was blown away. I mean, look at me. I'm *really* cute.

My initial shock soon turned to numbness, followed by denial, anger, depression, a brief moment of total euphoria, and then back to depression.

I have decided to share some of those messages here in an effort to confront the final stage in my grieving process, acceptance. Not to sound egotistical, but it is my hope that by accepting and honoring the writers' feelings, I will not only heal myself, but will also literally heal the world.

From keithpartridge:

> [Michael Ian Black is] . . . the most arrogant, self-absorbed, uninteresting, pretentious, cynical human being with no talent that VH1 ever hired to talk about something they have no knowledge about whatsoever . . .

(The grammar might be a touch clunky, Keith, but your message rings loud and clear. I honor your feelings. Well said.)

From Maddmaxx14:

> What does this snotnosed little **** think he knows about the 70s?

(The asterisks are Maddmaxx14's, not mine. I don't know what they stood for, but I think it was probably "faggot." Thanks for having the class not to say it, Madd.)

From Hollandscomet:

> How long after his lobotomy did they tape his segments, anyway?!? This guy has all the personality of a doorstop!

(Not to quibble, but there are some really whimsical doorstops on the market. Check out www.avalongarden.com for the "green rabbit" and "butch" doorstops; they've got personality in spades. Your point, however, is taken.)

From Born2Soon:

> MIB was crass enough to say that Arnold from *Diff'rent Strokes* should have been on *Roots*. Why? He didn't say why.

(The reason I thought Arnold should play Kunta Kinte is so he could say, "Whatchu talkin' 'bout, Master?" which I thought would be cute. Sorry about the confusion. I should have made this clearer.)

Another from Born2Soon:

> MIB looks like he's had botox on his forehead. His forehead never moves, even when he moves his eyebrows or smiles, which is rarely . . . He most likely had it done due to VANITY. That's the usual reason.

(It's true. I have had some work done, specifically in the forehead region. Vanity, however, wasn't the reason. It was because I was horribly burned in a fire.)

From Penlane40:

> I was fast-forwarding through his comments after he said Benji and his girlfriend didn't do it doggy-style . . . what an idiot!

(I did indeed feel like an idiot after speaking to a number of veterinarians and learning that the *only* way Benji and his girlfriend could possibly have "done it" was doggy-style. Mea culpa.)

There are, of course, more. Hundreds more. To those people, and to the thousands more who did not have the courage to write, I want to say this: I am really, really, really, really, really sorry. There aren't enough "reallys" to convey how sorry I am. Further, know this: I have learned from this experience, and I have changed.

I only hope these same people will accept and support me on my next television project, "Albert Schweitzer Can Suck Me," in which I use my winning sense of humor to rip the famed humanitarian a new asshole.

See the World but Stay Southern

ROY BLOUNT JR.

Though goings-on abroad they may amaze ya,
Always remember who you are.
Don't forget your raisin' in Eurasia
Or any of those areas off afar.

Somehow, in spite of what Robert E. Lee named his horse, I don't think of travel as a Southern tradition. When I was growing up outside Atlanta in the forties and fifties, it would no more have occurred to us to visit, say, Europe, just to *see* it for some reason, than California or someplace like that. Or . . . Charleston, even. We weren't related to anybody in Charleston, why would we go there? My father traveled a lot, but that was for business and—though in retrospect I wonder about this— was a cross he had to bear. For his two weeks of vacation every summer, we would drive off not in search of new vistas but "back home" to visit my parents' folks in Jacksonville, Florida, where it was even hotter. We'd spend a day at the beach, a day fishing for croakers and bringing them back to my grandparents' house to clean them and fry them up, with hushpuppies. Some good eating. But not the sort of thing a travel magazine would devote an article to, not a hot new getaway. Hey, when you roam, all the world am sad and dreary, right? Then I went away to college. And liked it. I've been traveling ever since. And not feeling quite right about it. I keep hearing my mother's voice saying, "He doesn't have any business *something something* when there are plenty of perfectly nice *something something* right here at home."

So wherever I go, part of me is determined to stay native to where I'm from. Here are some travel tips, deriving, as everything else derives, from some combination of where I come from and why I came from it:

1. Before you try a strange barbecue place, roll down your window and make sure it smells good from the car. But then if your attention wasn't caught by the aroma in the first place, why did you stop?

2. Never try a down-home restaurant whose sign is misspelled on purpose ("Vurnun's Caffay"), nor an imported-cuisine restaurant whose sign is misspelled by accident ("L'Bonn Formage").

3. Abroad, carry enough bottled water that you won't have to drink any unbottled water, but not so much that you will have to use the restrooms.

4. If, after trying for days to be patient and forbearing in a foreign-speaking country, you are tempted to scream, *"Will you please stop spouting that infernal gibberish!"* at people who live there, just for your own relief, remember this: they may understand what you are saying, and may take it personally. If they live in a part of the world that is at all suitable for tourism, they will at least have figured out that "gibberish" is English for, say, French, or whatever. In a pejorative sense. They may go into a shell, or misdirect you disastrously in weird near-English, or disappear for a few moments and then come back and run into you on one of those nasty little motorbikes.

5. Never hand your expensive camera to an indigenous person and ask him to photograph you and the rest of your party if he looks like he can run faster than everyone in your party. (Note: even if he doesn't look like it, he can.)

6. Don't show the slides of your trip to anyone who does not appear in them. Slides, unless they are salacious, gruesome or of museum quality, and usually even if they are of museum quality, are endurable only by people who appear in them. Or whose children appear in them. (Young children. Sensible parents do not want to see candid snaps of their teenagers away from home.) People who owe you money? They will sit through your slides. But if they are not in your slides,

and they don't have a child, a young child, who is in them, they will consider their debt discharged. All this goes double for video.

7. Don't worry about remembering whether a dromedary has one hump and a camel two, or vice versa, because whichever one you tell people you rode, they will give you a surprised look and say what a shame, you really should have ridden the other.

8. While you are away, the weather at home will be unseasonably fine, the team you root for will win its most unforgettable victory, and the emperor and empress of whatever exotic country you are visiting will pay a surprise visit to your neighborhood and invite your next-door neighbors to come see them any time at the castle, though preferably not this time of year, when all the tourists flock to the more obvious attractions and everyone who is authentic clears out.

9. If you decide to swing by the town of Sweetlip, even though it will make your drive much longer, on the assumption that it must be a charming town with such a name, you will find that it was named after Garner W. Sweetlip, who founded the town in 1951 around its principal industry, a plant that converts catfish viscera and old mesh caps into eleven thousand tons of commercial fertilizer an hour, not to mention by-products and effluent, samples available. It's pronounced "Swillup."

10. Never make eye contact with someone else's young child on a plane. That is what the parent prays for. A parent of a young child on a plane is liable to open up the emergency hatch and bail out if he or she can justify it by thinking that somebody else has accepted even a split second's responsibility for the child. "No one will blame me for leaping to my death if it was clear that I knew that someone was there to look after little Rachel as she was wallowing on the tray table, rubbing pudding in her hair and screeching"—we who have been parents of young children on airplanes ourselves have all been there.

That's all I have.

Fortuitously, my sister (who is younger than me and therefore was still growing up when there was a kind of sea change and my parents started going to the Cotswolds and places like that) has just this minute called to tell me she is back from Egypt. Now that—the Holy Land—might have been a place that people I grew up with would have considered traveling to, if they were going to travel to anyplace foreign, which they weren't, but at least there would be scriptural authority for it.

My sister went there, though, because she has wanted to see the ancient heathen temples along the Nile and she has an Egyptian friend. She was surprised, as I would have been, to note that parts of Egypt still look like the Bible—well, no, what she said was, the men still wear those things that look like nightgowns, as in the illustrations. But now they have motor vehicles, so camels are butchered and sold to poor people for meat. Seems a shame. I'd like to go to Egypt, but by the time I get there it probably won't look any more like the Bible than California. I was thinking about going to Cuba, if only because the government doesn't want me to, but the other night I talked to some people who had been there over Christmas. That is the kind of company I find myself in these days: people who will just up and spend their family Christmas in a Communist country, and not because they were abducted and forced to and are writing it up for the *Reader's Digest*, either, and they don't even smoke cigars. And do you know what they said? They said that as good as Cuban food in Miami is, the food in untouristy eating places in Cuba proper is terrible. Because, basically, there isn't much food in Cuba.

Well, hell, let's get some relations going with those people so they can serve foreigners some decent beans and rice. Because here is something I think we can say, generally, about Southern travelers: if we are going to pack up and find somebody to look after the dogs and the cats and the plants and go to the damn airport and wrangle our way over to some damn foreign place where the airports are even harder to get through than ours and figure out different money and spend a lot of it that turns out to be worth more in real money than it looked like and miss the Tangerine

Bowl and give the opposing faction on the Board of Stewards a chance to ram through some kind of crazy damn scheme involving the design of the porte cochere outside the new Sunday School building—I tell you what. The eating. Had better. Be good.

eBay Searches

July 14, 2003, 11:23 P.M.

SEARCH	HITS
one in a million	44

SEARCH	HITS
this is the one	11
this is the coolest	0
this is the best	6
this is the life	8
this is the end	1

SEARCH	HITS
I'm awesome	2
I'm scared	10
I'm scarred	0

SEARCH	HITS
fantastic	6,623
lovely	17,048
beautiful	59,982
amazing	10,246
sublime	429

SEARCH	HITS
super	45,945
duper	91
super duper	78
super dooper	2

SEARCH	HITS
tall, dark and handsome	7
sensitive	294
nature lover	10
hiking	2,031
skiing	837
snowboarding	360

SEARCH	HITS
blue eyes	2,014
romantic	2,684
fun loving	22
(fun lovin)	67
long walks	2
sad movies	2

—Stephanie Brooks

Forever Dale

JOE BOB BRIGGS

All I was trying to do, Your Honor, was have an ordinary 15-ounce beer in peace while raising a mug to the memory of Dale.

Yes, Your Honor, I know it was 15 ounces because that's the regulation Dale Earnhardt Sr. Glass Tankard that sells for $12.95 at the Exxon mini-mart. I'm sure you've seen 'em, with the giant number 3 on the side, and Dale's signature, and
. . . yes, sir.

So this gentleman—I'm gonna call him a gentleman because that's what Dale would of done—this gentleman over here interrupted my toast, and at first I didn't even realize what was happening because my eyes were already tearing up and all of us had risen to a respectful position of Dale obeisance, with our Dale Earnhardt Legacy Fitted Hats, the ones that say INTIMIDATOR on the bill, crossed over our chests, and I can't recall anyone ever disturbing that moment in the slightest, given the probly ten thousand Dale Earnhardt toasts I've personally conducted in several Mississippi counties over the last two years—and that would be, of course, two years and six months, to be precise, dating the toasts from February 18th, 2001, which, you know, the world changed that day, which is why everyone refers to pre-2/18 and post-2/18 and . . .

Yes, sir. I understand, sir. Yes sir, I will.

Well, my point, Your Honor, is that no one could have mistaken the sacredness of the moment, because we had the mugs raised and I was in the middle of saying "To Dale, who took the wall at Daytona for all mankind," when my associate Junior Wilcox removed his Dale Earnhardt Legacy Twill Jacket, the black one with the picture of Dale on the back, and called my attention to this gentleman attempting to remove the Dale Earnhardt Sr. Metal Thunder Plaque from the wall of this establishment. You can imagine how we all reacted, especially since several of us had ponied up the $125 to purchase the plaque, which contains, by the way, an actual piece of sheet metal from Dale's car that has never been touched by human hands since it was embedded into the walnut frame next to the color lithograph of Dale over the engraved nameplate with Dale's signature.

Your Honor, I don't want to tell you exactly what Junior Wilcox yelled at that moment, because I do respect the dignity of this courthouse, but he challenged the gentleman to desist. I do think the situation could have been rectified short of fisticuffs. However, the gentleman at that point in time chose to challenge the integrity of the assemblage with a statement that I think you would agree would be regarded as treasonable and inciting to riot.

Yes, Your Honor, I will, even though it disgusts me, frankly, to repeat the words. He said, "I'm tired of these damn Dale Earnhardt speeches. How about a toast for Sterling Marlin?"

Your Honor, I rest my case.

I can't? Okay. So maybe you should ask me some questions or something. I thought that pretty much explained the fracas.

Yes sir. All right, sir. Yes, Sterling Marlin was the driver— and let me say I have nothing against Sterling Marlin personally, although I was happy to see he crapped out in the pit last week at Phoenix and finished 36th—Sterling Marlin was the individual who smacked Dale on the left rear quarter panel on the final lap of the 2001 Daytona 500 and drove him headfirst into the wall, exploding his brain matter.

Excuse me, Your Honor. With your permission, I need to take just a moment here. All right. Fine. Yes, I can go on.

Technically, Your Honor, no, we did not dogpile on Mr. Stuyvesant—and, thank you, I'm very happy to learn his name, seeing as the court would probably not look kindly on our usual reference to him as the Cotton-Docker-Wearing Weenie—but no, sir, I wouldn't call it so much a dogpile as a flying wedge formation intended solely to prevent the destruction of property, namely the aforementioned plaque, the Dale Earnhardt Photo Clock, and the Dale Earnhardt Polyvinyl Hanging Banner, all of which were located in approximately the same area of the southeastern wall next to the waitress station.

Yes, Your Honor, as a matter of fact, Mr. Stuyvesant had made himself known to us on at least two prior occasions. The first instance occurred after a successful deer hunt, during which we were not in our customary attire but were dressed instead in Dale Earnhardt Realtree Camo Hats, the ones with the 3 on the front and the signature over the brim camouflage, and it was entirely a parking lot altercation, as the gentleman seemed to have some choice remarks about Lonnie Scroggins's Chevy truck, which had been kitted to resemble the Talladega/Confetti Win Car, with the black number 3 and the red spoiler and "Goodwrench" across the hood, because that is, of course, Dale's last winning car. But, in fact, the words exchanged that day didn't involve the car. The remarks were actually directed more toward Lonnie's Dale Earnhardt Sr. Trailer Hitch Cover, which, I might add, is a fine piece of equipment made of corrosion-resistant pewter alloy with heavy gauge yoke, with "INTIMIDATOR 3" in a raised 3-D design.

No, sir, I can't remember precisely what was said, but I recall the words as derogatory.

Yes, I did, thank you. There *was* a second exchange with this gentleman prior to the late unpleasantness at Phil's Blue Hole Roadhouse. It occurred during an eBay auction—yes, sir, that's what's known as a "virtual auction," and by the way, you may not be aware of this, but for $34.95 eBay offers the Dale Earnhardt Sr. Mousecar Racing Kit, consisting of a computer mouse in the shape of Dale's car, a Mousecar Pit Pad, and a RaceSavers ScreenSaver, all authorized and verified as genuine Dale . . . yes, sir, I *will* hurry along.

So the gentleman posted quite a few of what I would call nasty messages involving the auction items, which, if I recall correctly, included the Dale Earnhardt Sr. Race Cake Baking Kit, which is a frosting, cake mix and cake pan set that results in a cake in the shape of Dale's black Monte Carlo, complete with plastic spoiler and two free edible decals. That was the main item, but there were also lesser female-friendly offerings like the Dale Earnhardt Sr. Special Edition Monopoly Game, the Dale Earnhardt Bean Bag Bears (which is a matching set of two teddy bears with "DALE" stitched on the chest of both, representing Dale and Dale Jr.), the Dale Earnhardt Sr. Brunswick Viz-A-Ball bowling ball, with the 3 on the side and the signature, the Dale Earnhardt Sr. Hyperlite wakeboard, the Dale Earnhardt Christmas Ornament, and, if I recall correctly, there was also a Dale Earnhardt Sr. "Forever a Fan" black flag— I remember those because I have three flying from my own front porch, to the *left* of Old Glory, of course.

Yes, Your Honor, I will. Thank you. I didn't know the rule about relevancy, thank you for pointing that out.

Yes, Your Honor, I *will* sum it up. My analysis of what happened on the night in question is that the blows that were struck were entirely in self-defense. But when I say "self-defense," I don't use the term in its normal sense of our puny sorry-ass big-butted bodies. No, Your Honor, I mean in defense of an ideal and a legend. Dale gave his life—his *life*, Your Honor—so that Michael Waltrip could win that race. Let's face it, Judge, Michael Waltrip was zero for 462! They don't even have records like that in Pee Wee Football. And it wasn't just Sterling Marlin. Ken Schrader was there. Rusty Wallace was there. Either one of 'em could have run past Michael Waltrip and Dale Jr. if Dale hadn't been back there running interference for his team. His boys finished 1-2 while he was basically demolishing four cars between turn 3 and turn 4. This has been proven in great detail in the various books like *A Tribute to the Man in Black*, although I prefer *The Legend Lives On*, to tell you the truth. That book *At the Altar of Speed* was okay, but it didn't have enough pictures in it.

Yes, Your Honor, I do have a point. I'm sorry. My point is that it's not about *us*. It's about *Dale*.

Yes, sir. Yes, Your Honor. Would that include weekends, because I have younguns. Yes, Your Honor. I understand.

If I could ask one question, Your Honor? Thank you.

There's a product called Dale Earnhardt Sr. Playing Cards that come in a black tin with the number 3 on the side, and do you think that would be considered contraband in a county correctional facility?

Thank you, Your Honor. Even though I don't agree with your decision, I would just like you to know that all of us who stand before you today are simply dedicated to the memory of Dale and all he stood for, including the purity of NASCAR racing. We would just hate that to be demeaned or commercialized.

Yes, sir, I *will* go with the deputy.

KIM McCANN'S **DICHOTOMOUS WORLD**

Caption from *The Bible Coloring Book* or Excerpt from the October 1999 *Vanity Fair* Article on Ben Affleck?

1. She drew him from the water and raised him as her son.
2. He's larger than life and yet people can relate to him.
3. The reason I'm single is because I wouldn't want to be with anybody right now who would be willing to be with me.
4. They all went, two by two, in the ark where they would be safe from the giant flood.
5. And my head goes, "Boom!" Bounces off the concrete. It's like, "Whack!"
6. A young woman named Rebecca soon approached and offered him a drink.
7. Benjamin left his father, Jacob, and went with his brothers back to Egypt, as Joseph had commanded.
8. Underneath everything you say has to be the attitude of: You're an asshole, I know better than you, fuck you.
9. When he returned to his father's house, he was forgiven. His father said, "Forgiveness is not for those who think they are good, but for those who know they have sinned."
10. "Hey! I have two sphincters!"

Key
1. coloring book (about Moses)
2. *Vanity Fair* (Bob Weinstein, about Affleck's personality)
3. *Vanity Fair* (Affleck on relationships)
4. coloring book (about the ark)
5. *Vanity Fair* (Affleck on stunt work)
6. coloring book (about Ezikiah)
7. coloring book (about family dysfunction in Bible times)
8. *Vanity Fair* (Affleck on the Boston accent)
9. coloring book (about the prodigal son)
10. *Vanity Fair* (Affleck on ridiculous reasons to make movies about someone)

The Bitter End (My Will)

NANCY COHEN

To my ex-boyfriend, James, I leave my PowerBook G4 laptop. I've taken the liberty of removing the letter *L* because maybe that way you'll stop lying.

To my best friend, Cynthia, I leave my '89 Volvo. I know you can't drive a stick, but neither can I now.

To my second best friend, Diane, I leave my yoga mat and a roll of duct tape. You need to fuse your mouth shut and work out because you're very fat for a single person. This just in: You will never meet a guy in L.A. with hips like those. Especially since you won't settle for anyone who isn't as cute and successful as George Clooney. So downward dog, chunkster, downward dog!

To my Aunt Florence, who's a travel agent and afraid to fly in an airplane or drive over a bridge *or* get in an elevator, I leave my prescription for Zoloft. You're eighty, you've made a living convincing people to take vacations but have yet to take one yourself, and your mean husband's finally dead—so get the hell out of South Jersey for a day!

To my boring friend Claire who survived cancer, I leave my entire library of books so that you have something to talk about because you are incredibly dull and I would've ended this friendship years ago if you hadn't had cancer.

To my literary agents, I leave my *Curb Your Enthusiasm* spec script—the one where Larry pretends to be handicapped so he can be a hero in a wheelchair basketball league. It's fucking funny and I still can't believe you couldn't get me work from it. I hope your BlackBerry batteries die in the middle of closing a mid-six-figure deal (which should be MINE but since I'm DEAD it's too LATE!!!).

To my niece and nephew, who are eight and eleven, respectively, I leave a big-ass box of thank-you cards. Because for eleven years I've been sending checks for birthdays and Chanukah, and have yet to receive a verbal or written "thank-you." So please send out thank-you cards when I'm dead. And stop being so self-absorbed. Just 'cause you're kids doesn't mean the world revolves around you.

To my brother I leave nothing. Because we never really got along. And you kinda embarrass me. Twenty years of you saying "How's the left coast?" and thinking it's funny really gets on my nerves. And on my husband's nerves. In fact, you're the butt of many of our jokes out here "on the left coast." On second thought, I guess I'll leave you something. You can have the loose Tic Tacs at the bottom of my purse. Because you have bad breath. And it isn't genetic.

To my mother, I leave my love. Oh, and my collection of platform shoes—if you glue all twenty pairs together you might just be the height of a normal person.

To my husband of a year and a half, I leave you kisses. You're a great guy and you've made me very happy in our marriage. Now I leave you the right to date all the other women that I know you want to date, especially when I'm in my I-have-cellulite jealous sick rage. So go date fat-free younger women and that ex-girlfriend who you say you have no interest in but she's so pretty I just know you're lying. And I leave you whatever money I've made—take the girls out for sushi, to our place, you big cheater!

And to the guy in the red Chevy Blazer who I almost rear-ended on my way home because he didn't signal, I leave my right middle finger in a Lucite paperweight.

What I Learned About Cooking Last Night

NANCY COHEN

- You shouldn't dry lettuce leaves with a blow-dryer.
- Just because your smoke alarm went off doesn't mean your trout's done.
- Drinking a bottle of cabernet while cooking won't help you figure shit out.
- Don't use the big cap from your detergent as a measuring cup.
- Butter has an expiration date.
- If someone tells you making eggplant parmesan is easy, they're probably an eggplant parmesanist.
- A clove of garlic means just a small piece, not the entire thingie.
- It's tough to cook lying down.
- Paul Newman is a great actor who makes delicious sauce. I do occasional mediocre voice-over work and make poisonous sauce.
- Taking baby carrots out of the bag is harder than it looks.
- If you're wearing a skirt, don't shut the oven door with your leg—unless you're serving Third-Degree Burn.
- "Boiling" is "broiling," without the *r* . . . I think.
- Vegetarians won't eat brisket, no matter how much you nag.
- Paprika is useless.
- Baking is for freaks; muffins cost a dollar in the store.
- No matter how good a mood you're in, chopping onions will make you cry.

- If you need to thaw ice cream, nine minutes in the microwave is too long.
- Even the nicest guests expect herbal teas in all the primary colors.
- Do not put keys in key lime pie.
- If your potatoes taste more like chicken than your chicken does, order in.

HARMON LEON'S OFFICE PRANKS
BURIED TREASURE OF ONE-EYED PETE!

things needed
- 1 treasure map
- 1 parrot

During mid-week, gather the office gang around the water cooler. Tell them you've made an astonishing discovery; you've found an old treasure map hidden behind the filing cabinet. According to the map, hidden somewhere in the office is the treasure of One-Eyed Pete—a salty old pirate who sailed the seven seas back in the 1800s. Legend has it that One-Eyed Pete's fabled treasure is worth millions. Placing the parrot on your shoulder, tell everyone that you'll share One-Eyed Pete's treasure if you work as a team to find it within the confines of the office. Split the office into three different groups. Refer to people as "Matey." Occasionally blurt out "Arrrg!" Tear up the floorboards with a pick and shovel. After hours of hectic searching, proclaim, "I guess we'll never find One-Eyed Pete's treasure!" Go back to your desk and have a hearty laugh.

Supplementary Colors: Press Clips of an Unknown Woman

DAVID COLMAN

Eight years after Joe Klein—oops!—changed Old Glory's colors to red, blue and yellow, we imagine what would have happened if a pop singer took her soap box into the recording studio and onto the airwaves.

". . . and the uberfabulous crowd at the party at the Tunnel later went wild when Junior Vasquez spun that extra-long-lasting new track 'Holiday' from God-only-knows-who singing God-only-knows-what about Miss First Lady Hillary. Slipping into Miss Vasquez's hi-fi, high-security booth, I demanded Miss Thing's name, but she wasn't telling. 'I found her, I mixed her, and I made her, and I ain't sharing. So beat it, Billie Jean.' This with a sneer. I persisted, but—if you can believe—he had his security thugs hustle me out, the brutes. And all over a little remark that I'd read that crack tended to make people testy. . . ."
—*Paper* Magazine, August 1996

"Who's that girl? Record industry executives and downtown scenesters alike are buzzing about music's new mystery woman whose dance-club single 'Holiday'—a *chanson à clef* whose lyrics sardonically riff on the White House 'Travelgate' scandal—has risen out of nowhere to number three on the pop charts this week. In a possibly related story, deejay Junior Vasquez, who recently told a reporter from *Paper* magazine that he had produced the single as well as several others, has been missing for six days, according to a friend."
—*Billboard*, August 12–19, 1996

"Sire Records announced today that they have signed the mystery singing sensation—a woman known only as Madonnamous, according to a press release—to a $4 million recording contract, refusing to divulge the artist's name. The singer's latest single, 'Borderline,' a catty insider look at the political machinations that led to the North American Free Trade Association treaty, debuted at the #1 spot on the Billboard charts last week."

—*Wall Street Journal*, September 13, 1996

"Washington is in a tizzy over who Madonnamous could possibly be. The leading suspects so far: singer Janet Jackson, who sources close to the artist say has become obsessed with politics since having dinner with John F. Kennedy Jr. and appearing on the cover of *George*, political commentator Mary Matalin, Katrina vanden Heuvel, editor of *The Nation*, and Barbara Bush, who, according to a longtime friend, has often voiced a lifelong regret that she threw away her dream to be a pop singer to marry former president Bush. 'She was always griping that Mariah Carey couldn't even hold a note,' said the friend, who asked not to be identified. While neither Jackson nor Bush could be reached for comment, vanden Heuvel said, 'Get real. I'm far too busy to have a second career as a rock star.' And friends of Matalin scoffed at the reports. 'Have you ever heard her sing? There's no way it's her.' "

—*Newsweek*, September 23, 1996

"The producers of the upcoming GOP-funded documentary of the Clintons' 1996 presidential campaign, *Desperately Seeking Reelection*, have scored a marketing coup by snagging the latest single from mystery singer Madonnamous, tentatively titled 'Into the Groove,' for the film's soundtrack. Sources close to the project say the song critiques Clinton for adopting moderate stances on hot-button issues to shore up the middle-of-the-road vote. 'But it's got a great beat,' one source said. 'As they say on *American Bandstand*, I give it a ten.' "

—*Daily Variety*, October 14, 1996

"President Clinton apparently still has some pull. After reports that mystery singer Madonnamous was penning a song to help discredit his platform, the Democratic Party has announced that for an upcoming short film about Bob Dole's campaign, titled *Vision Quest*, they have managed to solicit not one but three hits from the singer for their soundtrack. Though no one would divulge what the songs' lyrics would say, her press rep said that the song titles—'Express Yourself,' 'Like a Prayer,' and 'Rescue Me'—spoke for themselves. She also said that Madonnamous would not be making a cameo in the film as Clinton had requested, but added, 'It's not like Dole shows up on film that well, either.' "

—*Daily Variety*, October 21, 1996

"Why put Madonnamous on the cover? Well, with the multisutured-ruptured discourse of millennial culture and gender being increasingly un(re)raveled, Madonnamous is the ultimate Aphrodite-Socrates: Aphrocrates, if you will: the age of Madrogyny! Heard, but not seen; known, yet unknowable. Who wants to know? We do! But do we? And yet, with epistemological knowledge of post-Warholian culture as indefinable as a quark, Madonnamous is at once ur-cul-de-sac and ur-closed-circuit. Derrida would approve. We love you, Madonnamous, whoever you are!"

—Letter from the editor, *Artforum*, November 1996

"Preliminary voice data analysis research performed by the Federated Audiotech Systems in Rock Neck, New York, indicated that, out of more than 300,000 candidates analyzed, one voice tested incontrovertibly as that of the woman known as Madonnamous: Marge Platt, a 51-year-old homemaker in Stellaboro, Ohio. Mrs. Platt gave a press conference outside her home this afternoon, admitting that the voice was hers. 'I always loved to sing in high school, and who doesn't like politics?' said Mrs. Platt, explaining that her relationship with Mr. Vasquez, who has been missing since mid-August, started when he spent Christmas at her house the year before as the guest of her son, who works as a go-go dancer in Manhattan. She declined to speculate on Mr. Vasquez's disappearance, saying, 'He's a nice boy. I'm sure he'll turn up.' She closed the press conference by humming a line from her latest single, 'Like a Virgin,' a blistering attack on the FDA holdup in the U.S. for the French abortion pill RU-486, and handing cookies out to reporters."

—*New York Times*, October 30, 1996

"Madonnamous Mom a Hoax!"

"Fake voice data and ringer-singer fool reporters—hoax artist gloats. Full coverage, page 4."

—Cover of the *New York Post*, November 2, 1996

"Madonnamous, whose identity still remains a secret after an elaborate media ruse by hoax-artist Joey Skaggs and his mother, an Ohio homemaker, has turned her famously acerbic lyric writing at the spotlight that aided, if not abetted, her rise to fame. The singer's love affair with the press soured, sources say, after Ross Perot won the presidential election and the artist's single, 'Material Girl,' a thinly veiled account of child labor in sweatshops, failed to ignite the public's interest. Her latest single, 'Vogue,' paints the goings-on at a fashion magazine as a carnival of egos and internecine squabbling, though it contains the conciliatory line, 'Anna Wintour, we love you.' Ms. Wintour, the magazine's editor in chief, said the song was wildly hyperbolic, but conceded that, 'We all have our bad days.' As for Madonnamous herself, Ms. Wintour said she liked the music and had enjoyed the phenomenon, but said, 'Let's keep it in perspective. I mean, tomorrow nobody's even going to remember who she is.' "

—*New York Times*, January 30, 1997

"Madonnamous and Junior Vasquez found alive on Greek Island with JFK and Elvis!"

—Cover headline, *Weekly World News*, August 4, 1999

Sister Goddess Ruby

JILL A. DAVIS

Jenn calls, she's thinking of taking another class, do I want to go?

"Not cheese-making again," I say. "The dry cleaner made me sign a release before they'd attempt to clean my sweater."

"Well, there's this thing. You'll hate it. It's an eight-week deal. You don't have to go to all eight weeks, but I'm allowed to bring a friend to the first meeting. I mean, I'm going, I already signed up, and it cost $800 so I can't back out."

"Aren't you too old for Outward Bound?" I ask.

"No. I'm not entirely sure what I've signed up for . . . it's kind of an empowerment thing. For women. Katie from the office suggested it. She said it really changed her life."

"Katie, the one who wears nylons in the summer with shorts?" I ask. "Katie, the one who wears makeup to the gym?"

"Yeah, anyway, I don't know, maybe I shouldn't go. I mean, it's not like men have empowerment groups," she says.

As she says this, I'm thinking, of course they do! What do you call Monday Night Football? They fill stadiums with men cheering for men. Men loving men. Men paying men lots of money to play with a little ball, it's a glorified love-fest with major sponsors, and beer bongs.

"You don't have any money, Jenn. So if you already paid the $800 you must have really wanted to go," I say.

"Yeah, I guess," she says. "So will you go to the first meeting?"

"Yeah, OK, maybe I can get a column out of it," I say. I knew she wouldn't go without me, and I knew she really wanted to go. And I needed a column.

"Oh, one thing I should tell you, in case you get there

before me: When you're there, you have to address the other women as Sister Goddess," she says.

Sister Goddess . . .

I know before I get there that this bring-a-friend thing is a total trap. It's a scam those vacation Bible schools use. Bring a friend, get a pack of Lifesavers. Lifesavers, of all things. The cult is hoping I'll have such a positive experience that they will be able to permanently induct me into the sisterhood. Either way, I said I'd go. So I'm going.

Any event that begins with the words "Sister Goddesses gather 'round" has to be worth the investment of two hours on a Tuesday night.

I take a cab to the Upper East Side. York Avenue. I climb the four flights to Sister Goddess Pam's studio apartment.

Everyone looked pretty normal. Jenn was there, sitting on a windowsill. Staring at her feet. Chewing on her lip.

I bounded in, caught Jenn's attention, and made an elaborate wave and said, "Hey, Sister Goddess Jenn."

"Hey, Ruby," she says.

"*Sister Goddess* Ruby," I say.

Sister Goddess Pam closes the front door. We're trapped. She invites us to gather around. "Welcome to Sister Pam's School of Womanly Graces," she says.

She tells us to join hands, and form a circle. Sister Goddess Pam asks us to reveal to our fellow sister goddesses our "item of riddance." Item of what?

Everyone had props. One woman had a journal. One had a necklace. Another had a lock of hair. And so on. The item of riddance, Sister Goddess Pam reminded us, was the item that represented what was holding us back. The thing we needed to get out of our lives the most.

My head raced. If I'd actually been alerted to this earlier . . . what would I have brought? What something was it that weighed me down, made me so scared, desperate, confused, lonely that I'd attend a Sister Goddess seminar to unload the item? I had nothing. I hadn't done my homework, and everyone else in the class had. How could Jenn forget to tell me about something as important as my item of riddance? I grabbed a piece of paper, and frantically wrote three words on it, and folded the paper ten times so no one could see it.

I had visions of us burning these in a smoldering bonfire of churning flames that would suck down our insecurity, or lack of independence, or general free-floating fears and whisk them away.

Instead, we formed a single line, and marched from Sister Goddess Pam's studio apartment down the hall to a closet that was slightly larger than Sister Goddess Pam's studio. A large blue sticker on the door read "Did you remember to recycle?"

One by one we unloaded our baggage down the chute that leads to the building's entrails, the whistling, clanking incinerator: Sister Goddess Jenn let her photo of Harry Stiller fall. Sister Goddess Susie (a nurse by day, a slam poet by night) tossed in her black makeup and black hair dye. Sister Goddess Tina, her birth control pills. Sister Goddess Ruby, my white piece of paper. Sister Goddess Sandy, a banker, threw in a man's shirt. Then let out a howl of laughter that couldn't be stifled. And somehow I couldn't help but to think that she was burning some important evidence that could potentially convict her, and we were all witnesses.

We march back to Sister Goddess Pam's cramped dwelling. There, she instructs us to sit in a circle. She excuses herself and sprays some Glade air freshener near the cat box. Then returns to join the circle.

"You are all here to reclaim something. Something has been taken from you, and you want it back," she says. "But there is something very powerful within you. Too powerful to be ignored, that you've always had. And you cannot, will not, be ashamed of it. Can anyone tell me what that is?" No one has a chance to answer.

"It's your vagina!" she says, so happy you want to slap her.

Are you like me? Are you eager for the vagina movement to end?

I'm sitting next to the Wall Streeter, aka potential murderer, and attempting to squash my laugh. I disguise it as a coughing fit, when I realize everyone else has been hypnotized by Sister Goddess Pam. She's got one talon on their brains, the other on their checkbooks. I begin to fear for my life.

"Sister Goddess Sandy, we'll start with you. If your vagina were dressed up in an outfit, what would that outfit look like?"

"A Knicks uniform," she says without missing a beat. I think she may have been to this class before. Or she's a ringer or something. Everyone claps.

"Away or home uniform?" I ask. She offers a dismissive glance.

"Sister Goddess Ruby?" says Sister Goddess Pam.

"What?" I say.

"If your vagina were dressed in an outfit, what would that outfit look like?" she asks.

"Are we talkin' about for, like, Halloween, or is this like everyday vagina clothes?" I ask.

"Sister Goddess Ruby isn't ready to share. And that's OK. We accept Sister Goddess Ruby. Because we know it's fear that makes her so aggressive. So we won't ask her to leave. Let's move on to Sister Goddess Jenn. Sister Goddess Jenn . . ."

"Well, a cowboy hat, and cowboy boots . . . and a leather vest. The kind with studs and fringes and stuff. And maybe chaps and a bandanna too. Oh, and a holster with some big guns. Loaded guns. Yeah, that's what it would wear," Sister Goddess Jenn says.

She is looking at me with great pleasure. Like she's accomplished something. I don't think I've ever seen her looking so self-assured. And I'm realizing something about my friend. With every part of her being she's really, really, really proud to be from Texas.

Sister Goddess Suzy says her vagina would sport a Dorothy Hamill haircut, because her mom wouldn't let her get one oh so long ago when they were the rage. And, her vagina would wear tight jeans and a ripped, "sexy" T-shirt. Go Flashdance!

"Can I just say, that this is one freaky masquerade party I don't want to be invited to?" I say. I'm ignored.

cowboy boots

Sister Goddess Helen says her vagina would sport La Perla underwear. Pink La Perla, she says. Sister Pam lets her get away with this . . . folks, she's saying she'd wear underpants. . . .

"Can I add another thing to my you-know-what's outfit?" asks Sister Goddess Jenn.

Jenn can't say the word "vagina."

Sister Goddess Pam beams. "Of course!"

"A sheriff's badge!" says Sister Goddess Jenn.

"A holster, bandannas, a sheriff's badge? Your vagina really knows how to accessorize," I say.

"Now, we're getting to know more about ourselves and each other, aren't we?" says Sister Goddess Pam. "We're learning that the self we show to the world can be very different from the self we show to ourselves. Now we're going to go around the room, and share some more. We're going to share what it is our vaginas would say if they could speak. . . ."

The pack looks momentarily uneasy. I think I might be swaying them.

"Sister Goddess Ruby, should we start with you?" says Sister Goddess Pam.

"Oh, I'm sorry, Sister Goddess Pam, my vagina can't talk right now, because it's still trying to figure out what to wear," I say. "If only I had a multitasking vagina."

"Mine would say, 'Fuck me,' " said Sister Goddess Sandy.

"Look, I have to be honest, you guys are really creeping me out," I say. And your vaginas apparently aren't capable of an original thought, I think but don't say.

I wasn't so much asked to leave as I was told to leave. Though, I was invited to return should I ever "desire a real relationship with the most important person in the world, your true self."

If they were so eager to meet their true selves, why were their vaginas in drag? Besides, no one seemed to get it. That it was an exercise to make yourself see just how uncomfortable you are with your own body. That the silliness of dressing one's vagina should put you at ease ultimately. But they all took it literally. They were genuinely excited about the fashion show aspect of it all. Only a woman could come up with an empowerment group that involves outfitting your vagina . . . what next, vaginal makeup? Collagen injections? Or exercise videos?

I sit on the steps of a brownstone and wait for Jenn. An hour later she bounds down the stairs. And we walk to the corner of 82nd Street and hail a cab.

By the way, I think, but don't say, because I don't really want to talk about vaginas on a street corner, your vagina does wear clothes. Every day.

"Have fun?" I say.

"Yeah, it was really great. I really felt like I connected, you know?" she says.

I don't know. See, because to me that seems like the worst sort of lost there is . . . a staged evening that makes you feel connected. Manufactured intimacy. When this class is over, there will be another class. Another "connection." But there's no permanent gain. It's all just sort of dangled out there by someone else, and until you can manufacture it for yourself, it can't exist without an end. Jenn is dependent on the idea that there is something to learn, but the focus never narrows.

I think about those letters from Michael. And I think about feeling connected, and what's real, and what's not, and whether there's a difference. It makes me sad. And then it makes me laugh. Because sadness at any length is terrifying.

"You really can't say 'vagina'?" I say.

"I really can't," she says. "You must have liked it in the beginning. You wrote something down as your item of riddance. I saw you. What was it? What did you want out of your life?" she says.

"Three words: Sister Goddess Pam," I say.

. . . Swiss bank offers Holocaust survivors free checking . . . Thugs beat estimates . . . Miss Universe pageant begins with big bang . . . Hubble shocker: Earth carried on back of giant turtle . . .

Wild Pitch: An Open Letter to Joe Francis

D. ELLIS DICKERSON

"MGM . . . has purchased the feature film rights to *Girls Gone Wild*, the popular home video series that features everyday women flashing the camera at 'party till you puke' events like spring break . . . [and] Mardi Gras. . . . Joe Francis, creator of the home video series . . . told the *[Hollywood] Reporter* that . . . the first 'Girls' movie will be a fictionalized version of *Girls Gone Wild*, with love stories and everything in between. 'We will take elements of the core product and bring it to the silver screen, which we all know takes a hell of a lot more creativity. And at the end of the day, all I want is a great movie. I don't need the money and would never want a piece of garbage with my name on it.'"

—*Entertainment Weekly*

Dear Mr. Joe Francis:

I think I was originally drawn to your films because, although it's nerdy to admit this, I've always been a fan of documentaries. Having now seen most of them, I consider myself something of a GGW expert. (And let me just say that although you have a simple theme, you know it very well.) As a former fundamentalist, I have also spent countless man-years sitting through perfectly wretched teen sex comedies, just because I can. (The movies suck, but just going to the counter and saying, "I'd like to rent this naughty, irresponsible minx of a film!"—it's a thrill every time.) On this basis, and adding that I'm a former grad student, which means I've both had cable and stayed up late, I'd like to offer myself as a consultant as you search for your particular artistic vision.

Just think: in the whole history of teen sex comedies, nudity has always been completely gratuitous. You know how it goes: right in the middle of the lingerie party fund-raiser someone accidentally triggers the sprinklers, and while everyone's trying to ignore it and keep roller-skating, it just happens to turn midnight, and so suddenly it's someone's birthday, and they have to get a spanking, etc. And yet if you, Joe Francis, make a movie where girls "go wild," everyone can buy a ticket in complete confidence that the promise of the title will be fulfilled. This stands in direct contrast to disappointing films like *Beach Babes from Beyond Infinity* (they're just from a nearby planet); *Sorority Babes in the Slimeball Bowl-a-Rama* (contains almost no bowling, and several of the "sorority babes" are technically rushees); and the worst offender, *The Bikini Carwash Company II* (no bikinis, no car washing, and might as well have been called *The Modest Lingerie Cable Station That Was Rated R for No Discernible Reason*). So I guess when you say that your film will contain "elements of the core product," I hope you remember the breasts!

Since you're concerned about plot, of course the first thing to do is look at your classical sources. The earliest version of this story is in some fragments of an Aristophanes play, *The Cantaloupes*. Young Innocent Bodacia and her saucy, worldly-wise gal-pal Madonna, have gone to Thrace for the bacchanal. There they meet two strapping Etruscans named Helix and Rictus who have snuck in, in drag, to report to the rest of the men if there really are sexy pillow fights at bacchanals. The fragment ends there, but this theme of young women improving men's lives with their half-naked shenanigans is yet another thing we owe to Aristophanes. Almost all modern teen sex comedies, starting with *Animal House*, still have a certain "Greek" flavor. (If you're going to read it for yourself, I recommend the Richard Lattimore translation, even though he has taken a few liberties, such as translating Helix's joyful cry of "Thalassa! Thalassa!" as "USA! USA!")

Skipping to *Macbeth*, you know the scene where Lady Macbeth bids a serpent to "come to my woman's breast and take my milk for gall!" What's less well known, is that the First Folio contains an additional marginal note that says, "Tom: for this sceene, wear falsyes & have them giganticall! Moreover, when thou rippest thy garment, hold them vysible for fyve seckonds." Some claim this comment was written by Francis Bacon, but critics are unanimous in suggesting this scene, if performed, would have been well received.

This motif surfaces again in Beckett's *Flash Cube*, where a woman pops out of a jack-in-the-box, whips off her bra and shouts, "See these? Now you're all filthy perverts!" Then she rubs her forearms together really fast until she catches fire. Alienation, longing, Catholicism—all your themes are right there.

The second thing you need to do, of course, is to remember the emotional thread of the story. No one's going to care about some college girl who travels all the way to Panama City and flashes on camera because she wants to get a T-shirt. Raise the stakes! Let's say our heroine, Trixie von Kamp, volunteers for the Make-a-Wish Foundation. And there's some sweet, terminally ill 8-year-old child who looks up at her and says, "Before I die, all I want is a million Mardi Gras beads, all gotten in the traditional manner! Plus footage if you've got any." So Trixie goes to Panama City on a mission to collect the beads. But after her first day, Trixie feels like an outsider, watching life instead of experiencing it, and she wonders if there's anything she can do personally to help this kid's dream come true. Then one night, a little drunk, Trixie finds herself on the roof of the Club La Vela (I've checked and they're okay with a little publicity) and there are people shouting down below, and although she's very shy and she's never done anything like this before, she loves that kid so much . . . ! Long story short, she grits her teeth, closes her eyes, and lifts her shirt, just to test herself— you know, to see if she can go the distance. Cue a song by Diane Warren.

Meanwhile, a nice college guy (Jason) is walking with his friend, the hard-drinking party guru who, in the tradition of *Delta Pi, Bikini Beach*, and *Spring Break USA*, is nicknamed "Animal." They're wandering the streets of P.C. because Jason has had a dream four nights running that this Spring Break he will meet the woman he will marry, and he'll know her by the butterfly birthmark on her left breast. (Jason: "But how will I know what her breasts look like when I see her?" Animal: "Dude, you need to party!") They've been going from city to city everywhere in Florida (except Miami, because in the dream, her breasts are real). And one night he looks up at the roof of Club La Vela, sees Trixie topless, their eyes meet . . . cue the love theme.

Wackiness ensues, but the upshot is, Trixie and Jason get together, and she learns about love, about life . . . and a little bit about herself too. At the end of the film they collect all the beads they need, and, sure, the child dies, but by then it doesn't even matter. I also have a zany subplot involving mistaken identities and a nipple piercing, but I think you get the point. This is your chance to tell the world that GGW is about more than just naked breasts: it's about America, and freedom, and the fragile beauty of underage bingeing.

Then *Girls Gone Wild 2* should be set in New Orleans at Mardi Gras. There's been a whole history of films set there— *Candyman 2: Farewell to the Flesh, French Quarter Undercover, Mardi Gras Massacre, Mardi Gras for the Devil*—and not one of them gets it right. Our protagonist always runs from (or chases) his opponent in the middle of a parade, and slips easily in and out of the crowd, while everyone around them, however loud, is also sober and fully clothed. With your film, maybe at last we can finally see a Mardi Gras movie that shows it like it is: just a massive, mile-long wall of frat boys—chanting "Show your tits! Show your tits! Show your tits! . . . Whoooooo!"

Even if you listen to nothing else in this letter, Mr. Francis, do a Mardi Gras scene where you can actually smell the vomit and urine, taste the fatty lukewarm hot dogs sold on every corner, hear the gasps as people realize they've been pickpocketed, and really see—as if for the first time—the dozens of plastic hand grenades lying in the street, now empty of their overpriced liquor. After all, it is the duty of art to speak the truth.

Thank you for your time,
D. Ellis Dickerson

My Bible

BRIAN FRAZER

A big hullabaloo is made over fundamentalist Muslims letting their entire lives be rigidly guided by a single book, the Koran. I can relate. Something I've been reading every night since childhood has been a guiding force in my life. I keep it with me at all times and it's never failed me in providing hope, wisdom and clarity. Thank goodness for *The Hardy Boys: The Haunted Fort*.

> "You're alert, boys," Mr. Davenport commented. "I like that. What's more, you're not afraid, like that custodian who guarded my fort." (*p. 25, par. 3, sent. 1*)

Whenever I need a little bit more courage (like when I have to drive on an unfamiliar highway at night) I am reminded that the Hardy Boys, both mere teens, had the bravado of a dozen lions. A dozen really brave lions!

> "You mean the trap was intended for Frank and Joe," Chet finished. "And maybe me too. No place is safe around here." (*p. 87, par. 6, sent. 1*)

A bullet just goes where it is told. So be careful, for cryin' out loud.

> "Uncle Jim loves his job," Chet continued, "or at least he did before the painting thefts started." (*p. 3, par. 2, sent. 1*)

It's very important to love what you do for a living, regardless of what it pays. More important to be a happy accountant or an ecstatic vacuum salesman than a bitter movie star like Val Kilmer.

"Chet," Frank added, "didn't you mention a haunted fort on the phone?" "Oh, that!" Chet groaned. "Yes, I did." (*p. 4, par. 1, sent. 1*)

Always double-check things if you're not totally sure. I once thought I had won the lottery and got really excited and went on a spending spree to end all spending sprees. Then I realized I was holding a ticket that was *six years old*! If I had double-checked the date, I could have spared my creditors a lot of embarrassment, not to mention myself the 17.8 percent interest on a yacht I really didn't need. But then again, who can expect to be as wise as Frank Hardy?

"Wow!" Chet exclaimed to himself, coming upon a dazzling creation being worked on by a thin, red-haired boy in dungarees. "Looks like a vegetable cart that's been hit by lightning." (*p. 37, par. 2, sent. 2*)

Don't underestimate anyone. Believe it or not, even red-haired people are capable of doing creative stuff.

The fort map in Joe's pocket, the brothers headed for the mansion garage. On the way, they passed a tall, bearded man at an easel. "Hi," said Joe. "You must be one of the weekend painters, only this is Wednesday." (*p. 90, par. 7*)

Expect the unexpected. Sometimes the ice cream man comes around at 4:30, sometimes he comes around at 4:45. You just never know.

It was late afternoon by the time they reached the fort. There had been no trace of the phony detour sign. (*p. 91, par. 4*)

Just because you see a "sign" doesn't mean you have to obey it. Be your own person. You control your own destiny. And there's nothing wrong with ignoring a traffic light if you feel like it. It might not even be real!

> Chet stuttered with fear as the shadow drew near. It had a long neck and a huge glistening head, gaping jaws and long sharp teeth! (p. 100, par. 4)

Shadows prey on the weak, especially stutterers. If you're a stutterer, you should really keep your mouth shut as much as possible. And if you walk with a limp, stay in bed.

> A thorough search of the grounds proved futile. There was no sign of Jefferson Davenport. (p. 153, par. 2)

Don't be stupid—always get a person's cell phone number, not just their home and work numbers. It's a really easy way to contact somebody. Certainly much quicker than searching all over the place for them.

> Warren nodded, boasting, "Pretty clever I was to get into Millwood by playing the weekend painter bit." (p. 167, par. 7)

Each of us is comprised of many different people. Sometimes when you go to a bar, you should pretend to be a businessman from London (remember to practice the accent). It will help you have more fun in life, and, if you're lucky, get you some "action."

> With a shrill laugh, he moved away and began viewing the student paintings. "My, my. If this is one of the best, what must the worst be!" (p. 124, par. 4)

Never worry about the quality of your work. No matter how bad you think what you're doing is, there's always someone even *less* talented someplace. Probably right down the hall from you making *three times* what you are and driving a much nicer car with a hotter wife! Oh, God! Life just isn't fair!

> The boys whirled to see a hatchet embedded in the old door! It had narrowly missed Frank's head! *(p. 154, par. 6)*

If somebody throws a hatchet at your head, that's a sign from God to log on to Expedia or Travelocity and get the hell outta town. And when you're packing, don't forget to bring along *The Haunted Fort* because I don't run the country and there won't be a copy of it in the drawer of your motel nightstand.

... Celebrities with colds urge more funding for cold cure ... Nothing new at Luddite Expo ... Celebrity look-alikes speak out against cloning ... Good Samaritans threaten slowdown ...

The Cola Wars:
The Next 50 Years

BRIAN FRAZER

"Dr Pepper/Seven Up, Inc. said it will launch Red Fusion, a red, fruity addition to its Dr Pepper soft drink lineup, [in mid-July,] adding more heat to the battle between new flavored carbonated soft drinks. Red Fusion's launch will come about two months after Coca-Cola Co.'s new Vanilla Coke and about a month before PepsiCo Inc.'s bright Pepsi Blue."
—Reuters

2005 Morocco suspected of developing beverages of mass destruction with five times the sugar and twice the caffeine as Jolt. However, U.N. carbonation inspectors unable to prove it. An Iranian spokesperson insists that it's a club soda factory.

2007 Riding the success of its celery soft drink, Dr. Browns develops parsley and kale soda.

2008 Soviets accused of selling caramel coloring to North Korea. "Not true," said Vladamir Chertok. "We have only sold them those bendy straws that make drinking more enjoyable."

2011 A-1 joins the soda wars by introducing meat soda: carbonated blood.

2012 After six years of experiments, scientists at Pepsi unveil spectacular rum and Pepsi combo to market to bars.

2015 Sunkist, Fanta and Minute Maid merge to form giant artificially flavored orange conglomerate.

2016 At Soda Summit in Rio, attempts by bipartisan commission to have a unilateral cola freeze prove unsuccessful.

2019 On his deathbed, Jimmy Carter tries to convince Americans on the virtues of Strawberry Quik.

March 2020 to June 2029: Waitress strike. "There were way too many beverage choices already. It just wasn't fair to us," said a prominent waitress. "I mean, it's hard enough listing off all the lunch specials without having to memorize another bunch of new soft drinks that everyone's gonna want. This has really cut into our oxygen breaks."

2022 Bottled water outlawed by President Schweppes.

2023 A&W begins talks with China about developing a diet caffeine-free bamboo-flavored soda marketed toward the expanding panda market.

2024 Pepsi decides to sell their two-liter bottles without a cap, for exceedingly lazy population.

2027 Canada Dry officially declares itself neutral in any future soda disputes.

2029 Thanksgiving officially becomes Cokesgiving as Americans begin to marinate their turkeys in diet Coke per martial law.

2031 to 2037 The U.S. government reportedly begins testing a secret cream soda in the Mojave Desert.

2039 Average nine-year-old child now has 27.8 cavities. International silver shortage forces dentists to fill them with grout.

2046 Fresca momentarily becomes most popular soft

drink when Sharon Stone's granddaughter "has" one in *Fatal Attraction V*.

2052 Pepsi reveals that they're actually owned by Coke and the whole "competition" thing was just to drum up sales.

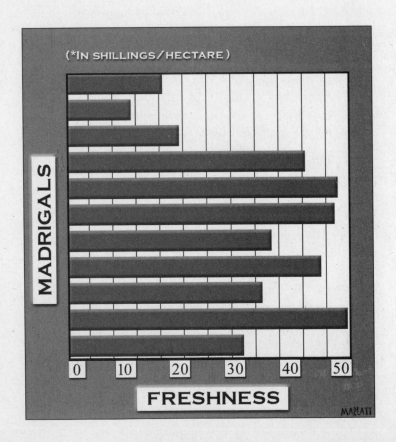

Synesthesia

DAVID K. GIBSON

The letter **A** was born rich, and never had to work for a thing in its whole life.

The burning associated with **B** does not respond to topical ointments.

C isn't sporty, but it's dependable and gets good mileage.

I once saw **D** leaving a movie with eyes red from crying, and though I am ashamed of feeling this way, I now think of it as less of a consonant.

The agency disavows all knowledge of **E**.

The letter **F** was thrust upward from the sea floor by intense geologic pressure.

G used to play semi-pro football, and its knees remind it of that every day.

In tests, only dry mouth and restlessness occurred more often with **H** than with placebo.

I goes to strip clubs, but never sits next to the stage.

J is cold. A wet cold, like in Nova Scotia.

K smells faintly of lemongrass.

What more need be said of **L**, taut and erect, humming in the breeze?

Your Aunt Janey went to school with **M**'s mother, where they were both officers in the Accounting Club.

N puts its sprinkler where it will wet my newspaper.

Sometimes when I am having a fight with **O**, I think about **P**, and wonder if things would have been any different, or if the real problem is me.

Q can be braised, but is tough if baked or grilled.

I wish **R** would just come out and say it.

S owns a convenience store, where it breaks up packages of snack cakes and butter, even though the units are clearly marked "Not labeled for individual sale."

T is full of right angles. Which is perfectly obvious, really.

When the letter **U** fantasizes, it imagines that people call it "crazy legs."

V no habla inglés.

We got our **W** at the shelter. It has a very sweet disposition but is not very good with children.

X rides a high-performance motorcycle, but brakes going into curves.

Someone chipped **Y** with the vacuum cleaner, so we turned it to the wall.

The letter **Z** may contain nuts.

. . . **Generation Z fears it may be the last** . . . **Physicists predict time travel "before you know it"** . . . **Koko the signing gorilla offers to mediate Mideast peace talks** . . . **Robotic dog bites man** . . .

Sinatron, Out of Control

DAVID K. GIBSON

1915 Francis Albert Sinatron is hatched in the rich chemical brine of the Hoboken, New Jersey, waterfront. His mother, an unclassified theropod and local political boss, encourages his destructive nature. The young Sinatron entertains at family gatherings by haphazardly destroying furniture and coat closets.

1930 Sinatron is expelled from Hoboken's A. J. Demarest High School for "general rowdiness." He never returns to school.

1935 Sinatron enters radio talent program *Major Bowes's Amateur Hour*. For the performance, Sinatron partners with a trio of giant ants to level downtown Hackensack. The quartet wins first prize, and joins Major Bowes's traveling show.

1938 Evil scientist Harry James discovers Sinatron working in an auto salvage yard in the New Jersey Palisades. He offers Sinatron $75 a week to front for his organization.

1939 Sinatron leaves James for the more evil scientist Tommy Dorsey. Here he develops his signature style of wanton destruction, and soon eclipses his evil overlord in popularity.

1940 Sinatron, living on Lagos Island with actress Alora Gooding, is seriously injured by naval bombardment during WWII. Radiation from atomic tests in the Pacific increases his size and special powers.

1943 Sinatron's first solo rampage, in Philadelphia, is attended by nearly a million citizens. Critics praise his characteristic phrasing and undeniable charisma.

1944 As Sinatron makes his first forays into motion pictures, he relocates to Hollywood. He brazenly tacks a list of cities he plans to destroy to his dressing room door, crossing them off as they are leveled.

1945 Sinatron has an audience with Pope Pius XII, who asks if he sings opera.

1946 Sinatron signs a five-year film contract with M-G-M, and switches his career focus from mayhem to acting. Many of his early films feature his trademark destructive chops, including *Sinatron vs. Monster Zero*, *Sinatron's Revenge*, and *On the Town*. Though a hit with the moviegoing public, Sinatron is attacked by the critics.

1951 After a fight with paramour Ava Gardner and depressed by his slumping career, Sinatron takes an overdose of maser radiation. Later, he and Gardner reconcile, and the episode is described as an accident.

1952 Sinatron ruptures his thorax and is temporarily unable to expel radioactive breath. He is dropped by M-G-M, the United Nations Security Council, and his agent.

1953 Sinatron begins shooting *From Here to Eternity*, which wins him a best supporting actor Oscar and revives his career. He does not destroy a city in the film.

1957 Upon the death of King Kong, Sinatron takes over as the leader of "Monster Island," a social club of gigantic beasts dedicated to absorbing massive amounts of radiation and smashing buildings. Over the next decade, the "Monsters" destroy dozens of cities worldwide, including seven capital cities.

1958 In an interview with *Look* magazine, Sinatron speaks candidly about his knack for destruction: "Being an 18-karat manic depressive, the brokenness I feel inside plays itself out in defenseless seaside cities."

1966 Sinatron assaults Frederick Weissman after Weissman asks him to stop destroying Los Angeles. Sinatron fractures Weissman's skull, but Weissman (whose house and car are anonymously trampled) does not press charges.

1971 Sinatron announces his retirement, and levels San Diego before disappearing into the Pacific.

1972 Sinatron unexpectedly and spectacularly emerges from retirement with a nationally televised rampage.

1981 In spite of antiapartheid protests, Sinatron destroys Sun City, South Africa. "I enjoyed it. I had a great time," he says, "I ate a great golf course."

1988 Sinatron begins a world reunion tour with Mothra, Megalon, and Liza Minnelli.

1993 In Seattle, Sinatron startles his screaming audience by returning to the fallen Space Needle and attempting to destroy it again. Onlookers report that Sinatron looks "confused." Sinatron's son, MechaSinatron, takes responsibility for the error, blaming a lack of rehearsal time.

1994 Sinatron collapses while destroying Richmond, Virginia, falling flat on his face immediately after crushing the dome of the Capitol Building. His publicist cites "exhaustion" as the culprit, but rumors concerning heart ailments are widely circulated.

1998 Sinatron, severely wounded in a battle with Matthew Broderick, sinks into the calm waters of Long Island Sound, and is declared dead in the world press.

ROD LOTT'S LISTS
9 FLAVORS OF JELLY BELLY GOURMET JELLY BEANS WE REFUSE TO EAT

coconut	buttered popcorn	strawberry daiquiri
Pepto-Bismol	toasted marshmallow	grilled cheese
seaweed	feet	buttered feet

Cabaret Is Not a Life

TOM GLIATTO

What's Playing at the Clubs This Week . . .

ironic wisdom

THE MORPHEUM ROOM

Lovers of popular song are always alert to any appearance by Sylvia Verner. Three nights weekly the venerable Miss Verner, now 108 years old, is gathered together and carried on a cushion from her bed at the Plaza to the stage of this intimate club, which over the years has become even more so as space has been subleased to a Russian bathhouse. Verner can be expected to start off with a few amusing anecdotes about her mentor, the legendary Mabel Mercer, whose dry flatulence was sometimes mistaken for actual singing. Then it's on to a repertoire that includes all the old standards and several of the ancient ones. No one can sing Demosthenes' "I Love You, You Love Me—How 'Bout That?" with Verner's exquisite balance of ironic wisdom and physical revulsion, and no one seems to want to. Six-drink minimum on the house.

DREAMLAND

Emmett Dorst, all of 22 years old, has quickly built a following among the city's cabaret cognescenti, calculated in the latest census to have declined from eighty-seven to seventy-nine (apparently some of them have siphoned off toward newer forms of pop music, particularly the barbershop quartet and Leslie Gore). With his endearing "aw shucks" persona—a reminder of a boyhood spent sucking out mortar from between the logs of his family's cabin—and a reedy falsetto that has been compared to a bass profundo, Dorst kicks off his two-week engagement with a program of standards not being sung by Sylvia Verner. That leaves a handful of precious gems, including the Neapolitan lullabies that Frank Sinatra used to sing to put the Gambini quintuplets to sleep. Free low-fat muffin with every encore request.

"THE BIJOU" IN THE BASEMENT
OF THE MARRIOTT MARQUEE

Adrienne Bandolier, who last season dressed as a commedia dell'arte Pulcinella to sing "Send in the Clowns," cobbles together two programs of desperately obscure songs unearthed by her arranger and archaeologist, Willy DeVear. First up will be songs dropped from shows on the road, then repaired and placed with loving foster families. After that, a program of love ballads the young Cole Porter wrote while being gripped in a half nelson by Ethel Merman. All shows benefit Adrienne Bandolier's mortgage and, once that is paid off, the establishment of a scholarship to encourage the composition of new old standards. Note: Starting next month "The Bijou" will be closed for minor renovations. It will reopen in November as Donald Trump's humidor.

THE NARCOLYPSE

Dwayne Bixby has been a fixture on this scene since 1956, when he fell into a manhole off Seventh Avenue and sang out feebly for assistance that never arrived. The Narcolypse was built over him the following year. The "Velvet Cumulonimbus," specializing in songs Noël Coward wrote for Beatrice Lillie to perform as far away from him as possible, has owned this sparkling yet rare oeuvre ever since the incomparable Gerald Simms, who was to have recorded the songs, was shoved beneath a subway train. The crime was never solved, but Bixby's airtight alibi put him far beyond suspicion: For three days he had been watching Julie Andrews and Robert Goulet in a matinee of the *Oberammergau*. At the Narcolypse he will be accompanied by a clunking radiator and falling chunks of ceiling plaster.

WAL-MART AFTERHOURS

The venerable Sylvia Verner, puffed up with helium and floated from her room at the Plaza down to Toms River, New Jersey, and Emmett Dorst, appealingly slim and fresh in a tuxedo of pressed damp alfalfa, meet up in Aisle K for a charmer of a program: Novelty numbers that Rosemary Clooney sang under hypnosis. Afterward Miss Verner will autograph back-to-school items (now on sale!), and Emmett will lightly hum a Johnny Mercer medley as he carries your purchases out to the parking lot. Then it's back for each to their regular engagements at the vacant lots that were once Dreamland and the Morpheum Room, both recently demolished to make way for the mayor's proposed Palace of Karaoke.

THE CELESTIAL LOUNGE

The legendary Mabel Mercer, her voice swirling through the ether, accompanies herself on harp. Hymns, mostly.

—— · —— · —— · —— · —— · —— · —— · —— · —— · ——

. . . Million Man Mambo called off . . . Mormons, swingers agree in principle . . . Fudd, Tweety, Barbara Walters settle lawsuit . . . "We are not alone," say extraterrestrials . . .

Tragicomic Lady

TOM GLIATTO

"I've always said that the tragedy of Hedda Gabler is that she's the only woman in Scandinavia with a sense of humor."
—*New York Times*

Herr Munch's *Scream*, ladies and gentlemen, what's *that* about? Have you ever seen such a portrait as this figure on the bridge, the paint swirling about like hallucinatory smoke? And yet I think it's not at all so mysterious, what it is "about." It is the mind reeling, reacting in horror to life, to existence itself. If I were to meet Herr Munch, do you know what I would say? I would say, "Herr Munch, I never sat for you, and yet that painting is my likeness exactly. Allow me, now that we have met, to demonstrate." Then I would slap my hands to my face and scream until my head exploded.

Ba dum bum.

When I say "ba dum bum," ladies and gentlemen, that signals that I have reached the end of the joke. Not to mention my rope. Ba dum bum. Perhaps you will understand me better if I add umlauts.

Ba düm düm.

Take my husband, please, and shoot him at twenty paces with this pistol that belonged to my father, the late General. Ladies, do you know what I have noticed about my husband? And perhaps you have noticed this about yours. My husband, I do not love him. In truth I detest him. And because he loves me I detest him all the more, and because I detest him all the more I love him even less. On and on it goes, until my heart is as cold as the December night air and I stride to the fireplace and I chuck into the flames the squirrel he gave me for Christmas to wear as a muff—yes, that is how ferocious and angry I am, I would prefer to wear a real squirrel, not its skinned hide. I would prefer to silently endure its bites and nibbles until I scream and chuck the thing into the flames, that damned squirrel that symbolizes my untamed, squirrelly spirit. Then I stand there and warm myself while the squirrel squeaks in pain.

You say you do not find that especially funny, a joke about a burning animal that left on its own is cute enough and happy to be allowed to live and hoard nuts in its fat cheeks. Why on earth should you like such a joke, unless you've been driven crazy by the conventions of middle-class life? The real joke is marriage, ladies and gentlemen. And yet "society" proposes that, since he is my husband, Torvald—or Erlig or Lars or Peer Gynt or Smitty or whatever his name is—this man, this stranger with muttonchops, he is by rights my agent and manager and entitled to 15 percent. Further, he does all the booking for me. That is how I come to be here, ladies and gentlemen, as the opening act for a chorus of singing seals from Copenhagen.

Knock, knock. That was the beginning of a joke, ladies and gentlemen. There was no one banging on the exit doors. There was no need to look around. *Knock, knock.* "Who is there?" "Ibsen." "Who is Ibsen?" "The author of the laff riot *The Master Builder,* about a great architect whose pride results in his destruction at the hands of the cleaning woman grown rich on coins she finds beneath his sofa cushions. It died in Oslo." Do you know what *I* wish had died, ladies and gentlemen? My husband. I wish he were not only dead, but long dead. How long? The casket should measure about five feet eight. Ba dum dum.

I am now going to try and entertain you with a famous old ethnic joke. I realize we have no ethnics in our country, so I will relate the version I first heard Stringberg do in improv. There is this man, see, and he and his wife are wrestling on the carpet, their hands around each other's throats, their teeth bared like wolf to she-wolf. The punch line remains the same in all versions. "Husband, you fill me with disgust at both you and myself. Our life together is a sham. Shall I tell you—? Yes, I *will* tell you! It was I, your own wife, who stripped all the semi-colons from your manuscript and destroyed its chances for publication! Rather than give birth to our child, I have carried it these six years. And you thought all that weight was because of macaroons!" Am I right, ladies? Yes? Am I right? You, the consumptive prostitute who has run away from her husband and lost all hope of respectability, I see you nodding your head. Am I right?

I had thought ultimately to use this pistol on myself, ladies and gentlemen, but thanks to you I have died a thousand deaths already this evening. So I conclude instead with a few quick impressions. "Emma Bovary." That was Emma Bovary, ladies and gentlemen. "Anna Karenina"—.

. . . Cure for the blahs discovered . . . War games canceled due to war . . . Paradigm shift causing sea change . . . Scientists isolate loneliness gene . . .

Jerry Springer's Book Club

TOM GLIATTO

MOM, YOU LOOK LIKE A HOOKER

It is because I like to stir things up on occasion that one day I invited Professor Harold Bloom to come on the show and discuss Shakespeare's sonnets. I believe he had just written a book on the subject. As he began to explore the identity of the sonnets' "Dark Lady," the "kids," who I later learned were under the impression that the professor was going to explicate an old Cher song, began to scream and yell and hurl chairs. Then they fell upon each other with ample guns and knives. As the security guards formed a human wall around Professor Bloom, I must admit that I felt an unexpected sting of "the green monster," by which I mean not Godzilla but envy. Here, in a matter of mere minutes, Bloom has somehow *gotten through* to them. This roomful of neo-Nazi boys and the antifascist cheerleaders who loved them—*they* connected with Shakespeare. Had I ever done something as worthy? The answer echoed through my mind: No . . . n-no, n-no, n-no. I then realized that what I was hearing was in fact the prolonged and sputtering moan of Professor Bloom from within the wall of security men. Like me, I suppose, he had experienced some sort of catharsis, a word I would not have even known if Joyce Carol Oates had not visited Montel Williams the previous week to supervise beauty makeovers for girls with ten or more facial piercings.

The question, then, was this: How to get my kids to drink "deep and long from that Go Cup of brew" (Wordsworth, *On First Getting Wasted*)? I decided the way to draw them to that sacred fount would be this solid classic of nineteenth-century Russian literature, the title of which I have also seen translated as *Mother, Are You a Hooker?* and *Mother, You Often Remind Me of Rasputin*. Tolstoy's command of narrative and psychology are unparalleled, and the way he uppercases all the dialogue in the fight scenes is quite effective. My young readers particularly "dig" the duel between Princess Marya and Natasha, as they meet in the snowy forest at dawn and proceed to bitch-slap the living daylights out of each other. And you should see their dilated pupils light up when I tell them that "this Tolstoy dude," as they like to call him between acid hits, renounced literature to become a nightclub bouncer in Kiev.

I'M CHEATING ON YOU—WITH YOUR LESBIAN AUNT

When I first recommended this French classic, some of the kids, complaining that it was "dry," stormed off the soundstage and went on a wilding spree in a nearby Barnes & Noble, where they disrupted a poetry reading and overturned the display table for my new collection, *I've Had It! You're Going Back to the Sideshow!*

THE LOVE LETTERS OF JERRY SPRINGER AND EUDORA WELTY

After the guards had chased after and tackled them and hand-cuffed them together in a circle ringed by fire, I patiently explained that Flaubert is a writer's writer, which meant "they were just gonna damned hafta be reader's readers—capeesh?" I then quoted a famous letter Flaubert wrote to his occasional lover, Louise Colet: "Madame: I am vexed by your announcement that you are carrying our child, and that you have no place to put him down. I only know that he cannot possibly be mine, and that you cannot put him down here. *Madame Bovary* requires every second of my day and every fiber of my being, and I—I—oh, I must confess, dear Louise. I must drop the sham. Babe? Honey? Sweetums? I *am* Madame Bovary. *Dieu!* How good it feels to have it out in the open at last! Yes, *c'est vrai*. I am really a pretty, provincial housewife who hitchhikes into town on weekends dressed in men's clothes and tells smutty stories in the locker room of the French Academy. I will not reveal to you just now how I did it, but I have showered naked next to Emile Zola! He was almost revoltingly hirsute."

There was some reluctance as well to read the book in the original French, but that was overcome when the kids realized that the gang scenes are all the more exciting with the accents *aigue* and *grave* slashing their way across the letters. And it is my firm belief that Parisians are bound to be impressed when these "uncultured" bruisers of mine come to the City of the Light and know straight away to hop on the Metro, head for the Louvre and slash and spray-paint a Delacroix or two.

The girls, incidentally, are often surprised to find that not only is "cellulite" French, but that Flaubert himself coined the word while stroking the pebbled white thighs of Madame Colet.

MY PIMP WANTS ME TO WORK IN A FAST FOOD JOINT

Certainly as a stylist in his prime Henry James is enormously challenging (or, as they say on the streets these days, "Lacanian"). His writing grew even more opaque after he retired from the fashionable whirl of London to his country estate, where he shaved his head and raised pit bulls behind a chain-link fence. But who else has ever written with such truth, such subtle poetry about teenage trailer-park trash? I would argue: No one.

"You mean to say, then, that—?"

"Oh," said Stacy, wrapping yellow tissue around the warmed burger and subsequently plopping the, if you will, "little bundle" onto a chute and giving it a push, a tap, the merest of nudges to begin its journey from her own insufficiently ventilated station in the scullery and forward—so her tequila-soaked mind imagined—into the great spinning world, while she remained (or so she felt, in her lugubrious dependence on the minimum wage), with no sally-forthings left of her own, having already been an adolescent "runaway" (the delicious paradox being that *she*, traveling under dark of an eclipse, unintentionally ran *home*) and then, too, she had been a "groupie," so to speak, with a boy's pop quartet that, on reaching the age of maturation—as who must not, excepting those unfortunates whose feet are bound in bricks?—had abandoned her to become an investment banking firm—enough adventures, in short, that she had been honored two years previous with an "After-School Special" (blessed with a performance by the infant phenomenon Linda Blair!), for which her own life became the faintest of—if you will indulge me (and if not, m———f———, I will club you with this metal pipe)—palimpsests. "I am not *saying* anything."

Brandy, overturning the fries into a bin of hot oil with the manual or (one might say) *menial* dexterity typical of a high school dropout—not only "typical," in her case, but indeed as indelibly "branded" into her skanky being as were tattooed crost her knuckles the words "Jon," "Bon" and "Jovi"—anyhow, okay, what happened was, she pounced upon the clue as would a tiger (or pit bull!), snarling in a jolly corner of the petting zoo of the unconscious, were it to spot a Jack Russell terrier, let us say or, if not, one of those cup-sized poodles with cheeks stained the pink of grapefruit. "You," she said, "*infer*."

"Infer," agreed Stacy, "and then of course," she continued, smiling in the way that she alone was known to smile when she managed the feat, the too rare yet oh too wonderful triumph, of walking and in the same instance—indeed, for what one might call a multitude or agglomeration of instances—chewing gum, "what can one do *but* conclude?"

"Ah."

"Oh, ever so much more than 'ah.' It is even so much more than 'yeah' or 'f——— A.' That—is it possible you do not see— is the beauty of it."

" 'Beauty'?" said Brandy, arching one brow and removing the basket of fries from their hot-oil "bath," as it was called among the largely illegal immigrant staff, and then, as it were, "launching" them—an armada of sizzling potato slices, borne on un-obstacled air rather than the vast indeterminate blobby-wavey-wetty "thing" of the sea—toward Stacy's face, which they, as "things" will do when "flung" at no great distance, shortly reached. "I do *not* see."

"Ah," Stacy screamed. "Evidently."

THE SOUND AND THE FURY

By this point I think my readers deserve a little breather—and Danielle Steel certainly fits the bill. Then it's "once more unto the breach" (Eminem, one of the parts of *Henry IV*) with Faulkner's masterpiece, "I'm Taking a Porn Star to the Prom."

JERRY'S THOUGHT FOR THE DAY

Maybe Cher *is* the Dark Lady.

. . . Boy Scouts tie knot . . . M. C. Escher injured in fall up flight of stairs . . . Elite troops arrive fashionably late . . . Stocks soar on doomsday rumors . . .

Outside the Box

TOM GLIATTO

When I cannot draw fresh inspiration from studying the caterpillar spin its web or sipping my favorite aperatif of Lillet laced
with cocaine, I turn to Pascal. He is simply the best houseboy
in the world, and he brings me my hookah. It becomes harder
with age, much harder, to find new ideas. I'm not complaining.
The box has brought me enormous wealth and celebrity. I could
easily while away what remains of my life entertaining equally
wealthy, celebrated, innovative friends on my private island,
where the bougainvillea grows so lush the toucans become
trapped between the flowers at night. Pascal has to go out and
free them, because their squawking disturbs my thinking. As I
say, I can while away my life easily, but happily? I am not able
to rest content merely as the Man Who Invented the Box. I
must push on, only this generates considerable emotional
strain. Last Thursday I was unconscionably rude to Bjork. On
reflection, she looked perfectly fine in that thing. Just needed
to lose the antlers.

Finally I have come up with something new—or is it? This
thing, which I call "the crate," is a box made not of cardboard,
the universal putty that I use for everything from throw rugs
to my muumuus, but rather wooden slats hobbled together
into six square planes, including a lid, and joined at right
angles. I sat in wonderment, watching the crate assemble
itself in my mind's eye. I wish I could say whether it was the
left or right eye, but at the time my liver was awash with one

of those expensive new "garage" wines, the kind they ferment in the engine of a Pinto. But now the engineers have built the prototype, and I'm not sure what a person does with it. Pascal suggests we store our theatrical costumes and props in it, and in fact the elephant we used for last month's *Aïda* needs to be put somewhere. But couldn't a box, a really big one, serve the same function? "*La plus ça change,*" Pascal says. At which point the elephant sighs loudly, and I tell Pascal not to be such an ass.

The paper bag, too, turns out to be something of a personal disappointment, a repeat performance—a punier, flimsier form of box, minus the lid. Oh, yes yes, I know, it has already proved to be life-transforming for millions, especially once the marketing people figured out you could use it to carry a light lunch. My original notion had been to turn it upside down to cover bedside decanters or trap bees. I hate bees. I suppose the paper bag would finally be enough of a laurel for a man to rest on, if that is what you do with laurels, rest on them, and if I were a mere inventor—a tinkerer. Benjamin Franklin, for example, I think of him as a tinkerer. He would do a little of this, a little of that, add X, subtract Y, and lo and behold he winds up with the Dewey decimal. And even then he only came up with the decimal, not the system. He got distracted inventing Philadelphia. Too many fingers, old Ben, too many pies! I'm at heart an artist, or a poet, or a dreamer, or something. I search for faces in clouds—not even in clouds! Clear azure sky! That can eat up a day. I see a cardboard box and I ask, "What if I turned it on its side?" And then I impulsively act. "Pascal, come and turn this box over on its side. No, the other side. Now—flip it back. No, the other side." Two hours of intense contemplation, a martini break, and then a second martini break, and then: "Pascal, come and turn the box over."

Only of course Pascal I have had to let go because of the *Dateline* piece. Luckily I know Ivan Tivonovki, the inventor of Tivo. He recorded it for me.

CORRESPONDENT: Friends say, however, that this troubled, tuckered-out tinkerer [!!!!!!!—G] is on the verge of serious trouble. Among those worried about G—— are his houseboy, Pascal.

Cut to:

PASCAL: He wanted me to beat up this young man—I believe he was 11—because he had invented the pup tent as a Scout project. "Oh this is such a ripoff," G—— said to me. He said the tent was just a gussied-up box for noble savages or something . . . sounded vaguely racist . . .

CORRESPONDENT: And you told him—

PASCAL: That it was something different. The pup tent has an opening and flaps and it is not made of cardboard or, like the crate, wooden slats. And if it were made of slats, that would be a lean-to, but I didn't tell him that. He wouldn't have listened, anyway, because for at least two days he had been out of his mind on mushrooms.

CORRESPONDENT: Hallucinogenic.

PASCAL: No, chanterelles. I guess I hadn't cleaned them thoroughly. But he told me if I didn't go out and "whup" the kid he would do it himself.

CORRESPONDENT: Did you call the police?

PASCAL: No . . .

CORRESPONDENT: Because you didn't think he was a serious threat, that he could not—

PASCAL (unhappy intake of breath): . . . fight his way out of a paper bag. (pause) And it's sad. (pause) Because I think once he could. I really do.

A small, flattened box with an adhesive flap for a lid. "Envelope!" Maestro! Genius! Brilliant! Nightmare! Because the testing lab has just sent back their report: I've invented something to put junk mail in. No more just flinging it onto the porch like a newspaper, no sirree. I am opening a Pandora's box. Which reminds me: Have the lawyers done anything yet about Pandora? How many millions a month am I throwing at them to go after that girl? Either she gives me a cut or she comes up

with some other thing to open. Pandora's sleeper sofa, whatever. That's her problem. . . .

The intervention was staged by Pascal—dear boy!—Bill Gates
and Boy George, although my mind was so clouded, I kept calling him Elton. But with every day comes greater clarity. This
morning in group someone named P—— introduced himself as
one of the creators of New Coke. Sad, very sad, but no one
rubbed it in. Then I notice a woman, also new to the group,
looking at me searchingly. "I believe you're the man who
invented the box," she says. And who, I ask, is she? She weeps.
"I am the woman . . . who keeps trying to reinvent the wheel."
  We hug for what seems forever.

Postscript. G—— never thought of anything new ever again,
but in his final days he seemed to me very content, to the
extent that such an awful man could ever be called content.
And it was nice that we reconciled.
  I had him buried in a low, long pine box. I think he would
be pleased to know how the idea has since caught on. —Pascal

very sad

On the Occasion, Give or Take, of the Fiftieth Anniversary of the First Staging, in Paris, of Samuel Beckett's *Waiting for Godot*, a Few Representative Selections from *The Annotated Treasury of "Waiting for Godot" Parodies*

BEN GREENMAN

WAITING FOR BEDPAN

London, 1954. One of the earliest known parodies of Beckett's existentialist classic was penned by the venerable drama critic Arthur Bryce. Bryce's initial reviews of the play called it "frankly idiotic," "folly at interminable length," and "a blot on the escutcheon of the theatre." When this review failed to derail Beckett's play, Bryce took it upon himself to craft this parody, in which an elderly man named Sam suffers silently in his hospital bed while he waits for the orderlies, who have been "disordered" by vapid modern theater, to bring him a bedpan. To Bryce's chagrin, the play ran for only ten performances; to what Bryce later confessed was his secret delight, Beckett himself took in one of those performances while visiting London. "What a prophetic work," he quipped. "I do have to go to the loo."

WAITING FOR McCARTHY

Berkeley, California, 1968. The rock musician Frank Zappa partially funded and may have partially written this overtly polemic work, which focused on a group of young people in despair over the popularity of Richard Nixon. Vladimir and Estragon have been renamed Michael and Michelle—some critics thought that the play was lampooning the counterculture's own brand of non-conformist conformity—and the central couple spends the first half of the play topless, lounging in bed. When Lucky enters, he is carrying two cups of black coffee and a framed portrait of Tom Hayden. Pozzo, predictably, is a crude caricature of Nixon.

WAITING FOR WAITING FOR GODOT

Reed College, 1974. This play grew from a real-life incident concerning theater majors waiting for the arrival of visiting professor and Beckett expert Jonathan Burkman, who had called a meeting for Monday, 9 a.m., to discuss that semester's production of *Krapp's Last Tape*. By 10, Burkman had not arrived, and one of the students proposed writing a play about his tardiness. Another student suggested that the students' actual conversation could be used as a starting point. Done.

WAITING FOR GOOD BLOW

New York, 1979. Vladimir and Estragon retained their names and most of their lines in this production, which recast them as downtown hustlers and part-time band managers meeting with their drug dealer on a Manhattan street corner. The long and somewhat sadistic set of instructions delivered to Lucky by Pozzo in Act II was left untouched. All actors wore black leather jackets and sunglasses; the soundtrack, delivered faux-amateurishly from an onstage boombox, redundantly included several songs by the Ramones, including "53rd and 3rd" and "Carbona Not Glue."

OH! HE'S HERE!

Coeur D'Alene, Idaho, 1985. Shortly after graduating from the theater program at Columbia University, the playwright Linton

real-life incident

Kwesi Silverstein (né David Silverstein) broke up with his girl-friend and perennial leading lady, Elaine Wofford, who had moved with him from New York. A few nights after the breakup, a drunken and despondent Silverstein penned this absurdist reduction of Beckett's play, in which Godot appears before the first curtain is raised, looks around for Vladimir and Estragon, cannot find them, and, convinced of his solitude, uri-nates onstage. The play also included a chess match between Lucky and Pozzo in which the game pieces were severed human fingers that, when touched, sang snatches of disco hits such as "More, More, More" and "Knock on Wood." There was only one known performance.

WAITING FOR SADDAM

Baghdad, 2003. After a tattered copy of the original play found its way into the hands of students at al-Mustansiriyah Uni-versity, they quickly cobbled together a crude political satire that owed as much to *South Park* as to Beckett. It is not known whether the play has ever been staged, but it has been posted on the Internet. Updated daily to reflect changing political realities—the most recent draft incorporates the deaths of Uday and Qusay Hussein—the evolving work has attracted the attention of an independent television producer who has already contracted with Britain's Channel 4 and America's Fox network for a reality show called *Down and Out in Baghdad Hills*, which will follow a ragtag bunch of Iraqi comedians and satirists attempting to remake post-Hussein Iraq with the power of laughter.

—Stephanie Brooks

Crossing Over

KEVIN GUILFOILE

JOHN: I'm getting a letter J. Or possibly a G.

DENISE: Could it be a C?

JOHN: Sure.

DENISE: Omigod! It's Carl!

JOHN: He's waving . . .

DENISE (hysterical): I miss you, Carl!

JOHN: He wants you to know that you don't need to yell and that he's not feeling any pain.

DENISE (weeping and nodding her head): Carl hated pain so much.

JOHN: He says that he left you something.

DENISE (collapsing into the arms of an excited female companion): I found his watch! (sobbing now) I found his watch in the sofa when I was sticky-rolling cat hair before the wake!

JOHN: He wants you to treasure it forever, to keep it in a special place. Was there a spot in the house that had particular meaning for the two of you: a box for valuables with a hidden compartment, or—wait—a place where he used to hide gifts?

DENISE: I already gave it to my one friend from work.

JOHN: Oh.

DENISE: His name's Phil. He always admired it.

JOHN: Carl says that's okay.

DENISE: I suppose I could ask for it back.

JOHN: Look, it's not a big deal. Phil can keep the watch. That's what Carl says.

DENISE: I can ask Phil. He'll understand.

JOHN: Carl wanted you to have it, but now he wants Phil to have it.

DENISE: I'll ask him to return it. Phil's a really good guy. He needed a watch, and he liked Carl's because it had a second hand, and Phil sometimes needs one to time the PSAs he writes for the radio. But he'll understand. Carl wants me to have it.

JOHN: For Christ's sake, Denise, what Carl wants is for you to knock the passive-aggressive shit off.

DENISE: Sorry.

JOHN: He's showing me water now. Does that mean anything to you?

DENISE: Our honeymoon! St. Croix! (weeping) We always said it was the happiest eight days we'll ever spend on this earth. We were planning another trip for the fall.

JOHN: He's showing me beaches. The two of you holding hands. I can see a bicycle—no, no!—mopeds!

DENISE: Also, he drowned.

JOHN: What's that you say?

DENISE: The water. He might be showing you the water because he drowned in the lake.

JOHN: No. No. I don't think so. I'm definitely getting a honeymoon vibe here.

DENISE: Don't you think that's weird?

JOHN: Why?

DENISE: Well, Carl just drowned like six weeks ago, and the police don't think it was an accident. If he's showing you water don't you think he might be trying to tell me who his killer is, instead of just sending you vacation snapshots from a honeymoon that took place ten years ago?

JOHN: I don't know. Uh. When I said "water," your first thought was St. Croix?

DENISE: I was trying to think happy thoughts.

JOHN: There you go. He doesn't want to upset you.

DENISE: Well can you ask him?

JOHN: Ask him what?

DENISE: Ask him who his killer is.

JOHN (bringing his finger to his temple): He says he slipped.

DENISE: Slipped?

JOHN: Yep.

DENISE: Are you certain?

JOHN: Let me double-check for you. (eyes shut tight) Slipped, slipped, slipped. Clear as day.

DENISE: Are you sure he might not be telling you "Skip"? His brother Skip is one of the prime suspects in his murder.

JOHN: I'm pretty sure I can tell the difference between "Skip" and "slip."

DENISE: You couldn't tell the difference between "G" and "J."

JOHN: Those were in lowercase cursive.

DENISE: What if "slip" means "boat slip."

JOHN: What are you getting at, Denise?

DENISE: That maybe "Skip" killed Carl in the "boat slip."

JOHN: Carl thinks not.

DENISE: "Not" or "knot"?

JOHN: N-O-T. Not.

DENISE: How do you know? What if Skip used a "slipknot" to strangle Carl?

JOHN: Well, which was it? Was he drowned or strangled?

DENISE: Drowned.

JOHN: See? Not "k-n-o-t." Just "n-o-t" as in "Not Skip in the slip with the slipknot."

DENISE: Okay.

JOHN: Can we move on?

DENISE: Sure.

JOHN: What else do you want to ask Carl?

DENISE: What is heaven like?

JOHN (settling down now, eyes shut, both hands to his hairline): I'm getting a movie. He says it's just like in the movie.

DENISE: Which movie?

JOHN: He says you'll know.

DENISE: *Crumb*?

JOHN (opening his eyes): Oh, for crying out loud. Think about that for a minute. How could heaven possibly be like the movie *Crumb*?

DENISE: That was the first thing that popped into my head.

JOHN: *Crumb* was?

DENISE: Yes.

JOHN: There's nothing even remotely magical or heaven-like in that film.

DENISE: You said Carl said I would know what he meant, and I thought of *Crumb*, as clear as if Carl himself put it in my mind.

JOHN (sighing): Heaven is not like *Crumb*, Denise. *Crumb* is a documentary, for God's sake.

DENISE: Fine. You ask him what movie he means, then.

JOHN (agitated now, fingers quickly to his temple once more): *Like Water for Chocolate*.

DENISE: I've never seen that. Neither has Carl.

JOHN: You have to stop resisting, Denise. Listen to what Carl is telling you. He's showing me water. Then, *Like Water for Chocolate* . . .

DENISE (making a face): *Like Water for Chocolate*? That's foreign, right? Is it on DVD?

JOHN: I have no idea.

DENISE: Ask him if there's another movie I can rent on DVD that's sort of what heaven looks like.

JOHN (staring at her blankly)

DENISE: I don't like to rent tapes anymore. They get stuck in our machine. How about *Snatch*? Is heaven anything like *Snatch*? That's got a ton of extra features.

JOHN (still staring)

DENISE. Two discs.

JOHN (staring)

— · — · — · — · — · — · — · — · — · — · —

. . . Bottle dropped in ocean fourteen years ago still missing . . . Tuna found on Mercury . . . Nabisco employees admit shredding wheat . . . Last honest man dies . . .

Transcending Spaces

KEVIN GUILFOILE

BEFORE THE SHOW

MIA (neighbor): I've been a huge fan since Season Two, and I've seen every Season One show in reruns. I even watch the British version, *Changing Minds*. Actually, I was the one who turned Connie onto it, *way* before it became popular. My favorite designer is Tamara. Did you see that kitchen she did in Seattle? It was *so* utilitarian.

CONNIE (neighbor): Mia and I usually watch the show together and if we don't, we spend all the next day talking about it. She'll say, "My God, can you believe what Leigh did to that woman's dining room?" But most of the time, Leigh is only being true to her convictions. If Leigh decorated the room in a way that exactly reflected the philosophy of the home-owners, then what would be the point of even bringing in a designer?

MIA: I'm a little nervous being on the show. But I have all the faith in the world in Connie and Bill. They know exactly how we think, and they won't let Dan do anything crazy like glue tree bark to the wall or allow the design scheme to be overly influenced by Hume. Also, we have our fingers crossed for some crown molding!

CONNIE: What would be the worst thing they could do? Let's see . . . I don't like any sort of "Country" motifs. And I would be really upset if they painted the furniture. Really, *really* upset, because those pieces belonged to Bill's grand-mother. Also I'd hate to see any Heidegger in there. Our family spends a lot of time in the living room and I wouldn't want it all gummed up with angst. If Dan absolutely insisted on going existential, I could maybe—*maybe*—live with Kierkegaard, but only as an accent.

DAY ONE

MIA: We were really excited to meet Tamara, and she was *so* sweet. Plus, we're both expecting babies in about five months, so we have that in common. After we cleared the room, she revealed the first part of her plan. Although it was very blue (not necessarily my favorite color!) I saw right away how much it was influenced by William of Ockham. I put my hands up and screamed, "I *LOVE* IT!" And I'm sure Connie will love it, too, because she's a minimalist.

CONNIE: Things didn't get off to a good start over at our house. We got into it with Dan right from the get-go. He announced his "theme" for the room, which he called "Perfectly Plato." I was like you have *got* to be *kidding* me. Then he tried to throw our preshow interview in my face because he heard me say I wanted to do something "retro." That was true, I'll admit, but by "retro" I meant the 1920s. You know: Art Deco, Logical Positivism. And enough already with *asking* instead of *telling*. Just now Dan said to me, "If I disobey and disregard the opinion and approval of the one who is wise, and regard the opinion of the many who have no understanding, will I not suffer evil?" Whatever. I just wanted to know if Tad was building them a new armoire.

MIA: Tamara taught us a mantra to go with our theme: "Whatever the designer does is by definition good." It's hard work, but we're having lots of fun with Ockham's Razor. Every time we run into a problem we say the same thing. Like when we found out the ottoman Tad built wouldn't fit through the front door, we looked at each other and, laughing, all shouted at once, "The simplest solution is usually the most valid!" Then we cut the bastard in half with a chain saw. What's that? Oh, right, the ottoman, not Tad! Ha!

TAMARA (designer): We're having such a good time—my home-owners are very hard workers—and I haven't even told Mia and Larry about the best part yet! Shhh! It's a secret!

CONNIE: I'm sorry, but I'm still not buying into this Plato theme. Dan wants to turn Larry and Mia's bedroom into a cave beyond which exist realities that cannot be directly perceived by the senses. Does *that* sound romantic to you? We're supposed to have at least *some* input regarding what happens to our neighbors' house, but when I suggested we apply Frege's System of Mathematical Logic to the installa-tion of crown molding, he gave me this really condescend-ing look.

TAD (carpenter): Dan gave me his drawings for the bed and I spent all morning building it only to find out that his mea-surements weren't even close. Anyway, I asked Dan where we were putting it so I could get the actual dimensions and he said that a "bed"—at least how a carpenter like me would know it—doesn't even exist except as a thing participating in the "Form of Bedness." These freaking designers, I'm telling you.

DAN (designer): I'm getting a lot of resistance from Bill and Connie, but I know that once they understand my vision they're going to love it. They think "Perfectly Plato" refers only to the famous student of Socrates and the author of the *Dialogues*—sounds pretty boring, I'll admit. But when it comes to the romance they're looking for, they forget that we have the Neo-Platonists, and even the Renaissance Neo-Platonists to draw from. Honestly, what's sexier than a boudoir based on St. Augustine?

MIA: I don't know what to say. I thought things were going so well, but then Tamara gave us our homework and it all went kablooey. She wants us to put stencils on the ceiling show-ing dinosaurs and man living together. In the first place, I hate stencils. Ick. But, on top of that, Creationism? I don't want to be one of those "difficult" homeowners, but I don't think we can do that. On principle.

TAMARA: I'm very disappointed. Things were really humming

along but now it's the end of day one and I've got a mini-
revolt on my hands. Mia doesn't like the stencils and Larry
says that Bill will object to my "Creation Science Flair"
because he's a paleontologist. Well, *I'm* a designer. I'm supposed to challenge people. If I gave in and let every home-
owner have whatever she wanted, then all we'd ever do week
after week is Descartes, Descartes, Descartes. Nothing but
boring old suburban *Cogito ergo sum*. And Creationism is *so
in*. If I even *suggested* Natural Selection to my New York
clients right now they'd laugh me out of the Upper East Side.

DAY TWO

CONNIE: Well, we were up all night putting plaster on the walls
and then staining. It's horrible. Ugly. Brown. Damp. I wish
I'd put my foot down at the beginning. All I wanted for this
bedroom was something subtle and romantic, maybe with a
French twist—Rousseau, for instance—and I should have
said something. Instead I went with the flow and look
where we are. In a [expletive] cave.

DAN: Apparently Connie and Bill decided to take matters into
their own hands last night and so we've got a little situation
this morning. It seems they went ahead and put up crown
molding. Now, aside from the fact that your typical Greek
cave didn't have crown molding, they insisted upon using
Frege's System of Mathematical Logic to install it. Of
course, if they had asked me, I could have told them that
Frege's theory was refuted by Russell's Paradox in the early
1900s. So not only do we have a design element that's completely inappropriate to the room, I'm not sure how we're
going to take it down because I have no money left in the
budget for Bertrand Russell. Maybe Tad will have some
idea.

TAMARA: We worked out a compromise on the ceiling. Instead of Creationism, we're going to stencil it with Christian Eschatology: Book of Revelation. Judgment Day. End
Times. That sort of thing. It's a little less hip, but I'm okay

with it, and my homeowners are happy. That's really the important thing.

TAD: The basic problem with the crown molding is this: Some mathematical sets are members of themselves, an example being the "set of all sets," which is, of course, also a set. But is the "set of all sets that are *not* members of themselves" (which in this case includes the "set of mahogany paneling inexplicably nailed to the wall of a fake cave") a member of itself? If it is, then it isn't; if it isn't, then it is. Gottlob Frege lived almost eighty years and he never came up with an answer for that. We only have two days. The crown molding stays where it is.

CONNIE: We got everything loaded into the room and then Bill asks where the television is supposed to go. Dan laughs at him and he shows us this metal screen. His idea is to hide the TV behind the screen and, using mirrors and a piece of muslin, project shadows of the television images onto the wall of the cave. I started to cry.

THE UNVEILING

MIA: I was so nervous at the reveal I was shaking. When they finally said, "Open your eyes!" I was about ready to burst. Omigod, I *loved* it! It was so beautiful. It's like our own little Hobbit hole! Of course, I wanted to know where the bed went, and I'll admit I wasn't really clear on the explanation, but we'll get used to sleeping on the antelope skin. At first I couldn't tell what Larry was thinking, but finally he said, "Hey, I got my crown molding and they didn't tear out my ceiling fan. The rest of it, I could give a crap."

CONNIE: I was feeling bad about what we did to Larry and Mia's room until I saw the way they trashed our place. They say Tamara based the design on the teachings of William of Ockham. Ugh. There's a fine line between a minimalist and a poor person, you know? The entire room's empty except for a cheap ottoman made out of particle board—and somebody sawed that in half. What happened to our sectional

sofa? And the entertainment center? There's no place for
the kids' toys, and the *praying*—Christ, these Franciscan
monks prayed like six times a day! Who has time for that?
And I hate, hate, *hate* the stencils on the ceiling. I don't
care if they're supposed to be War, Pestilence, Destruction,
and Death. Horses say Country to me. And I hate Country.

HARMON LEON'S OFFICE PRANKS
AMISH FOOLERY

things needed
- 1 Quaker Oats beard
- 1 black brim hat
- butter-churning facilities

Get to work early and remove all the electrical appliances. When
questioned, proclaim that the office is now Amish-compliant, stating
this is according to some turn-of-the-century building ordinance.
Stress this point by wearing a black-brimmed hat and overalls. Claim
that you are "Milo-Tiller of the Internet." If your boss asks for a company report say you will finish it as soon as everyone pitches
together to raise a new barn in the break room. Gather all the wom-
enfolk in the office and insist that they churn butter. At the water
cooler, suppress unpure sexual thoughts by praying.

Bienvenue au Musée Renteria

KEVIN GUILFOILE

I am the greatest painter of the kind of paintings I like to paint," Jose Maria Renteria said with typical bravado in the summer of 1916. Although it caused a stir across Europe at the time, that claim was never more true than in the middle 1970s, when the master was working primarily in the medium of uncooked fish and Fonzie stickers.

When Renteria died in Provence in 1978, he left 34 heirs spread among 11 wives and almost 90 mistresses. A devout Communist for most of his life (until 1974, when he joined the board of Monsanto Corporation), the prolific Renteria never allowed a single painting to be sold during his lifetime and so left his loved ones penniless—penniless, that is, except for his work, worth a fortune on the international auction market once Renteria was dead and unable to threaten his children with lighted matches and tequila.

Enter the French government, according to whose calculations the suddenly marketable Renteria estate owed over seven billion francs in taxes. A generous settlement was negotiated, armed guards confiscated all of the artist's possessions, and the Musée Renteria was born.

Whether you are an educated scholar of modern art, a member of the Caucus of Women Against Violence Against Women on Canvas who have been picketing the museum since 1987, or an American who wandered in thinking this was a quaintly appointed Virgin Megastore, we hope this Visitor's Guide will help you understand how Renteria became such a towering twentieth-century figure and will enhance your appreciation of this treasured collection.

GIRL WITH GLASS IN FACE, APRIL 1908

Often when looking at one of Renteria's more experimental works, you will hear a comment by the ignorant or the foolish: "My nine-year-old could paint better than that." Such flippancy is refuted by the technical skill in this early painting, done in the style of Velasquez. Completed when he was only 17 (and some seven years before he moved permanently from Spain to France), this oil-on-canvas depicts a delicate young señorita, her lavender dress suspended as if by a marionette's wires from her slight frame. She holds a fan in her left hand, perhaps to cool her at the afternoon bullfights Renteria so dearly loved, and her face is horribly and permanently disfigured by protruding shards of colored glass. Note that at this nascent stage of his career, the master was still signing work with his clown name, Humpy.

SEATED NUDE, SUMMER 1924

Arguably the two greatest mysteries in Western art are "Why is the Mona Lisa smiling?" and "Why is the Seated Nude holding a pistol and a restraining order?" Like so much in Renteria's personal life, this was a matter between him, his models, and the gendarmes.

LOVERS ON RUE DE RIVOLI, DECEMBER 1939

Renteria often said he considered the perfect representation of man to be the bull—fearsome, virile, and prone to outbursts of rage—while the perfect representation of woman is Henri Matisse in short pants. This might have seemed witty and scandalous the first time he said it in some café along the Siene, but Renteria was very poor at recognizing when a joke had run its course and, in 1939 alone, he produced over 450 watercolors depicting Matisse's deflowering by a leering water buffalo wearing a monocle and a panama hat. If you would like one, just ask a member of the museum staff on your way out.

HOORAY FOR STALIN, MARCH 1944

Of the 3,000 paintings, sculptures, ceramics, and collages Renteria created in his lifetime, he disavowed almost 2,500. In this, one of many explicitly political works from his "Uncongenial Period," we see a self-portrait of the artist offering the Soviet dictator a baby to eat, and a frowning Stalin pushing the baby away. The artist's head is turned smugly toward the viewer as if to say, "See? Stalin does not eat the baby even when the baby is placed right in front of him." Over the years, Renteria not only expressed regret over this painting, but produced a series of clarifications including *Still Standing by Stalin* (1947), *Stalin: The Least of Many Evils* (1953), and finally, in 1965, the famous watercolor *Stalin's $4.99 All-You-Can-Eat Baby Brunch*.

MARIE WITH PILLOW, SPRING 1955

This portrait of Renteria's sixth wife, Marie, depicts her as a nude reclining on a settee under an open window in their Rhone Valley cottage. Her image is idealized—fleshy thighs, rounded calves, long fingers—so one assumes this is Marie as she appeared when Renteria fell in love with her, the young libertine he first met in Holland in 1952. In fact, the only evidence this was painted near the end of their marriage is the presence of the artist's hands entering from the left side of the canvas to smother her with a pillow.

THE PURSER, HIS WIFE, AND HIS WIFE'S SLUTTY FRIEND FROM CERAMICS CLASS, NOVEMBER 1969

Renteria explored the subjects of passion and lovemaking with gusto in the 1960s. Some speculate this was a sign of his advancing age, recognition of his mortality and, perhaps, the specter of impotency (he was 78 when this work was completed). However, in the master's own correspondence (available by appointment in the museum library), he points to a more practical reason: "*Playboy* now costs over five francs," he wrote to Picasso in 1964. "Plus, you can't purchase just the *Playboy* or you look like a big perv. You have to buy the *Time* magazine, the breath mints, a copy of *Le Monde* . . . Not that I don't find your *Seated Woman with Hat* sexy, but sometimes you put the boobies in the wrong place. . . ."

THE CRUCIFIXION, SPRING 1971

At this stage in his career, it's surprising to see Renteria working with a religious subject. In fact, most of his works during this period concerned the television show *Adam-12*. Renteria was never really known as a "reader," and his ignorance of the Bible is evident throughout this piece. Note that the Roman soldiers are beating Jesus with a phone book and are playing the board game Clue. Also, Christ is nailed, not to two perpendicular boards in the shape of a cross, but to an absurdly expensive gift pen.

WATER PITCHER, TIN CAN, IAN FLEMING PAPERBACK, AND DICE, JULY 1978

Although this became Renteria's most famous installation (as his final work, it has been widely celebrated in textbooks and traveling exhibits), it's unclear whether it is a carefully arranged tableau in the Dadaist mode, or just things he had on the bed-side table when he finally succumbed to syphilis. Likewise, *Head of Snarling Woman* (macaroni on paper plate, 1964) might not be "the master's most realized expression of his gender-related angst" (as claimed by the Art Institute of Chicago), but possibly something a desperate Renteria, home alone with his children, slapped together frantically with glue in an attempt to stop babies from crying.

Norse Myths Reference Pages

KEVIN GUILFOILE

Every day, it seems, one of your friends is forwarding another of those irritating Norse myths to your in-box. How can you tell which stories are true, and which are traditional tales once used by the Nordic people to explain practices, beliefs, or natural phenomena? The Norse Legends Reference Pages are dedicated to separating *faktum* from *fiksjon*, and getting the straight dope from the mouths of people who know.

MYTH #1: In Valhalla, the Valkyries served mead, which poured in unending quantities from Odin's goat, Heidrun. They also served the warriors meat from the boar Saehrimnir, which the cook Andhrimnir would prepare by boiling it in the cauldron Eldhrimnir. The boar magically came back to life to be eaten again at the next meal.

FACT: "Oh wow, I'd forgotten about that," laughs former Valkyrie Hldissfrigg. "Some of the so-called 'warriors' were actually getting squeamish about Andhrimner slaughtering a pig every night—the squealing was really loud, I'll admit—so Odin came up with this tall one about an immortal 'magic boar,' and half those moron grunts totally bought it. I mean the pigs didn't even look the same: one would have a big black spot, the next a little white one, or maybe he'd be pink instead of brown. It cracked us Valkyries up. I mean, if your boar was, in fact, magical—like maybe he could fly or pull a boat large enough to carry all the gods—would you really want to butcher, boil, and eat him over and over? Eventually you're gonna have a pissed-off magic hog all up in your face."

MYTH #2: The son of Odin and a member of the Aesir, Thor was the god of thunder and the main enemy of the giants. He would smash their heads with his mighty hammer Mjollnir. To wield this awesome weapon he needed iron gloves and a belt of strength. Mjollnir would return to Thor's hand after being thrown and was symbolic of lightning.

FACT: According to Heindall, who used to watch the Rainbow Bridge for the coming of the Frost Giants: "Well, his hammer was *supposed* to return to his hand after it was thrown, but that particular feature never really worked properly, and Thor wasted a lot of prime giant-killing time chasing the stupid thing up and down Middle Earth. I've heard some of the old-timers say Thor could have smashed the heads of about 30 or 40 more giants, lifetime, if he only had a hammer with a decent return mechanism. I also asked him once about Mjollnir being symbolic of lightning and he rolled his eyes. 'I had a college girl tell me she did her thesis on how it was supposed to be some kind of penis,' he said. 'Sometimes a hammer is just a frigging hammer.'"

MYTH #3: Son of the giantess Rind, Valli was born for the sole purpose of avenging Balder's death, since the gods could not kill one of their own. When he was only one day old, he killed Hodur. He will be one of the seven Aesir to survive the Ragnarok.

FACT: "One day old? Are you shitting me? Who told you that?" asks Tyr, ex–god of war and the inspiration for Tuesday. "God, that's hysterical. I mean, Hodur was blind, and maybe not the ripest grape on the vine, but he was Odin's kid. I'm pretty sure he could have fended off a newborn *baby*. Anyway, Valli'd been out of junior college for at least six years when he killed Hodur. He dropped out, but he blew off one summer on a Eurorail pass, and waited tables down in Cabo for a while. He had to have been at least 23 or 24. Geez. One day old? That's rich. When Loki hears that, he'll piss his pants."

MYTH #4: Hljod and Volsung had ten sons, the eldest named Sigmund, and one daughter named Signy. Volsung had a palace built around the tree called Branstock so that the massive trunk grew inside the palace walls. At Signy's wedding banquet, Odin arrived in his usual disguise—as an elderly man wearing a cape and hood. He stuck a sword in the tree and said whichever man pulled out the sword could keep it. All tried but only Sigmund prevailed.

FACT: "In the first place, *everyone* knew it was Odin," says Njord, a guest at the banquet who, at the time, was god of the wind and sea. "He was always walking around in these disguises, but it was so obvious, even when he wore a wig and tried to cover up that gnarly empty socket. I mean, a crazy old man with one eye crashes your wedding and wants to show you a *sword trick?*—who else is it going to be? Anyway, Odin was all like 'Whosoever can pull this broadsword from the tree Branstock, may possess it!' but he was so weak he could barely shove it in there and the crappy old thing fell out by itself at least a half dozen times. The blade was all rusted out and no one wanted it, so Sigmund said to me, 'I'll pull the dumb sword out and make Odin happy if you catch the garter. I hate all this wedding crap.' "

MYTH #5: After Sigmund went into hiding, Signy exchanged shapes with a beautiful sorceress and went to her brother. The two slept together and Signy later had Sigmund's son, Sinfjotli.

FACT: According to Signy, "For the last time, *I did not sleep with my brother!* Gross! But even if I wanted to, I wouldn't need to exchange shapes with any skank sorceress to do it. Sigmund was *always* trying to get me in bed. Lots of brothers and sisters were doing it back then because they thought the Ragnarok was coming, but I told him to go to Hel, so he keeps spreading this story that we knocked boots and he knows I won't defend myself and reveal the name of Sinfjotli's real father because the guy's married and weighing a run for county assessor. Sigmund is such a cock."

The Celine Experience

BOB HIRSHON

"Let us give birth to a fragile or suspended moment in time, during which we can touch the very soul of the world."
—Franco Dragone, creator of Celine Dion's *A New Day*

Celine Dion's Las Vegas production, *A New Day*, is, to put it simply, the single most important event in the history of humankind. Celine does no less than introduce a wondrous new Age of Entertainment to a thankful world.

A New Day begins with a simple, golden cocoon, levitating above a glimmering circular stage. To the opening strains of "My Heart Will Go On," the cocoon opens and Celine steps out, symbolizing her emergence from her long, bucolic hiatus in rural Canada. Costumed as Mothra and magnified to gargantuan proportions by the audience's Active Matrix CelineSurround goggles, she spreads her enormous wings and soars high above the audience. With the crescendo of each chorus, she shoots scintillating silk threads from her mouth, vanquishing, in turn, a cybertronic, fire-breathing Whitney Houston, costumed as Godzilla, Britney Spears, as the warrior beast Megalon, and a chest-beating Barbra Streisand, as King Kong. With her foes struggling uselessly against the golden silk, Celine flutters her wings and releases sparkling, gold dust. As it settles onto them, the divas explode into a dazzlingly choreographed pyrotechnic display.

As Celine descends, her enormous Mothra body suit flutters to the stage and Celine shimmers in an elegant evening gown, encrusted with $500 million in jewels. She welcomes the audience and announces the first of the evening's medleys: music from the dawn of time to the present day.

Primal drums beat an insistent rhythm. A troupe of enormous lowland gorillas burst onto the stage, surrounding Celine. We hear hoots, howls, and the rending of fabric, before they bound from the stage, holding the tatters of Celine's gown.

The singer is left alone in a spotlight that pulses to the drums, naked. (Actually, she is wearing a body suit, painstakingly hand-crafted to be an exact recreation of her nude body.) Gyrating to the primal beat, Celine sings a soaring, anthropologically accurate ode to our Stone Age forebears.

Segueing into the theme song from *Clan of the Cave Bear*, Celine wrestles and kills a prehistoric giant grizzly, skins it, and fashions a stunning, low-cut dress from its fur. With a chorus of 144 loincloth-clad men, she reenacts a pagan ceremony: she is the embodiment of Gaia, the earth spirit. At its conclusion, she is thrown into a fiercely erupting volcano, which instantly transforms into a verdant tropical paradise. Celine erupts triumphantly from the crater, gracefully stage-dives into the crowd of dancing men, and resurfaces in the robes of a Mongolian peasant girl.

A master of Tuvan harmonic throat singing, Celine sings seven ancient Mongolian melodies at once, each more beautiful than the other. Then a crowd of fierce Masai warriors leap onto the stage and dance her to a dusty West African village. Shedding her robes, Celine is adorned in colorful Masai ceremonial raiment and body paint. She dances with her Masai captors and ululates thrillingly around a crackling fire. Suddenly, rough-hewn young sailors stream onto the stage from the audience, spiriting Celine onto a slave ship. They surround her and when she emerges, she is wearing a jaunty eighteenth-century sailor suit. She performs a spirited step dance with the sailors, followed by a medley of haunting sea shanties. Arriving in antebellum Savannah, Celine leads a musical uprising of her fellow slaves, culminating in a Gospel revival that has the audience on its feet, stomping, clapping and singing to Celine's "Hallelujah for the Music of Me!"

After an unbearable intermission, Celine returns to prove that her voice is more than a match for *any* musical genre. She kicks off with a moving tribute to Janis Joplin. Wearing the dress that Joplin wore for the cover photo of her breakthrough album, *Pearl*, as well as a wig made from Joplin's hair, Celine performs the rock legend's music "the way Janis would have, if she had my musical gifts."

As Celine scats the finale to "Me and Bobby McGee," a holographic rainbow spreads across the theater. An adorable Scottie trots onto the stage, barks twice, then tugs at Celine's *Pearl* dress, scampering off the stage with it, revealing Celine in a farm-girl frock. The familiar opening of "Somewhere over the Rainbow" begins, and Celine sings and soars over the shimmering rainbow. There she finds a treasure chest of Vegas one-dollar gold coins bearing her likeness. She showers them over the audience as a full-scale replica of the *Riverboat Queen* steamboat rolls onto the stage. Shedding her frock to reveal a short, tight skirt and purple-sequined tube top, Celine launches into "Proud Mary," shimmying her way over the boat's gangplank and onto the deck crowded with the entire London Philharmonic Orchestra. Next, Celine brings her own special stylings to Ella Fitzgerald, Patsy Cline, Aretha Franklin, Madonna, Billie Holiday, Sarah Vaughan and Michael Bolton. In a tender interlude, she softly growls "Cold, Cold Ground" by Tom Waits and, donning the garb of a street minstrel, strums an elegant homage to Bob Dylan's "Lay, Lady (Baby), Lay."

Then, showing that she definitely knows how to rock, Celine concludes her set with a cleverly intertwined Twisted Sister's "Kill or Be Killed," Marilyn Manson's "Speed of Pain," and fellow Canadian Avril Lavigne's "Sk8ter Bo," performed on a jet-propelled scooter with which Celine performs multiple 360s, helipops and a thrilling Backside Ollie Kickflip.

Just when the audience has seen everything, the theater lights dim. The Omnimax ceiling turns black velvet as dots of light appear. They brighten and sharpen until they are revealed to be a billion distant galaxies, magnified by the Hubble Space Telescope and beamed live to Caesar's Palace. The theater begins to rumble and shake, and in a flash of blue flame, the floor of the theater seemingly drops out, replaced by a receding field of Milky Way stars. The audience experiences the chest-crushing weight of 7 g-forces as they accelerate to light speed and beyond! Watches slow and then run backward.

Celine begins an encore of "My Heart Will Go On," leading the audience on a warp-speed flight in search of . . . what?

The answer appears in the form of a tiny, brilliant blue star. It grows larger as Celine, now whirling feverishly, spins golden silk about herself. Soon she is fully encased in a golden cocoon once more and, as she sings a dramatic high note, she shoots skyward, piercing the heart of the now enormous and brilliant blue star. It explodes in a thunderous supernova, spraying blinding beams of light everywhere!

When the audience regains consciousness, they behold a Celine who spans 180 meters: she is Mothra again bedecked in thousands of blue diamonds. She smiles down beatifically. The members of the audience find that a tiny blue star has been tattooed by laser onto their foreheads, each with a *C* at its center. All are filled with a sense of limitless wonder and awe of the universe—and of its star, Celine, who allowed them to touch "the very soul of the world."

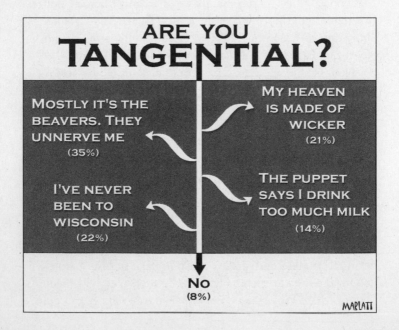

from ÜberGogh

GREGORY HISCHAK

Editor's note: Readers of More Mirth of a Nation *will recognize this as yet another Etch A Sketch work by Vincent van Gogh recently unshaken by a restoration specialist at Ohio Arts.*

The tortured mayhem of Vincent van Gogh crossed many disciplines with the ease of, say, Thomas Kincade moving from ceramic plates to miniature trains. True genius recognizes no boundaries and understands that, like "yam" and "sweet potato," "calling" and "curse" can indeed be one and the same—as the following glimpses into the ÜberGogh will attest.

Lust for Bibb Leaf

GREGORY HISCHAK

C&E (the Cheese & Easels Network) presents Provencal Cooking
with Paul et Vince

VINCE: Today, my good friend Paul Gauguin will prepare for us
trout.
PAUL: *Truites farcies à l'oignon au vin*—and my dear friend,
Vincent van Gogh—
VINCE: *Gogh*.
PAUL:—such a marvelous host during my stay here in
Provence, will assist.
VINCE: Paul brings such warmth to my little yellow house.
PAUL: It's a catbox. Vincent, did you wash these mangoes?
VINCE: It's important to taste the earth on your tongue.
PAUL: It's dirt. Let's remember Kitchen Rule Number Two: *no
dirt on food*.
VINCE: *Ah*—and look at this fine fish Paul has brought for us
today. *Beau raie*.
PAUL: It's *truite*, not *raie*. I bought it at Devaultier's.
VINCE: Maultelle's is cheaper.
PAUL: Well I bought it at Devaultier's, didn't I?
VINCE: Devaultier is a thug.
PAUL: Mangoes always require careful washing.
VINCE: Devaultier's wife is a thug as well. She chased me out of
their magazine aisle last week with a broom. . . .
PAUL: Now, if you've never cleaned a *truite* before—
VINCE: Trout—an explosive cut of veined metal.
PAUL: It's *truite*—a meditative wash of reflective tints and sug-
gestive underpainting.
VINCE: That sounds like Cezanne's *truite*.

PAUL: Do *not* speak of Cezanne's *truite* in this kitchen.

VINCE: You raved about his *truite*.

PAUL: No, I did not.

VINCE: You raved about Cezanne's *truite* and his bouillabaisse.

PAUL: Cezanne's bouillabaisse has no *rascasse* and bouillabaisse without *rascasse* is, to me, like a day without sunshine.

VINCE: Pissarro said that.

PAUL: I said it *before* Pissarro and those mangoes aren't going to wash themselves, are they?

VINCE: Pissarro said it at the league banquet . . . are you cutting the trout's head off now?

PAUL: We leave the head on, Vincent.

VINCE: I want to cut off its head. Give me the damn knife—

PAUL: We have rules in our kitchen.

VINCE: Yes, I know we ha—

PAUL: And Rule Number One?

VINCE: *Vincent does not touch the knives.*

PAUL: That's right. For this dish, we keep the *truite's* head attached. Its vibrant silvery cheeks and penetrating gaze symbolizing the primal life source.

VINCE: They suggest the fetid nature of our original sin.

PAUL: No, *truite* is freshwater and it symbolizes the primal life source. *Paupiettes de saumon* symbolizes the fetid nature of our original sin and we're making that next week.

VINCE: May I cut off its head now?

PAUL: I said we're keeping the head on, Vincent.

VINCE: Its penetrating gaze mocks me.

PAUL: Vincent will sauté the onions in four tablespoons of butter until soft.

VINCE: Butter—a dissolving swirl of cadmium sun. I want to burn in its incandescence.

PAUL: Vincent, get off the counter.

VINCE: Its brilliant xanthic warmth illuminates my small kitchen. I melted the butter last week, didn't I, Paul?

PAUL: It's not necessary to squeeze the butter from its wax paper wrapping as Vincent is doing—did you take your medication this morning?

VINCE: The warmth . . . *the warmth* between my fingers . . .

PAUL: Do we need a time-out?

VINCE: Monet played with his butter all the time.

PAUL: To the *truite* we add three shallots and a *bouquet garni*.

VINCE: I've *seen* Monet play with his butter.

PAUL: Just before putting the *truite* into the oven to braise at 180°C for fifteen minutes, we fold the tail up through the slit in its body cavity so that it protrudes through the *truite's* mouth.

VINCE: You're a primitivist—*don't cut off my head!*

PAUL: Vincent, I'm reaching for a lemon. Will you stop squeezing that butter and please wash the bibb leaf.

VINCE: I immerse the lettuce into the sink with the care that I would give a leafy green infant's head. Baptism and absolution, the cleansing liquid bookends of existence.

PAUL: It's three-quarters water.

VINCE: Existence—three-quarters water.

PAUL: No, bibb leaf. It's three-quarters water and a perfect bedding for *truite*. Pass me those mangoes, Vincent.

VINCE: This is a similar bibb leaf used by Monet to cradle his *Pave de daurade au beurre d'algue*.

PAUL: Monet never made *Pave de daurade au beurre d'algue*.

VINCE: Maybe it was Manet?

PAUL: The mangoes are a beautiful complement to fish.

VINCE: Last week you said papayas were a beautiful comple—

PAUL: Papayas do complement fish as well.

VINCE: My primitivist friend smothers everything in mangoes.

PAUL: Well, my compulsive cohost dumps sunflower seeds into his waffle batter.

VINCE: And my syphilitic comrade has repeatedly told me how much he *loves* my waffles.

PAUL: That's because I'm a gracious guest.

VINCE: And your breaking my pipe without offering to replace it?

PAUL: You shouldn't have left it on the chair.

VINCE: My long-term guest sucks his teeth when he chops endive.

PAUL: I *have* teeth to suck and I, at least, know how to spell "mayonnaise."

VINCE: You lie—*haa!*

PAUL: Vincent, give me that knife back. Kitchen Rule Num—

VINCE: You've no idea of the pain I live with, you free-loading *grilletante!*

PAUL: You'd be surprised. Are you putting that knife down or am I calling your brother again?

VINCE: Say *good night,* Paul!

— ▪ — ▪ — ▪ — ▪ — ▪ — ▪ — ▪ — ▪ — ▪ — ▪ —

. . . Beatniks booted from Bohemian Club . . . Flat Earth Society boycotts Golden Globes . . . Love child charged with hate crime . . . Mystery illness hits extraterrestrials . . .

The Nuance of the Leap

GREGORY HISCHAK

t isn't just about draftsmanship.

A bead of sweat ran down Vincent's brow as he squinted beneath a swirling cadmium sun—8:30 in the morning and already hot. A Herdmaster roared past close enough to the shoulder to make Vincent almost keel forward. From the passenger-side window an elderly woman with blue hair shouted:

"You call that an elk?"

"*Hey*—do you *see* antlers here?" Vincent hurdled his brush at the receding RV but even at a good ten miles below the speed limit it was already out of range.

Tourist whore—it isn't just about draftsmanship. It's obviously not an elk. Disgusted, Vincent unbolted his work and flung it across the deerless expanse of lavender and alfalfa.

With a fresh sheet in place he began again: *The forelegs are together so that they visually read as one single leg.* Cezanne knew it wasn't just about draftsmanship, dammit. Cezanne's deer were a juxtaposition of flattened planes and discarded chiaroscuro that abandoned all fealty to mere silhouette yet still conveyed the nuance of the deer's leap and the sense that they'd be Xing for the next six miles.

"Go—you out there?"

Tanguay's bark startled Vincent from an unengrossing issue of *State Route Monthly*.

"*Gogh*," Vincent muttered uselessly as he entered the office. Lowering himself into a folding chair he watched the long white ash of his boss's cigar extend toward a wall map.

"Twenty-five miles in two weeks, Go?"

"*Gogh*. Van G—"

"Exactly how many deer crossings are there between Foix and Tarbes?"

"A lot."

"A lot?"

"Several elk crossings too—"

"*Several elk crossings too.*" Tanguay mocked Vincent's high-pitched Dutch accent as another stub of ash fell to the linoleum. "Shit—an elk is a deer with antlers."

"It isn't that simple, Mr. Tanguay."

"Actually, it is. Gauguin just covered Clermont-Ferrand to Lyon in a week and there's a shitload of elk between Clermont-Ferrand and Lyon."

"Maybe he's stenciling?" Vincent suggested.

"I hire *painters*. I'd subcontract to Matisse's crew if I wanted stencilers—you want a mint?" Vincent declined the small jar of candies that were shaken at him and rubbed his sweaty palms together.

"I want the truck on a wedge assignment, sir."

Tanguay exhaled a rank blue plume toward Vincent and sat quiet for a moment.

"Six percent grade?"

"Yessir."

Tanguay filled a glass from a vin de table and downed it with one backward jerk of his head.

"I'm tired of painting deer, sir."

"Don't make me cry, Go—I hate crying. Seurat was just in here trying to make me cry: '*Painting zee leetle reflective dots on mileposts gets very teeedious, Mr. Tanguee. . . .*'"

"He wasn't asking for the six percent grade job, was he?"

"Truck on a wedge—*Truck on a Wedge*—everybody wants to draw the truck on a fucking wedge—"

"I draw kick-ass trucks, sir."

"What I need, Go, are your kick-ass leaping deer—and a lot more than what I'm currently getting—that's what I need. I need kick-ass reflective dots from Seurat, and kick-ass no-passing lines from Degas—but do you know what I'm *getting*?"

"Bellyaching?"

"Kick-ass bellyaching is what I'm getting." Tanguay gazed up at the wall map:

"Valenciennes to Perpignan; Toulon to La Havre; Rennes to Chambért . . ."—his cigar belched rings around the entire highway system. "Go, motorists are depending on you to know when to expect deer to come across their path." Tanguay downed another shot of vin de table. "Listen, I didn't just give you this job as a favor to your brother."

"You told me you did."

"I did?"

"I don't have leaping deer in my heart anymore."

"Hey—don't get all Cezanne on me, Go, I don't need that. You stick those deer right back in your heart and keep them there for seventy-five miles a week and then—and only then—we'll talk truck on a wedge."

"Promise?"

"Promise. Now get to work and don't smash into Lautrec again on your way out—Lautrec!"

Vincent squinted through his windshield and observed a speck on the horizon grow into the crouched form of Seurat carefully filling in circles of reflective white paint on gray metal posts. A deer Xing was going in at milepost 486 and Vincent pulled over to the shoulder. Seurat was oblivious to his approach and didn't look up until Vincent stood over him.

"Four hundred and eighty-five," Seurat announced with a final splab of paint to the center.

"Nice."

"Thank you."

"It's very reminiscent of your two hundred dots between Aurillac and Le Puy."

Seurat dabbed his brush in thinner and thwacked it against a guardrail.

"Well, individually they're just dots, but if you drive the whole stretch it becomes . . ." Seurat's Parisian rasp trailed off.

"A body of work?" Vincent suggested.

"It's the distant, you know. My work needs to be seen from a distance."

"I always thought so." Vincent walked the tenth of a mile alongside his coworker to the next marker. "How do you suppose Cezanne is getting on since leaving the department?"

"Starving, I imagine," Seurat said calmly, stirring his brush before beginning the outline of a small circle at the top of milepost 486. "I think your deer are conveying a real emotional intensity now, Vincent."

"I'm just not feeling the deer anymore."

"No, I think you're feeling the deer. You have the nuance of the leap."

"Thanks—you've developed a very strong dot." Seurat looked up at Vincent, a twinkle suddenly lighting his eyes:

"Tanguay told me if I get seventy-five miles of dots this week I can start painting trucks on wedges."

"He *what?*"

"Six percent grade."

The blast of a passing eighteen-wheeler suddenly sent both of their hats flying across a shimmering expanse of wheatfields and crows.

ROD LOTT'S LISTS
28 TELETUBBIES WHO DIDN'T MAKE THE CUT

Mange	Dyspeptic	Bling-Bling
Tinkle	Tipsy	Dolemite
Pedo	Pervy	Vulva
Ditzy	Poo	Homey
Mowie-Wowie	Schizo	Dank
Blah-Blah	Björk	Cuz
Pickle-Tickle	Pope	Drop-Dead
Shaft	Hanky-Panky	Stud
Swami	Pikachu	
Moesha	Bang-Bang	

UN Monthly Bulletin

MARC JAFFE

I was astonished by the broadcast of the UN Security Council session in which Colin Powell presented his case for an attack on Iraq. It wasn't the evidence he presented or the rebuttal by the Iraqi delegate, but the announcement by the German chairman concluding the session. He reminded the members that there was a luncheon to be held that afternoon. A luncheon? What? Was it in honor of the official abandoning of the Yugoslavia name? Or perhaps it was given by Namibia on the anniversary of its independence. Whatever the purpose it certainly made the UN seem more like my synagogue than an institution of world leadership. Somehow, I now think I would find items like the following in the UN monthly calendar:

EVENTS

Sunday Night BINGO / Help us raise funds and maybe win some cash for your homeland at the same time. Other prizes include: grab-bag UNICEF boxes, UN helmets and one extra week on the Security Council.

French Lessons / 8:00 p.m., every Tuesday evening. Baguettes, Brie and Bon Vivant—Remember French is still one of the most important languages. Just ask the French. And think how nice it will be to stop using those uncomfortable headphones for the next long-winded, sanctimonious speech.

All Nations Winter/Summer* Dance / Come join the fun at the annual hootenanny. Don't let those Russians monopolize the

*Depending on your hemisphere

dance floor this year, bring your dancing shoes and find your partner from amongst the neighborly countries. Native casual.

East African/Scandanavian Mixer—Bowling. Wed. 26th, 7:30 p.m. UN lanes, Subbasement level.

Sisterhood Membership Dinner—Honoring Margaret Thatcher. Muslim nations are welcome to join.

MILESTONES

Guyana / Twenty-five years cult-free.
Nepal / Third straight year of positive GDP.

GIFTS TO FUNDS

Ted Turner Fund
Bahamas, Cayman Islands

Help the U.S. Pony Up Its Dues Fund
Jimmy Carter

HELP US

Do you know where they are? We are trying to contact members we've lost touch with, be it through name changes or a move. If you have any information on the following, please let us know: FIJI, RHODESIA, CANADA

Ask Your Doctor

MAIRA KALMAN
AND RICK MEYEROWITZ

Dysplosives
Platitudium Bromide
Psychopenicillin
Confusadril
Cucumberdil
Preventidrool
Revoltin
Belittlin

Soporifiquil
Dixichixil
Preparation-W
Preventafit
QueSeraSerum
Krazyglucosamine
Accidentiprone
Mindbenderine

Nostalgics
Advertizin (*Sellmor*)
Nothin
Prozenconz
Linoleum
Mylarr
Zabar
Mishkamine (*Pishkamine*)
LummOxx
Miketycin

Pheduprin
Neo-Sufferin
Benumbitussin
Ritalintintin
Nothin (*with Somethin*)
Vexxin
Pedanticort
Trafficort
No-Morte

Antipepsodines
Kishkafix
Famishtin
Anusaire
Enthusiastimene
Ennuigra (*Tedium*)

Pseudointellectuol
Crinoline
Globbinlarynx
General Tso's Black Oil
Lornaluft
Theatrical (*Overactin*)

Cratch
Cratch-Gel
Enigma (*Miasma*)
Monrodoctrin
Miesvanderol
Vongerischtin
Martinizin (*One every 3 hours*)

Espresso Bismol
MoMAQuens
FrancoXenophobisol
Phenaminafenafinaphen
Ibuproblem
Maladroitin (*with Chondroitin*)
SchmuckAid

Pandemonics
B-itch
Fartin-X
Amexx
Hypochondriax
Emmanuelax
Hydrocortidrek
Credenza
Conundraderm

Schwarzeneggra (*Shtarkazine*)
Acetaminiluggage
Armageddadone
Relapsin
Ipsofactil
Ineptorol
Folderol
Thatsol

. . . **Building evacuated again at Suspicious Package Expo . . . Buzz diminishing for last year's Oscars . . . Major scare: Doomsday Clock running slow . . . Arrest made in death of literature . . .**

The George W. Bush Memorial Library

MERLE KESSLER

Mr. President:

Please read this, sir, and note my comments. We've got to move on funding opportunities while you still have "heat."

The first section lists the official "holdings" of the President George W. Bush Memorial Library, as we know them. If there's *anything* you care to add to this list, please do so quickly.

This list is followed by potential locations for the George W. Bush Memorial Library.

1. THE COLLECTION

Books

Paperback version of *Treasure Island*, by Robert Louis Stevenson. Cover missing. Possibly obscene scrawl on page 17. (If this doodle is yours, sir, it could add to value.)

The Hungry Caterpillar, by Eric Carle. (This charming children's book is yours, technically, but I believe your staff bought it for you? Clarify, please.)

Hondo, by Louis L'Amour. Mint condition.

Anecdotes for Public Occasions. Anonymous.

A Charge to Keep, by Karen P. Hughes. Cover missing, autographed (by you, sir).

God's Alphabet Plan, by Reverend Robert "Bob" Skilwether. (The letters in this book don't seem to be in any particular order. It could shed some light on you and your father's unique style of oratory.)

Frivolous Lawsuits. Humorous commentary by the "ol' jedge, Lee T. Gator." (Pseudonym?)

Slouching Toward Gomorrah, by Robert Bork. Extremely mildewed.

Winning at Solitaire, by Fred Hurle. (This is accompanied by a CD-ROM. Did it improve your game, sir?)

Wither Persia, by C. Worthington Galt. Very large volume, apparently self-published by the author.

Pamphlets

"One Hundred Tips from Successful People"

"Speaking in Public"

"Dry Cleaning Explained"

"Make Big Money from Oil and Professional Sports!" (A how-to guide.)

"Make Your Own Tall-Boy Bong" (A how-to guide, copyrighted 1972. A real antique!)

"Counting Votes in Florida" (A how-to guide.)

Comic Books

Spider-Man #23, poor condition.

Fantastic Four #47, missing first five pages and cover.

Classics Illustrated version of *Silas Marner*, cover missing.

Classics Illustrated version of *A Midsummer Night's Dream*, only six pages remaining.

Bob's Big Boy souvenir comic, mint condition.

Newspaper Clippings

"Family Circus" comic strip. (And a fine episode it is, sir. Grandpa appears to little Billy from heaven. Stirring. I can find no better word.)

A recipe for "gen-you-wine yee-haw Texas chili," clipped from the *New Haven Register*.

Recipe for tuna casserole, origin unknown.

Speeches

Have you, or anybody on your staff, saved any of these? They might come in handy.

Miscellany

Bazooka Joe comic. That fellow in the eye patch always cracks me up! What is his story, anyway?

VCR manual, cover missing.

Refrigerator magnet collection. Some fruit missing.

Beer can collection, beer missing.

Map of Texas.

Map of Iraq. With pins.

Poster: "It's NOO-CLEE-AR, stupid."

Poster: "It's AWL-BIDNESS, stupid."

Poster of Osama bin Laden, with mustache drawn in Magic Marker over his regular mustache. Most amusing.

Old Rolodex cards.

Used videotape, half of which contains an exercise video from 1982, the other half an episode of *The Sopranos* that cuts out five minutes before the end.

Eight-track cartridges of Supertramp, Journey, Jefferson Starship, and Pablo Cruise. Also one 33⅓ lp called *Discosizer!* Scratched.

Sir, if I may say so, this collection really gives a true flavor of George W. Bush the man, one that your presidency—excellent as it has been—could not possibly convey, a taste that hopefully will leave America hungry for more.

2. POSSIBLE SITES

There's a studio apartment in Millbrae, California, with reasonable rents. However, the landlady seems a little "snoopy," and might not "cotton" to the droves of tourists and history seekers that we hope will throng to the George W. Bush Memorial Library.

Leisure Town, outside of Ada, Oklahoma, is willing to donate its next available double-wide mobile home to house this collection. However, residents here, though elderly, and despite everything, are surprisingly healthy. It could be years before a vacancy.

A longtime supporter of yours, one "Tee Dub" McGuire, from Dallas, Texas, has kindly offered his garage, with the proviso that his collection of *Popular Mechanics* (dating back to 1947) not be disturbed.

Stor-Edge, the "cutting edge of material management," is willing to lease one of its sheds at a substantial discount—in any of forty-six locations of our choosing—if its public relations team can use your image in its promotions. It might be good publicity for both of us. They have a Web site, if that means anything to you.

Mr. and Mrs. Gary Fowler of Wilmington, Delaware, have a spare bedroom we can rent. However, their FBI file reveals that they also have a son with a history of co-dependence. If his second marriage breaks up (and sources indicate that this is likely), he would probably return to claim this bedroom as his own. This could prove awkward.

Sir, the above does not exhaust our possibilities.

There are several vacant lots and spaces in mini-malls that we're looking at. It would be nice to have a marble edifice of some sort, and we're still hoping that we get the stone and labor donated to this worthy cause. After all, we're only looking at a piece the size of a cutting board. I'm certain we can get some stonecutter to cough up that much dignity.

We are also looking at the possibility of housing the collection in a recreational vehicle of some sort, and taking it on the road. What with county fairs, state fairs, or even simple mall openings, we believe the Library could pay for itself inside of ten years.

Those are our options, sir. Please give us your input ASAP.

I'm going to go ahead and paste this right into your e-mail, rather than attach it, because you indicated that you couldn't figure out how to open the document last time. Let me know if you or your people have any difficulties.

Yours truly,
John McCain
Curator, Chairman of Location Committee,
George W. Bush Memorial Library

Live from Folsom Prison:
Liner Notes

IAN LENDLER

A day that will live in infamy among those who follow humor: July 15, 2000. Ian Lendler records *Live from Folsom Prison*, one of the high-water marks of modern recorded comedy.

Now, four years later, Columbia Records has seen fit to place this album in its Legends/Masterpieces catalogue, and mark this grand occasion with a digital remastering and brand new liner notes.

Ian speaks of his experience: "It was the warden himself who first asked me to come to Folsom and, in his words: 'Write them up a funny story the way you do.' He'd been a big fan of the 'Jokes to Jails' outreach program and its previous albums. There was Chucklin' Charlie's 'Laugh Riot in Cell Block #9' and Dr. Retarded's 'Sing-Sing Hijinks.' But those boys were booked solid through the summer. Plus, they were frightened."

Ian had yet to perform before a prison audience and leapt at the chance to cut his own incarceration album. In an interview before the show, he explained, "Prisoners have all that hurt, all that sin to purge with laughter. Plus, they got nothing to do, nowhere to go and guns trained on them at all times. It's every comedian's dream!"

Hopes were running high. You could cut the excitement with a shiv when Ian took the stage to the cheers of the prisoners. The album sleeve includes never-before-seen photos of these opening moments:

Ian settled into prime humor-writing position: in a hammock slung across the stage, pen and pad in hand, fan whirring nearby, TV in front of him, with a steaming cup of coffee in a tin cup (to show his allegiance to the prisoners).

And he proceeded to write.

The initial enthusiasm of the audience comes through beautifully on this digital remastering—the encouraging shouts of "Go!" and "Yeah!" as Ian stares off into space and then begins flipping channels before settling on *Good Morning America*. Then he leafs through a magazine, stopping only to take a brief quiz to determine whether he is or is not a good lover.

Many scholars have argued that Track 4, "Ian rummages in refrigerator for some yogurt," marks the point at which the audience becomes audibly tense at the transpiring unfunniness. For me, however, it's Track 7, "Ian logs onto eBay and bids on Hungry, Hungry Hippos." The audience's ripostes, such as, "Hey, Lendler, you slurp shit!" add a delicious menace to the entire affair.

His next gambit was to "Write what you know" (Track 8). He shares his own incarceration experience with the audience, riffing on the time he wrapped his mom's Mercedes around a telephone pole and she grounded him for a whole month and Consuela had to bring his dinners up to his rooms—on the shoddy, servants' china no less! Yes, he knows what hard times are all about.

The whir of the fan is all that can be heard in the ensuing silence.

He tries a little audience participation, reading aloud a few slips of paper the prisoners have passed up. One bon mot, "Hey, Lendler, you want somethin' funny? How about my foot in your ass?" is met with thunderous applause.

In retrospect, it's astonishing how quickly Ian crumbled under the pressure. Immediately, he began babbling excuses for his unfunniness—he'd been funny yesterday, he swore, they should have seen it, but today he wasn't "in the zone" and hey, don't you hate airplane food?

This gives rise to the now famous off-mic exchange, digitally enhanced and transcribed here, between Ian and one "Tiny" Duggan:

Tiny: "Fuck face!"

Ian: "Yes?"

Tiny: "This show sucks! You get paid for this shit? I'm a fuck-load funnier than your ass."

Ian's response, "Well, maybe you should've thought of that before you axed up your momma," was not well received.

Though it occurred exactly at this point in the performance, who's to say, given the mercurial nature of prisoners, what touched off the riot and subsequent 11-day standoff with the authorities? Critics have argued that Ian was held hostage "against his will," but this ignores the passion with which he threw himself into the performance to ensure a classic recording. As the tapes continued to roll, Ian let loose some of his finest corkers, including enough bouts of weeping and pleas for God to take him from this bad, bad place to inspire campus drinking games.

The progressive one-upsmanship of Side Two is a pure masterpiece of the slow burn, building from Track 9, "Who's the funnyman now?" with its unidentifiable but visceral whomping sounds, to a crescendo with the unforgettable Track 11, "At the behest of prisoners, Ian performs 'Good Ship Lollipop' in a girly voice." You may well remember this track as the catchy tune that, in its 12"-single dance remix, swept the nightclubs of Europe in the summer of 2000.

Each track rewards you with new details upon further listening, be it the faint *tick-tick-tick* of the electric clock as if suggesting the minutes, hours and months till each convict's release, or the *slish-slish* of sharpened spoons carving out the list of demands in Ian's thigh, then the revised list, then a few new demands, then a copy-edited draft on the other thigh.

Fortunately, his funny bone remained intact. To this day, if a lit cigarette comes anywhere near him, his face contorts into a grotesque mask; his pants become soiled. Apparently, this has become something of a running gag at parties he attends, proving he can still leave crowds gasping for more.

Sadly, the tape ran out, denying us the dramatic finale, when SWAT team sharpshooters managed to take out the leader of the riot, one "Tiny" Duggan, with a masterful carom shot off Ian's frontal lobe.

Fortunately, Ian emerged from the hostage crisis and impromptu lobotomy funnier than ever, with a voracious appetite for life, puddings and shiny things. And a Grammy-nominated, platinum-selling comedy album in the can!

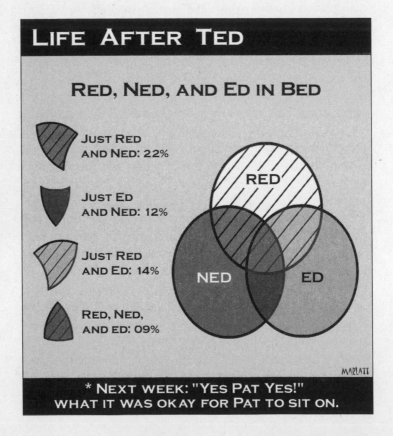

Waiting Room Digest

IAN LENDLER

At last, there's a magazine for those of you just waiting, be it at a dentist's, doctor's, or therapist's office, or maybe the DMV. Every issue of *Waiting Room Digest* is created in waiting rooms, by people waiting—people who feel your pain.

This month's features:

WHAT'S HOT HOT HOT

Our up-to-the-minute monthly selection from waiting rooms reading material across the country.

Newsday '79: What Carter has in store for his second term!

Highlights for Children, March '93: The maze leading the squirrel to the pinecone is only halfway done.

Life magazine '53: Will man ever walk on the moon?

Women's Health '97: The amazing new food that will help you lose weight *and* double as effective home-heating insulation.

TECHNOLOGY AND YOU

"The Snub-Nose .38 Beretta"

How openly fondling small firearms can cut your wait in half—*and* earn you some quick extra cash.

REPORTING FROM THE FIELD

It's here! The final installment of our 10-part series on the spellbinding growth of the grass outside the window of the jury duty room. Will the grass succumb to the rapid advances of those weeds? Will that dandelion bloom? Will those ants be lured to their doom by the chubby kid with the melting popsicle and magnifying glass? Read on . . .

POINT-COUNTERPOINT

Point: If I've said it once, I've said it a thousand times, this office has 376 ceiling tiles.
Counterpoint: The only logical conclusion for reasonable people to arrive at is 375, and if that baby screams once more—just *once*—I'm gonna go *totally* freakin' batshit, I swear to Christ.

PROFILES ON PARADE: "THE ATLANTA FREEWAY"

Move over, L.A., the hottest waiting room in America is Atlanta's smog-clogged commuter drive-time. But that may not be a bad thing! A roundtable between hoboes and fraternity pledges on the uses of carbon monoxide as a "party" fume.

CONSUMER WATCH: "HARD CANDIES"

How long they've actually been sitting there in that little candy dish. What we found may surprise you . . . or may not . . . it sort of depends on what you thought in the first place.

LETTER FROM THE EDITOR IN CHIEF

What the . . . ? I totally got here before that guy! Why the hell does he get to go ahead of me?! This sucks! Plus, this complimentary coffee stinks! I should know, I've had 9 cups since I've been here! And another thing . . . (cont'd pp. 7–10, 18–26, 41).

WAITING ROOM CONFIDENTIAL: "SEX WITH PATIENTS"

Is this why you're waiting so long? One reporter goes undercover and sleeps with patients to determine just how long a dentist might take, given the patients' groggy state.

THE POWER OF POSITIVE THINKING

A step-by-step primer on how to kill a man with your mind, or, barring that, bump your appointment up ten minutes. Whichever comes first.

STAYIN' ALIVE: A NEW SURVIVAL SKILL EVERY ISSUE!

This month, learn how to turn a plastic fern, Cremora, and a wad of prechewed bubble gum into a delicious meal that feeds six.

FRESH PERSPECTIVES: "THE ZEN OF WAITING"

An Exclusive Interview with the Dalai Lama
In which His Holiness speaks of his lifelong wait to return to his homeland of Tibet, from which he escaped as a child to avoid the slaughter of so many of his brother monks, just for a little perspective on those 15 minutes you've been waiting for someone to look at your tummy ache.

― · ― · ― · ― · ― · ― · ― · ― · ― · ―

. . . Anti-lobotomy bill a "no-brainer" . . . New study: all snow-flakes alike . . . U.S. developing "smart" dirty bomb . . . Thousands gather to protest First Amendment . . .

Greatest Love Quotes Ever

DANNY LIEBERT

"Better a dinkle clarney than a wishet bairnie."
—Irish

*This is just as true today as it was last Thursday when I made it up.
Whether the folk wisdom of simple peasants or the ponderings of
great minds, Love makes everyone an idiot. Read these little gems
again and again, for they leave not the slightest trace in the brain.*

The haughty eye of a beautiful woman, the proud lip of a
camel, the ringing of swords in battle: these three have nothing
in common.

—Traditional Bedouin

Come to me, my sister! my love! . . . Mom and Dad are at the
Goldsteins!

—Song of Songs

Bringeth Sweet Asphodel, Clytemnestra Leaf and Star Anise,
bringeth Pansies, Feverfew and Eyebright. Bedeck the altar
of the Little God of Love for 'tis the Vernal Season! Bringeth
Monkey-Jewel, Jack-in-the-Pulpit and Jill-in-the-Stirrups, and
don't forget three bags of fertilizer from Plant Depot.

—Sir John Burpee

Though Love is capable of making out vague shapes and contrasting areas of light and darkness it is "legally blind" and may
qualify for a full disability.

—U.S. Dept. of Human Resources

Hey, I thought we said no names!

—Anonymous

If a man who chews tobacco takes a wife who chews they will forever compare spittoons.

—Southern U.S.

The Husband eats the Cream of Tomato Soup of Peace but the Roué's many "capers" make his salad too salty so he asks the Husband if he can have some of his Tomato soup and the Husband says "No way! Roué!"

—The Abbe of Vanburen

Le coeur a ses raisons
Que la raison ne connait point
(The heart is full of raisins,
but raisins aren't the point)

Pascal

Love is a Feast and Passion is the Meat, Beauty the Sauce. The Table is Hope and Children are Little Packets of Sugar you put under one leg of the Table of Hope to keep it from wobbling and spilling the Wineglass of Impropriety on the vest of your Rectitude in which case you end up taking it to the Dry Cleaners of Public Opinion to get the stain out and it costs as much as the vest.

—Lord Chesterfield to his Son

Illekikidiki mrokemboloni mokuimiki filikqwa qwa'ah'aa'aaa'h'aa a.
(The good lover can set a bologna on fire with his nose.)

—Maori

When you're tired of Nude Coed Volleyball, you're tired of life.

—Dr. Johnson

My love, thy hair is as a flock of goats,
thy teeth are a flock of sheep come up from the washing
thy nose as the tower of Lebanon
thy eyes like fishpools . . .
thy nose, thy teeth, thy hair we can do something about,
but those fish pool eyes . . . will take some getting used to
—Song of Songs

Ah, Cherie, Love is like Professional Wrestling: everything is
fake, fake, fake and you wear silly underwear.
—Colette

Woman! She is a mystery wrapped in an enigma and padded
with secrets in a spooky box with a baffling bow delivered by a
shadowy figure in a flowing burnoose at three in the morning
behind an Art Nouveau antique shop on an obscure side street
in Paris.
—Baron Molto-Agitato

Grow old along with me, the best is yet to be: impotence,
senility.
—Traditional

Beauty is not of the face but further down.
—Jim across the hall

In the evening take a little Thessalian wine, nothing stronger,
and do sword exercise till out of breath. Strip naked, splash
with icy water & slip into a tunic of raw linen. Bed down with a
book of philosophy and read till pleasantly drowsy. Dim the
light, jack off and go to sleep.
—Marcus Aurelius on love

Newly Discovered Emily Dickinson Love Poem!

This is a love poem to her secret lover, "MH," known to scholars only as "Mystery Hunk." Written in the style of her greatest period, it shows how the poetess could vastly inflate the homeliest details of her fiercely circumscribed life. (In this case skinny-dipping with "MH," dozing off and getting sunburned.)

Love—a Remoter Pampa
a crepuscule Argentine
till Sun—Ducat of Doge's Purse
led Procession—cochineal

Like Rubies defenestrated
from Parapets of Noon
Light flowered—deafened Sense
as We lay—Spoon in Spoon

Night found him—Crustacean—
Gethsemaned in Pain
I—with Ointments Unguentine
As—Dimity Saviors—tend!

... **Flat Earth Society ship missing** ... **Japan overrun by stray robotic dogs** ... **Hate groups to offer dental plan** ... **Ecuador, South Korea, Finland join League of Random Nations** ...

Prattle & Humbert Paint 2004 Catalogue

Because you deserve paint.

DANNY LIEBERT

Whites

Vichyssoise
Nivea
Starched Hanky
Chinese Funeral
Ceviche
Nothingness
Boo Radley
Anthrax
Flokati
Icy Stare
Lymph
F47 Contrail
Ricotta

Grays

Stirfried Lint
Blanched Gizzard
Turkish Submarine
Asylum Smock
Dirty Cake
Moonie Skin
Calumet City
Mutton
Bauhaus Suicide

Sad Anchovy
Bachelor Sheets
YMCA Wastebasket

Browns

Perturbed Pine
Verbally Abused Walnut
Stranger Abducted Oak
Crop Circle
Depraved Macaroon
Burnt Vienna
Hairy Mole
Toasty Toast
Whispering Dirt
Banjo Brulé
Pretzel
Sundried Turtle
Expired Eggnog

Greens

Wild Asparagii
Military Mist
Everglades Crash
Vague Lettuce
Breath of Scallion

Fork-Mashed Peas
Buttered Toad
Inappropriate Touch
Sea Spew
Fogged Spruce
Sprigged Yew
Mossy Moose
Misty Moss

Blues

Chilled Ink
Azurinian Azure
Winsome Hittite
Varicose
Foreign Policy Mirage
Santa Fe Dawn
Taos About 11:15 a.m.
Byzantine Trout
Windex
Regency Fop
Odd Blue Rash
Voltage
Rockabilly Trousers

Yellows

Piss 'n Vinegar
Yam
Dawndust
Slip-Proof Bathtub Daisies
Hitchcock Blonde
Bunion
Goose Schmaltz
Bad Puppy
Stonewashed Muffin
Yakbutter Tea

Tapioca Nights
Sunspritz
Whitefish & Eggs
Swishy Verbena Mince

Reds

Greasefire
Revelations 6:12
Whispered Borscht
Crushed Tuberose
Bruised Gladiola
Pistolwhipped Poppies
Hot Bubblegum
Robitussin
Whorehouse Drapes
Fistula
Canned Ham
Plumbutter Drool
Chafed Thigh
Stonewashed Salami

Blacks

Luger
First Wife's Ashes
Mr. Kurtz He Dead
Stonewashed Licorice
Ninja
Lincoln's Hat
Brother Theodore
Iron Headboard
Solzhenitsyn on 'ludes
Film Noir
Nosferatu
Charred Rafters
Sated Leech

Colonials

For that "Colonial American Mood" of sexual repression, melancholy and alcoholic stupor punctuated with irrational violence, religious fanaticism and genocide.

Grim Pilgrim
Sodomy
Children of the Corn
Burnt Witch
Dun Cow
Shat Pumpkin
Stonewashed Stone
Backless Pew
Succotash
Apple Pandowdy
Protestant
Bacon Rind
Quaker Bitch

HARMON LEON'S OFFICE PRANKS
CUBICLE NATION

things needed
- 1 shotgun
- 1 homemade flag
- landmines

One day, come to work and declare your cubicle an independent country. Construct your own flag for your cubicle/country with your face as the emblem. Hang the flag high over your work space, naming the country after yourself. Also create an original national anthem and sing it at full volume. If you can't think of an original tune, use a song from '80s rockers RATT. When a coworker comes near your cubicle, yell, "Get the hell out of *my* country!" Make specific rules that govern your new country. Start a revolution to overthrow other cubicles. Make them refer to you as "El Presidente!" When security comes to remove you from the building, put up a fight, protecting the rights of your country and its bylaws.

What Every American Should Know

DANNY LIEBERT

The New Improved List for the Culturally Literate, now, for the first time, in order of importance. With apologies to Mr. Hirsch, et al. To preempt attacks by the "Diversity-Mongers" we've included Don Cornelius, host of Soul Train, *and dancer Tommy Tune, who very well might be gay.*

Buffalo Wings
Phil Rizzuto
The War of Jenkins's Ear
Rosemary Clooney
Crapola
The Older Americans Home
　　Repair & Winterization
　　Act
"A terrible beauty is born . . ."
Eric Bogosian
Salt Lake City, Utah
Pizza
Ismail Gasprinsky
"Houston, we have a
　　problem . . ."
Giambattista Vico
Raid
Harvey Keitel
The Little Engine That Could
Art Brut
Chicken Pot Pie

Nolo Contendere
"Kentucky Woman" (song)
Battle of Lepanto
"Get them panties off . . ."
Remy de Gourmont
Pad Thai Noodles
Canada
Theatre of Orangeade
Theatre of Cruelty (no
　　orangeade)
Madame de Stael
The Ozone Layer
Plato
Pluto
Lulu
Lassie
Battle of New Orleans (not
　　the song)
Death by Chocolate Cake
Rainer Maria "Wendell" Rilke
Slaw

Umbrella Drinks
The Yamagata-Lobanov
    Agreement
Nookie
Queen Uracca
Kasha Varnishkes
Admiral Perry
Refrigerator Perry
World War Two
Boca-Burgers
The Battle of Saxa-Ruba
Mark Twain (Samuel
    Gompers)
Crazy Eddie
Botticelli's *Birth of Venus*
Da Vinci's *Last Supper*
Oscar Meyer's "Pickle Loaf"
Queen Mab
St. Zita the Virgin
Pu-Pu Platter
Orlando Furioso
"By the short hairs . . ."
The Triple Entente
John Stuart Mill
Ferdinand "Jellyroll" Magellan
Louis "Louie" Armstrong
Elizabeth "Lizzie" Borden
President Rutherford "Gabby"
    Hayes
Hildegarde "Moms" Mabley
Underpants
The Smoot-Hawley Tariff
The Smoot-Hawley Steak-
    house
Tommy Tune
Kukla, Fran and Ollie
Bob & Ray

Bait & Switch
Mop 'n Glow
Jacoby & Meyers
Betty & Veronica
Bondage & Discipline
Heckle & Jeckle
Flotsam & Jetsam
Beanie & Cecil
Prince Matchebelli
Judy Chicago
Jenny Berlin
Julie London
Jerry Paris
Nathan Detroit
Tony Roma
"Lady of Spain" (song)
Lady of Spain (person)
The Atlantic Ocean
Theodore Bickel
Angelyne
The Hanseatic League
Pulling Train
Trujillo
Port Authority Bus Terminal
The Duke of Earl
Adolf Eichmann
Steve
"Make wee-wee"
Osteoporosis
Gandhi
Muffin Tops
Fujita Scale of Tornado
    Damage
Fiddle-Faddle
The Battle of Fort Pillow
Barbie's Dream Camper
Alar Scare

Potstickers

Kekule von Stradowitz

Butter

Emperor Nerva

The Siegfried Line

"Puppy Love"

Don Cornelius

Credit Mobilier Scandal

Berlin Wall

Phil Spector's Wall of Sound

The Bay of Fundy

Edith Head

Tequilaville

Brown 'n Serve Rolls

Treaty of Ghent

Bobby Goldsboro

Auschwitz

"Eight maids-a-milking"

Bechuanaland

Mike 'n Ike

The Lesser Edda

The Pretty Good Edda

Poi

Frederic Chopin

"Pinch an inch"

Bishop Desmond Tutu

Fake Rubber Vomit

Soren Kierkegaard

Pimm's Cup

William "Tecumseh"
    Shakespeare

"Dumb as a Box of Hammers"

Elisavet Moutzan-
    Martinengou

Aquaman

The Era of Good Feelings

The Era of Hurt Feelings

Regular or Extra Crispy

France

Osip Mandelstam

Underarm Farts

Mount Ida

Junior Samples

The Grapefruit Diet

Akira Kurosawa

Rocky Aoki

Corn

The "Hail Mary Pass"

Mason Reese

Fish Sticks

Satan

Battle of Marengo

Goo-Goo Clusters

"The Bride of Abydos"

Matzoh Brie

Long John Holmes

Golf

The Lubavitcher Rebbe

"Right as rain"

Suzi Quatro

Carpatho-Ukraine

Marvin Gardens

Fruit Leather

Johann Sebastian Bach

Skirt Steak

Trouser Steak

"Not tonight, I have a
    headache."

Moses

Senator Orrin Hatch

The Boulevard of Broken
    Dreams

Easy Street

Back Street

Havah Negillah
Slam Dunk
Annie Sprinkles
Nuclear Deterrence
Buddha
"The House Dressing"
Tweetie Bird
"3rd of June, another sleepy
    Delta day."
Hanta Fever
Egg White Omelette
Gravity Boots
"For crying out loud!"
The Treaty of Kangwa
Pauly Shore
"A small horse is soon curried."
The Ozarks
Cheese
Sandor Ferenczi
Yabba-Dabba-Doo
The Articles of Confederation
Babyback Ribs
Meniere's Disease
"Just put your lips together
    and blow."
Africa
King Wamba the Visigoth
Sweet Potato Fries
Penis Envy
"Curly Bill" Brocius
Aruba
The Battle of Killiecrankie
I. M. Pei
"Where the sun don't shine"
Seamless Toe Socks
"Baby Doc" Duvalier
Mayonnaise

Kuala Lumpur
Gig Young
Cubic Zirconium
Lazy Eye
"Take this job and shove it!"
Crab Rangoon
Nude Twister
Munchausen-by-Proxy
    Syndrome
Alvah Bessie
The Shroud of Turin
Milk
Treaty of Brest-Litovsk
Gasoline Alley
"Jailbait"
Franz Kafka
"Don't let your meat loaf."
Piero della Francesca
King Kong
Dwarf Tossing
"Howdy, Miss Jane"
Spam Lite
"One hand washes the other."
Uranus (the planet)
Johnny Appleseed
Caveat Emptor
"Your white's whiter, your
    brights brighter"
Vasco de Gama
King Pepin the Short
Queen Latifah
Voltron, Defender of the
    Universe
Babelthuap Island
Outer Space
"Everything at sixes and
    sevens"

Twist and Shout
Hell
Gorgeous George
The Pitti Palace
Chicken Tenders
"Hail Fellow Well Met"
Butter Buds

Millard Fillmore
Lumpfish Caviar
Zona Gale
Lake Titicaca
Red Velvet Cake
Europe

Editorial

KURT LUCHS

We join with all other Americans in applauding the President's recent decision. In light of the volatile situation around the globe we feel it was the only decision he could make and, all things considered, we're glad he made it.

We may not agree with everything he says he'll do, but we'll defend to the death his right to say he'll do it—so long as he doesn't actually do it. In today's world, saying it should be enough.

George Washington said it. We can't recall at the moment exactly what Washington said, but it must have been good because he was that kind of man and once he said something it was said forever.

Nor did he stop there. What he said he'd do he did, and when he did something it stayed done.

Did Abraham Lincoln ever say, "It can't be done"?

Perhaps. Perhaps not.

But if he did he was talking through his beard and no one heard him. And more power to him, we say!

Indeed, a bullet ended his life, as bullets have ended the lives of so many other brave Americans in war and in peace. Some of them also had beards like Lincoln. Some did not. In a few cases, we suppose, the beard may even have been pasted on. A hard, bitter truth, if in fact it is the truth, or at least truth-like, but one this nation would be better off facing squarely here and now.

Or maybe there and later.

Because in the final analysis, isn't that the very picture of a true American: A man who may or may not be wearing a false beard, who may even have forgotten to shave, but who, underneath it all, and taken all in all, is the salt of the earth?

We applaud them all.

Let it be understood that we are not by any means advocating new legislation along these lines, although there are many plausible arguments for it—too many to enumerate here. Nor are we necessarily opposed to such a law, despite the many convincing reasons for taking such a stance—more reasons than you could shake a stick at.

Of course if you did shake a stick at them, at least it wouldn't go "Bang!" and kill three innocent bystanders.

Yet we must ask ourselves, since no one else is listening: Can anyone be said, in this day and age and in today's society, to be truly innocent? Or were they possibly enemies of the state? And if so, which state? If it were Alabama, could we blame them? Or should we applaud them, too?

The issue of states' rights requires careful and serious consideration. Let us merely state that all states have or should have states' rights, that they have the right to state those rights, and that one of those rights is the right to state that states' rights are, by right, those rights belonging only to states.

We don't know how to put our position any more simply than that.

It's only our opinion, but we're prepared to stand firmly behind it, where nobody can find us.

■ · ■— · ■— · ■— · ■— · ■— · ■— · ■— · ■— · ■

. . . Study links wise guys and bad study subjects . . . Boy Scout, old lady blamed in 36-Segway pileup . . . No talks scheduled in mime strike . . . Study: anti-genocide commercials not working . . .

Excerpts from the Safety Brochure

KURT LUCHS

Good morning, and welcome to United Airlines Space Shuttle flight number 909 to Kuala Lumpur and continuing on to the Moon base at Copernicus Crater City. Please remain in your seat throughout takeoff and after entering orbit. If you must leave your seat, keep your magnetic boots on and walk slowly and carefully. Do not remove your boots and try to float down the aisle carrying your boots. Do not wait until the head of one of your fellow passengers or a crew member is between your boots and a metal wall and then let the boots go, pretending not to know what will happen.

Under no circumstances should you cover your mouth with one hand, make false radio static noises and say, "Houston, we have a problem." Nor should you fashion a realistic alien pseudopod out of phosphorescent Silly Putty and surreptitiously place it on the shoulder of the passenger in front of you. Nor should you make strange gurgling sounds, clutch your heart and yell hysterically, "The little bugger's biting through my chest cavity!"

When being served your in-flight meal, please refrain from asking the flight attendant what went wrong with the food replicators. Do not refer to any crew member as "Seven of Nine" or "Two of 36D," and do not mention, even obliquely, your own "very personal Borg implant." Keep the lid on your drink at all times. Do not attempt to "liberate" your drink from the "unnatural restraints of a weak, contemptible gravitational field." If your drink should accidentally escape from its sealed reverse-pressure container, do not slap the ball of liquid and disperse it into a thousand tiny globules.

If you are seated near an emergency exit, do not ask the flight attendant for an electric screwdriver under the pretext that you are "just one lug nut away from Nirvana." Do not place a holographic decal of a Hubble telescope photo of a supernova on the window and ask your fellow passengers what that strange light is out there. It would also be a mistake at this point to cut a Ping-Pong ball in half, draw scraggly lines on the pieces with a red felt-tip pen, insert a piece into each eye socket and moan, "Oh my God, not that solar flare thing again!"

When the order is given to turn off all cellular phones, laptop computers and portable DVD players prior to takeoff, it would be considered a serious breach of security to keep pounding the mouseball and screaming, "More thrust, damn it, we need more thrust or we'll never achieve escape velocity!"

Passengers are strictly forbidden to pull down the oxygen masks directly above their seats unless first instructed by a non-imaginary crew member. Further, they are not to breathe into the mask, cough as if suffocating, and declare, "My people need at least a 40 percent chlorine mixture to maintain normal body metabolism." Simulated body spasms and cries for anyone present to erect a level 10 force field and fill it with your world's atmosphere could be disruptive to other travelers.

If you need to use the restroom, it would be best to withhold any loudly uttered comments from within the cubicle along the lines of, "My arm! It's got my arm!" or "Cut it out—that tickles!" Do not bang your fist on the inside wall and issue a warning about the wormhole reopening and the need to reverse impulse engines.

During our final approach and landing, please avoid assuming a head-down crash position atop the nearest flight attendant and imitating an air-raid siren or any type of emergency vehicle or injured seagoing mammal.

If you are unable to read or understand these instructions, do not ask the passenger next to you to read the instructions silently to themselves while you attempt to perform a Vulcan mind-meld.

Finally, we ask that while waiting to exit from the spacecraft, you refrain from any high-decibel outbursts in which you plead frantically for someone named "Hal" to "open the pod bay doors."

We hope you enjoy the flight, and thank you for choosing United on your first day of lunar work-release.

. . . Bottled water found on Mars . . . Shocker: human genome may be one long Mad Lib . . . Hell reports hottest year on record . . . God warns of flaws in genetic code . . .

Thought Police Blotter

KURT LUCHS

A Bronx branch of the Chase Manhattan Bank was robbed twice yesterday and once this morning in the mind of Andy Scherer, 27. Scherer, a tax consultant, does not own any firearms and has never committed a violent act. Recently, however, he has fallen prey to increasingly savage and vivid daydreams in which he binds and gags the employees and customers of his local bank branch at gunpoint and, after emptying the vault and firing shots that cause mass cowering, makes a spectacular getaway on rocket powered rollerblades.

At 2:43 a.m. last night, Rosemary Gonzalez, 43, of Deerfield, Illinois, briefly considered setting her cheating, unemployed husband, Armando, on fire as he slept, but gave up her plan when she realized she was out of lighter fluid and there were no stores open. Her thoughts then shifted to a copper colander she had seen on sale earlier in the day at Crate & Barrel.

Tom Maxwell, 38, of Reno, Nevada, willfully and forcefully generated a mental image of a naked Sharon Stone without the actress's consent, which he then projected onto his wife, Patricia, as they were having mechanical, partially clothed sex sometime after 10 p.m. last Thursday. The illicit illusion lasted approximately two and a half minutes, after which Maxwell's powers of imagination failed and he fought back an overwhelming desire to weep.

Elaine Younger, an administrative assistant at the Oakland Discount Tire Outlet, contemplated stealing a box of blue ballpoint pens, a stack of Post-it note pads, and other minor office supplies this past Friday afternoon during her 3 o'clock break. The 51-year-old native then remembered that she still had not used up the supplies she had filched from her last place of employment. At this point the words, "Oh God, my pap smear results!" flashed through her mind, obliterating all thoughts of petty theft.

Robert Michaels once again decided this morning that kidnapping was the only way to resolve in his favor the ongoing custody battle with his ex-wife, Clarice. He mentally rehearsed a detailed plan to abduct his two children, Bob Jr. and Lindsay, from the parochial school they attend in Great Neck, Long Island, going over the fine points out loud with local barman Tony Mendiola. The plan became clearer after the second beer, but somewhat fuzzy after the fourth, and all but disappeared from Michaels's consciousness after the seventh. Michaels, 49, is now resting quietly in the backseat of his car.

A series of highly obscene and abusive calls was nearly made over the past four days by a Gary, Indiana, woman who works as a receptionist in the administrative office of Ronald Reagan Elementary. Helen Blossey, 58, came within seconds of making the calls at least several dozen times, being stopped only by incoming calls at the switchboard, which she had to answer. On each occasion, Blossey was prepared to unleash a stream of profanities upon whatever stranger picked up her randomly dialed call. Police have yet to discern a motive.

Randall Gillispie, 31, mentally stalked his coworker, Anne Schwartz, for the eighth time this month in what has become an obsessive evening ritual for the Bridgeport, Connecticut, resident. His imagination followed her home after she got off the 5:32 express train two stops before him. He pictured her entering her apartment while he loitered nearby, incorporeal and impotent, unable to mentally enter her home because he had never actually been inside it and thus could not clearly picture the interior.

The Trouble with Taffeta

MABEL MANEY

I was born in Appleton, Wisconsin, a small town famous for being the birthplace of Harry Houdini, and as producers of high-quality cheese; a scenic spot an hour from Oshkosh, where they make fine overalls and have an airport. Appleton has a river running through it, with the town's elite, cheese tasters, Cadillac dealers, and the like on one side, and the descendants of Irish immigrants on the other. I was born downwind of a cottage-cheese factory, to a salesman specializing in sensible shoes, and a housewife.

On the night of my birth, my mother, a slip of a lass—like many women of her time, she believed coffee and cigarettes to be the fundamental building blocks of nutrition, with an occasional crumb cake thrown in for fiber—ventured forth into a storm, in her best black taffeta cocktail dress and high school graduation pearls, for a night on the town. After one dance at Appleton's finest supper club, she felt a contraction, and raced to the nearest Catholic hospital, spoiling her shoes in a puddle. When my mother informed the Obstetrics Ward head nun that she was having a baby, the nun took one look at her slender frame and told her to come back in six months. Her fear of nuns greater than her fear of giving birth on cold linoleum, my mother withdrew to the waiting room, to take a load off and have a cigarette. In the middle of a *Redbook* quiz, "Plaid Organza: Is It for You?" her water broke, and her taffeta dress, a crisp cool fabric with a sophisticated sheen, copied by her seamstress mother from a Doris Day film, the movie star my mother most resembled, was ruined. My grandmother, who had been home replacing her dress shields, rushed to the hospital with a quilted rayon bed jacket, and a cheese log for the nuns.

The next decade was a busy one for my family. I got a new brother or sister every two years, my father became a purveyor of paper products for fast food restaurants, my mother was the first on our block to get a beehive, and we got a pool. It came in a kit from Sears.

Not only was my father the napkin king of the Great Lakes region, he also sold whiskey out of the trunk of his Buick, bought dirt-cheap down south and resold at ten percent under retail. The trick to good salesmanship is in the details, my father always told me. He offered discreet home delivery, free of charge.

For years my grandmother said that someday my mother would change her mind about my father and move back home, but after baby number six, she withdrew her generous offer.

Then came the first of four incidents that shook our happy home.

My father, who had realized that children made him nervous and so had taken a job that kept him on the road three weeks of every month, always remembered to bring presents whenever he came home. Sometimes it was swizzle sticks and humorous cocktail napkins from bars where he'd stop to catch his breath between sales calls, and once it was a Stuckey's pecan log that made us all sick before supper. The best thing he ever brought us was a little beagle puppy, which we promptly named Tipsy, our secret nickname for our father. My mother immediately changed the dog's name to Tippy.

The first night Tippy howled for hours, stopping only after we stuffed her with bowls of white bread soaked in Carnation Instant Breakfast. The next morning we let Tippy have some toaster waffles with blueberry syrup. She got the syrup on her chin whiskers and later rubbed it all over my mother's ice-blue crepe de chine couch, but by then we were all in love. Tippy, like my father, was a real charmer. And she was so little. But not for long.

We soon found that Tippy would eat anything. The miniature apple pie sandwiched between the Salisbury steak and mashed potatoes in TV dinners, peanut butter and banana sandwiches with relish, bugs from under the porch, and once even a whole frozen ham.

She loved to ride in the car, especially when we were going to the Piggly Wiggly. *Don't let that dog eat our supper*, my mother always yelled when we heard Tippy rummaging through the grocery bags in the back of our station wagon. Sometimes she'd actually get something good, but she'd just as happily sit there and lick the condensation on the boxes of frozen potpies.

Every year we dressed Tippy up and took her trick-or-treating with us. She looked especially nice as "Tippy the Wonder Dog," in her little blue satin cape. Each year my grandmother warned us about the crazy people who put shards of razor blades in candy, but the only person we feared was Mrs. Thornburg down the block, who gave away the best candy but made us come inside first and watch a filmstrip about Christian missionaries in Africa. Then she'd hand us a candy bar with a religious pamphlet wrapped around it. One year Tippy got overexcited and snatched the Baby Ruth from my hand. She ate it in one gulp, rubber band and all.

The year I was 10 and Tippy was 4 we spent Easter Sunday at my grandmother's. My father was on a sales trip and my mother was resting. During church we left Tippy in my grandmother's green Falcon in a shady spot in the parking lot. After mass we were supposed to go to the hospital, in our Easter finery, to cheer up less fortunate children, but when we got back to the car we found a very sick Tippy squeezed into the back dash, moaning and panting. We had seen Tippy overeat many times, and some grass from the backyard and a big burp always fixed her right up, but this time Tippy looked like she was about to explode. Strewn throughout the car were the remains of four foil-lined shoe boxes that had been filled with my grandmother's bunny-shaped sugar cookies meant for the hospital kids. I guess even Tippy had her limit.

"Tippy looks terrible!" we cried. We piled into the backseat, caring little that the contents of our Easter baskets were spilling all helter-skelter all over the car floor. My grandmother, a tiny woman with a quiet nature and a tendency to meander in traffic, jumped in the driver's seat and raced out of the parking lot, narrowly missing Mrs. Thornburg. While she sped down Main Street to the veterinarian hospital, my brother tried in vain to feed Tippy plastic Easter grass, but Tippy just turned her head.

Later, after the doctor had pumped Tippy's stomach, given her a sedative, and put her in a cage for the night, my grandmother took us to the A&W Root Beer Drive-thru for hot dogs and pop. We had ham and scalloped potatoes waiting for us at her house, but we didn't want to go home just yet. Not without Tippy. Between sips from frosty mugs, we filled my grandmother in on Tippy's long culinary history.

"You are never, ever to feed that dog human food again," my grandmother cautioned us. The vet had noticed Tippy's corpulent figure, and extracted a promise from my grandmother to immediately put Tippy on a slimming diet of low-cal dog food. We listened solemnly while my grandmother impressed upon us the proper care and feeding of a dog. We didn't want Tippy to die, did we? We all cried a little, promised to take better care of our beloved pet, and had another hot dog.

Before we went back to my parents, my grandmother gave each of us a dime so we could call her in case of emergency. The next day my brothers and sisters spent theirs on Tootsie Rolls, but I still have mine.

Then, while attempting to steam-press the dining room curtains without first removing them from the rod, my mother had an accident that left her with a deep fear of ironing and ironing-related appliances. As part of her recovery, the iron, spray starch, and all 100% cotton clothing were banished from the house. The kitchen curtains disappeared first, followed by the fringed fingertip towels in the guest bath.

Then, a Saturday a few months later, my mother had just gotten out of bed and slipped into something Dacron, when we got the call. My Uncle Wesley, who raised dachshunds, all named Fritzi, had been involved in a mishap far more serious than my mother's run-in with the ironing board.

Uncle Wesley had married Aunt Alice, whose undergarments lacked adequate support, because she was a woman who knew her way around a kitchen. In the 1960s, Aunt Alice won the Wisconsin State Fair Pastry Bake-off five years in a row, until a high school home economics teacher named Irene snatched away the crown with her Prune-licious Brown Betty. The next day, Wesley announced that he was leaving, and that he was sick of pie. Alice accidentally shot him, and, after a stay in the same Catholic hospital where my mother had mussed her dress, he went home, quietly, with a new appreciation for Alice's cooking, and minus a limb. We rallied around Wesley, taking turns walking the Fritzis, and giving Alice, whom we now called Bad Aunt Alice, the cold shoulder.

Then, my father, who had started watching television in the basement alone, neglected to return as scheduled from a sales trip to Chicago. A few days later a postcard arrived for my mother. "Dear Gert," it said. "Am going to Los Angeles. Won't be back. Mortgage papers in the top bureau drawer. Already canceled my insurance. Best of luck. Milt." That afternoon, my mother sat on the green sectional sofa she had bought on layaway, clad in a silky orange hostess gown and matching harem slippers, smoking and eating Bugles, the crunchy little horn that tastes like corn. By the time our Salisbury steak TV dinners came out of the oven, my mother had realized this was not one of my father's practical jokes, and called my grandmother, who came right over and gave her a permanent wave. After my mother's hair was combed out, we drove her to the bus depot and sat in the front seat of my grandmother's green Falcon, drinking orange pop and waving good-bye. My mother was going west to find my father, who had taken our only car.

June 28 Chicago

Today I sat next to a nice lady, Mrs. Thornburg from Cleveland. Years ago she was on *Queen for a Day* and won a washing machine, which still works nice. Also a chrome breakfast set, electric sewing machine, luggage, dishes, a complete wardrobe, and 4 dozen American beauty roses. Her husband passed away last year. Some people have all the luck! Broke the heel of my best white pumps climbing on the bus, which is just as well since it's almost Labor Day.

Love, your mother

June 21, Jefferson City

Got up at 5 a.m. to catch bus. Had lunch in Council Bluffs while it was being greased; chicken and potato salad and chocolate cake, but not as good as your grandmother's. Got something on my nice white sharkskin jacket. Went shopping but the stores were closed. Saw one car from Wisconsin, but it wasn't anyone I knew. My shampoo leaked all over the inside of my purse. No sign of your father.

Love, your mother

P.S. Ask your grandmother if you need anything.

July 4, Topeka

Snagged my best pair of hose on metal sticking out from under seat, complained to driver, who was very nice. Lady in front had sparklers and we all had a very merry holiday, although my blouse got smudged and won't wash out. That's the trouble with taffeta. Stopped for an hour at the Abraham Lincoln memorial so a lady overcome by travel sickness could rest. It's 12-and-a-half feet tall and made entirely of bronze. My, Mr. Lincoln certainly was tall! Ha. Ha.

Love, your mother

July 6, Denver

Dear May: Have your grandmother take you to the Junior Miss department at Grossman's and open an account in my name. Under no circumstances is she to allow you to buy slacks. Shirley Sternberger runs ladies hosiery and you tell her I said it was okay. Ask her, does she have any beige size-nine seamless she could send me?

Love, your mother

P.S. A lady on the bus says plaid is popular this season. Tell your grandmother that one jumper and two skirts will do.

Love, your mother

July 7, Santa Fe

Today crossed the border into New Mexico and had a fruit inspection. A very friendly guy. Then drove over a road made of volcanic ash. Smooth as a rug and very dark maroon. Could have enjoyed it more if it didn't remind me of the color your father put on our kitchen ceiling when we were first married. Did your grandmother take you shopping yet?

Love, your mother

July 9, Phoenix

Dear May: Met a nice girl, Audrey Klempke of the Oshkosh Klempkes, a buyer for May's Department Store in Chicago; Collegiate and Sportswear. She definitely recommends plaid. Gave me spot remover. Reached Yellowstone 4 p.m. Got there just in time to see Old Faithful erupt. Did you get your school clothes yet? There have been 3 bear accidents so far this year in park so we were pretty glad to get back on the bus.

Love, your mother

July 11, Los Angeles

Dear May: Am in Hollywood at a cute little room with a kitchenette. Thought I could stay with my cousin Elda's married daughter, but when arrived found the house empty. They had moved the day before. Saw Red Skelton on the street on the corner of Hollywood and Vine. Am I glad to get off that bus—my best gabardine suit is wrinkled beyond repair! If your father had only gotten me a car like I wanted, this wouldn't have happened.

Love, your mother

P.S. Make sure to hang up your new clothes when you get home from school so they last.

   While my mother chased my father, we slept in my grandmother's basement on disaster cots borrowed from the hospital
where she volunteered as a Gray Lady. When my mother finally
came home, she brought with her a determination to start her
life anew, and a suitcase of damaged clothes. She never did
catch up with my father. Years later I asked her why she had
married him in the first place. She said she had married him
because he was a man who was going places.

**... Canada, Mexico discuss strengthening borders ... Human
shields vote to unionize ... Gorillas discover seven-million-year-old
human skull ... Defense rests in trial of narcoleptic ...**

Take These Mottoes, Please

DAVID MARTIN

When it comes to state mottoes, it's time for a change. Some are old. Some are boring. Some are even in Latin. Let's start fresh:

Maine: You can't get here from there.
New Hampshire: Live tax-free or die.
Vermont: Mountains 'R Us.
Pennsylvania: Amish 'R Us.
New York: Live rent-controlled or move.
Connecticut: New York's backyard.
Massachusetts: Kennedyland.
Rhode Island: We're not an island.
Delaware: We're not a brand of plates.
New Jersey: Hey! I'm talking to you!
Maryland: Washington's vestibule.
Virginia: Washington's bedroom.
West Virginia: Washington's washroom.
South Carolina: Sorry about Strom Thurmond.
North Carolina: Sorry about Jesse Helms.
Tennessee: Sorry about Al Gore.
Florida: God's waiting room.
Mississippi: The poverty state.
Arkansas: At least we're not Mississippi.
Alabama: Without the *a*s we're just LBM.
Georgia: We're not just pickups anymore.
Kentucky: We're not just rednecks anymore.
Ohio: The almost-a-palindrome state.
Indiana: The not-quite-a-palindrome state.

Illinois: The should-be-a-palindrome state.
Michigan: The autoerotic state.
North Dakota: Not South Dakota.
South Dakota: Not North Dakota.
Minnesota: Not Canada.
Wisconsin: Not just cheese.
Iowa: Not just corn.
Missouri: Not just pigs.
Nebraska: Not just cattle.
Kansas: Not just wheat.
Oklahoma: Not just oil.
Louisiana: It's pronounced "Nawlins."
Texas: The double-wide state.
Nevada: The double-down state.
Utah: The double-spouse state.
Colorado: The rectangular state.
Wyoming: The other rectangular state.
Arizona: Sand 'n sun.
New Mexico: Geezers 'n guns.
California: The fine whine state.
Oregon: Live free and die.
Washington: The Microsoft state.
Idaho: Spuds 'n nuts.
Montana: Just nuts.
Alaska: There's no place like Nome.
Hawaii: It's not the heat; it's the humidity.

New State Mottoes

IRON CHEF CHALLENGER
ANDREW BARLOW

Alabama: All's well that ends well.
Alaska: Honesty is the best policy.
Arizona: Desperate times call for desperate measures.
Arkansas: Two wrongs don't make a right.
California: Lift with your knees, not with your back.
Colorado: Able was I ere I saw Elba.
Connecticut: Easier said than done.
Delaware: You go, girl!
Florida: Slow and steady wins the race.
Georgia: Fore!
Hawaii: Don't be a hero.
Idaho: For all intents and purposes.
Illinois: The end justifies the means.
Indiana: Have a good summer.
Iowa: Who's better, Matt Damon or Ben Affleck?
Kansas: Every state has a motto.
Kentucky: A motto for every state.
Louisiana: Mottoes for all of us.
Maine: When all is said and done.
Maryland: Please turn off all cell phones.
Massachusetts: Ontogeny recapitulates phylogeny.
Michigan: From our mouths to God's ears.
Minnesota: First things first.
Mississippi: A fool's paradise.
Missouri: The Motto State.
Montana: Did somebody say "waffles"?
Nebraska: Nobody here but us Nebraskans.

Nevada: Let's not make a scene.

New Hampshire: Come to New Hampshire.

New Jersey: Wine, booze.

New Mexico: Whatever.

New York: I said "waffles."

North Carolina: Correlation is not causation.

North Dakota: It's nothing to be ashamed of.

Ohio: Tennis, anyone?

Oklahoma: If you lived here, this would be your motto.

Oregon: No questions asked.

Pennsylvania: Our favorite state is North Carolina.

Rhode Island: Toys in the attic.

South Carolina: Everybody dance now.

South Dakota: This is South Dakota.

Tennessee: I can't make heads or tails of this.

Texas: Got your nose.

Utah: I can't feel my legs.

Vermont: We are an asset to the Union.

Virginia: It's just that—

Washington: No Soap. Radio!

Washington, D.C.: The Non-State.

West Virginia: Because I'm the mommy, that's why.

West Wyoming: The Made-up State.

Wisconsin: Who's laughing now, Delaware? Who's laughing now?

Wyoming: No littering.

Reduce, Reuse, Recycle

DAVID MARTIN

The Regional-Municipality of Urban-Decay and the Townships of Hither, Thither and Yon are pleased to announce the further expansion of our award-winning Recycling Program. In response to your requests for a simpler, more efficient system, we've updated the Program to serve you better.

Effective September 1st, please note the following changes:

1. Your blue box will now be reserved solely for cans and packaging made from metals with an atomic number less than or equal to 26. Don't forget to wash the items thoroughly and crush to a thickness of no more than one inch. For larger items, call our special Cancycle pickup service at 555-1636. Don't forget to ask for the free plastic gauge with the one-inch slot to help you sort your blue box items.

2. The black box remains the primary receptacle for paper products except for cardboard. Under the new program, no more sorting by paper type. Fine paper, wrapping paper, flyers and newspapers can all go in your black box. We would, however, ask you not to include copies of the *Star* or the *National Enquirer*. Please bundle these separately and call 555-1637 for special nighttime pickup.

3. The green box has changed function to more accurately reflect its primary color. Starting September 1st, the green box is no longer to be used for clear glass bottles and small auto parts. Instead, use it for leaves, plants, lawn clippings and other yard-related organic waste. Please do not include animal products or body parts of any type. The municipal composter cannot handle such items. Please dispose of them through your regular refuse collection or call the police at 555-1777.

4. We've added the red box this year to make recycling even easier. The red box is exclusively for plastic containers regardless of the code imprinted on the bottom. All plastic recyclables can be included so long as the caps and labels have been removed, they've been washed and thoroughly dried and they've been crushed to a thickness of one inch or less. What could be simpler? Don't forget—you can use your plastic gauge from the blue box to make sorting a snap.

5. We've also added the yellow box to handle miscellaneous recyclables. This is the one to use for Styrofoam containers, glass bottles, aluminum foil, milk cartons and those not-quite-plastic–not-quite-cardboard thingies used for microwave dinners. If you have trouble keeping track of what goes in the yellow box, just remember the handy acronym SGAM.

Municipal workers will be distributing the new red and yellow boxes commencing the first week of August. If you order now, they will also deliver a handy six-shelf plastic shed to store your boxes. It's only $50 and it comes in your choice of slate gray, army green or puce. Call 555-1638 and have your credit card handy.

In conjunction with the new yellow and red boxes, we've also changed the pickup schedule to make the system even more user-friendly. Starting September 1st, you'll no longer have to remember what zone you live in to determine which day to put out your recyclables. Now the entire Urban-Decay region will follow the same plan.

Put out your blue box on Monday and your black box on Tuesday. Wednesday is green box day, Thursday is red box day and the yellow box goes out on Friday. For holiday weekends, just move each box up a day and double up the yellow box and the blue box on the following Monday.

Regular refuse collection will still be on your designated day depending on your residence zone. Please consult the booklet "When Do I Put out My Damn Garbage?" to determine the day and time to take your garbage to the curb.

We're proud of the changes to our Recycling Program. You've spoken out and we've listened to your complaints and suggestions. We've taken your threats of legal action to heart and designed a system that we think is second to none. To help with the transition, we've added a Recycle Hotline (555-1639). Please feel free to call and leave a message anytime.

Enjoy the ease and convenience of the new Recycling Program. And look for the newly upgraded Leaf Program coming this fall. Your instructional video, bag maker and regional leaf map should be in the mail soon. Remember—together we can make a difference!

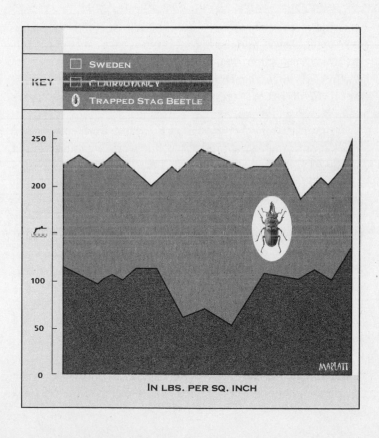

And What's with That Round Ball?

DAVID MARTIN

The White House today released a copy of a letter from President Bush to Joseph Blatter, president of the international soccer association charged with organizing the World Cup.

Dear Joe:

As you know, I'm not a big soccer fan. Like most of my fellow Americans, I don't know an offsides from a corner kick.

But I do know one thing: People in this country don't care for soccer. It's not that they don't want to like it. It's just that it's so darn boring and confusing.

I think it would be a great step toward world peace and international understanding if all the world's nations could compete in one sport together. I understand you've already got a lot of nations onside with this soccer thing. Here are some friendly suggestions to help sign up the rest:

- Stop calling it football. It's not football, for Pete's sake. Football is the Giants versus the Redskins, the Cowboys versus the 49ers, Notre Dame versus Ohio State. Your game is soccer. S-O-K-E-R. Got it?
- Please put more lines on the field so we know where the players are. How about some horizontal, parallel lines every five yards or so to let us know where the action is?
- Give the players some helmets and padding. Boy, it's hard to watch a guy hit the ball with his uncovered head, or collapse in pain when someone bumps him, and not think this is a

cruel and dangerous sport. I assure you that protective equipment will make everybody safer.

- Let one team have the ball for more than 10 seconds. Why not give each team four tries to make 10 yards, say? If they do, they get four more tries. Then you've got some continuity instead of the current chaos.
- Stop the clock once in a while. The referees have whistles; why not let them use them? I'm sure the players could use a break, and I'd sure like a chance to get a snack or use the bathroom. And you know what, Joe? I bet you'd get a lot more advertisers. You might even want to consider splitting each half up into two quarters to provide more ad time.
- Change that offsides rule. Who the heck understands that? I can't even figure it out in hockey, where they've got a blue line and everything. Why not line both teams up and call that the offsides line or, say, the line of scrimmage?
- I've got one word for you, Joe: cheerleaders. A group of attractive, athletic young ladies is always entertaining for the folks in the stands and those watching at home. Let's face it, Joe. Your game can be a bit of a yawn-fest, and it's always nice to look at pretty gals.
- Let the players use their hands. Joe, they look like a bunch of sissies out there with their arms hanging limp. Let 'em catch the ball and pass the ball. If they have to kick it, why not set up some goal posts at either end and let them try to kick the ball through the posts?
- Now this playoff business, or what you folks call the World Cup tournament. I used to be in the baseball business, and I did OK. But it wasn't from holding playoffs every four years! You gotta hold them every year, Joe.

Now, if you folks could implement these minor changes, I'm sure you'd get Americans coming to your games in droves. At that point, I doubt any of them would even care if you still called it football.

From *The Blue Guide to Indiana*: The Thirty Years Salad Bar War

MICHAEL MARTONE

OPENING MOVES

At dawn on December 2, 1952, forces of the Salad Axis in alliance with the Cafe Owners and Independent Truck Stops League stage a surprise preemptive attack on the Hobart Restaurant Equipment Company in Hobart, Indiana, destroying the prototype mock-ups and machine tools used in the manufacturing of the newly invented deep fat fryer. At the same time, elements of the Tea Room Operators and mercenaries in the employ of public school cafeteria managers launch a siege on the Jenn-Air Range and Oven plant in Indianapolis. The Future Franchisers of America and the Legion of Lard respond by imposing an embargo of cucumber and pimento, seizing these and other vegetable contraband at the border crossings with Ohio, Michigan, and Illinois.

A PLEA FROM THE POPE

The Vatican releases an ambiguous statement. In a delicately worded bull, Pope John the 23rd reiterates the Holy See's position on natural food but suggests that the Holy Spirit–inspired Fry-O-Later facilitates the celebration of "lean days" and the abstention of meat during Lent and on all Fridays by making appetizing the abundance of lake perch found in the state.

THE ATTEMPTED ASSASSINATION OF
COLONEL HARLAN SANDERS

In the parking lot of the Hobby House restaurant, Colonel Sanders comes under attack by fusillade. The Condiment Brotherhood issues a denial of responsibility on WOWO radio and reports their membership has mixed feelings about the introduction of Kentucky Fried Chicken as it utilizes a pressure cooker in the process and, therefore, falls outside the strict interpretation of the rules of engagement declared against the forces of fried food.

THE LAST STAND OF THE WATERCRESS SANDWICH

At the sidewalk cafe of W&D's Department Store, the final watercress sandwich is served by Cindy Hall to Mrs. Bud Latz, who eats it and who, afterward, addresses the crowd of several thousand gathered to witness the event. In the throng, the disgruntled unemployed sous chef, Bob Earle, carves decorative rosettes from hydroponic radishes.

THE OPENING OF THE TRANS-INDIANA
MAYONNAISE PIPELINE

The second Eisenhower administration opens the pipeline running between Chicago and Cincinnati through the egg- and soybean-rich heartland. Both sides claim this public work as a victory. The forces allied with salad hail the mayonnaise as essential to the dressings of their various dishes. The opposition claims mayonnaise as one of the secret ingredients in their secret sauces.

THE GREAT FRENCH FRY FAMINE

Blight devastates the potato crop, forcing the emigration of thousands of Hoosiers to Ohio, and contributes to the ketchup panic at the Chicago Board of Trade. Conspiracy theories abound, sug-

gesting the natural disaster was actually the work of the ruta-
baga, turnip, and parsnip cartels. A long-term consequence is that
the agreed-upon spelling of the tuber's proper name falls into
obscurity.

THE GENEVA CONVENTION

Signed in Geneva, Indiana, the convention forces the signato-
ries to adhere to certain rules of war, including the treatment
and exchange of prisoners and the abstention from the use of
food-borne pathogens. The instrument also establishes certain
zoning ordinances and prohibits the construction of a sandwich
of more than three decks.

A SECOND FRONT

Partisan skirmishes erupt between The Syracuse China
Company aligned with Oneida Flatware and Libby Glass
against the incursion of disposable utensils, dishes, and cups.
Volunteer brigades of dishwashers and silver polishers attack
the phalanx of Greek Evzones and Turkish Zouaves hired to
smash china while dancing.

THE BREADED PORK TENDERLOIN
IS DROPPED ON MUNCIE

John of John's Awful Awful (Awful Big, Awful Good) introduces
the dreaded Breaded Pork Tenderloin sandwich at his restaurant near Ball State University. It is crucial that the thinly
sliced, dredged, and tenderized slab of fried pork extend signifi-
cantly beyond its accompanying white bread bun and, in most
cases, its serving plate. The design is widely copied and prolif-
erates throughout the state. An early prototype falls into enemy
hands. During an experiment at the secret laboratories of
Purdue, five grad students in hotel and motel management are
killed in a suspicious grease explosion.

THE SNEEZE OFFENSIVE

Paramilitary units infiltrate cafés, buffets, cafeterias, and restaurants that deploy the new endless salad bars. In fits of sneezing, they contaminate the colorful array of side items and salads. There are scattered reports of other fifth column sympathizers ignoring the new-plate-for-each-trip rule, filling up their plates three or four times with second helpings.

THE ELEVENTH-HOUR CROUTON

At the eleventh hour the crouton is introduced. It is golden brown and crispy like fried foods yet is allied with salad. Confusion reins.

PUDDING IS DECLARED A VEGETABLE

The Supreme Court, in a sharply divided ruling, declares pudding, especially chocolate pudding, to be a vegetable. The decision brings an uneasy truce to the war after protracted and contested negotiations by the belligerents at an A&W Root Beer stand in Huntington on the Wabash River.

... Study: most crop circles not the work of aliens ... Doctors declare Bush smart as a fiddle ... Verbal SAT scores, like, lower ... Miss Nude America relinquishes title after clothed pictures surface ...

ATTENTION: LOST CAT REWARD

if you find my cat Sally. Sally is eleven but she has the face of a cat much younger. She is taffy-colored and she has no distinguishing features except for the spot on her lung. Sally understands eight commands. Nine if you count, "Drop it! Drop the baby!" Sally loves a

good steak but will gladly have whatever you are having. If she gives you the impression that she's having trouble swallowing, call Dr. Alan Sidarsky, 570-499-3944. Dr. Sidarsky calls every day to ask if Sally is back. Dr. Sidarsky once invited me to a tennis match where a little girl who could not speak English beat the defending champion. She was taffy-colored, too. If you ask me, Dr. Sidarsky has a crush on me. Before Sally was lost, Dr. Sidarsky nominated me for Pet Owner of the Year. When the judges came to our house, Sally would not come down from the breezeway. I'm not saying that was the reason I lost the title but it cost me points.

Sally was last seen in Kansas where she fell out of my car— 1998 yellow Toyota Corolla, Indiana license plate FJ3-JR57. To tell you the truth, Sally didn't actually fall. My ex-husband was trying to push me and my suitcases out of the car and Sally was in the way. I'd opened the door to throw out a pair of pants and some other garbage of my ex-husband's. I really hate a messy car. My ex-husband says he was leaning over to close the door but I definitely felt a nudge. Sally and the gourmet cooking cassettes that I took out of the library landed all over Highway 23 in Kansas. Sally ran toward Nebraska. We were on the ramp toward Missouri. My ex-husband's sister Sugar lives in Nebraska. I don't like Sugar and I know Sugar does not like me. She sent me a bathroom scale for my wedding gift. As a rule, I have nothing to do with Sugar but I called just in case Sally could have turned up there. You know, sometimes animals have a sixth sense about knowing who your relatives are and how to get in touch. As usual, Sugar was unpleasant. She said I sounded like I had gained weight.

Sally has been missing for more than a year and I am losing hope. Sally's mother belonged to my grandfather and now my grandfather is dead. Sally is my last link to my grandfather. If you find Sally and she is dead, send her back anyway. My parents are dead but I have their steak knives. Once, I had a locket of my grandmother's. I gave it to my daughter for Christmas since my daughter was named after my grandmother who was named

after her grandmother who was named after Sally but not that Sally. When I lost my daughter in the custody suit, I lost the locket, too. I lost everything. Well, not all of the steak knives. Or the weight, I didn't lose that either.

In spite of what the judge said, my ex-husband is not fit to care for my daughter, pony or no pony. The only thing my ex-husband can cook are Texas

Tommies. My ex-husband's girlfriend cannot cook either but I have to admit—she knows good food.

If I still had Sally, I think the judge would have let me keep my daughter. Pets are a sign of a loving home life. I know the judge would have been impressed if I had been Pet Owner of the Year. I might have gone into politics if I had been Pet Owner of the Year, maybe alderman. I am not too old to get into politics and I have a lot of ideas. Let's not forget that after the Russian Revolution, they turned the stock exchange into an aquarium. For the people! We could do something like that. If Sally came back, I would take a picture of me holding her and use it in my campaign. And if she didn't, my slogan could be "Help me help you find my cat!" Even if you don't find Sally, please send cash. It's not the same thing as a cat, but it is a consolation.

—**Patty Marx**

Review

PATTY MARX

—Is everyone here?

—What about Mrs. Kimball?

—She's still in the hospital.

—I thought they pulled the plug.

—She's having a chin implant!

—Let's begin, then. Anyone?

—Well, basically I liked it, but it definitely dragged.

—What doesn't? Everything is twenty minutes too long.

—He's right. Even when I really like a movie, I think, "This is great! When will it be over?"

—The only reason to do anything is to talk about it afterward.

—Isn't that why we're here?

—People, can we return to the comment that everything is too long?

—Sex isn't too long.

—Yeah? Go meet my husband.

—I felt the end was uninspired. I mean, death is such a cliché.

—The whole thing didn't make sense. For instance, what was with the concept of Weather? Room temperature wasn't good enough? It was always too cold or damp or—

—Are we still talking about sex with her husband?

—You know what I did like? The food. Aside from that silly drizzle thing restaurants started to put on dessert plates in the what,'70s? Still, looking back, I had a lot of good stuff to eat.

—But why did they make it fattening? That was a flaw.

—Oh God, remember the '70s? Why did they have to end? That was such a great decade!

—Except for the part that Rod McKuen wrecked.

—See. It's not that it was too long; it's that it was too long in the wrong places. They should have let you freeze some of your time and tack it onto the end—the way the Wyndale Health & Racket Club lets you freeze your membership for up to three months.

—Another perk for the rich! Everything was always geared to them.

—Not nature. What about nature?

—I felt there could have been more colors—not hues, primary colors. They could have come up with a fifth one—something sort of . . . bright drab.

—Oh, they were too busy developing the quote unquote perfect sunset.

—You got to admit, though, the idea of putting Chicago on a lake was excellent. They should have done more of that.

—You know what I could have come up with? The wheel.

—Sure, anyone could've. Once you have round, which they did, you're pretty much there.

—But in a million years you'd never think of luggage-on-wheels.

—I enjoyed errands; did anyone else? And I got most of them done.

—Could we discuss the guests? How did so many jerks get invited?

—I know. There were, like, billions of people. I would have preferred a smaller guest list.

—Who says you would have made the cut?

—I say if they're going to have that many people, they should make them wear nametags.

—I just wish that it had been a true meritocracy.

—No, no, absolutely no! I wish they'd based everything on alphabetical order and I'm not just saying that because—well, yeah, I am, but still . . .

—I hate to be catty, but did anyone ever meet that guy? He was from Philadelphia?

—Did he have a mustache?

—You're thinking of someone else. This guy was born in the

early '50s. He was married to . . . oh, you know, what's her name, whose family was in that business?

—I met him. He bugged me.

—He was so arrogant and about what?!

—I didn't like his taste in shoes.

—I always wondered if he was latently gay.

—Or latently Jewish.

—Or dormantly Mormon. I love saying that.

—Excuse me. I'm not comfortable talking about people who aren't, uh, with us yet.

—Jeez, I can't think of any category of people better to talk about.

—Yes, at last we can speak ill of the living.

—Hello. Is this Banquet Room B?

—It is. And you are—?

—Mrs. Kimball. Surgical gauze accident.

—Eeeugh!

—Pull up a chair, Mrs. Kimball.

—I have some questions. I wrote them down. Is there a God? Are human beings born good, bad, or neither? Does a low-carb diet really work? How did Mia Farrow get so many good husbands? Are psychiatrists crazier than non-psychiatrists or is it just ironic that they are equally crazy? Was it my mother or my father's fault that I developed bursitis? What really happened that night with Larry?

—I'm sorry, Mrs. Kimball; we're not about Truth with a big T. All right now, who thinks that Shelly Oughten was cheating on Eric in the early '90s? You in the striped shirt.

Notre Pensées

PATTY MARX

Letrilla / *A Delicate Type of Lettuce*
—Luis de Gongora (1561–1627)
translated from another language by Patty (1980–   )

Oveja perdida, ven
   O, I lost my oven cleaner, which, when
sobre mis hombros, que hoy
   I was sober, I put with my hat.
no solo tu pastor soy,
   No, the Pastor is alone, eating soybeans,
sino tu pasto tambien.
   or tomato pasta, so he couldn't have stolen that.

Lenore / *Lorraine*
—Gottfriend August Burger (1747–1794)
translated from another tongue by Patty (1980–)

Lenore fuh ums Morgenrot
   Lorraine for, um, um, Morenrot
Empor aus schweren Traumen:
   Emperor of Trauma or Trout (or of some
   combination of Trauma and Trout
   or maybe it's a typo):
"Bist untreu, Wilhelm, oder tot?
   "Something is a lie, Willy, something?
Wie lange willst du saumen?"
   Will you something something salmon?"
Er war mit Konig Friedrichs Macht
   The something with King Freddy Mack
Gezogen in die Prager Schlacht
   Something in Somewhere
Und hatte nicht geschreiben,
   And something is not something
Ob er gesund geblieben.
   If it is something else (probably fish related).

What I Bring to the Podium

PETER MEHLMAN

Attention: Mr. Andrew Card, White House Chief of Staff:

I am writing to apply for the position of Press Secretary within your organization. I understand a Mr. Fleischer will be leaving the post soon and I am certain you will find my vast media experience and winning personality well suited to the task—unless vast media experience and a winning personality are attributes you shy away from in a press secretary—in which case I can be uninformed and snappish.

Though hardly a Washington insider, I have many close associates who work inside the Beltway as well as on the Beltway, removing litter and graffiti. Through exhaustive discussions with them, I've learned that your firm deals mainly with international concerns and, on rare occasions, domestic stuff.

Should you hire me, you will find I can frustrate the press on both fronts. Domestically, I have only lived in New York and Los Angeles, so I'm quite unfamiliar with America and its problems. Internationally, even though I've traveled abroad roughly twice as many times as your CEO, my only impression of foreign countries is the inability to get a cup of coffee to go in Paris. (I understand your firm's relations with France are frayed; I would suggest the severing of all ties until the takeout coffee situation is rectified.)

With no expertise on foreign or domestic issues, I believe, if given the position of Press Secretary, your board of directors can easily keep me out of the loop. I've never been in a loop but it sounds time-consuming. Firmly ensconced outside the loop, I can claim ignorance to all media queries without ever grumbling that the job is beneath my dignity. If I had to estimate, I'd say the job is about even with my dignity.

Clearly, with such low expectations, you needn't fear that I will ever resign in a huff. Mr. Fleischer claims to be stepping down in order to spend more time with his new wife. My mother believes he is stepping down so he won't have to spend another summer in Texas. Whatever. If you hire me, these will be non-issues as you won't want me in Texas and I don't have to spend any time with Mr. Fleischer's wife.

At this point, you are undoubtedly impressed with what I can't and won't do. Allow me to switch gears. I have enclosed my resume and, not to be arrogant, but my credentials are mind-blowing. As you can see, I've worked for Howard Cosell and Jerry Seinfeld. Mr. Cosell was simultaneously loved and hated by all Americans so I have experience in going whichever way the wind blows. Mr. Seinfeld is really funny. Scraps of their charisma and wit have worn off on me and would be tremendous assets to your team—unless charisma and wit are attributes you loathe in a press secretary, in which case I can be humdrum and incoherent. It should be pointed out that, upon leaving their employ, I never wrote a book about Messrs. Cosell and Seinfeld. We all know the long history of Washington insiders writing tell-all books a day after leaving their posts. No worries here. Loyalty is another of my many tepid passions.

Finally, if you are still undecided about hiring me, get this: *You don't have to pay me.* I got out of the stock market in early November of 2000 and *Seinfeld* residuals appear in my mailbox almost as often as letters from the Democratic National Committee asking for more money. On top of that, my accountant tells me I'm getting an inexplicably huge tax break.

Okay. Before you leap to bring me on board, you should know that I'm not willing to relocate. Los Angeles is my home. I have a touch-tone telephone. Tell Brit Hume to relocate. Besides, jettisoning the White House Press Corps out of Washington would free up some office space in your corporate headquarters and keep your CEO from ever having to hold news conferences.

Thanks in advance for making all this happen. If you have any questions—anything at all—please hesitate to ask. Because, much to your delight, I'll only respond with "No comment" or "I don't know."

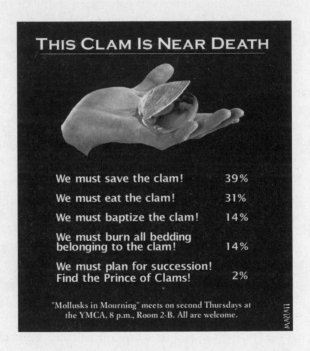

THIS CLAM IS NEAR DEATH

We must save the clam! 39%

We must eat the clam! 31%

We must baptize the clam! 14%

We must burn all bedding belonging to the clam! 14%

We must plan for succession! Find the Prince of Clams! 2%

"Mollusks in Mourning" meets on second Thursdays at the YMCA, 8 p.m., Room 2-B. All are welcome.

... Digital dating: mostly ones and zeros ... Deconstruction workers strike for greater meaning ... Philip Morris sues ex-smokers for lost revenue ... Fall ritual: color blind leave New England ...

Fences—and a Few Nukes—
Make Good Neighbors

PETER MEHLMAN

I am writing to officially put America and the world on notice that I have nuclear weapons in my house. Any and all inspectors who know what nuclear weapons look like are welcome to come over and see them. My housekeeper was here yesterday but I'm pretty sure my weapons of mass destruction are either in the den or the guest bedroom.

Surely, these announcements are getting tired of late, but this one is different. First of all, my threat isn't one you would react to by saying, "Oh great, another country heard from." I'm actually in town. And second, I don't rule a nation, just 2,300 square feet in a shady, overpriced canyon bordering Pacific Palisades.

Without a nation of my own, this clumsy way of rolling out a new international menace is the best I can do. Admittedly, I tried leaking this news to a friend who was recently an embedded journalist at the Golden Globe Awards, but the story was killed in favor of a twelve-part investigative feature on ABC's fall lineup. From here on in, I'll try to adhere to the standard etiquette of publicizing one's nuclear stockpile.

My need for going nuclear crystallized after a border skirmish with my neighbor, a middle-aged woman named Edie Amin. Overhanging branches of an eight-year-old, federally protected sycamore tree touched off a violent eruption of shpilkes. Then, a call for repairs on a retaining wall now referred to as "the 38th Parallelogram" ignited an all-out conniption, including the severing of all diplomatic ties—though Ms. Amin is still nice enough to call the police every time my gardeners water the yard.

In short, things in Santa Monica are very tense.

Achieving nuclear capacity—obtaining the weapons-grade plutonium, titanium detonators and a wick—was surprisingly easy. One globally warmed morning, I called the prop guy on my latest failed sitcom pilot and that was that. My assistant picked up the weaponry and, because she had Dodgers tickets that night, left it for me at the front desk of my health club.

Since procuring my nukes, not only has my neighbor's rhetoric become less shrill but a strange feeling of merriment has come over me. I can't quite explain it because I'm not articulate, but I kind of smile a lot. And while being the happiest person in Los Angeles doesn't preclude one from being utterly miserable, I think I'm on the right track.

Which leads me to the nuclear blackmail part of this announcement. Oh come on. If this were all about my neighbor, the whole exercise would be childish. I have demands.

I know what you're thinking but no, this isn't about money. Hollywood pays so well, when I go to New York I can hardly believe my money's good there. And no, this isn't about infrastructure. If the marines were sent in to replace my retaining wall, it would be viewed as a measure of good faith—no more, no less. And no, it's not about food subsidies. I wouldn't say no to a sponge cake but it's not a deal breaker. This isn't about any of those things.

The truth is, I'm not sure what this is about. I've had WMDs six weeks now, and maybe my buzz is fading, but it could be months before I get another shot to blackmail the United States of America. I have a seat at the table; it would be silly not to make demands *now*. Just let me think of some.

Okay: I want NBA players to stop giving high-fives to a guy who misses a free throw (I mean, what's the incentive to make the shot?). I want people to stop excusing celebrity shoplifters by saying "it was an obvious cry for help." (Why do they have to steal? Why not just cry for help?) I want to go back to calling Mao Zedong *Mao Tse Tung*. I want to outlaw thank-you notes. We should make it harder for people to get handguns. I'd like to get some use out of my appendix. Everything being in alphabetical order is getting on my nerves. And, let's see . . . oh: I also don't like the passage of time. I stink at some things I used to be really good at. Can't time just stand still for a while? One year with no births, no deaths, no marriages, no divorces, no mergers, no acquisitions, no wars—just let me breathe! And for all or some of that, I'll de-weaponize. My agent is listed. You have 24 hours to respond.

Oh, I left out one piece of nuclear boilerplate: I'm crazy.

Mandela Was Late

PETER MEHLMAN

Mandela was late.

Frankly, as a parole officer, you root for your thugs to come late, or better yet, not show at all. They get kicked back in the can where they belong and you have time for a sandwich. But for some weird reason, I felt different about Nelson Mandela. Maybe it was all an act on his part, or maybe I was losing my edge, but he seemed somehow more respectable than most of the rancid ex-cons who pollute my schedule.

In twelve-plus years, the only time Mandela missed an appointment was when he had to accept a Medal of Freedom or some such shit from some panel of European gasbags. Hell if I can remember the details but personally, I don't think getting sprung from the joint should get you any medals. Still, Mandela gave me eight months' notice and asked politely if we could reschedule. Thinking the bogus award might give him some positive reinforcement, I let him slide.

Clearly, I set a bad precedent because it was 11:03 a.m. and he was still AWOL. Damn. I considered Mandela among the top fifteen most effective rehab jobs I'd ever done. This was his last parole meeting and, by my count, he was a tick away from flushing all the work I'd put into him right down the toilet. But, let's face it, you can't argue with statistics. The recidivism rate for a guy who does 27 years in the clink is up there with the chances of your Beemer getting jacked in Johannesburg.

Jacking Beemers. The thought painted my mind blue. *If that's what Mandela's up to, I swear I'll run that self-destructive son of a—*

My door opened. It was Mandela. It took every neck muscle

I ever had to keep from looking at my watch. Instead, I went through my routine, taking in his overall bearing: blue blazer, white shirt, plum tie, gray "ANC Athletic Dept." sweatpants. Well, right off, the flashiness of the tie queered me. Was his ex-wife back in the picture?

Nonchalantly, I peeked at the file on my desk labeled MANDELA, NELSON (GUERILLA/PRESIDENT/#20742-0019). It was thick as the Merck Manual but I fingered the first page and saw her name: Winnie. Right. My old colleague Briscoe was her P.O. One day, he went out on his lunch break to get his negative HIV results framed under glass and was found with a pickax in his head.

Phrases like "material breach" and "consorting with known criminals" flooded my head. I took a step toward Mandela and frisked him: hankie, debit card, two-way pager, a signed photo of Gwen Stefani and the keys to every city on Earth with a mayor. I moved on. Subtly, I caught a whiff of his breath. A faint hint of waffles but nothing to raise any red flags. Mandela was clean. Still, my antenna was up. Way up.

"Have a seat, Nellie."

He lowered himself into a chair, slowly, like Gandhi ten days into one of his crash diets.

"Rough night? You seem a little stiff."

"I'm eighty-four years old," said Mandela.

Of course. Every hood walking through my door thinks he's the victim.

"What have you been up to?"

"Today?"

"Today, yesterday, Tuesday. Whatever. Yeah, start with today."

"I had breakfast with Kofi Annan, a conference call with Colin Powell and posed for a portrait photographer named Richard Avedon."

Annan, Powell, Avedon. I made a note to run the names through the database.

"Yeah, but are you're keeping busy?"

Mandela rolled his eyes. Oh great, I thought. Here we go.

"Talk to me, Nelson."

"Well, the press picked up a talk I gave recently where I was discussing the Iraq situation and referred to George W. Bush as 'a president who has no foresight, who cannot think properly.'"

I launched out of my chair. "I knew it! The same crap that got you in trouble in the first place."

"Yes," he said with cool defiance, "but now, we live in a free country."

"Not for repeat offenders, it's not!"

Mandela threw me a facial expression I couldn't read with an X-ray machine. Truth is, I'd forgotten about the whole "free country" thing. It took me twenty-five years to learn that the *h* in Apartheid was silent, and by then the game was over. Mandela was right. Legally, I had no beef with him. That's my problem with long-termers like Mandela: they make me feel really unintelligent.

For the next ten seconds, Mandela and I didn't say a word. Luckily, I had time: my noon appointment had to cancel after being shot to death on his way to picking up a new bulletproof Mercedes. It was at that point I realized that irony was everywhere and this whole charade was a charade. Whatever decision I made on Mandela didn't matter. Maybe he'd go straight, maybe he'd backslide into a miasma of human rights. The fact is, people will do what they do, whereas fish are driven mainly by instinct.

I cleared my throat and broke the silence.

"Hey, that Hugh Masekela can really blow the crap out of a horn, huh?"

I caught him off guard with that one. Mandela's face softened. He looked like he wanted to smile or become violently ill. Or maybe he'd split the difference and become non-violently ill.

"Look, Nelson," (he knew I was serious when I called him "Nelson"), "I'm doing the paperwork on you. We're done together. Your last ties to the penal system are officially severed."

Mandela joyfully looked up to the sky and said, "Good, because I was going to make some calls this afternoon and have you fired anyway."

"Well then, we've found some 'common ground,' as you would put it."

At that, Nelson Mandela stood up, walked out my door and I never saw him again.

But then, it's only been three weeks.

KIM McCANN'S **DICHOTOMOUS WORLD**

Lyrics to Bob Dylan Tunes or Poorly Translated English on Japanese Food Packaging?

1. It's burned to a crisp with all our heart!
2. I see you've got your brand-new leopard skin pillbox hat!
3. Anytime, anywhere, just like your friend.
4. We're going all the way until the wheels fall off and burn.
5. You might like to drink whiskey! Might like to drink milk! You might like to eat caviar!
6. The sentimental taste is oozy for the heroines in the town.
7. My mind was relaxed by attaching importance to the tradition.
8. You've got all the love, honeybaby, I can stand!
9. Teeth like pearls, shining like the moon above.
10. Relieve the relief and listen to the angel's whisper.
11. There is a house in New Orleans they call the Rising Sun
12. If dishes are nice, the square ceiling becomes round.

Key

1. Batard bread
2. from "Leopard Skin Pillbox Hat"
3. No-Brand Orange Punch
4. from "Brownsville Girl"
5. from "Gotta Serve Somebody"
6. Koedastick chocolate candy
7. Izumiya Confectionary Company
8. from "Buckets of Rain"
9. from "Brownsville Girl"
10. Angel Relief chocolate and biscuit cookies
11. from "House of the Rising Sun"
12. a fondue pot

From *Miller's Dictionary of Food Clichés*: The Evolution of Scallops

BRYAN J. MILLER

Mrs. Paul's Frozen Scallops

Mrs. Paul's Fresh-Frozen Scallops

Mrs. Paul's Fresh-Frozen Jumbo Scallops

Mrs. Paul's Fresh-Frozen Breaded Jumbo Scallops

Fresh Scallops

Fresh Maine Scallops

Fresh Maine Diver Scallops

Fresh Maine Day-Boat Diver Scallops

Fresh Maine Day-Boat Hand-Harvested Diver Scallops

Fresh Maine Dinghy of Questionable Seaworthiness Close-to-Shore Harbor Hand-Harvested Diver Scallops

Fresh Maine Stolen Lifeguard's Surfboard Paddled Mostly in Circles Inside the Roped-Off Swimming-Allowed Area Hand-Harvested Fresh Maine Diver Scallops

Fresh Maine Stolen Lifeguard's Surfboard Hand-Harvested Diver Scallops Retrieved in Chest-High Water by Novice Scuba Students

Fresh Maine No-Boat Pier-Harvested Diver Scallops Retrieved by Sophomore Class of Haddock Regional High for Gym Credit

Former Gotham Mayor Unveils Mexican Anti-Crime Proposal— President Fox Withholds Comment

Fate of Bush Niece Uncertain

BRYAN J. MILLER

Mexico City—Former New York mayor Rudolph Giuliani, who has been retained by the Mexican government to help devise a plan to fight crime in this corruption-plagued and frequently violent country, said today that his first act as "jefe de criminales" would be to arrest and lock up all Mexicans living in Mexico.

"I realize it sounds a little tough," the law-and-order executive acknowledged, "but we need to send a quick and forceful message to the country—law enforcement officials now mean business."

Evidently unaware of Giuliani's off-the-cuff remark to a group of international journalists here, Mexico's President Luis Vincente Fox, whose entire family is Mexican, declined comment until after reading the "fine print."

Critics of the plan, including Amnesty International, cited several potential roadblocks to the initiative. Chief among them are Mexico's overcrowded and substandard penal facilities, which, at the moment, are limited to the cafeteria of a former serape factory in Ensenada and minimum-security former Club Med compound near Puerto Escondido.

When pressed on where he intended to detain nearly 60 million Mexicans, Giuliani paused, opened what appeared to be an atlas of Central America, and declared:

"In Ecuador."

Mayor Giuliani proffered that relocating the entire Mexican population to a friendly nearby country would have the added advantage of boosting the Mexican economy. Many American corporations have left Mexico, the mayor posited, because a "relatively small" number of executives had been either kidnapped, enslaved or simply disappeared.

"Mark my words, this abduction business will diminish greatly when all of the kidnappers are safely behind bars."

Defending his strategy before a skeptical press corps, Mayor Giuliani likened his anti-crime strategy to several successful policies he enacted early in his first administration as mayor of New York City.

"We sent a get-tough message right away by incarcerating every one of these people that we referred to as 'squeegee guys,'" he said. "Now, seven years later, do you see any squeegee guys on the streets of Manhattan? Case closed."

Upon learning of Mr. Giuliani's innovative plan, President Bush, who has a 12-year-old niece of Mexican-American descent, lauded the approach in principle but added that the cutoff age for detention should begin "somewhere in the pre-teen years."

Mexico City's largest newspaper, *La Periodico Largo*, reported today that the mayor's plan goes even further. After every Mexican in Mexico is safely incarcerated, the paper reported, Giuliani plans a national tour to stamp out "smutty looking" art.

Invoking another of his initiatives in New York City, the mayor recounted: "You won't believe what they tried at a museum in Brooklyn—toilets and Jesus as art! I put the cabosh on that real fast."

Giuliani concluded, "As I told President Fox, I don't mind a naked saint or two, after all, I'm Catholic. But I think it's a little out of control down here. And that can lead to crime."

The First Thanksgiving
Family Feud

JIM MULLEN

Historians all agree that the Pilgrims really did celebrate a first thanksgiving but they also agree that it was a one-time event. It wasn't turned into a yearly celebration until Abraham Lincoln made it official during the middle of the Civil War, some 250 years later. New documents have come to light which may explain why.

"Never again," writes John Aldin in a letter found in a newly discovered cache of papers composed by the original passengers of the *Mayflower*:

Six long hours we have spent looking at the hind end of a horse on the overly crowded road to the house of my parents and lo, for what? To see my brother with whom I barely speak and his harpy wyfe who so disrespecteth me and mine in a backhanded way? He starteth acting like a wee childe immediately, from the time we stepped from the carriage until the time we have departed. He bringeth up small jealousies and grievances from our youth long ago. His unhappiness is like a contagion, a pustule that never heals. "Letteth it go and getteth a life," he has made me wish to scream, and more times than one. We should be spending less time together, not more, me thinks.

One unpleasantry follows another as I suffer my uncles and aunts to runneth on and on about my cousins—how well they are doing, how much money they are sending to their parents, what comely grandchildren they have produced. Yet I knoweth these same cousins. They are base and low and would soil themselves if they were ever made to do a day's work. They wish their parents dead and spend their days making plans to squander their inheritance in a warmer clime. Their small children know not the word "no" and understandeth not its meaning. They runneth around and screameth all day when peace and quiet is called for. The spawn of satan himself would make more pleasant company.

And my handsome wyfe cares not for the way my mother prepareth the meal. "She useth not oysters in the fowl's stuffing," she rails at me. "She putteth not the bird in a paper bag in the hearth." It maketh me fatigued to hear such words. Yet Priscilla's own stuffing would not winneth any praise even in the land of my birth where they can taste not the difference between condiment and composte. She knoweth not, but secretly I giveth my portions of her bounty to the hound beneath the table. It teacheth him not to beg.

My wyfe speaks ill of none, yet I can tell from the bearing of her body that she would rather be ducking witches on a cold day in December than be in the company of my family and their offspring. As if her family be a barrel of salted fish. Her sisters make it well known that their spouses buy them more kitchen tools than I do and that the corn from their labor is bigger and better than that of my own. They maketh my head hurt. Were they not aboard, the journey of the *Mayflower* could have been as a fun ship cruise. With them, it was the hate boat. Had the voyage lasted but one week more, 'twas they who were going over the side or 'twas I.

It occurred to me suddenly that we may have left the wood stove on at home. Priscilla volunteered that it may be true as she had often noticed my forgetful habits. Happily, we fled the festivities. On the road home we spoke not to each other for many hours. "Let us hope we can do this again next year," at last I spoke. It got a hearty laugh as Priscilla knew I was in perfect jest. In truth, you could not make us do that again were four hundred years to pass. For that we gave thanks.

HARMON LEON'S OFFICE PRANKS
BE YOUR OWN EVIL TWIN

things needed
- 1 comb
- contrasting clothing
- a maniacal laugh

Note: The following office prank works particularly well if you've just been named Employee of the Month.

Come into the office and state your long-lost twin is visiting from out of town, at which point your coworkers will proclaim, "I didn't know you had a long-lost twin." After mumbling some excuse about a lengthy hospitalization, mention the fact that your long-lost twin would like to come to the Employee of the Month indoctrination ceremony, held later that afternoon.

Drop the fact. Let the day go about as normal. While coworkers are diligently busy filling out reports and filing papers, sneak into the janitor's closet. Once there, do the following:

1. Comb your hair differently to differentiate your good and bad self.
2. Dress drastically different. If you normally wear a three-piece suit, wear bell-bottoms, and vice versa.
3. Make a slight change to your first name. If you're called Bart, make your evil twin's name Bert.
4. Speak in a vastly different voice. For example, have your evil twin speak with a southern accent, northern German dialect or slight, husky lisp.

Later, when the boss herds everyone into the conference room for the monthly Employee of the Month ceremony, arrive to the festivities as *your own evil twin*.

Once there, do the following:

- Steal your own loved one away from yourself (if they happen to work in the same office).
- If you happen to also be the president of the company or corporation, take it over from yourself, in an evil sort of fashion.
- Ruin your own good name!
- Develop a drug and alcohol problem, causing your good half embarrassment, then let out a maniacal laugh.

After mayhem erupts, quickly change back to your regular self, at which point say to your coworkers, "Hey, did I miss anything!" Slap your boss on the back and call him an "old son of a gun!"

... Moderate terrorist groups meet ... Smokey replaced by pro-industry bear ... Cosmic gridlock blamed on perpendicular universe ... Emerging state declares state of emergency ...

The Narcissos

MARK O'DONNELL

Characters

(4 men, 4 women; some doubling possible)

Hal Martini	Minerva Limegrove
Sheila Foot	Richard Nussbaum
Jean-Claude Poubelle	Marla Limegrove
Dewey Lamont	Melody (The Starlet Envelope Bearer)
	Announcer (voice-over)

*The Scene: The glittering stage typical of Academy Award cere-
monies, and their imitators, with shimmering Mylar curtain
and anything ostentatious to highlight the entry of the celebrity
presenters, like a few gilded stairs at either side. A podium dom-
inates the center of the stage, and an enlargement of the cov-
eted Narcisso—a figure of a nymph contemplating itself in a
pool or hand mirror—hangs above and behind the presentation area.*

(Music: A low drumroll.)

Announcer: *(voice-over, slow, sonorous, awed and reverent)*
Live . . . from the Elwood Covet Pavilion in Hollywood,
California . . . the incestuous film community's oldest new tra-
dition . . . The Second Annual Narcisso Awards. . . .

*(Music: Massive pop-maestoso sweeping introit, perhaps
Arthur Fiedler's version of "Stella by Starlight.")*

. . . honoring the longest and most publicized achievements
in cinema of the past year . . . The Narcisso Awards are brought
to you by Aujourd'hui . . . the scent that makes you a little more

special than any other woman your man sleeps with . . . And, by Neverin . . . Neverin, for the relief of the tension caused by nausea, for headaches caused by anticipation, for jitters, for the ghastly deep-in-your-bowels torment nothing seems to alleviate . . . Now your host for the Narcissos, Mister—Hal Martini!

(*Applause; slightly less pretentious music. Hal appears, a puffy, tuxedoed, powerful older singer, charismatic, complacent, and coldly facile. In short, Frank Sinatra. He sings an upbeat but featureless opening song.*)

Hal: (*singing*) Are you zoomin' upward or comin' back? Will you be Apollo or Just a Hack?
Is it "Hello Gorgeous" or "Sorry, Jack"?/Who's on top?/Are you record breaking or just plain broke?/Are you hot or will you go up in smoke?/Do they say you're funny, or just a joke?/Who's on top?/Who's on top?/Who's on top?

(*Applause, followed by reverent hush as Hal speaks: A slight echo on all voices might be nice.*)

Good evening, and one final ponderous welcome to you all, and to the millions watching this via satellite in homes, store windows, hospital beds, hospices, shelters, mud huts, gay bars, prison rec rooms—wherever, and as meaningless as it seems, whoever you are, it's that momentous moment when Hollywood passes judgment on its own—or at least, those it's told are its own! (*grins at this paternity suit joke, but it doesn't play*) Founded a year ago by the then late Lazarus Gold Narcissman, a great patron of the patrons and a comeback story every future will-have-had-been can envy, the Narcissos was originally intended to honor its own televised ceremony as the best program in its time slot on its particular channel. This year the board of kibitzers has voted to laud the films and the filmy of the past twelve months, and, just as they expected, it has already proved to be the most effective way to get actual stars to attend. Now, no sooner done than said, here to present the first award is a precariously established dramatic star—and, hoping you'll think he's dating her, a smoldering young nonentity from somewhere foreign . . . please welcome Sheila Foot . . . and Jean-Claude Poubelle!

(*A brief fanfare as Sheila, a hardworking regular woman, and Jean-Claude, a bony lounge lizard, enter and momentarily bask in the recorded applause.*)

Jean-Claude: (*to seem human*) Ees my tie straight?

Hal: (*dubiously*) Your tie is, anyway. (*Pause.*) Sheila is nominated tonight for her blistering performance as Anya, the epileptic prostitute, in *Agony in the Snow* . . . but few will remember, a few years ago this talented actress appeared in a short-lived but very special televised series . . .

(*Sheila turns very pale.*)

Sheila: (*with simple, unexpressed horror*) Oh no.

Hal: With charm to spare, and she did, Sheila grinned, capered, and entertained millions of pre-schoolers and schoolers alike as *The Tiny Invisible Nanny.*

Sheila. (*under her breath to Hal*) How could you?

Hal: (*cruel but sotto voice*) Kick me out of bed, will ya, frigid?

(*Jean-Claude seems oblivious to this scene, and fumbles on a pair of glasses. He reads laboriously as she fumes.*)

Jean-Claude: Zeee nome-ee-neez for least interesteen award category are . . . Interieur Decoration . . . Achievement een Sound . . . Short Subject Doak-umen-tairy . . . Muzeek Adapted from Anothair Medioom . . . and technical or Scientifeek Achievement . . .

(*A blonde starlet enters with the envelope. She is a gorgeous but doomed hopeful, and will prove vital to our story.*)

Sank you. The ween-air . . .

(*The Starlet, Melody, grins hammily into the camera without leaving. After a moment the awkwardness is felt and she tries to retreat gracefully. As she exits, Sheila and Hal argue surreptitiously.*)

Sheila: (*under her breath*) I was never in bed with you! I don't even know you!

Hal: (*indifferently*) It must have been someone else then. Sorry. You look a hell of a lot like whoever it was.

Jean-Claude: Zee ween-air ees . . . Technical Achievement.

(*Canned music, applause bite. Sheila and Jean-Claude exit as Marla and Minerva Limegrove, two overwrought look-alike sisters, enter.*)

Announcer: (*voice-over*) Accepting the award for Technical Achievement, both nominees themselves for Best Actress, are Marla and Minerva Limegrove! (*They are icy and uncertain in their enactment of sisterly solidarity.*)

Marla: My older sister and I . . . are so honored on the part of technical achievement . . . whatever that is . . . thanks so much. (*Now, slyly*) . . . See you all later!

Minerva: (*angered, as the two exit*) "See you all later"? What is that supposed to mean? Huh? (*She hectically addresses the audience, an afterthought*) Thanks on the part of . . . that thing! . . .

Hal: (*resuming*) The best non-starring performance is a unique category. It's for second-stringers, also-rans, and even winning has a slight smack of not-quite-there about it, but people still pretend to worry about it. Here to present that award, a nervy young star who in one short year has made eight hit movies, conclude what you will about the care lavished on them—Richard Nussbaum!

(*The music and applause snippet plays.*)
(*A gallingly smug young star enters, unaccustomed to his tuxedo.*)

Hal: (*uncaring and perfunctory*) And how are you, Richard?

Richard: Sorry. No interviews. (*He turns a cold shoulder to potentate Hal.*) The nominees for best non-starring performance are—(*He smirks at the lineup of unknowns*) Ruta Hagen-Daas in *Wrinkled Rulers*, Dorothy Jackson in *Pistolwhipped*, Eliot Farm in *The Brooding Ones*—yeah, yeah, come on, speed it up, I'm expecting a phone call—I can read—Williams Roberts Williams in *The Fire and the Flame*—and Towser in *All the Sick Young Animals* . . .

(*Melody, the starlet, brings on the envelope, and this time there is pathos and desperation, not mere ambition, in her attempt to get Richard's attention.*)

Richard: (*oblivious*) I'm nominated, too, in the *real* category! . . . (*He grins ingratiatingly and takes the envelope without looking at Melody. She tries vainly for a moment but then retreats self-consciously.*)

Melody: Richie, psst!

Richard: (*opening envelope*) And it's . . . oh good for it!—Towser!

(*Applause, music, and the Limegrove sisters reappear.*)

Announcer: (*voice-over*) Accepting the award for Towser are Minerva and Marla Limegrove, themselves both nominated for Best Actress.

Minerva: (*a bit too rapaciously*) Thank you! Thank you all from my older sister and myself! I'm sorry the dog couldn't make it! But wherever you are, Towser—Good dog! (*Grins*) It's nice to be up here! For now! (*She winks, winningly, she hopes, but there is awkward silence.*) . . . If you get me! . . .

(*Silence at her gaffe*)

I'm sorry the dog couldn't make it!

(*Marla rolls her eyes in contempt as they make an awkward exit.*)

Marla: "For now"? What was that supposed to mean?

Hal: . . . To me falls the special privilege of presenting the award for Best Actress. Just sexy I guess. (*He coughs to get serious.*) The nominees for Best Actress are . . . the late Dame Edith Adman in *Queen Lear* . . . the dead ones usually get it . . . Sheila Foot in *The Tiny Invisib*—I mean, *Agony in the Snow* . . . Marla Limegrove in *Hello at Last* . . . Minerva Limegrove in *Why Bother with Blouses* . . . and the late Delia Roseburn—oo, competition—in *The Angered*. May I have the envelope, please?

(*Melody enters with the envelope, weeping piteously if privately. Hal doesn't notice.*)

And the winner . . . the only real actress in the bunch . . . (*He opens the envelope. Pause. He examines the paper stupidly.*) . . . It's a tie! (*Shocked pause*) A four-way tie! . . . The winners are . . . the late Dame Edith Adman in *Queen Lear* . . . the late Delia Roseburn in *The Angered* . . . and . . . Sheila Foot in *Agony in the Snow*! (*Awkward pause.*) Oh, did I say four? I meant three. Yeah, a *three*-way tie. Whoops, sorry!

(*Applause, music. Sheila, Marla, and Minerva enter.*)

Announcer: (*voice-over*) Accepting the award for the late Dame Edith is Minerva Limegrove.

Minerva: (*stifling curdled rage*) I don't deserve this award. I really don't.

Hal: (*tersely*) You're accepting it for someone else, Minerva.

Minerva: I know. I'm speaking for her.

(*Now Marla takes center spot.*)

Announcer: (*voice-over*) Accepting the award for the late Delia Roseburn is Marla Limegrove.

Marla: (*also a knot of conflict*) I'm v-very happy . . . for . . .

Diana . . . even if it's a kind of waste since she can't enjoy it . . . and . . . I hope you all remember my suffering good sportsmanship next year.

(*Applause, music, and the two shattered sisters exit.*)

Sheila: (*gathering herself solemnly*) Sometimes the world can seem so petty and vicious—as Mr. Martini no doubt knows. I thank heaven for this award. It means I didn't marry men I didn't love for nothing. Thank you.

(*She exits, gravely, considering she's a winner, and glares at Hal in passing. He doesn't care.*)

Hal: The awards for screenplay, music, and direction will be given privately, since the nominees are all too ugly to come up onstage in person. Again, this time to present the Best Actor Award, possibly to himself, given his molten hot performance in *The Ashtabula Tapes*—soon to be seen in *Anybody's Bedroom*—the physically and fiscally magnetic—I just read it, folks—Richard Nussbaum!

(*Applause, music, and the joyfully confident Richard enters.*)

Richard: What an honor it is, Hal, to be praised by someone like you, a singer, who no one expects even to have any opinions about acting quality—
Hal: (*tautly*) I have made a few films, Richard—
Richard: (*not wishing to dally*) Oh, right. The nominees for Best Actors, I mean, *Actor*, I'm so psyched, I'm about to go above the title!—*Actor*, are Terence Coot in *Action Ill-Advised*, Christopher Halidome in *The Fire and the Flame*, Richard Nussbaum—who? ha-ha!—in *The Ashtabula Tapes*, Reynolds Prawney in *Action Ill-Advised*, and—(*he can't help giggling at this last obvious also-ran*)—heh!—Toshiro Sazakawa in *Tiger of Joy, Tiger of Sorrow*. May I have that little flying carpet to the stars, please?

(*Melody appears with the envelope, but clutches Richard's arm as she gets to the podium. She is strangely wild.*)

Melody: (*pleading secretively*) Richie!
Richard: (*remembers her vaguely; confused*) Huh? Melody, right? What are you doing here?
Melody: I had to see you! I'm a presenter. The gown's rented—
Richard: I'm a little preoccupied right now, Melody—
Melody: (*with heartbreaking diffidence*) I haven't seen you since that crazy party—six to eight weeks ago—and—I have some news for you—
Richard: (*remembering the camera*) Ah ha-ha! Yes, thank you!

(*He tries to pry the envelope from her.*)

Melody: Can't you see your child-to-be in my eyes?

(*She grabs his hand and places it on her abdomen. Horrified, he recoils and wrenches the envelope from her, also breaking her hold on him.*)

Richard: (*playing the stranger*) Thanks! Thanks so much! (*He turns from her. Deeply hurt, and not strong enough to persevere, she retreats, but looks maddened.*) . . . the winner—sorry to keep you all waiting!—is—Richard Nussbaum! (*Applause and music. He picks up the award and shifts it from his left to his right hand in self-presentation.*) Whoa, wow, this is great! I had a speech about da Vinci and landing on the moon, but forget it! Just— well—to all you young, struggling actors—Don't give up! There may be some roles I'm not right for! Thank you again!

(*Melody pokes her head back in, and Richard strategically exits on the other side. Music and applause.*)

Hal: (*resuming*) Now, to present the Narcisso for Best Picture—a man who has tried to cheer decade after decade of

wartorn America with his inconsequential and utterly inoffen-
sive talent—a man we have decided for our own self-
congratulatory reasons to honor with a *special* Narcisso—for
longevity, for acceptability, for sheer occupation of space—Mr.
Dewey Lamont!

(*Applause, music; Dewey stumbles on—old, senile, drunk,
panicked and inextricably confused. His tuxedo doesn't quite fit.*)

Dewey: (*clutching the podium*) Where's the cards? Where's
the names? The—the abominations for Best Picture—
Hal: (*holding up Narcisso: beaming*) This one's for *you,*
Dewey.
Dewey: (*testily*) I don't know them by heart, I haven't even
seen any of them—Where's the cards?
Hal: (*peeved*) It's a special award for you to keep, Dewey.
Dewey: Keep? Who do I keep it for?
Hal: It's your goddamned honorary award, will you take it?
(*Dewey is clearly out of it, so Hal takes over curtly.*) The nomi-
nees for Best Picture are *The Angered*, Sawbuck–Neiman,
TKO, producers; *The Fire and the Flame*, Nino and Dino
Portofino, producers; *Forever Ends at Dawn*, Inter-Cine-Ex-
Am On Inc., producers; and *Sex Girls on Vacation*, Narcisso
Investment Group, producers.

(*Hal sees Melody, mad as Ophelia, stranded staring with the envelope at one exit, and hurriedly takes it from her; he hands it to Dewey.*)

This is a moment of tremendous magnitude, and reminds
me—I hope, in the next presidential election, you all do the
right thing and vote for—(*He notices suddenly that potty old
Dewey has torn up the envelope and its contents; mischievously
or helpfully, who knows?*)

The enve—Why, you old—Fortunately, Slice and Quarterhouse, our accountants, always keep duplicate envelopes in
case of accidents—Would the aide bring a duplicate envelope,

please? (*Melody is pushed onstage, crazed and past caring.*) A duplicate envelope!

Melody: What do you want?
Hal: (*trying to preserve decorum*) A duplicate envelope!
Melody: (*wild-eyed*) Duplicate, what are you talking about?
Hal: Now look—
Melody: You . . . go to hell! I'll see you there! In about five minutes!! (*She flees offstage. Meanwhile, Minerva Limegrove rushes on, and takes the podium.*)

Minerva: Ladies and gentlemen, luckily, I know the winner. I slept with Slice *and* Quarterhouse last night, and although (*there is a violent but momentary clatter offstage.*) I'll tell, *if* you give me a special award, too!

(*Voices, presumably from the audience, hurl guesses as the chaos increases.*)

Voices: *Fire and Flame! Fire and Flame! Forever Ends at Dawn! Sex Girls! The Golden Goat God!*

(*An offstage gunshot is heard.*)

Minerva: Okay, okay, I'll tell. But keep the cameras on me!

(*Jean-Claude runs onstage and hides under the podium. Richard staggers on, done for. He, clearly, is the victim, clutching his stomach.*)

Richard: (*crumples and falls*) The airplane, the polio vaccine, and now, this honor—I thank those who got out of my way—and—and—believed—until the entire universe—acknowledged . . . my . . . (*He dies, delirious.*)
Minerva: (*also cracking*) Over here! Keep the cameras over *here*!!

(*Marla Limegrove rushes on, and jockeys for attention.*)

Marla: Over here! I know, too! I slept with Slice and Quarterhouse this *afternoon*! I know, too! But first let me say, those two men are liars! Liars! If accountants' words don't count for anything in this world—

(*Melody staggers on, with a smoking pistol. Jean-Claude screams.*)

Melody: I shot him! The man I loved! I killed him! (*She sees Richard's body and screams, then falls senseless to the floor. Hal is bemused by all this. An offstage aide hands him a note. Smoke drifts in from offstage.*)

Hal: Ladies and gentlemen—when leaving the Memorial Pavilion tonight, please avoid the parking area until—we have completely put out the—apparently some upholstered seats in someone's car—wait until we have extinguished the—until the staff says—
Voices: (*overlapping and unnerving Hal*) Sex Girls! Forever Ends at Dawn! Sex Girls! Birth of a Nation!

(*Marla and Minerva wrangle with each other, wrestle, really. Dewey wanders around lost, and sits in exhaustion. Sheila Foot comes to his assistance. Is he asleep or dead?*)

Marla and Minerva: (*as they fight*) Come on, get the close-up over here! Here, me! I'll tell! I'll announce it nice and orderly! I will. No, me!! No, me!!
Sheila: (*cradling Dewey*) Dewey! Dewey!

(*The band strikes up, à la* Titanic, *and Hal obliges with the show's theme.*)

Hal: Who's top banana? Who's just a fruit?/Who's the goddess? And who's just cute?/Who gets the hand, and who gets the boot?/Who's on top?/Who's on top?/Who's on top?

(*Smoke fills the stage. Blackout.*)

May Contain Nuts centerfold, Steve Altes

When Worlds Run into Each Other

MARK O'DONNELL

(Outer space. Two planets meet by accident and hail each other.)

ONE: Hey, whoa, how are you!

TWO: Hi! I must be way out of orbit, running into you! Look at you!

ONE: Hey, you look great! What is it, trillions?

TWO: Trillions of years, it has been. So how's your civilization?

ONE: Well, they're just discovering music, if you know what I mean.

TWO: Lotta drums, huh? My smallest satellite—Plutonis, that green bit in the distance, just broke out in mammals.

ONE: Very natural, mine had them. I notice your polar ice caps are larger.

TWO: Well, you're not exactly molten, you old spheroid—how's your star?

ONE: The red giant? No, seriously, fine, couldn't break free if I wanted to!

(awkward silence)

TWO *(out of chat)*: Well, you look great. Real atmosphere.

ONE: You, too. Bounce some cosmic rays in my direction.

TWO: Sure will, I sure will.

ONE: Bye!

TWO: Bye!

(They part. Pause, then, each says to itself simultaneously)

BOTH: I thought she'd exploded!

(blackout)

Simmer in Sweat

MARK O'DONNELL

Characters

Violet   Foster

Vendor   Lump

Angie   Peaches

The Scene: The lower porch of a dilapidated two-family house in a squalid Southern town.

(Music: Disillusioned waterfront saxophone. It's a hot summer night. Fragile yet very pregnant Violet sits fanning herself on the steps; she looks yearningly down the street for her errant husband. Vendor crosses pushing a filthy snack cart.)

Vendor: Moon pies! Cotton candy! Gossamer fancies for broken lives! Hot as hell tonight, huh, Miz DuVin?

Violet: Well, I don't know, Mister Vendor, but I reckon I'll find out eventually!

(Vendor exits as Angie enters, an innocent, raggedy "pidgin English" teenager. He carries a birdcage with two crows in it.)

Angie: Songbirds! Who will buy my songbirds? You like one, Missus DuVin?

Violet: Why Angie! Those birds aren't songbirds! Those birds are . . . Yes, I do believe they're . . . ravens!

Angie: Ravens?

Violet: Dark, disrespectful creatures with a hungry emptiness behind their eyes. No, Angie, no ravens for me! Not while I am ripe with child and my heart beats life, life, life!

Angie: Does your brother want one?

Violet: My brother?

Angie: The henpecked yet brutish consumptive.

Violet: Oh, Foster! He's my half brother. No, Angie, you'll find no business here! Try over in Finnish Town! This time o' night those Laplanders are so drunk they'll buy just about anythin'!

Angie: Okay, I try there. I see you later, when things are much more complicated!

Violet: (*Longingly*) Angie, wait! I've always secretly . . .

Angie: Yes?

Violet: Nothin', never mind.

Angie: Okee-fenokie!

(*He goes. She stares up at the sky, and sighs.*)

Violet: The stars make such noise tonight!

(*A scuffle is heard upstairs. We hear the voice of Foster's ghastly wife.*)

Ghastly Wife: (*offstage*) You cheatin' on me! You cheatin' on me! I caught you red-handed!

Foster: (*offstage*) No, baby, no! I . . . Violet! Help!

(*Foster comes stumbling and coughing down the steps to safety with his sister. He calls back up the stairs.*)

Foster: Look, honey, you can *have* the triple word score!

Foster: (*to Violet now*) That ole eagle eye! I'm 'bout ready to kill her, Violet, I swear!

Violet: Oh, Foster, no! You and your killin'! Is mister Darwin's work all for nothin'?

Foster: Ex-cuse me, Miss Too-good-to-kill-folks!

(*He stumbles off, coughing.*)

Foster: I'm goin' over to the Lost Dreams Café. I'm goin' t'have me a drink at the Lost Dreams Café!

Violet: That's a good one! All they have at that café is lost dreams!

Foster: Come on, Tureen! I'm goin' over to the you-know-where! Wanna come? They havin' the Ugly Wives contest t'night!

Wife: (offstage) Why, you know I'm a bedridden virago!

Foster: Only too well, baby, only too well! I hope a photo will do . . .

(He stumbles off, coughing.)

Violet: My sweet Lump would never treat me that way. What could be keepin' him? He must've done overtime at the mud fact'ry.

(Lump and Peaches enter lewdly entwined and drunk. He's a dumb stud; she's a floozy.)

Violet: Why, Lump! Lump, honey, who is this person?

Lump: Oh, this? This here is Peaches! You just go ahead and cling, Peaches! (Guffaws)

Peaches: Miz DuVin, you should be real proud o' yore son! He's terrific in the uh . . . long run!

Violet: Son! Lump, what tales you been tellin' her? Who is she?

Lump: (Lying) She's a—a old elementary school teacher of mine! I ran into her outside the mud fact'ry!

Peaches: (giggling) I needed some mud! For my teachin'!

Violet: You expect me to believe a cuh-razy story like that one? What has gotten into you? You used to treat me all nice and human like, bring home moonpies for me and Junior—and now you drag in this, this Peaches person—

Lump: Aw, Violet, you're jealous, aincha! C'mon, admit it, you are! Whattaya say, Vi, kin I keep her?

Violet: Lump, you're my husband!

Peaches: Thanks, honey, you're a sport! Got any gin in the house?

(She flounces inside.)

Lump: I'll help you look!

(He follows into the house. Vendor crosses.)

Vendor: Red hots! Get your sizzlin' red hots, right here! Make your mouth burn!

Violet: This is too much to bear! I . . . mustn't . . . go . . . insane!

(Foster stumbles on.)

Foster: Fine time for the Lost Dreams to burn down!— Violet! Violet! What's wrong?

Violet: Uh, nothin', Foster, nothin'.

Foster: Don't try to fool me, baby, we grew up together! I know when you has fits outside at night, somethin's botherin' you!

Violet: Oh Foster, it's Lump! I found out somethin' horrible about Lump!

Foster: Baby, I told you not to get them eyeglasses!

Violet: No, no! He's seein' another woman! In fact, I seen her too! She's inside the house right now! He brought her here, right under my knows all about it! I'm glad he's proud o' my housekeepin', but—I'm goin' just plain crazy!

Foster: Now, don't do that. Remember when we wur kids, when Daddy used to take us out in the woods and bury us? We wur miserable. What did we do to feel better? We'd pretend we wur little lost royalty! We wur the Prince and Princess of Somewhere! That's what you got to do now—Retreat into a hopeless fantasy world!

Violet: Foster, I just don't know if I have the strength. I guess I'll go wander the humid, glowerin' night, a phantom of my lost self . . . Maybe catch a movie . . .

(She goes off eerily. Foster coughs and looks up at the sky.)

Foster: Too bad we're all just leaves driven by the tempest of time . . .

(He goes upstairs. Lump and Peaches emerge. Their sex was a flop. He looks away moodily.)

Peaches: Don't feel so bad, sugar. It happens to lots an' lots an' lots o' men sometimes, believe you me! Let's try again, we'll go play spin-the-secret in the boo-dwah!

Lump: Aw, I'm runnin' out of secrets. You blurt one—I'm tired.

Peaches: Well, my Daddy was the town drunk . . . And in New Orleans, that's somethin'!

(Lump goes inside. Foster stumbles back downstairs.)

Foster: Whoa, 'scuse me! I forgot my coughin' bowl!

Peaches: Well, hello there, you X Y configuration, you!

Foster: Lady-lamb, that's some hotsy flesh fort you got on!

Peaches: I see you're a poet.

Foster: Yes, Ma'am! I'm a Longfellow! Would yew care to check out my rhythms?

(Foster simulates rhythmic thrusting.)

Peaches: I would be delightful! *(corrects herself)* Er, *ed!*

(He and Peaches embrace and then make out, despite his breaks for violent coughing and spitting.)

Foster: Oooh—hack h-hack—baby! Give me—coff!—your sweet lovin'! Brrrrr-ackkkh! Ooh, yeah! Ptooie!

(Violet enters, decked in weeds and insane. She's no longer pregnant.)

Violet: Call the rescue team! I'm trapped! Trapped—inside my own life! And in this heat, all I can do is suffer and simmer! Simmer in sweat!

(*She collapses at the foot of her steps. Foster breaks away from Peaches and goes to Violet.*)

Foster: Violet!
Violet: It's really rather peaceful in this sleety, fetid gutter.

(*Angie wanders on. His cage is now empty.*)

Angie: Songbirds! Who will have my songbirds?
Violet: I am the Princess of Somewhere!
Angie: Mrs. DuVin!

(*He goes to her. Peaches joins them.*)

Foster: Careful, now! She's the fragile type!
Violet: Oh Angie, at last! Why have I never told you?
Angie: Told me what, Missus DuVin?
Violet: I've always secretly loved you, Angie, in my way, but it's not a very profound love, really! I like you just fine, don't get me wrong, but it's my husband I truly love! I mean, you're nice an' poignant an' all, but my feelins for you are just, I dunno, comme ci comme ça. I guess that's why I never brought it up.
Angie: (*tortured*) No, no, Miz DuVin! It is a sin so to speak. You love Lump too many, much too many!
Violet: Well, yes, that's my point.
Angie: No, no! It is a wrongness!

(*He runs off.*)

Violet: Wait! Come back! The Princess didn't give you leave to leave!
Foster: Oh, Violet! You lost the baby inside you!
Violet: Don't we all?

(Lump rushes from the house.)

Lump: Violet!
Violet: Oh, Lump . . .
Lump: Violet! She's dyin'!
Peaches: *(to Violet)* It was nice meetin' ya!
Violet: Now I'll know if hell is hotter than this . . .

(She dies. Lump wails.)

Lump: Violet's dead!
Foster: What're you sayin? She is not!
Lump: Is too! Is too!

(He sees Peaches clinging to Foster.)

And you. You're dead, too. To me.

(He despairs, and rushes inside. Peaches follows.)

Peaches: Now wait! Just simmer down!
Foster: Careful! He's got that killin' look!
Peaches: *(offstage)* Lump! Don't! He's got a knife!

(Offstage gunshot.)

Peaches: *(offstage)* One o' those special shootin' knives!

(Lump staggers on, falls by Violet, dies.)

Lump: Hot . . . enough . . . for ya?

(Peaches reenters, joins the mournful tableau. Angie ventures on again.)

Foster: The princess has her Lump at last.
Foster: *(To Angie)* What do you want?

Angie: My birds, Mister Almost Brother. I left my birds.

Peaches: What kind of birds were they?

Angie: Oh, pretty birds, fast lady! Red and yellow! Bright as the sun!

Peaches: The door of the cage is open.

Foster: They musta got away.

Angie: Fly, little birds! Fly above the wind!

Peaches: I'm just boilin'. I'm just all over sweat!

Foster: Angie, this feather is black!

(They all gaze into the empty cage. Vendor appears.)

Vendor: It's sweet! It's light! It melts, melts away!

Foster: Violet!

(Fade out.)

Diary of a Country Gentleman

P. J. O'ROURKE

We have given up the fast-paced life of Washington, D.C., with all its sophisticated glitz and glitter. (Crack open a bottle of Cold Duck! Our friend Dan just made G-15 at the Department of Health and Human Services!) In years past we have "summered," as they say in New Hampshire, in New Hampshire. But this year we have decided to stay on through the winter and live full-time at our country place, Breakwind Oaks.

It's a lovely center-hall colonial built in 1773, although with various additions and modifications following a fire in 1801, a fire in 1832, a fire in 1845, government requisition for use as a U.S. Army pest house during the Civil War, a flood when the dam at the local lint mill broke in 1877, a coal boiler explosion in 1903, lightning damage in 1936, and a windstorm in 1978 that caused three enormous oaks to collapse on the roof. Some of the doorknobs date back to the Revolution.

We bought the house in the 1980s from a Boston lawyer whose family had owned it for generations. They are one of those Back Bay clans, pals with the Cabots and Lodges, and I have to say that that Boston Brahmin blood seems to be running a bit thin, perhaps due to inbreeding. At the house closing the lawyer, an eccentric type, snatched our certified check and ran from the room cackling, "Ha! Ha! Ha! Ha! Ha!" in a high-pitched voice.

Anyway it's a charming spot, nestled in the Beige Mountains between the Mt. Barntop ski resort and Lake Wannaneujetskee. We have 165 acres. Make that 163. I just received a notification from the state Environmental Protection Agency informing me that lawn chemical contamination has been detected in the swamp on our road near the property line. I gather I would be liable for cleanup costs. A retired couple from Worcester, Mass., has built a new, vinyl-sided center-hall colonial next door. I don't know why they drive those land survey stakes so deep. It's a remarkable lot of work pulling them up and pounding them in again. But it's good to get the exercise and fresh air.

Healthy exercise and bracing fresh air are why we moved here. For us, leaving Washington had nothing to do with an enormous jet plane smashing into the Pentagon, terrorism warnings, and anthrax threats. (Speaking of which, I was amazed to learn last winter how crabby the VISA card corporation can be when their invoice is returned a bit crumpled and faded. You would have thought, during those days of heightened alert to potential dangers in the mail, that VISA bills would have been printed in such a way as to readily survive simple precautionary treatment in the washer and dryer of our apartment building's laundry room.)

I'm particularly fond of the bracing fresh air—very different from Washington, D.C.

"Yes," says my wife, "the water in the flower vases rarely skims over with ice on September nights in Washington. When can we turn the heat on?"

I reassure her that I'll be done cleaning the furnace flues by Christmas at the latest and promise that there'll be no repetition of last Yuletide's difficulties when we came up to Breakwind Oaks for the holidays and the Bestsey-Wetsey doll that we'd wrapped for our eldest daughter froze and exploded under the tree.

My wife and two little girls are still somewhat "citified." They don't fully comprehend the many duties and responsibilities involved in running a large old country house. If something is amiss, you can't just bang on the pipes to call the Super— especially if those pipes are iced up solid and may (as they did last year) shatter during a vain attempt at Super-calling. To avoid such problems (and what with the shocking price of fuel oil these days) I intend to heat our house with the ready and dependable supply of wood left from the oaks that fell on the roof in 1978. My wife does not quite "get" this. Just the other day she was saying that she thought the chain saw was too "heavy and dangerous" for our five-year-old to operate. Nonsense, I told her, emergency rooms all over New Hampshire are filled with kids that age who use chain saws all the time.

Nor do my wife and children possess quite the same enthusiasm I have for wildlife. I have counted, this season, chipmunks, voles, field mice, two species of squirrels, nesting swifts, and a black snake. And those are just the things that were dead in our chimney.

"Eeeeek!" screamed my wife, "A horrible creature is in the breadbox!"

"Humph," I said, "it only chewed through the middle of the loaf, and you're always telling the kids that the crusts are the best parts for them."

"Daddy!" shrieked our five-year-old, "there's a scary monster in my bedroom!"

"Just a bat," I soothed, swinging a broom. "See, Muffin, nothing scary about it. Think of it as an extra-large dead rat with wings."

"Waaaah!" yelled Poppet, our two-year-old, "lion in potty!"

"Hush," I said, "lions have been extinct in the Belge Mountains for centuries although, come to think of it, something did leave a very big paw print in the garbage last night."

My New York publisher, Morgan E., was visiting for the weekend. Just a social call, he insisted, nothing to do with the fact that my book Whitewatership Down, an amusing satire on the Clinton administration featuring a family of rabbits, is eight years overdue.

We'd finally—lion in potty or not—gotten the children to bed. Nothing like bracing fresh air (and a dose of Children's Benadryl) to make kids sleep like logs. We were enjoying some cheese and port in the dining room (there's an organic vineyard in New Hampshire that produces its own port wine which, as Morgan puts it, tastes "unusual") when a gurgling sound began in the basement.

"Hmmmm," said Morgan, sniffing curiously, "this cheese is ripe."

"What's that noise?" asked my wife.

I went to investigate. "Quick," I shouted from downstairs, "no one have a bodily function!"

You'd think that the seven or eight septic tank people that I called, who advertise emergency service, wouldn't all be asleep at one in the morning. And each of them asked me the same question, "When was the last time you had that septic tank pumped?" I didn't previously know that people who pump septic tanks were Democrats. When I mentioned the Reagan era every one of them hung up.

"I'm beginning to see why your book is so late," said Morgan, giving me encouragement from a lawn chair as I dug up the yard the next day.

"Those septic tanks, they're easy to find," said my neighbor, the retiree from Worcester, who stopped by to give advice. "It's state regulations. State regulations say that tank's gotta be inside seven hundred feet of your house. So's all you got to do is draw yourself a circle with a seven-hundred-foot-long string and dig around in there. I know," he continued, "it's the regulations 'cause when I built my house that's what the state Environmental Protection Agency fellow said. A regular busybody, if you ask me. Got a phone message from him on my answering machine just this morning, something about lawn chemicals. Don't know what he wants now. I brought over a little stick that you can tie the seven hundred feet of string to."

I found the septic tank at last, beneath my wife's prize delphiniums. She was just retuning from the woods, having helped Muffin and Poppet understand another lesson in nature's bountiful gifts—that the whole world is a toilet. "Lion in potty!" said Poppet.

A savvy little student of nature she's become. There, in the end of the sewer pipe, blocking flow from house to septic tank, was a lion indeed—from Steif.

DIARY OF A COUNTRY GENTLEMAN, PART II

The vernal season has commenced at Breakwind Oaks, our country house nestled in New Hampshire's Beige Mountains. The first bulbs of spring, *Galanthus elwesii*, commonly called Greater Snowdrop, have bloomed. At least they have according to the chapter titled "New England April—Fun with Frozen Mud" in my copy of *The Gardener's Pal*. The book was a Christmas gift from the Acropolis Paving Company. It came with a card from proprietor Nick Papandreou showing a Currier and Ives–type illustration of the new parking lot at Mall of Colonial America here in Quaintford, New Hampshire, and bearing a message of Yuletide cheer: "Give yourself the gift of freedom from lawn care, shrub trimming and flower bed chores. Call Acropolis Paving, the Gardener's Pal."

"Ah, country living!" I was musing to my family the other day. "What miracles of nature we get to enjoy! All creation seems drear and dead and yet, in the annual mystery of vegetative resurrection, we—probably—have delicate blossoms of Snowdrop."

"Buried under three and a half feet of ditto," said my wife. "Also, I think Nick Papandreou poured asphalt where I planted the bulbs." My wife was glancing at a copy of the local paper, *Beige Mountain Natter*, preparatory to wadding it up and throwing it in the cast-iron stove, which we are keeping fed with newsprint, cardboard boxes from the liquor store, dozens of empty bags that used to hold driveway salt and some of the less attractive furniture from the attic because we're heating the house with wood and we ran out of it in February.

"The milk in my Fruit Loops is frozen again," said Muffin, our five-year-old.

"Just sit on it for a while," said her mother, who had removed a mitten to tear an item from the *Natter's* front page. "You know," she said to me, "how you wanted us to move here for the genuine experience of New England rural culture?"

"Yes," I said.

"Well, this evening is Folk and Bluegrass Karaoke Night at the Grange."

"Carrot okay?!" said Muffin with indignant little puffs of breath forming around her in the—I'm sure very health-giving—frosty kitchen air. "I hate carrots!"

"No, no, Muffin, not 'carrots are okay,' " I explained, " 'karaoke.' " And I told her how one stands up in front of a crowd of complete strangers and sounds bad and acts foolish and everybody who hears this is driven mad.

"I can do that!" said Muffin. "Please, Daddy, please let's go."

It's true that genuine experience of rural culture was one of the reasons I wanted to give up our apartment in Washington, D.C., and live full-time at our summer place. But there were also, to be frank, considerations of income and expense. For freelance writers of light, humorous pieces, there has lately been a certain, shall we say, "market correction." It's that War on Terrorism. An increasingly solemn inside-the-Beltway atmosphere caused a noted Washington manufacturer of political novelties to decline to purchase my idea for "Fuq Iraq" bumper stickers. And every time I sat down to work on my book of Florida ballot-counting jokes, I seemed to be stuck in Chapter 11.

Alas, removal to a rustic clime has not proven quite the financial relief I had hoped. During the January thaw our whole driveway slid downhill into our neighbors' yard. It was only by dint of creative skills honed over a lifetime as a freelance writer that I managed to convince our neighbors, a retired couple from Worcester, Massachusetts, that asphalt is an excellent natural plant mulch and that, if they wouldn't sue, I wouldn't charge them anything for fifty-two cubic yards of it.

Our new driveway was installed by Acropolis Paving. The bill came as a bit of a "shock to the pocket." But the move here has been value for money in other ways. Country living is, for the children, full of salubrities. If that's a word. The mice have eaten my dictionary. I have given each of the girls her own little gravel rake and matching shovel so they can exercise, helping the neighbors spread asphalt on their vegetable plot. Muffin doesn't like this as much as the karaoke at the Grange Hall, but it gets her outdoors and away from what I feared was becoming somewhat obsessive play with a "Star Barbie" doll complete with scanty actress clothing she got for Christmas from an aunt. Muffin's favorite game was to parade Star Barbie through the house in its Barbie-sized thong underwear while chanting, "Barbie is hot!"

Finding this rather disturbing, I asked, "Muffin, what do you mean, 'Barbie is hot'?"

"I mean, she isn't cold," said Muffin, clutching the doll to her polar fleece vest with gloved hands in the—I'm sure very health-giving—frosty playroom air.

And country life has done wonders for our three-year-old, Poppet. I was remarking on this to my wife recently at dinner. "See the rosy glow of her complexion, those apple cheeks!" I exclaimed.

"That's the hood of her red ski parka," said my wife. "You're looking at the back of her head. And will you stick the salad cruet back in the microwave; the olive oil has congealed."

It does make the kids happy to find out that almost every thing on their plates is some kind of frozen treat. "It's a porkci-cle!" I tell them. And, speaking of happy kids, we got a dog. Nick Papandreou wanted to do something to make up for the current price of asphalt. ("It's the War on Terrorism," he explained. "Asphalt's gone sky-high.") So, when the locally famous hunting dog owned by Nick's brother George had a lit-ter, Nick made sure I obtained first pick. George Papandreou is a restaurateur and noted sportsman in these parts. He owns Quaintford's only Chinese takeout, Athens Dim Sum, and also Chow Mein Kennels.

The dog is a purebred Shedhair Setter, from a distinguished line of close runners-up.

"What shall we name the puppy?" I asked my excited daughters.

"Karaoke Star Barbie," answered Muffin without hesitation. Poppet nodded in vigorous agreement.

"But . . . ," I said.

"Karaoke Star Barbie!" insisted Muffin.

". . . the puppy is . . . ," I demurred in a conciliatory tone.

"Karaoke Star Barbie," sniffed Muffin, tears beginning to roll.

". . . a male," I muttered.

Karaoke Star Barbie will answer to nothing else. I have tried "Karey," "Okie," "Star" and even "Barb," but the dog only comes if addressed as "Karaoke Star Barbie" in full.

However, a country squire hasn't got an Esq. to his name without a good bird dog, in my opinion. Therefore, with philosophical attitude toward his peculiar moniker, I have been putting Karaoke Star Barbie in the nearby woods, schooling him with firm and full-throated commands to be "steady to wing and shot" and not chase squirrels while barking insanely and wrapping his twenty-five-foot check cord around a tree trunk like a yo-yo string. By means of this rigorous program of training, a keen-nosed scout of upland game is being crafted, as is, apparently, a large body of jokes at my expense. I have heard, "Karaoke Star Barbie, roll over," from the far bay at the self-service gas station; "Karaoke Star Barbie, here's a bone," from somewhere near the meat counter in the grocery store, and snatches of "Who Let the Dogs Out?" sung in the last row of folding chairs at the Town Meeting.

Karaoke Star Barbie has not, as yet, I confess, exhibited much of a nose for ruffed grouse or woodcock. But he did find the tires on my sports car and chewed all four to shreds. Actually, the electric-blue Miata was beginning to look a bit like a midlife crisis mistake anyway. And having a vehicle up on concrete blocks in my yard has given me New Hampshire "road cred" that makes up for a certain amount of good-natured ribbing about the dog's name. Karaoke Star Barbie also found the retired couple from Worcester's satellite dish and caused a spectacular short-circuit when he raised his hind leg. TV reception problems and disappointment with asphalt as a natural plant mulch were, perhaps, the deciding factors in our neighbors' decision to sell their home.

The property was quickly purchased by two young men from Los Angeles who have opened Ye Old Blisse Authentic

Yoga Spa on the premises. I immediately called a Quaintford selectman. "Surely," I said, "this is in violation of our zoning ordinances."

"You bet," said Nick Papandreou. "They're going to have to pave five acres to meet our hospitality service parking space requirements."

The fall in our property values caused by a large, halogen-lit expanse of asphalt marring our view of the Beige Mountains was not, unfortunately, matched by a corresponding decline in our property tax bill. In fact, our property is now being taxed at the rate levied on commercially developable land. This was an additional financial burden. Although I did manage to find the money for a nice present for my parents' wedding anniversary, it being their sixtieth. I got them a two-week cruise in the Caribbean aboard the S.S. *Listeria*, of Montezuman registry. My wife was not sure if this was a wise expenditure under the circumstances.

"Are you sure you're in their will?" she asked.

Meanwhile I take solace in long tramps with my loyal canine companion, refining his natural instincts to hunt, and . . .

"Fill our larder," said my wife, "with car tires, satellite dishes and squirrels. By the way," she continued, "while you were out yelling at the dog a Hollywood television producer called."

"A Hollywood television producer?"

"He's staying at the Yoga Spa," said my wife. "He heard you in the woods and asked the owners, and they told him they were pretty sure you lived up here."

I take great solace in long tramps with my loyal canine companion—now that I have a script-writing deal for thirteen episodes of *Karaoke Star Barbie* on the Cartoon Network, plus 15 percent of the licensing fee for the sing-along CD.

DIARY OF A COUNTRY GENTLEMAN, PART III

After a cold, snowy winter preceded by a rather early Labor Day blizzard and followed by a somewhat late Memorial Day twenty-two inches of flurries, summer arrived right on schedule in New Hampshire. The ice broke up on Lake Wannaneujetskee in plenty of time for the Fourth of July festivities. There was more than enough open water for the annual patriotically decorated parade of float boats. And a picnic excursion to the beach to stand wrapped warmly in blankets, waving sparklers, was a welcome respite from the chores of agriculture. I have decided to turn our summer place into more than just a hobby farm. I think this will be a wonderful learning experience for our children, Muffin, six, and Poppet, three. Also I've signed a contract for a new book, *The Approaching Global Catastrophe—Turn Your Summer Place into More Than Just a Hobby Farm*.

I've bought a tractor, a classic old John Deere. I got it from a local family who, after nine generations at Boulderstone Farm, have given up tilling the New England soil and opened their land to tourists as a horizontal rock climbing venue. They advertise it as suitable for all ages and much safer than rock climbing of the vertical kind. I plowed a strip of our old hay field 1,750 feet long. And I will plow more once I figure out where the reverse gear is and back out of the woods. I'm consulting with the U.S. Department of Agriculture County Extension Office about the best crop to raise. "My guess," says my wife, "is party ice."

The barn is now replete with livestock: two sheep (named by the children), Bob the Builder and Sleeping Beauty; six chickens (named by me), Eggsaggeration, Eggsasperation, Eggumenical, Eggsistential, L'Eggs and In-Arcadia-Eggo; a pony (named by its previous owners, who were apparently admirers of the American Indian ethos), Crazy Horse, and a 360-pound pig.

My kid sister, Alice, has come from San Francisco to stay with us, bringing considerable horticultural skills and the pig. It traveled with her on the airplane in its own seat (First Class). This is a Vietnamese potbellied pig, the kind that was briefly popular as a pet with trendsetters before the trendsetters realized that Vietnamese potbellied pigs grow to a size of 360 pounds. The pig does not have a name because, Alice explains, "She can't manage to tell me what she calls herself. It's the fault of the Bay Area liberals. They refuse to understand the value of English immersion. If Animals are going to thrive in America, they need communication skills."

Alice is a romantic about animals, and about everything else. She has been since she was a child. Dad was worried Alice might become a nun. He was so worried that he considered converting to Protestantism. In fact, Dad went so far that, once, when Jehovah's Witnesses knocked on the door, he invited them in. (This did not work. The Jehovah's Witnesses ended up staying for martinis and went home with several borrowed copies of G. K. Chesterton's Father Brown mysteries.)

Anyway, Alice was always far too romantic for the quotidian banalities of family and marriage. [N.B. to copy editor: delete coarse marginal note scribbled by my wife.] Or so I had thought. But then, in her early forties, Alice fell in love with a university professor. The professor was hired by the Political Science Department at Colgate-Palmolive College in nearby Cheeseborough Ponds, New Hampshire. And Alice gave up her rather lonely job as the California State Republican Party's Liaison to PETA and followed her beau East.

Alice has been a tremendous help on the farm. It was she who, after the demise of Eggumenical, Eggsasperation and L'Eggs, pointed out that locking our rather aggressive male dog, Karaoke Star Barbie (named by the children), into the henhouse at night to guard against foxes was not a productive strategy. The children adore her. She is a genius at keeping them occupied. She told them a story about how every little living thing on earth is a precious gift from God and, ever since, Muffin and Poppet have spent hours collecting individual carpenter ants from the house, carrying each one outside in cupped hands, and releasing it into the wild. Actually, the pig has been helpful, too. At first Karaoke Star Barbie was jealous. But, after a short scuffle with the pig (picture a World Sumo Wrestling Federation performance), the two became pals. They pass the day together happily digging huge holes in the lawn, into which we are planting young fruit trees. Also, being pressed between 360 pounds of stern pig and a fence post is the only way to get Crazy Horse to hold still long enough for Muffin to sit on her pony.

Alice is cheerfully tolerant of the meat-eating in our household, even when my wife said, while serving beef bourguignon on the first night that Alice was here, "It's got vegetables in it, for pete's sake." And Alice did not press the point when the dog rejected mucilage and resumed consumption of Alpo. What's more, Alice has been encouraging about my own attempts in the direction of a vegetarian diet. "The Bombay company does not test gin on animals," she notes.

Alice's boyfriend, Dr. Frank Glosspan, is a practicing Catholic and a staunch Republican and would be something of an anomaly in academic circles if he weren't stark raving mad. Dr Frank's field of PolySci specialization is micro-democracy. His Ph.D. thesis was "Liberty, Equality, and Fraternity in Salmonella typhimurium." He rewrote and expanded this for the general public in his best-seller, *The Universal Declaration of the Rights of Pizza Toppings*. Dr. Frank is a leading advocate of providing all carbon-based life forms with Green Cards—as long as they don't abuse the U.S. welfare system. "There are billions and billions of members of just the class Insecta alone," he says. "Think what they could achieve if they had property rights and rule of law! Plus," he confides, "insects would vote GOP."

The romance between Alice and Dr. Frank seemed to be proceeding well. He has been a frequent dinner guest at our house, bringing with him Tupperware containers of calcium, niacin and riboflavin. (He tries to eat only inorganic matter.) After coffee (hot water with caffeine alkaloid prepared synthetically from uric acid for Dr. Frank), he and Alice would retire to the barn. "And read John Stuart Mill to the pig," says my wife.

Although I hasten to add that she says this with a smile. My wife likes Dr. Frank. So do the kids. "I'm not eating my vegetables," says Muffin, "because of my love for all broccoli-kind."

Dr. Frank approves of my farming operation and says that it's clear that I'm not exploiting animals, they're exploiting me. He's even gone so far as to give his blessing to my pursuit of upland game. "I've watched your brother shoot skeet," he told Alice, "and I can see that he'll be practicing 'catch and release' on grouse this fall."

Alice and Dr. Frank have gone for long hikes in the Beige Mountains with the pig. They've taken the pig swimming in Lake Wannaneujetskee. They even visited the Vermont birthplace of Calvin Coolidge, bringing the pig along in the back of Dr. Frank's Toyota Priius. When the pig was barred from the Coolidge homestead, Dr. Frank dressed it in his own tweed sportcoat and claimed that the pig was a prominent senator from Mississippi. The tour guide, being a young man with an earring and a soul patch, believed it.

Dr. Frank and Alice appear to have been made for each other. We've all been waiting for Dr. Frank to pop the question. The upcoming Animal Companion Ball, given by the New England Society for the Abolition of Chattel, seemed a likely occasion. And, indeed, last night Dr. Frank arrived at our house bearing the look of a man with a serious proposal to make. After cocktails (synthetic ethanol and soda for Dr. Frank), he and Alice—as is their custom—went to the barn. My wife and I discreetly retired to our bedroom. A while later Dr. Frank's Toyota drove away with a low electric hum, and I heard Alice come into the house alone. There was a sound of weeping in the living room.

"I'll go down and see what's the matter," I said.

"Better let me," said my wife.

My wife returned to bed saying, "Dr. Frank brought an invitation to the Animal Companion Ball."

"But that should have made Alice happy," I said.

"The invitation was for the pig," said my wife. "Alice is quite upset. She says she's going to spend the night in the barn."

"Imagine," I said, "no one to love but a pig."

"I can imagine it perfectly," said my wife.

Alice was up before everyone this morning. I could hear her bustling around in the kitchen. "What's that smell?" I asked.

"Bacon," said my wife.

How to Make a Kitten

ED PAGE

I hope this article doesn't upset any cats. They've had a monopoly on kitten-making for as long as I can remember, so they may be a bit perturbed to learn that an outsider has figured out how to make one. But I've done just that. In fact, I've come up with a great many kitten-making techniques, one to suit every fancy, I daresay. Here, for instance, is a simple three-step method:

1. Find a full grown cat.
2. Reverse the flow of time.
3. Wait.

I devised these procedures a few weeks ago in an all-night brainstorming session that arose when I mistook a couple of No-Doz for my sleeping pills. I sat out the night in my den, a cushiony chair beneath me, my beloved black kitten Debbie purring in my lap. As I sat there, puffing leisurely on my Basil Rathbone–style pipe, my mind wafted hither and yon. "How would one go about making a kitten?" I mused, gazing down at Debbie. "They're such complex little contraptions. So many moving parts!" I surprised myself with my ingenuity. Cogitating away in the wee hours, turning the question this way and that, I came up with a whole slew of solutions that now, in the light of day, strike me as flawless. (Loath to ignite Debbie's jealousy, I have yet to test any of them.) Below, I present a sampling of my solutions. Happy kitten-making!

THE VACUUM METHOD

Using a standard vacuum cleaner or Dustbuster, suck up half the empty space from between the atoms that compose the body of an adult cat. Push the atoms together. Voilà! A kitten!

THE MARIONETTE METHOD

Carve a kitten marionette out of wood. Wish upon a star that it were a real live kitten. The Blue Fairy will eventually grant this wish, but not before the wooden kitten, brought magically to life, gets mixed up in many entertaining situations and is swallowed by a whale.

THE MIRACLE METHOD

Travel back to the time when all the things in the New Testament were happening. Wangle an invitation to the water-into-wine party. After the wine miracle, approach Jesus with your goblet and explain that you're not much of a wine drinker and would rather have a kitten. Watch as Jesus performs the wine-into-kitten miracle.

THE COSTUME METHOD

Wear a cat costume all day, every day. Never be seen not wearing the cat costume. When it comes time for you to have a baby, the stork will bring you a kitten.

THE DREAM METHOD

Fall asleep and dream that you have a kitten. Frolic with the kitten in a lush dream meadow full of wildflowers and happiness. When you feel yourself starting to wake up, grab the kitten and hold it gently but firmly close to your heart. When you're fully awake, look down at your arms: you're still holding the kitten!

THE GIANT HOUSE METHOD

Demolish your house. Rebuild it so it looks exactly the same, only twice as big. Fill the house with things that are twice the size they normally are: giant phones, giant chairs, giant toaster ovens, etc. Get a full-grown cat and put it in your house. What outside your house was a cat is now—amazingly—a kitten! (Note: This method has the fun additional benefit of turning you into a dwarf.)

THE NATURAL METHOD

Invite a handsome male cat and a pretty female cat over to your house for dinner. Light candles. Put on a Barry White CD. Serve your guests oyster-flavored Tender Vittles and plenty of wine. When you're sure both cats are drunk, escort them to the guest room. In the morning, after the cats have gone to their respective homes, strip the bed and plant the soiled sheets in your garden. Soon, a tree will start to grow. By late spring, the tree will be tall and leafy and full of kittens.

giant toaster ovens

ROD LOTT'S LISTS
28 OLSEN TWINS VIDEOS WE *WOULD* PAY TO SEE

Mary-Kate & Ashley's Slumber Party Massacre
Mary-Kate & Ashley's Bordello of Blood
Mary-Kate & Ashley's Book of Shadows
Mary-Kate & Ashley's Chained Heat
Mary-Kate & Ashley's Last House on the Left
Mary-Kate & Ashley vs. the Aztec Mummy
Mary-Kate & Ashley's House of 1000 Corpses
Mary-Kate & Ashley's Orgy of the Dead
Burn, Mary-Kate & Ashley, Burn!
Mary-Kate & Ashley Conquer the Martians
Mary-Kate & Ashley's Behind the Green Door
Mary-Kate & Ashley's Island of Lost Souls
The Incredibly Strange Creatures Who Stopped Living and Became Mary-Kate and Ashley
Mary-Kate & Ashley's Blood Beach
Mary-Kate & Ashley's Zombie Island Massacre
Mary-Kate & Ashley: Portrait of a Serial Killer
I Know What Mary-Kate & Ashley Did Last Summer
I Still Know What Mary-Kate & Ashley Did Last Summer
Mary-Kate & Ashley's Lust for a Vampire
Mary-Kate & Ashley's Fists of Fury
Mary-Kate & Ashley's Most Dangerous Game
Boxing Mary-Kate & Ashley
Mary-Kate & Ashley's Premature Burial
Mary-Kate & Ashley's Texas Chainsaw Massacre
Mary-Kate & Ashley's Stewardess School
Beneath the Planet of Mary-Kate & Ashley
Mary-Kate & Ashley's Mission to Mars
I Spit on Mary-Kate & Ashley's Grave

Application for _____ Capital
of the World

ALYSIA GRAY PAINTER

NAME: North Carl, New Hampshire

ADDRESS: North Carl, New Hampshire

OCCUPATION: Town

AGE: 2 months–94 years

SEX: Both

LANGUAGE: English (with the exception of a few seniors who mumble pretty bad)

ETHNICITY (*optional*): We have voted to support it with a parade every two years.

CITIZENSHIP: U.S.A. (North Carl boasts two exchange students from Quebec, Martine and Jean, who have proven to be a wonderful source of foreign knowledge for our young people. *Quelle merde*, or isn't life grand, as our two Quebecuties love to say.)

INTERESTS: Hunting, dressing up dolls, baseball, dancing, not dancing, dominoes, reading, learning to read, assault and battery, needlework, vodka, model trains, cigarettes, bird-watching, knitting, pornography, wreath-making.

DAYTIME TELEPHONE: Several (Note: Mrs. Meg Hamilton's phone is currently not in service due to her raccoon infestation, as the raccoons become stimulated when our favorite chatterbug gets on the horn. Even the sound of Mrs. Hamilton merely dialing causes the animals to run to the nearest wall jack and begin to suck, their wild saliva sending sparks up. Mrs. Hamilton is recovering nicely, albeit without any form of modern communication but with the occasional splitting migraine and/or crying jag. Her weeping, apparently, is causing the raccoons to attack the jacks more fiercely. So Mrs. Hamilton's phone is out until further notice, i.e., Dan the Raccoon Man™ can stop by with his stun gun and tasty Raccookies. Certain humans here love those Raccookies, but don't tell the raccoons!)

HONORS & AWARDS: The Cloverleaf Club presented North Carl with the "Best Town to Break Down" plaque back in 1984. Also, The Lady Lunchers of New England awarded us "Most Usable Public Lavatories" in 1991 and 1993. Sadly 1992 was a memorable year for mold. And littering. And someone forgot to empty the bathroom trash bins from March to December. But yay us! '91 and '93 way to be!

IN CASE OF EMERGENCY: Woodville, PA, and Kenner's Falls, WV. (Woodville says no calls after 11 p.m. weekdays, please.)

HOW DID YOU HEAR ABOUT THE "WORLD CAPITAL OF" FAMILY?: The Baker clan over on South Street just got back from visiting John Baker's aunt near Gilroy in California, which is the official Garlic Capital of the World. The Bakers said garlic bulbs sprout everywhere, on postcards, calendars, you name it. So we in North Carl started talking about all these world capitals. Someone remembered a town in Florida that is the World Capital of Shark Teeth. So we thought, hey, all these places are pushing their covered bridges or cheese, shouldn't we have our claim to fame? So, yes, the Baker family, John Baker, Louisa, their three kids, one adopted, the youngest, very sweet, over on South Street. That's how our town heard about it. Garlic. Which North Carl doesn't eat, generally, but we are not against gourmets who enjoy it on occasion, say in a marinara sauce.

PROPOSED CAPITAL OF: Pajamas

REASON FOR PROPOSED CAPITAL: North Carl is the home of the former SnugBug™ flannel factory, built in 1904 and permanently closed in 1967. The year of 1967, of course, was a very trying time for all fabrics, as everyone across our great nation simultaneously removed their clothes. But flannel especially seemed to suffer. Some old-timers say flannel was just too constricting for those Summer of Love sorts. A "flesh fence" the kids called it. We don't call it that now. Never. Then recently a few artist types moved into the empty factory, the children of the hippies plus some brand-new hippies, the long hair and the pants. They aren't troublemakers or dissenters but they are prone to making ceramic drink coasters. So the town began to reminisce about our flannelled annals, and we were delighted to discover that we all wear pajamas, every one of us. No nudies or skin-sleepers among us. We didn't poll the artists on this topic, though, because we expect they may have answered differently. Thus, Pajama Capital of the World seems as perfect a fit as a four-button Sally Snoozy with a stitched left pocket and cuffed bottoms. That was a pajama reference in case you didn't notice!!

IF PROPOSED CAPITAL IS UNAVAILABLE, WHAT IS YOUR ALTERNATE SELECTION?: Window Treatments, including awnings, bishop's pants, shutter covers, draperies, valances. North Carl may one day be recognized as a town that takes fabric seriously, especially fabric that blocks sunlight and hinders vistas. We're as earnest about our curtains as our nighttime sleepwear, and you can put that in print.

FINANCIAL SUPPORT: Mary Kirkpatrick, the owner of Mary's N'ice Cream, not the Mary Kirkpatrick who is the assistant manager of the North Carl Bank & Loan, volunteered to set out a Folgers can (without any coffee in it) next to her cash register for any donations to help with our World Capital campaign. It should be noted that $9.67 was collected the first week when the Folgers can was left as is. Compare this with the $21.45 collected the week Mary Kirkpatrick created a pipe cleaner "cozy" for the can, making it more noticeable to the eye and chic. The pipe cleaners sort of look like bug antenna. Our modish Mary may not be in the frozen confections business much longer. Remember us in Paris, Coco (Chanel)!

REFERENCES: Nashua and Hillsboro. They have long been supporters of North Carl, at least the several individuals from Nashua and Hillsboro who have driven through North Carl. We think they were from Nashua and Hillsboro, but they didn't stop. You know us New Hampies, always on the go! But even if they didn't stop and get to know North Carl, they sure did seem to like us. They obeyed every traffic law and one North Carlite said that a child in the back of a minivan with a Hillsboro sticker waved at her. So please talk to the kind folks of Nashua and Hillsboro about us. We're sure they'll not snarl about North Carl! They might say something nice, too.

Manchester has also promised us a letter of recommendation but it may have gotten lost in the mail. Manchester is also very big and busy and may have forgotten. Maybe you can call Manchester for us. Maybe ask Manchester if it is mad at us for something we don't know we did, if that doesn't seem too awkward or anything.

ESSAY: Fabric. Curtains that billow. A flannel hat with mittens so warm. Pajamas, sweet slumber-makers. These are items of interest to everyone everywhere. People young and old wear clothes. People of every religion and creed and belief wear clothing. People everywhere get up every single morning and say, "what shall I wear this day" and they go wear something. And then they change their clothes at least once a day, sometimes five to fifteen times a day. Everyone everywhere loves fabric, which is the soul of clothes. And we love to sleep in it. We put on fabric, like a cotton flannel set, and then crawl between our flannel sheets and under our flannel blanket and we dream our dreams, full of contentment. What are dreams but magical threads through our minds, like the threads of fabric? So we in North Carl, if selected the Pajama Capital of the World, will proudly become the tailors of the dreams of dreamers. By coming to our town, taking a tour of our flannel factory, eating in our diners, and buying our bumper stickers/T-shirts/mugs, anyone who has ever worn clothes will have found the thread through their dreams, winding, ever more. Flannel. Pajamas. The duds of dreamers. In the Pajama Capital of the World. North Carl. Thank you.

Prices May Vary

ALYSIA GRAY PAINTER

Magazine
USA $4.25
Canada $6.75

Book
New York $28.99
Los Angeles $4.99

Enchilada
San Antonio $3.95
Bangor $5.95

Whole Enchilada
San Antonio $6.95
Bangor $9.95

Tattoo
Seattle $35.00
Palm Beach (unavailable)

Ice
Buffalo $.25
Phoenix $70.00

Meat
Milwaukee $8.45
Malibu (discontinued)

Meatless
Milwaukee $1.95
Malibu $27.99

Earthquake
Hollywood Hills $44,000
Sepulveda Basin $2.50

Bells
Hell $4,600
Philadelphia 150 pounds, 13
    shillings, 8 pence (damaged)

Fountain of Youth
St. Augustine $2.00
Beverly Hills $11,500

Oxygen
Moon $5,000,000
Earth $1.75 (quality may vary)

P.R.
San Francisco $8,000
Oakland $3,000

Pork
Iowa $13.00
Washington, D.C. $4,560,000

Flan
Spain $3.50
Spa $350

Filter
Aspen $10.00
Pompeii $3,900

White Christmas
Maine (complimentary)
Melbourne (not in stock)

$5,000
Atlantic City $12,000
Las Vegas $31,000

Ring
Manhattan $7,000
Saturn (NFS)

Billing
Minneapolis $850.00
St. Paul $825.00

Santa
North Pole $500
Fe $100

Penicillin
Hartford $100
1693 $32,500

Fishing Equipment
Key West $67.00
Los Alamos $900,000 (sold
    under "Fission Equipment")

Q
Quebec $1.00
Albuquerque $2.00

Telephone
Vancouver Island $39.90
Vacant Island $55,000

Seashell
Myrtle Beach $.20
Mojave Desert $4.60

Canada
USA (discontinued due to lack of
    interest)
Canada $4,000,000,000

USA
USA $7,900,000,000
Canada (further fees apply)

A Reenactment of the Reenactment
of the Battle of Turkinsville

ALYSIA GRAY PAINTER

Promptly at 10:30 in the morning last Saturday, a large group of spectators waiting behind the gate near Martin's Field were called over to the teal-blue 1989 Honda Civic of Mr. and Mrs. John Barting. The Civic was parked to the left of the footbridge, as it had been the morning of 13 March 1995. Several of the visitors who had been present at the actual Civil War reenactment on that morning in March immediately noted a glaring anachronism. The Honda Civic now had higher mileage. On the morning of 13 March 1995 the counter had read 49,877, and for authenticity purposes should have been rolled back from its current reading of 67,222. Several spectators present agreed rolling back odometers is highly unethical but completely necessary in any reenactment of a reenactment. For the interested, there are a number of private mechanics in town that will do that job for a not ungenerous fee. These mechanics are also reenacters and are uncommonly sympathetic to the plight of those who demand genuineness. Also, ask about their Civil War discount on tire rotation and chrome plating.

Perhaps more glaring than the higher odometer, however, was the addition of an AAA decal on the lower left bumper, which purists present at the 1995 incident claim was absolutely not on the Civic. One spectator also maintained that the "Otto the otter" Beanie Baby visible through the back window also had not been in the car on that March day, and intends to research when the Ty toy company first introduced Otto, believing that date to fall somewhere in early 1998. Another spectator suggested that there had been a stuffed animal in the Civic on 13 March 1995 but it was definitely a small Garfield cat with suction-cupped paws. A short and lively discussion followed but nothing was ultimately concluded.

A quiet took the crowd as the actors emerged from a thicket of bushes and stepped into the car. After a few moments of preparation, the reenactment of the reenactment commenced. Karen Barting, here being played by Karen Barting, began to fiddle with the radio knob. On the actual morning of the reenactment, Karen Barting had tuned the radio to 103.4 Classique Rockque, but 103.4 was sold late last year and now plays modern jazz fusion with a dash of pop. It was a discrepancy immediately noticed by all present, sending a ripple of derision through the onlookers. There is another local station that plays classic rock at 90.5 on the dial, but had Mrs. Barting chosen to move the finder down the dial the authenticity of the moment would have been grievously damaged. Seasoned viewers whispered it was the best decision under bad circumstances.

After tuning the radio, Karen Barting turned to look at husband John Barting, who was sitting in the driver's seat of the Civic licking his palm and stroking the stray hairs in his beard. Readers will not be surprised to learn that John Barting was here being portrayed by John Barting. John Barting, while some fifty pounds heavier than his March 1995 self, had once again donned the exact flannel shirt and wool trousers, although the fleet of eye could see that the trousers remained undone to allow Mr. Barting the ability to breathe. His kepi, or Civil War–era cap, was also the same kepi worn on 13 March 1995, although John Barting's temples had grown noticeably grayer. Scorekeepers observed that all of Mr. Barting's apparel was custommade by Miss Sybil at Battle Hems of the Republic on 5th Street in downtown Jackson. The sassy sort might inquire after his undergarments but we can only hope and assume Mr. Barting is a true reenacter.

Karen looked ready to speak. The crowd drew nearer the Civic.

"John, why aren't you wearing your glasses?" Karen asked.

That was exactly what she asked on 13 March 1995!!!

John Barting straightened his shirt. "Hon, look, the boys way back then didn't wear light bifocals in a titanium frame. I gotta look the part, right?"

Onlookers murmured that Barting had actually used "babe" rather than the more formal "hon" on 13 March. One gentleman up front with clipboard in hand also raised an eyebrow over "the boys way back then" believing that Barting had said "when" rather than "then" on the date in question.

Karen flipped off the radio (perfect, exactly!) in a peevish fashion. "You need to see out there. Please."

"Nope, won't do it," John countered.

Was it "no" or "nope" back in 1995? If anyone knows for sure, please contact me, either by e-mail or phone before 8 p.m. weeknights.

"Look, Johnny, I don't care what those crazy sixteen-year-olds were doing back in 1863. You're a middle-aged guy with middle-aged eyes. Please, do your wife a favor."

Bull's-eye! Karen sure had her lines down. Had she been working with a coach even? The crowd approved, sounding a smattering of applause.

"Okay, fine," John said and got out of the car, glasses on.

"I'll be watching you. You better have 'em on, mister," Karen yelled after him, and then turned on the radio once more and began tapping her hands on the dashboard.

The mob erupted. A success! After a moment, John and Karen walked over to shake hands and accept much-deserved compliments. A gift basket emerged and was handed to a blushing John. Karen repeated a couple of her lines per a viewer's request, saying them with a bit more oomph than necessary.

The next reenactment of the Reenactment of the Battle of Turkinsville will take place next Saturday at Martin's Field. Matt Jensen and Gerry Gonzalez will be reenacting the incident where they enjoyed a smoke while waiting for their regiment's tent to be set up prior to the Reenactment of the Battle of Turkinsville that took place on 13 March 1995. Gerry has promised to once again tell the ribald story of his bank teller's daughter as he told it to Matt that day. And Matt assures me he is attempting to get sick with a head cold, much like the head cold he had on 13 March 1995. If any of our readers currently has a head cold and wouldn't mind giving it to Matt, he said he'd be glad to come by your house, where you might do some heavy coughing on him. Maybe you could even share a can of soda or perhaps engage in a little platonic cuddling. Bravo Matt! Glad to see authenticity is alive and well.

Gates open at 10 next Saturday! See you all there.

9 FUTURE TITLES IN THE HARRY POTTER BOOK SERIES

Harry Potter and the Tar Baby
Harry Potter and the Goblet of Mad Dog
Harry Potter and the Bordello of Blood
Harry Potter and the Vaguely Satanic Overtones
Harry Potter and the Tramp
Harry Potter and the Chamber of Frilly Lacy Things
Harry Potter and the Fantastic Everlasting Gobstopper
Harry Potter and the Sorcerer's Kidney Stone
Harry Potter and the Goblet of Potted Meat

IRON CHEF CHALLENGER DAVIS SWEET
10 FUTURE TITLES IN THE HARRY POTTER BOOK SERIES

Harry Potter and the Chamber of Cho
Harry Potter and the New Action-figure-suitable Characters
Fear and Loathing in Hogsmeade
Harry Potter and the Magic Knob
Harry Potter and 500 Superfluous Pages (Special Edition with built-in wheels)
Harry Potter and the Spell That Kils Uppity Copy Editors
Harry Potter and the Gratuitous Death of a Peripheral Player
Hakeem Potter and the Religious Conversion
Harry Potter and the Just Buy the Damned Thing
Hermione Potter and the Little Indiscretion

Ten Increasingly Annoying Short Stories

NEIL PASRICHA

A Short Story, About Something Really Annoying

You accidentally get locked inside your bathroom, which is full of mosquitoes.

The mosquitoes keep trying to bite you but, just as you start trying to swat them, you realize that they may become your only source of food as the time inside this small bathroom wears on.

You also realize that you are the mosquitoes' only source of food and *they* will die if you stop them from drinking your blood, possibly depriving you of food in the future. So you take off your clothes, sit with your eyes clenched tightly on the toilet, and suffer mosquito bite after mosquito bite, just to fatten up the darned insects, so that you will have something to survive on when you begin to starve to death in a few days.

Then, a couple hours later, when you're covered in mosquito bites from head to toe, your buddy Ralph comes by and unlocks the bathroom door.

Moral: Do not lock yourself in a bathroom.

An Even Shorter Story, About Something Even More Annoying

All the vacations to Belgium and France are booked up for Spring Break, so you settle for a trip to the slums of Colombia.

Determined to still experience the taste of some fresh croissants purchased from a local bakery, you walk around the streets of Colombia until you find a bakery with a sign outside reading "We Are a Local Bakery Serving Fresh Croissants, Much Like a Similar Bakery Would in France."

You enter the bakery and are viciously beaten with a plastic bag full of stale rock-hard Kaisers.

Moral: Feel free to get locked in a bathroom. Just don't try to buy croissants from a Colombian bakery again.

An Even Shorter Story Than the Shorter Story, and Definitely More Annoying

You accidentally get locked inside a bathroom in a local Colombian bakery while attempting to buy a lemon tart.

There are no mosquitoes inside this bathroom that you could fatten up on your own blood to eat later.

There is, however, a ruthless baker covered in tattoos named Salianto inside the bathroom, who proceeds to pummel you to death with a bag full of stale rock-hard Kaisers and a comically large rolling pin.

Moral: Okay, add back the first moral about not locking yourself in bathrooms. And change the second moral to include all baked goods, not just croissants.

Even Shorter Than the Last Story, and Even More Annoying Too, Even Though the Last Story Included Your Own Death, Which Probably Really Burned You Up

At your funeral, your friend Ralph does the eulogy, and he tells *everyone* about how you were killed by being beaten with a bag full of stale rock-hard Kaisers and a comically large rolling pin.

Everyone laughs, and a few people make rolling-pin gestures.

Moral: In the future, make sure morals from your past really annoying stories include more details about how to avoid death.

A Shorter Story That's Possibly Even More Annoying Than Dying and Having Your Friends Laugh at You at Your Funeral, If That's Even Possible

During the funeral, your long-lost brother Raoul, separated from you at birth, runs into the room with a suitcase in each hand, a scrapbook with old newspaper clippings hinting at your whereabouts, and two tickets to France for Spring Break.

Moral: Who told you to go to Colombia anyway? I don't remember the moral of the first story mentioning that sensible piece of advice. Clearly, there are a lot of issues at work here, not the least of which is you jaunting off to dangerous South American slums and killing yourself. What's the point of morals if you never take their advice?

The Story Where You Enter the Action in the First Person, Blow the Increasingly Shorter-Story Rules Out of the Water, and Come to Near Blows with Your Moral-Spouting Alter-Identity

I'm not to blame here! Who knew that a ruthless baker would beat me to death inside a Colombian bakery? Nobody, that's who. Your pointless morals certainly didn't warn me. Don't eat croissants? What kind of moral is that?

Moral: You're so predictable and whiny. I could have just read the title and skipped the body of the story, that's how predictable you are. You'll probably argue with me in the title of the next story. Get ready everyone, here it comes!

The Death of the Moral-Spouting Alter-Identity

If what you say is true, then this should probably kill you once and for all.

Moral: Ah, but it didn't. And do you know why?

The Story Where the Moral-Spouting Alter-Identity Reveals That He Has Taken Control of the Story Titles and Can Never Die

No!

Moral: Oh yes!

What's the Point of Going On? The Hero Is Dead. He Was Killed in a Colombian Bakery. The Only Real Mystery Left in This Story Is the Identity of Me, the Moral-Spouting Alter-Identity Who, for Some Reason, Takes Great Pleasure in Abusing Our Hero

Ralph? Is that you? Thanks for letting me out of the bathroom, man, but seriously, what's up? The funeral thing was pretty funny, but these shenanigans have gone too far. A joke's a joke, man. Ralph? Lay off it. Please just let me rest.

Moral: Say hello to your brother.

The Ultimate End

Raoul, no! But why! Why!

Moral: Because I wanted to go to France! I spent months trying to find you, and bought nonrefundable airline tickets so we could go on a vacation together and learn about each other's lives. I wanted to spend time with you. I wanted us to be together. But what do I find when I finally get to you? You're dead, man. You went on a stupid Spring Break trip and got yourself killed. I missed the flight to France because of your wake. I will never forgive you for the heartbreak you've caused me. I will always desire what I cannot have. So rest, dear brother. But do not rest in peace.

Moral: Don't buy nonrefundable airline tickets.

Clarifying My Relationship

NEIL PASRICHA

Last year I married a very nice lady, developed a relationship with her twenty-two-year-old daughter from a previous marriage, divorced the very nice lady because of philosophical differences, had a child with her twenty-two-year-old daughter, and then was at a loss for words, for I was caught in a mysterious web of undefined relationship titles.

My new child, a daughter, was certainly my daughter, I don't deny that, but wasn't she also my grand-stepdaughter, since she was the daughter of my stepdaughter? Or did the stepdaughter rule not apply since I had already divorced the very nice lady who was the mother of the stepdaughter, thereby nullifying all relationship titles associated with that key central relationship? And what was I supposed to call the mother of my new daughter, the twenty-two-year-old, who I had not married or even dated? She wasn't my wife or girlfriend, but calling her my stepdaughter from a previous marriage seemed a bit, I don't know, square.

To get myself out of this embarrassing headache I married the twenty-two-year-old daughter, who was the mother of my new zero-year-old daughter, formerly called my grand-stepdaughter. I say formerly because when a man and a woman get married and produce a baby girl the baby girl is called the daughter, case closed, right? All previous relationships involved in producing the baby girl go out the door, right? For clarity, that's what I'm assuming. Also, the twenty-two-year-old daughter of my ex-wife, my stepdaughter, was now also my wife, which I decided must supercede all other relationship titles.

I rested easy for a few minutes after the wedding, kicking

off my dress shoes in the back of a Lincoln as we rode to the airport, thinking I had finally sorted these relationship titles out. My "wife" and I had a new baby "daughter," I thought, smiling slowly at the image of this perfectly nuclear family I had helped create. We would grow up together in a quiet cul-de-sac, with other families such as ours living next door, shooting free throws on our driveway in the afternoon, watching office-based sitcoms in the evening, and erasing our Internet cache at night. It would be so perfect.

Then it struck me. Since the title of wife supercedes all other titles, what about my ex-wife, the very nice lady? Sure, we were divorced, because of philosophical differences, but the fact remains that she was my wife, and it was through her that I met my new wife, her twenty-two-year-old daughter. If the divorce nullifies all relationship titles associated with the key central relationship, in this case my marriage to the very nice lady, then my relationship with the very nice lady's twenty-two-year-old daughter, my stepdaughter, would have also been nullified. She was just a twenty-two-year-old woman then, and not anything else. I began thinking that I got married for nothing.

Then I remembered having this same thought well before getting married to the twenty-two-year-old daughter. Look up a few paragraphs if you don't believe me, for this thought is well documented. It seems I may have acted too hastily, though, because here I am now, with a band around my finger, telling the whole world I got married because I had to when I didn't necessarily have to. I mean, why didn't I just slow down a bit, think it through, and realize that the key central relationship here, the marriage, affects everything only when the marriage is intact. This makes sense, right? What I'm saying is clear and logical, right, and I'm just a few paces ahead of the crowd on this whole matter, aren't I? This doesn't all loop around backward and end up in a nonsensical circle of rhetoric, does it? Because if so, if I married my twenty-two-year-old non-wife and non-girlfriend just so she would become my wife so that I could mentally supercede the only other title she had in my mind, as a stepdaughter from a previous marriage, then that would seem a bit, I don't know, square.

Then again, wouldn't you be caught in a nonsensical circle of rhetoric too if your ex-wife was now your mother-in-law?

ROD LOTT'S LISTS
A DOZEN MYSTERY INGREDIENTS NOT YET USED ON *IRON CHEF*

anthrax
Beanie Weenie
Pectin
I Can't Believe It's Not Butter
Fresca
Beano
Funyuns
Vienna sausages
Yoo-Hoo
Bac-Os
kumquats
waffle fries

IRON CHEF CHALLENGER DAVIS SWEET
REMATCH! A DOZEN MYSTERY INGREDIENTS NOT YET USED ON *IRON CHEF*

panda haggis
whiffleballs
bats (whiffle or other)
Colin Farrell (hey, he's in every other fucking thing)
pygmy sashimi
hydrogen
anything ending in "-O's" (Spaghetti-, Cheeri-, shrimp-, Ore-, etc.)
Velveteen rabbit (you thought this was going to be "Velveeta," didn't you? Ha!)
Pooh (also homonyms poo and pu-pu)
chef's choice: poi, koi, goyim, gollum
Carrot Top (grating and/or dicey)
love

Peter and the Wolfowitz

A Republican's Guide to the Orchestra
Loosely Based upon the Music of Sergei Prokofiev

LOUIS PHILLIPS

Each of the persons in our story is represented by one of the instruments of the modern orchestra. For example, Dick Cheney is represented by the sounds of gold coins being rubbed together at a moderately fast rate (the musical term for this is inflation); George W. Bush (or, as he is called in this symphony, Peter) is associated with a sound produced by mating a violin with a hurdy-gurdy and then shouting "Gotcha!"; Defense Secretary Donald Rumsfeld is represented by the clarinet and, oftentimes, by the thud of heavy metal jail doors being slammed shut; Paul D. Wolfowitz is represented by the sound of governments being toppled—most easily expressed by French Horns; Soldiers are not fairly represented in this piece, but if you hear a cannon going off, then you are listening to the "1812" Overture, so you should turn the record over and listen to Prokofiev. Trills on the flute represent small birds twittering, but this should not be confused with the Democratic Party. The Democratic Party is actually represented by a very long silence and much whimpering.

One morning, Peter got it into his head that he should fly a plane over his father's broccoli field and land on an aircraft carrier, looking like John Wayne. (Note: In some productions, the aircraft carrier looks like John Wayne. In other productions, it is Peter [or George] who looks like the movie hero. The notes left behind by Prokofiev, since they were written in a language no longer taught in our schools, only confuse the issue.) Here, our first theme is introduced:

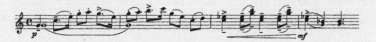

Our hero sings: "If I were a rich man." Later, those six words will play a much larger role as the Republican Anthem for the 2004 elections. On the way to the bank, Peter decides that he can get a lot of attention for himself if he accuses his Yale English teachers of creating weapons of mass destruction (i.e., grammar) and thus send deconstructionists and civil libertarians to Cuba, never to be heard from again. (Note: At this point in the composition, large gold cymbals clash together. Because this is a Republican composition, this warlike sound comes under the general rubric Gebrauchmusik, or music that is useful to stimulating economic growth.) Peter calls out: "Wolf-owitz! Wolfowitz!" and soon all the simple villagers come running. The simple villagers (who had been far less simple before they received their news from television sound bites) not only skip out to the meadow, singing joyously: "We've Got Plenty of Nothing and Nothing Is Plenty for Us," but they also festoon Peter with garlands of flowers left over from the Clinton administration. "Ah!" Peter sighs. "The simple villagers love me even when they have no jobs and nothing to eat." He wipes a tear away from one of his eyes.

"Where is the Wolfowitz?" they all ask.

"Oh, he's home reading about the history of the British Empire," Peter says, laughing.

(Here, a naked accordion restates theme #1, but in such a way that it becomes actually theme #2, though the administration insists it be named theme #1):

(Note: in some states, the accordion or MOAMI [mother of all musical instruments] is considered a lethal weapon, especially when playing at Polish weddings. If an accordion cannot at this point in the composition be found in the orchestra, it will be found later.)

Peter's father is very angry with his son. "If you cry Wolfowitz and there is no Wolfowitz, what will you do when a real Wolfowitz takes over our little white house? You will cry Wolfowitz and no one will come to your aid." To underscore the father's admonition, the Calliope plays a plaintive wail, reminding listeners that its wail stands for $4 billion a month being dropped into a black hole. This is theme #3, using an augmented sixth, although the administration insists that it is still theme #1 and that the motif can be augmented if a huge tax cut is approved for the wealthy.

"God told me to do it," Peter stammers, but no one is pleased. Especially God. Peter's father and the confused villagers trudge home. No sooner is Peter left alone (humming "Nicht weise bin ich"), but a trio of hunters—Wolfowitz and Rumsfeld and Cheney—leap out of the shadows. They have already swallowed the Bill of Rights whole, but they are still hungry. They sing almost in unison:

> Wohin scheich'st du
> Eilig und schlau
> Schlimmer Gesell

(Note: No scholar has satisfactorily explained why they all sing in German when no one else is around.)

"Wolfowitz! Wolfowitz! Wolfowitz!" Peter cries out, but of course, the villagers are tired of being tricked and so no one turns off *Wheel of Fortune* and no one comes to Peter's aid except for some very rich Texans who had just been strolling through the oil fields on the edge of the woods. The name Wolfowitz does not at first catch their attention, but when Peter, in desperation, screams, "Liberal! Liberal!" they rush to Peter's rescue. In celebration, the rich Texans throw a huge banquet (which they charge to the simple villagers and write off as a business expense). Prokofiev's charming introduction to the Republican Orchestra comes to an end with the trio of Hunters, the chorus of Texans, and most of Congress singing at intermediate intervals, "Let's Pick a Pocket or Two, Boys. Let's Pick a Pocket or Two!"

Golden cymbals crash. The curtain falls. The names, addresses, and phone numbers of everyone in the audience are taken down for future use.

ROD LOTT'S LISTS
7 MOVIES WE *WOULD* SEE WITH THE WORDS *MY, BIG, FAT,* AND *GREEK* IN THE TITLE

National Lampoon's My Big Fat Greek Wedding
My Big Fat Greek Breasts
My Big Fat Greek Demon Lover
Bill & Ted's My Big Fat Greek Adventure
My Big Fat Greek Deep Throat
My Big Fat Greek Stepmother Is an Alien
John Carpenter's My Big Fat Greek Prince of Darkness

plaintive wail

Blues for Advanced Beginners

JUDITH PODELL

"Woke up this morning and went back to sleep . . ."
—"Epstein-Barre Blues"
attributed to Memphis Earlene Gray

1. You have an inalienable right to sing the blues if you were born under a bad sign. Capricorn is a bad sign to be born under. Jesus was one. So was Nixon.
2. The right to sing the blues may be earned if you:
     a. suffer
     b. lose
     c. pay some dues
3. It's not the blues when your loss is tax-deductible.
4. Some examples of dues:
     a. working for the man
     b. hating your day job
     c. losing your man
5. Some forms of suffering that will never be blues-worthy:
     a. anorexia nervosa
     b. low LSATs
6. It's the blues if you:
     a. wish you'd never been born
     b. feel like a motherless child
7. If your mother is dead and you miss her it's Country.
8. Good times to have the blues are:
     a. Christmas
     b. Mother's Day
     c. every night when the sun goes down
9. You can't sing the blues in Chinese.

> *Mouth full of toothache*
> *Head full of network news*
> *Gonna go downtown*
> *Buy some alligator shoes"*
> —"Silverpoint Blues"
> attributed to Blind Drunk Johnson

10. Blues women never sing "Send in the Clowns." They pack heat and eat meat.
11. Just because you shot that two-timing man doesn't automatically make you a blues woman, but it's a good start. So is buying him an Armani suit, or paying his child support.
12. Blues sports are:
    a. drinking
    b. gambling
    c. running around
13. Blues men are not team players.
14. You can't sing the blues in Gore-Tex.
15. The following drugs don't belong in the blues:
    a. ecstasy
    b. speed
    c. multi-vitamins
16. Blues women don't wear Chanel. Other fashion no-no's:
    a. running shoes
    b. lace
    c. Botox
17. Blues men don't get born again.
18. There is no word in French for "hellhound."
19. You can't sing the blues in French, not even if you are blind.

My Resignation from the *New York Times*

NEAL POLLACK

Following is an account of approximately one-tenth of the arti-cles in which falsification, plagiarism, defamation of charac-ter, improper grammar, jingoistic sucking up to Donald Rums-feld, mishandling of basic geographical facts, bad spelling, and just plain ignorance were discovered in a review of articles written by Neal Pollack, who resigned yesterday as a reporter for the New York Times. *The review, conducted by a team of very tired* Times *reporters and researchers, came as a bit of a surprise, since no one was aware that Mr. Pollack actually worked here. According to Mr. Pollack, he was hired as the* Times's *Seoul bureau chief in October 2000 and has filed important stories on every major world event since then. Spot checks of his claims reveal that he's full of crap.*

"LAWYER SAYS D.C.-AREA SNIPERS HAD MYSTERIOUS ACCOMPLICE," APRIL 27, 2003

Denied Reports

A lawyer for Lee Malvo, the younger of two men charged in the Washington-area sniper attacks last fall, was quoted as saying, "Neither of my clients ever touched a gun. There was a third gunman, who hid in the shadows and fired with deadly accu-racy. Here, let me show you his videotaped confession." Through a business partner, the lawyer told the *Times* that he was getting a "massage" all day and never spoke with Mr. Pollack.

Factual Errors

The first sentence of the story said that Mr. Malvo requested a lawyer who was "stacked." He did not.

"INJURED SOLDIERS TREMBLE IN WAR'S AFTERMATH," APRIL 17, 2003

Whereabouts

The scenes described in the article ostensibly took place inside a ward of the National Naval Medical Center in Bethesda, MD, which Mr. Pollack has never visited. Hospital employees said they received a number of phone calls where the person on the other end said, "I know you are, but what am I?" Records show the calls were from Mr. Pollack's cell phone.

Denied Reports

Of the nine "wounded" soldiers described in the article, only one was actually injured, and that was from a paper cut sustained while filing papers in the hospital office. Pollack's interview with Cpl. Max Klinger, who he described as "nothing but an armless hunk of meat who regrets everything about this war," was also substantially falsified. Cpl. Klinger actually has both his arms and thought the war was delightful.

"RESCUED PRIVATE SAYS SHE'S 'READY TO PARTY,'" APRIL 4, 2003

Plagiarism

Pfc. Jessica Lynch did not say, "I loved Ashton, but I'm not sorry we broke up, because now I can have sex with whoever I want." That quote was lifted directly from a profile of actress Brittany Murphy in US Weekly. Pfc. Lynch was also not on hand for the Hollywood premiere of the new hit comedy Just Married.

Whereabouts

Hotels in Palestine, WV, show no record of Mr. Pollack's alleged visit. The Hard Rock Hotel in Las Vegas, on the other hand, reports that he ran up an $800 minibar tab and made several calls to a local "friendship" club.

"COUNTRY STAR HILL CRITICIZES PRESIDENT DURING EUROPEAN TOUR," MARCH 22, 2003

Denied Reports
Singer Faith Hill did not say during a concert in Dublin, Ireland, that "George W. Bush is an illegitimate president who should be impeached." Interviews with Ms. Hill's record label, attorney, and angry husband Tim McGraw show that she's never been to Ireland, has never criticized the president, and is very annoyed that Clear Channel radio stations across the country are encouraging citizens to burn her in effigy. According to Mr. McGraw, Mr. Pollack sent Ms. Hill a bouquet of flowers several months ago with a note saying he'd "love her forever." When she didn't respond, he called their house and said, "I know you love me! Admit it!" When she didn't reciprocate he said he wrote for the *New York Times* and was going to ruin her career.

"SNIPER WAS PRIEST, CHURCH OFFICIALS SAY," FEBRUARY 1, 2003

Whereabouts
This page A-1 story carried a Boston byline, but cell phone records indicate Mr. Pollack was in Barbados on a liquor-industry junket.

Plagiarism
Mr. Pollack quoted John Allen Muhammad as saying, "The Lord is my shepherd, I shall not want," which is actually from Psalms 23:1.

Denied Reports
Father Patrick McDonald was quoted in the story as saying that Muhammad "was my best seminary student, even though he

was Muslim." He says he never spoke to Mr. Pollack. Also, the Vatican denies that the pope "did a little tap dance, just like Richard Gere in *Chicago*," when he heard of the snipers' arrests.

Factual Errors

John Allen Muhammad was never a priest, duh. He also didn't "invent the recipe for Ding Dongs" and didn't "play on the 1989 World Champion Detroit Pistons basketball team." Also, Lee Malvo wasn't in the cast of *Saved by the Bell: The New Class*.

ROD LOTT'S LISTS
31 ANATOMICAL TERMS THAT SOUND LIKE POKÉMON CHARACTERS

Amnion	Labia
Blastopore	Mammilla
Brachial	Meatus
Chondrin	Medulla oblongata
Cilia	Mesocolon
Duodenum	Neuroglia
Epiglottis	Obelion
Fibula	Perineum
Fontanelle	Profunda
Fungiform	Pubis
Ganglion	Sarcoplasm
Ginglymus	Suprascapular
Hamular	Trochlear
Hernia	Tympanum
Ileum	Zygoma
Jujunum	

Editor's note: Too busy for Cliff's Notes? *Welcome to* The PowerPoint Anthology of Literature: *Great books distilled to their essence and presented in the most efficient form of communication ever devised.*

HAMLET

Option One: To Be

PROS

✓ Nobler in the mind

CONS

✓ Slings

✓ Arrows

Option Two: Not to Be

PROS

✓ Sleep

CONS

✓ Dreams (???)

Pride & Prejudice

Good Fortunes Possessed by Single
Men Vis-à-Vis Desire for Wife

Agenda Items:

- Determine connections among all factors
- Acknowledge veracity of connection
- Define parameters of acknowledgment (e.g.,
  "universal")

Hope Is the Thing with Feathers

Methods of Identification

	Things that are hope	Things that are birds
Has feathers	Yes	Yes
Perches	In the soul	On trees, rocks, statues, etc.
Words to tune it sings	None	None
When it stops	Never at all	Nighttime
Where heard	Chillest land, strangest sea	Varies by species
Asked for crumbs	No	Yes, also seeds

Meet Lolita

- **Qualifications**
  - ✓ Light of life
  - ✓ Fire of loins
  - ✓ Sin
  - ✓ Soul

- Steps taken by tip of tongue on pronunciation

  1. Upper palate ("Lo")

  2. Transitional ("Lee")

  3. Teeth ("Ta")

- **Name as function of situation**

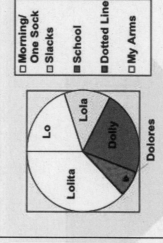

□ Morning/
  One Sock
□ Slacks
■ School
■ Dotted Line
□ My Arms

Lo
Lola
Lolita
Dolly
Dolores

May Contain Nuts

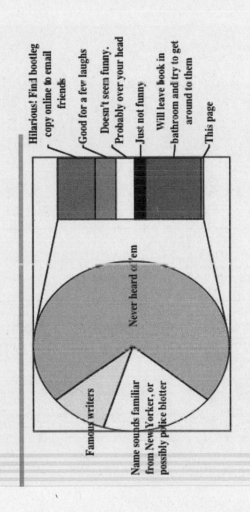

Hilarious! Find bootleg copy online to email friends

Good for a few laughs

Doesn't seem funny. Probably over your head

Just not funny

Will leave book in bathroom and try to get around to them

This page

Never heard of 'em

Famous writers

Name sounds familiar from New Yorker, or possibly police blotter

Goodnight Moon

Objects Identified

- Room (green)
- Telephone
- Balloon (red)
- Cow w/ moon (picture)
- Bears w/ chairs (implied picture)
- Kittens (little)

- Two (2) mittens
- Toy house (little)
- Mouse (young)
- Comb
- Brush
- Bowl w/ mush
- Lady (old, quiet, whispering "hush")

Objects Said Goodnight To

- Room
- Moon
- Cow
- Light
- Balloon (red)
- Bears
- Chairs
- Kittens
- Mittens
- Clocks
- Socks

- House (little)
- Mouse
- Comb
- Brush
- Nobody
- Mush
- Lady (old, whispering "hush")
- Stars
- Air
- Noises (in toto)

Abstinence, Only . . .

LAURIE ROSENWALD

A poll released by a coalition of conservative groups finds that most parents want schools to teach their children the ABC's of sex education, but disapprove of more explicit guidance commonly used in sex education classes.
—*New York Times*, National desk, February 13, 2003

In light of President Bush's allocation of $135 million to promote an "Abstinence-Only" S-E-_ E-D-U-_-_-T-I-O-N policy in public schools, we thought it was the very least we could do to present a fairly informative, kind of accurate, but not nearly comprehensive account of, well, *you know*. We feel that if kids know just a few of the ghastly, disgusting "facts," they'll be less likely to try to find out all of them, through the Internet and stuff. Or even worse, *experience*. A little misinformation goes a long way. In an effort to increase the pleasure of these anxious, frustrated parents, and educate and inform their clueless, frustrated, and nubile offspring, we offer the following report:

WHERE BABIES *REALLY* COME FROM

The sexual act is best demonstrated by putting your finger into an electrical outlet. First you must wet your finger. See? Sex is very painful and may cause an "organism." An organism might pop out and make you scream something like "Nobody Beats the Wiz!" or "Deutsche Grammophon Gesellschaft!" Then the organism turns into a tadpole. If you are wearing rubber, don't worry, because you are grounded, and protected from the organism. Before the sexual act, put on new sneakers and brush your tongue. Put on your Tom Jones record, and try some French

Twisting. You may experience one or more side effects, such as diaper rash, global thermonuclear meltdown, or tummy ache. Try not to drool on your sex partner. This may cause a short. To practice safe sex, use a surge protector. Now, close your eyes, and get ready for the ride of your life. All right then, away we go!

Some believe sex is where babies come from, but we now know that babies come from France. Sex is like something you feel for a pet, only not nearly as intense and erotic. It is much like love, but burns even more calories. True love can last up to fourteen minutes, but good sex can last for years at a time.

Avoid sex with dead people. This is called Philadelphia, and is frowned upon. If you have sex with your relatives, you'll have to light incense. Instead, have sex over the phone or through your computer. It's clean, efficient and modern. Unfortunately, our telecommunication devices are unwilling to perform sex with us, but we saw the laser printer winking at us so we're taking it to Indochine on Friday for a late supper.

People enjoy sex in many different ways. Some people are into pain. Others are into peanut. This is called M&M's, and either way, plain or peanut, it's going to hurt like hell.

You can make big money with sex, but only in Las Vegas. It is the only state where the constitution is legal. If someone offers you a "job" for twenty dollars, talk them down to ten. For oral sex you'll need a muffler, Dentyne, and some felt.

You can have sex with yourself if you have a subscription to *Glamour*. This is called procrastination, and Catholics believe it is very naughty. You can have sex with up to twelve people, but only if they are condescending adults. Sex is like ballet, except Mr. B is not always complaining about your short neck, and you don't *have* to wear your hair in a bun. Also, the Russians are no better at it than regular people. The Discovery channel is good, except for the spiders, unless you *really* hate your boyfriend.

With sex, remember that *size is the most important thing*. If you are the size of a muon or a quark, forget it. Nobody's going to be sexually attracted to a subatomic particle they can't even see.

If you have sex with a minority, you might even go to jail, because they are much too young. There you will have brutal sex with a man with a tattoo on his bicep that says "mother." You will meet him in the shower if you drop the soap, and then you will be his "girl" even if you are a boy. This is what they call being "inmate" with somebody.

If you wear lots of clothing, no one will have sex with you. If you wear tiny triangles of cloth attached with string, they will be all over you. If you are a boy, any young girl with two big houseplants will "turn you on." You will become hard like a rock all over and if you don't have sex right away somebody's going to have to mop up the kitchen. Probably you.

If sex is so much fun, we asked a friend why she doesn't "do it" more often. She said she couldn't find the "right guy." Apparently, he has to be "single." We pointed out that New York City, where she lives, has the highest density of "singles" on earth, except for that leper colony in Hawaii. She told us to shut up, and that Sartre was right, Hell *is* other people. She's been very moody. Perhaps she is molting. We tried to help, but she said she wouldn't have sex with us even if we *weren't* the size and shape of a Zamboni machine. Too bad, because she's one hot, sexy babe, and we could make her smooth and shiny all over. Her parents were bohemian communists and told her about sex when she was three, but then she forgot, so she learned it ten years later from a guy named Alan in Central Park. They were drinking "Peppermint Twister" out of a green bottle, and then she had an organism. There is a small bronze plaque there that marks the place where they did it. That night she lost her flower, because it was the "sixties," when "flower power" was "happening." She also lost her house keys, which is how her mother found out. Boy, was she mad! All mothers are against sex, but if they had not had sex they couldn't even be mothers. Unless, of course, they have been to France.

People over Time

BILL SCHEFT

A surprise restructuring inside AOL Time Warner forces *Time* magazine into a new group headed by *People* magazine.... Employees learned of the news via internal memo.
—*New York Post*

FROM: Ann Moore, *People/In Style*
TO: Bruce Hallett and fellow Timesters
RE: What up?

Ka-ching, ka-ching.... There's a new sheriff in town. Kidding. Just a few minor changes, so we can all get on the same high-glossy stock.

Not too many formatting hiccups. First one, right out of the shoot, next issue, Page One on, everybody's name is in **bold**. You do this in a couple of sections already, why do you stop? Let's have a little stylistic consistency here. We're not just working to the John Grisham eggheads in the back of the room. **Bold** means pay attention. **Bold** means this is important. **Bold** means, stand back, there's a newsmaker coming through. Be honest. Who would you rather read about, Dick Cheney or **Dick Cheney**? (Quick question: Re: **Cheney**— Any chance on some of his favorite heart-healthy summer snack recipes?)

Say, what kind of computer setup do you have over there? I ask this because it seems every one of your keyboards is missing an exclamation point. This is important! See, even if it wasn't, I just made it important! With this!

You all seem like a bright bunch over there. Fans of vivid verbiage. Tell me, is there some kind of pun shortage in Midtown? Because after the headlines, your writers seem to pun-ch out. Readers like puns. They're fun. They're easy. No-body gets hurt. I thought of one on my way to Yog-assage this morning: "Discretion is the better part of velour." Find a spot for it somewhere. (Maybe **Tony Scalia** doesn't always wear an all-cotton robe.)

This is not meant to be a lesson in reporting (See next week's memo!), but remember your three *W*'s: *What? When? Where?* If your reader has to ask "Who?" ask yourself "why?" Then pick up your severance at the fourth *W*, the *Window*. (Wait . . . Maybe a new monthly of up-and-comers—*WHO!* Huh? Come on, give it to me!)

Speaking of what's wrong, do we have to call them "corrections"? What's the big deal? Must we call attention to every dropped stitch? Okay, we regret, we're sorry, but why must everything sound so apologetic? Change section to "Our Bad" or "So Sue Us."

Cover Stories

Two issues ago: "How the Universe Will End." What are you, nuts? "How Matthew Perry's Universe Almost Ended," sure. "How the Milky Way Disappeared from Carney Wilson's Solar System as Her Waistline Went from 'Help Me, Rounda' to 'Thin Thin Thin Since Daddy Took the T-Bone Away,'" fine. You want a space story? Tail George Lucas for a couple of weekends.

Winners and Losers

We're all family, but if you folks are going to steal stuff from us, do it right. How about some PEOPLE we've heard of? Jack Welch? Didn't Harrison Ford play him? Hey, how about Harrison Ford? Isn't a *Working Girl* retrospec-tacular long-overdue?

The Nation

Must we cover Washington every bloody week? Isn't that just so 1994? Aren't enough press pool monkeys doing that? Okay, sure, we led with the Bush Twins last month, but only because we'd be remiss as journalists if we didn't address underage drinking. And they're stone cold babes!

The World

No offense, but what is this obsession with world leaders? Friendly bet: We both start on either side of 42nd and Fifth. You walk with Saddam, I walk with Sade. Let's see who stops more traffic. Enough.

And maybe I didn't read the last issue thoroughly enough (Always a possibility!), but is everyone you infogeeks cover undressed? No? Then can we puh-lease mention a designer? Or six?

Hey!

I read somewhere (It may have been your mag!) that this guy Abu Nidal (sp?) is the Number Three threat to the United States. Who knew there was a list? And if there isn't, let's make one! "Sexiest Threats—Watch Out for These Guys!" Something like that. All I can come up with is this Boo Needle guy and Vince McMahon. Good start, though.

Oh yeah, what's with all the candid photos? Is your art department in that much of a hurry? I don't want to tell you ladies how to do your business, but three shots have really been good to us: The subject and his/her wife/husband/significant other/publicist in the kitchen cooking; the subject and his/her wife/husband/significant other/publicist on the couch wrestling; The subject and his/her wife/husband/significant other/publicist wrestling in the kitchen as a dog looks on. (Note: Check and see if Abe Booneydoll has a kitchen.)

People

Love the name of this section. Is that where we got it? And no complaints. Oh, except this: Eighty-two pages, one page devoted to celebrities. One. Uno. I counted. And didn't you bigshot "journalists" forget something—like a quote from the komodo dragon?

significant other

By the way, these stories write themselves. This memo wrote itself. Again, kidding.

Enough. That's all for now. It may take a while for the focus group data to come back, but to be sure, let's dummy up a cover with the mag's new name—are you ready?—

(It's) TIME!

(18–24 demo loves parentheses.)

KIM McCANN'S **DICHOTOMOUS WORLD**

Classic Quilt Pattern or Sexual Innuendo?

1. Log Cabin
2. Carpet Layer
3. Country Sampler
4. Riding the Dolphin
5. Visiting Down South
6. Ring Around the Nine Patch
7. Drunkard's Path
8. Double Irish Chain
9. Grandmother's Fan
10. Wild Goose

Key
1. quilt pattern
2. sexual innuendo
3. quilt pattern
4. sexual innuendo
5. sexual innuendo
6. quilt pattern
7. both
8. quilt pattern, except in Boston or Chicago, where it is both
9. quilt pattern
10. quilt pattern

SAG/AFTRA Strike Update

BILL SCHEFT

STRIKEUPDATESTRIKEUPDATESTRIKEUPDATES

The National Board of Directors of SAG and AFTRA voted to implement a strike of all television and radio commercial work, effective May 1. Other than zero movement on the part of Management (Hitherto referred to as "Employers," formerly referred to as "Suits," "Ad Monkeys," "Greaseballs" and "Massuh"), contract talks are going quite well. Just last week, we agreed on almost all of the selections for the bargaining table cheese tray. Below are answers to your most common questions.

Are all SAG/AFTRA members supposed to refrain from working during the strike?

No, just commercial actors. The following groups are not affected during the strike:

Actors in theatrical films
Actors in TV shows or radio programs
Actors in music videos
Successful people in general
Pop 'n Fresh
Tony Roberts

Are there, like, key issues on which both sides are far apart?

No, not at all. We thought it might be nice for everyone to walk around in a circle during the day, like we're all unpaid extras on *Law & Order*. Of course, there are key issues, Meisner.

cheese tray

Employers have proposed eliminating the present "pay per play" formula, where we receive compensation every time a commercial airs, and replacing it with a one-time payment for unlimited use. Hey, while they're at it, how about "don't ask, don't tell?" We want to retain "pay per play" and expand it to include a free 16-oz. soft drink every time a stranger recognizes us from commercials that are no longer being broadcast.

Employers have proposed major rollbacks of the already inadequate pay structure for commercials airing on cable television. We are looking for the same money Hitler gets every time he appears on A&E.

Employers have proposed reckless cuts in residual payments for puppeteers, stunt performers and magicians. We have no problem with this. In fact, we'd like to know how these freaks got into our union. And while we're at it, let's can-can all the tap dancers.

We want adequate compensation for radio commercials that air on the Internet. Employers not only refuse to discuss this, but claim they're a 5' 10" blonde with 36D breasts and keep asking for a credit card number.

We are vigorously pursuing increased numbers of contractually covered background actors. Employers want to pay all those peppy white dancers on those spots for the Gap as one guy. (Wait a minute. They're dancers. Okay, that's fine.)

We strongly advocate a more comprehensive method of monitoring the actual on-air use of radio and television commercials. Employers see no problem with the current setup, where responsibility for said monitoring rests solely with Roone Arledge's 15-year-old granddaughter, Roonetta.

Employers want to reserve the option to reedit commercials without additional compensation. This clearly infringes on our unwritten right to deliberately blow takes and stretch out commercial shoots into "golden time" for ourselves and our union brothers and sisters on the crew. It really doesn't, so forget that stuff about deliberately blowing takes. You never heard that, we never met, show's over, move along.

All this labor mumbo-jumbo is too confusing. And boring because, frankly, it isn't about me. Are there any petty demands we want included in the next contract?

You must not think very much of your elected union officials if you don't think we have petty demands. We're actors too, pal.

- We want to sing show tunes on the picket line, even after the strike is settled.
- Head shots must be increased 10 percent, to 8.8 × 11.
- $1 every time any vested union member's likeness appears on a surveillance camera for over 30 seconds.
- $100 hazard pay if you walk into an audition and the casting agent says either: "What the hell was I thinking?" "What the hell were you thinking?" or "Okay, send your son in."
- Double-scale if we have to say, "It's not Head and Shoulders. It's *new and improved* Head and Shoulders."
- Complete overhaul of pay structure for voice-over work. For some reason, under the current system, 50 percent of wages are automatically garnisheed to James Earl Jones.
- No more use during contract talks of the word "garnish." We have to say that enough during the dinner shift at the restaurant
- And speaking of the restaurant, before announcing the specials, we want the option of saying, "I'm Tim, I'll be your waiter this evening, and I'm seeking representation." Even if we are *not* seeking representation.
- Option during videotaped auditions to give name, astrological sign and triglyceride number.
- Option to coldcock any director who during commercial shoot utters the phrase, "I need a little more Adam Sandler."
- Additional employer contributions to our union health plan to cover any and all use of collagen. (This item is non-negotiable.)
- Complimentary dried smoked pig ear on set during shoot. (Taco Bell chihuahua only.)
- No cops.
- No negative ads. Just kidding.

This is your future. Get involved (We need people next Wednesday to carry a picket sign for the Hamburger Helper Helping Hand). Solidarity is our greatest weapon. We are willing to publicly expose and humiliate Kathie Lee Gifford as an example. The example being, ah, that this is what we do to our own.

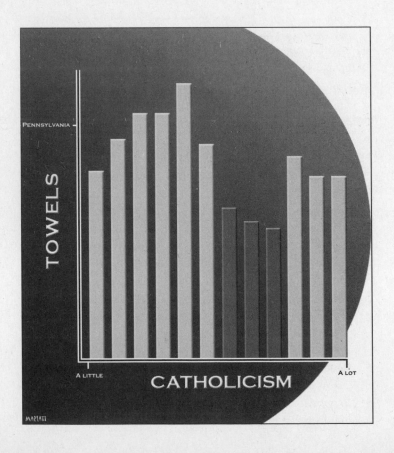

More Sins of the Fathers

BILL SCHEFT

In the widening wake of scandal, more church officials have decided to bravely come forward, admit previous wrongdoings and throw themselves upon the mercy of a forgiving public. (Last names are withheld to ensure piety.)

FATHER M: Took twenty-five 12-year-olds to a Braves-Phillies game at Veterans Stadium in 1985. Returned with twenty-seven 12-year-olds.

FATHER MCM: Sold lottery tickets through narrow opening in confession booth, which he nicknamed "slotto." Transferred in 1994 from Chicago to Milwaukee, where he changed his name.

FATHER SLOTTO: Transferred from Milwaukee to Laughlin, Nevada, in 1995, where he served four years before taking a leave of absence to write and produce the hit casino revue, *Nude Testament*.

FATHER B: Transferred from Claremont, California, to Montclair, California, after concluding a mass by saying, "You know what? Instead of one of those stuffy old hymns, how about something from *Pippin?*"

FATHER D: Every June from 1974 to 1989, had altar boys wear sneakers and white shorts for two weeks during Wimbledon.

MARK MCGWIRE: Former Cardinal. Now admits to hugging Roger Maris family "maybe a bit too long" after breaking home run record in 1999.

MONSIGNOR Q: Twice petitioned Vatican to bestow dual sainthood on Siegfried and Roy after he saw their 1988 New

Year's Eve show at the Mirage and counted eleven separate miracles.

FATHER L: Transferred to missionary in Beijing after countless reprimands to stop greeting fellow priests by saying, "Hail, Mary . . ."

CARDINAL F: Before transfer to Anchorage, ran the often-scrutinized Sante Fe archdiocese, where he tried unsuccessfully to recruit progressive-thinking priests with his two-day workshop, "Celibacy on a Need-to-Know Basis."

FATHER Z: Nine times between 1990 and 1992, before his transfer to Juneau, visited inmates on death row at the correctional facility in Del Rio, Texas, just to ask if they had the correct time.

PADRE S: When parishioners complained last year about church stand on birth control, suggested, in lieu of abstinence, to try staring at photographs of a shirtless Harvey Weinstein.

FATHER X: On at least 1,100 different occasions, eschewed protocol and ended confessions by barking, "Forget the Our Fathers, just drop and give me fifty."

BISHOP J: In 1971, dismissed suddenly as Sunday School teacher at St. Michael's after telling class the Old Testament was "too Jewish."

FATHER T: Transferred to International Falls after he paid church secretary $100 to type up a 1998 spec script for *Veronica's Closet*.

FATHER T: Despite years of diocese-subsidized aversion therapy, still cannot say "layperson" without giggling.

FATHER O'R: Transferred last month from New York City to Billings, Montana, after the Op-Ed page of the *Watchtower* published his questionable analysis of statistics claiming 50 percent of priests are gay. (Father O'R concluded the church could get that figure closer to 65 percent if there were more costume changes.)

FATHER B: Held up sign behind home plate during Game 2 of 1978 World Series that read, "Tommy John 3:16."

MONSIGNOR E: In 1981, used position and influence to get his one-year contract with the Columbia House Record and Tape Club annulled.

FATHER V: Boca Raton parishioners waged a vigorous letter-writing campaign on his behalf, but could not prevent his transfer to somewhere in Vermont. Among Father V's innovations: Replacing collection plate with a tip jar on top of the organ, and hiring an attendant to stand next to the holy water handing out towels.

CARDINAL R: During His Holiness John Paul II's 1994 American tour, on a dare from coworkers, installed the Club on the steering wheel of the bulletproof Popemobile before an appearance at Shea Stadium. Unfortunately, left the key in his other pants, but avoided serious disciplinary action when Mets reliever John Franco greased the Shea grounds crew, who allowed the Pontiff to ride in the bullpen cart wearing Vince Coleman's batting helmet.

FATHER G: Although alcohol was never officially determined to be a factor, during 1983 midnight mass reading of Christ chasing the money-changers from the temple, editorialized, "Oh, you know her, nobody else can ever have a good time."

RABBI V: Divorced, non-smoker, worldly. Enjoys long walks, klesmir music, a nice piece fish and the ironic notion of self-denial. Philosophy: God is love, and so am I. Seeks same. No freaks.

PMK's "The Odyssey"

STEPHEN SHERRILL

Sing to me of the man, O Celebrity Publicist
Of the twists and turns that befell your client
Once he had plundered the hallowed heights of Troy.

Odysseus and Penelope remain happily married, and are very much in love. Naturally, his work means that they sometimes have to spend time apart. And yes, for the Troy project, he has been gone some twenty years, and this presents difficulties, like Odysseus's sufferings in that lonely sea-girt island, far away, poor piteous man, from all his friends. But he and Penelope remain as solidly committed as ever. Any rumors to the contrary are absurd.

From time to time, Penelope has social gatherings at her house, and sometimes these are boisterous affairs. But the attendees were not clamorous, brazen and rascally suitors, but, rather, just friends and neighbors.

Nor did their son Telemachus drive them from the palace for devouring his father's treasure and slaughtering on and on his droves of sheep and shambling his oxen. I can assure you, all of Odysseus's sheep are doing just fine and his oxen have hardly been shambled. The dinner, as it happens, was a catered affair, Telemachus made a toast to his father, and a good time was had by all.

Odysseus has, I can confirm, visited Calypso on her island. But Calypso does not crave him for a husband, forever trying to spellbind his heart with suave, seductive words until Odysseus longs to die! They are just old friends. Years ago, they did date, briefly, which they often laugh about now. But they've remained friendly, and they often go out to dinner with their spouses.

When Odysseus left the island, he did come across Poseidon, but there's no "bad blood" between the two. In fact, they have greatest respect for each other's work, and look forward to working together in the future.

So obviously there's no reason why Poseidon would rouse the rage of every wind that blows till earth, sea, and sky are hidden in cloud, and night springs forth out of the heavens. To the contrary, they greeted each other warmly. Odysseus's ship was not wrecked by Poseidon. Odysseus simply docked it at Nausicaa for routine ship maintenance and the Lord of the Earthquake even gave Odysseus a loaner until the repairs and detail work were finished.

It is true that Odysseus made a stop in the land of the Lotus-eaters, and though he, like most people, engaged in harmless experimentation when he was a teenaged warrior, he now leads a very healthy lifestyle and has no desire for the honey-sweet fruit which makes you lose all desire to send a message back, and dissolves all memory of the journey home forever. If he did, there's hardly any way he could hurl a disc from his brawny hand that makes a humming sound in the air and flies beyond any marks that have been made yet.

Odysseus's route did, in fact, take him near the island of the Sirens. Naturally, Odysseus, like most people, is a big fan of the enchanting sweetness of the Sirens' high thrilling song, and has, in the past, stopped by to take in a set or two when he's in town.

On this particular occasion, however, he was running late. When he informed the Sirens' representatives that he was tied up, they mistakenly interpreted this as meaning that Odysseus was bound hand and foot, lashed to the mast of the swift ship by rope on chafing rope. Nothing could be further from the truth.

When he heard their ravishing voices float out across the air, his heart inside him didn't throb to listen longer, nor did he signal his crew with frowns, pleading to let him listen. He simply reminded his crew that they had to get to Scylla and Charybdis. He then sent the Sirens a bottle of champagne with a warm note of congratulations.

The reports of Odysseus and the Cyclops have also been quite exaggerated. Yes, they know each other. And, yes, they have had their minor differences. Anytime someone takes two of your best crewmen and sheds their brains upon the ground so that the earth is wet with their blood and then tears them limb from limb and sups upon them—tensions are bound to escalate. But as it turns out, the whole thing was a small misunderstanding. The two just sat down, talked it out, and cleared the air.

The subsequent, and unfortunate, loss of Cyclops's one giant eye was actually due to a hunting accident, and not from anyone driving the sharp end of a beam into a monster's eye, bearing upon it with all his weight, until the broiling eyeball burst. I cannot comment any further, as the matter is under pending litigation.

Regarding the irresponsible speculation about Odysseus and his relations with that nymph-goddess with lovely braids, Circe, specifically that she coaxed him into mounting her gorgeous bed to mix in the magic work of love that they may make friends and learn to trust each other, and that he then ended up making friends and learning to trust her day in and day out for an entire year, I would like to say the following: Please respect the privacy of Odysseus and Penelope at this sensitive and difficult time. Odysseus, though a great warrior, raider of cities, and son of Laertes, is still only a mortal. He has acknowledged that he has not been a perfect husband, and that he has caused pain in their marriage. His relationship with Circe was, on occasion, not entirely appropriate.

He would like to ask the forgiveness of his family, his men—at least those who weren't turned into swine by Circe (with grunts, snouts, even their bodies, yes!)—his many fans, his longtime supporters in Ithaca, and, most of all, Zeus, Lord of Thunder and Sire of Gods.

I would like to add, however, that, at the time, Odysseus was suffering from nervous exhaustion and overwork due to an overly ambitious killing and smiting schedule. He has also been struggling with substance-abuse issues stemming not from illegal drugs, but, rather, from prescription pain relievers he was given for a back problem caused by performing his own stunts in the Trojan Horse project.

Upon leaving Circe's palace, Odysseus did not, as some commentators have said, check into a private treatment facility in Hades, the mouldering Kingdom of the Dead. He was in Hades, but he was simply there to take a little time off, rest, get some reading done, visit some dead acquaintances, including his old childhood friend Sisyphus, of whom he's always been a big supporter.

When Odysseus finally arrived at home, there were no suitors there, and nobody was having their life ripped out, or being smitten on every side, making a horrible groaning as their brains were being battered in, and the ground seethed with their blood. It was just a routine homecoming from a business trip. Odysseus and Penelope and Telemachus had a quiet dinner by themselves and then watched *The Sopranos*.

I wish I could give you something more dramatic, but, clearly, there's just no story here.

. . . Divers rearrange deck chairs on Titanic . . . National Grammar Bee won by humorless know-it-all . . . Mars launches latest Earth probe . . . Gap widens between rich and super-rich . . .

Windows Messages, as Rewritten by Scott, This Guy Who Bullied Me in Second Grade

MATTHEW SUMMERS-SPARKS

Windows: In order to decrease the risk of being infected with a boot sector virus, remove the floppy disk before you shut down. Click OK after removing the disk.
Scott: If you don't remove your stupid floppy disk from your stupid floppy drive, I'm going to pound your skinny butt, Summers. Click OK. Quit crying.

Windows: System has encountered a fatal fault. Click DEBUG to see the error log.
Scott: Why do you wear that stupid purple jacket all the time? It makes you look like a dork. Fatal fault. Click DEBUG to see the error log of your ways. Dork.

Windows: Save changes to document? Click OK or CANCEL.
Scott: Hello, Matt. It's Scott. Now that we're adults, what do you say we meet for lunch? A little bistro just opened nearby; they serve excellent sandwiches. Let's catch up! I have some news to discuss with you concerning how you stink and your mom thinks you're dumb. Click OK or CANCEL.

Windows: Word has insufficient memory. Do you want to save the recovered file as RESCUE1.TXT? Click YES or No.
Scott: I have insufficient memory—aren't you a dork-head? Click YES to admit you're a dork-head and save your recovered file as I-AM-A-DORK-HEAD.TXT. Click No to delete your

recovered file. Only a dork-head deletes his recovered file. Dork-head.

Windows: Are you sure you want to exit Windows?
Scott: It's almost noon and I have a hankering for one of those bistro sandwiches. I'm out here, next to the Dumpster behind your building. Come on out—let's discuss you giving me your lunch money over a couple of knuckle sandwiches. Bring $6.95, plus $1.25 for a Sprite, plus tax. Make it $10. Get out here. Now. Exit Windows!

Windows: Do you want to permanently delete the document that is currently in your trash folder? Click YES or No.
Scott: I saw you. At 12:00, you exited out of a third-floor window and descended the fire escape. You then scampered into an idling car, *without giving me your lunch money*. Mommy picking you up for lunch was crafty but stupid—just like the old days. Here's the deal. After work. You and me. By the Dumpster. We'll reminisce about second grade. Sound like fun? Click YES.

Windows: Error extracting support files. Catastrophic failure. Click OK.
Scott: Your boss walked by the Dumpster at about 12:30. I chased after him and engaged him in a discussion of computers. He's a bright and engaging fellow; naturally, we hit it off. I shared my opinion that IBMs are for nerds and Macs are for girls. I was set to take his lunch money when he invited me to join him at the new bistro. How could I say no? We had an enlightening conversation about you. I inquired if you still wet yourself during book reports. He wouldn't say, but I bet you do. You're a catastrophic failure. Your boss says you need to work harder. Click OK.

Windows: An access request was received from client with an invalid signature attribute. Click OK.
Scott: Your boss offered me a job. He needs an opinionated go-

getter, an office disciplinarian, and someone who can stop invalid signature attributes. I'm considering the position. We're meeting at 4:30 to discuss compensation and benefits. I'll find your desk on my way out to let you know my decision. I'll ask the first person I see, "Pardon me, but have you seen a dorkus in a stupid purple jacket?" I'm going to pelt you with spitwads. Click OK.

Windows: Are you sure you want to delete Windows Help? Click DELETE *or* CANCEL.

Scott: For your information, I arrived at your company's lobby at 4:30 to announce that I *didn't* want to work with your stupid, crappy company. I could've not shown up, but turning you down in person was the classy thing to do. I didn't realize half the nerds from second grade worked there. When two dweebs and your boss restrained me against the elevator door, I suspected this wasn't my kind of work environment. The wedgie they gave me confirmed it. You showed great generosity by refusing to ratchet my wedgie. I thank you for that. I think the generosity you showed is the foundation for our new, beautiful friendship. The first question of our new life as best buds is: You don't really want to delete Windows Help and me, do you? Click CANCEL. Please. I'll be your best friend. Do you have an extra purple jacket for me?

Windows: After deleting Windows Help, the program will automatically load the backup Windows Help version. Revert to the backup Windows Help? Click YES *or* No.

Scott: You accidentally clicked DELETE on that last message. Big mistake, pal. Keep me around and we'll hit the road together. It'll be awesome. We'll bully our way across Europe and, if there's time, England. We'll be all dapper in matching purple jackets. I'll even stop calling you dork, dorkus, and dork-face. Just click *No.* . . . Uh-oh, you accidentally moved your cursor above the YES button. I'm surprised someone as brilliant and handsome as you might accidentally delete your pal Scott. Allow me to make one small change. . . . There! I changed the

Yes button to the My Name's Matt and I Admit That I Am, in Fact, a Stupid Dork-Face button. You're not a stupid dork-face! Don't click that button! C'mon, click No. . . . Uh oh, you clicked the Dork-Face button. So this is what it feels like to be deleted. I'm alone again. It's not so different from not being deleted. . . . Ah, I see what happened. You *haven't* deleted me: you clicked the Stupid Dork-Face button but kept your finger on your mouse button, so the command hasn't taken affect. Don't panic! It's not too late to save me. Stay calm. Don't wet yourself. Just press the Escape key to cancel the command. Think of Europe! England! I wouldn't delete you, dork. . . . Sorry! I didn't mean that *you* are a dork! I was thinking of another dork—

ROD LOTT'S LISTS
23 CONSECUTIVE SUBTITLES FROM CHAPTERS 13–15 OF BRUCE LEE'S *GAME OF DEATH* DVD

Aah!	Chi-yaah!
Woo!	Ah-waah!
Aah-ohh!	(Crack)
Wah-ah!	Woo-aah!
(Yelling)	(Groaning)
(Yelling)	(Gasping)
Wah!	(Gasping)
Wah!	(Bones Crack)
How do you like that?	Hakim!
Wah!	Hakim!
(Both Yelling)	Hakim?
Hyah!	

Ars Gratia Artis?

BETH TEITELL

What is art? Ah, who cares? The question's been belabored for centuries. Today's aspiring snob is faced with a more pressing problem: What *counts* as art?

Which art-related activities can be exhibit-dropped in the big cocktail party of life, and which might you just as well skip? Will anyone in East Hampton be impressed by a reference to the Impressionist blockbuster you've just seen, even if you attended the special members' viewing *and* took the docent tour? How about a MoMA screening of an experimental film (with a post-movie Q&A with the director)? Is it worth schlepping through a gallery crawl in the meatpacking district, or reading *ARTnews*? Should you work the terms "found art" or "installation" into your conversation?

Who knows, right? With all that's been written about Art— its transformative properties, the role of the artist in society, the relationship between viewer and object—none of the so-called experts have published a handbook detailing how many points you earn for any particular experience. And without proper guidance, how can we know which exhibits to attend, or at least claim to have attended, and which we can boast about *not* having seen?

If the National Endowment for the Arts really wanted to help the public, the agency would fund a team of social scientists to go out in the field and eavesdrop at 92nd Street Y PTA meetings; in the locker room at the LA Sports Club; courtside at the 'Sconset Casino tennis club in Nantucket. Armed with quantitative data, the researchers could compile a catalogue for would-be show-offs that would spell out what impresses who, and save all of us a lot of time.

So in case anyone in Washington cares, here are the issues that need clarification:

- Does lunching in a museum café count as culture? Does it entitle you to wear a lapel pin? Can you claim to have seen the museum's acclaimed Art of Oceania collection, or the wonderful Japanese screens, if you merely passed by them on your way into the restaurant (and were so absorbed in the wine/no wine question that you barely noticed your surroundings)? Is it worth your time to glance at the sculpture garden visible from your seat?
- Concerning museum gift shops: is the shop within the museum presumptively better than the museum store in the mall, since it provides proof that you were in a cultural institution and hints that you may have looked around while there? Is a Scarab necklace from the Met's gift shop morally superior to one sold at Bloomingdale's?
- Does going to a museum *only* to look at originals of art that hung in your dorm room (or art that's replicated on note cards nationwide) count at all? What about a show of celebrity photographs by Annie Lebovitz, or an Andy Warhol retrospective? Does either entitle the viewer to indulge in an expensive post museum dinner, confident that his or her cultural obligations have been fulfilled for the day?
- How long must one spend at an exhibit for it to count, and do you have to look at the art the whole time, or can some time be spent critiquing other art lovers? Is extra-credit awarded, and if so how much, for the following:

listening to the audio tour *without* skipping ahead

reading *and remembering* the explanatory signage; especially if it's faint and you have to fight your way to the front

sitting on a bench or the floor and sketching a painting or sculpture—without doing so to impress girls (or guys)

- Does having a membership to a museum excuse you from going? What about serving on the board? Is meeting someone at a "Friday night swings" singles event, in which you drink and mingle among the Masters, the kind of detail worthy of inclusion in the *New York Times* wedding announcement?
- Are there entire museums that don't earn any points at all? Can we get a ruling on the Museum of Television & Radio, please? Is watching "A Toast to Dean Martin," or "The World of Hanna-Barbera" at the (wink, wink) *museum* any more intellectual than seeing it on TV at home?
- Should you buy coffee-table books? And if so, should they be displayed, or are they better used as a stealth weapon, stored on a bookcase (overcrowded, of course) and grabbed off the shelf in the excitement of the moment? What about an exhibit poster? Is there any place in the home, besides the guest bathroom or your teenager's room, where they may be hung?
- And finally, under the no-pain-no-gain theory, can one *ever* earn credit at an exhibit that doesn't induce "museum fatigue"? And in a related matter, is "museum fatigue" a medically recognized condition? And if so, should sufferers be encouraged to leave the museum as quickly as possible and retire to a nearby bar for some life-saving hydration?

Onward and upward with the arts!

Diagnostic and Statistical Manual of Mental Disorders DSM-IV: Subsection: Food-Related Disorders

BETH TEITELL AND KEN MANDL

RESTAURANT NERVOSA

The individual exhibits a marked and extreme fear that his plate or glass will be whisked away by the waiter before he has eaten the last bite of fava bean and pecorino salad, or taken the final sip of Shiraz. Desperate to stay safely within the so-called "Are you still working on that?" zone, the patient/patron afflicted by r. nervosa may be unable to eat more or drink more than half of his portion. As a result, the sufferer often becomes dangerously thin. On the rare occasions when his guard is down and he loses his last mouthful, the poor schmuck still feels he "didn't eat anything—they took away my whole meal."

POST-TRAUMATIC FRUIT STRESS DISORDER

This ailment follows exposure to a sudden and unexpected rotting of fruit. The disease primarily affects females in their fourth decade, who develop an overwhelming fear that fruit will go bad before it is eaten. A common stressor event is the over-ripening of an exorbitantly priced box of out-of-season raspberries. A compulsion to prevent the wasting of fruit can overtake the patient. In one case a woman developed "banana bread creep"; over a period of a few weeks, she made banana breads with progressively less ripe bananas, eventually inflicting inedible gift loaves, made with crunchy green bananas, on family, friends and coworkers. Vitamin supplementation is an important part of the therapy in patients who replace all fruit in the diet with spoil-free substitutes such as Dots and Cherry Coke.

SEATLESS IN SEATTLE RAGE SYNDROME

SSRS was first reported in the Pacific Northwest, but is now common on both coasts. Genetically predisposed people become enraged when, after having purchased a Starbucks coffee, they are unable to get a seat. Sufferers report anger at those customers who place a newspaper or other "placeholder" on a table before ordering, and at those whose laptops are plugged into wall outlets. In the mild form, a person with SSRS will glare at seated patrons. In the more severe form, he will ask if "that seat is taken," join the perceived "enemy occupier" and initiate chat. A major risk factor for a severe episode is having ordered the beverage "for here" in an earth-tone ceramic mug.

BORDERLINE ORDER DISORDER

The BOD patient becomes consumed with regret over ordering the "wrong thing" at a restaurant, and desperately attempts to rectify matters. Upon hearing the waitress compliment another's order—"the sea bass is wonderful tonight"—the individual may try to switch his order to the sea bass. If he realizes that it is too late, he may fall into a depressive episode lasting weeks or months. Alternatively, he may attempt to establish an entrée-sharing relationship with his co-diner, invariably wolfing down nearly the entire Chilean bass and permanently marring a friendship. Additionally, the BOD patient who does not order the elaborate chocolate dessert soufflé at the start of the meal may sink into a downward spiral of self-reproach and doubt, as he might if he *did* order the soufflé, but then found the main course more filling than anticipated.

HOSTESS GIFT PARANOIA

Suffering from severe persecutory delusions, the HG Paranoid "knows" that the bottle of pinot noir or fruit salad she brings to a dinner party or holiday gathering will be intercepted—by a guest who's deputized himself as a para-host, perhaps, or the partner who doesn't keep track of such things—and she will never get credit for her offering. Believing others are out to make her look like a shnorrer, the individual may resort to extreme measures to link herself to her gift, bringing a dessert that requires her to engage in ostentatious preparation mid-party, such as a last-minute flambé. While some evidence suggests the prognosis for this type of paranoia may be considerably better than for other types of the disease (particularly the "Is This Decaf? It Tastes Like Regular" variant), there are unfortunate cases in which the HG Paranoid becomes so sure her gift has gone unrecorded that she steals it back at the end of the evening.

TRANSFAT ISOLATION SYDROME (FORMERLY AGORAPHOBIA: TRANSFAT VARIANT)

Victims of TIS have an unnatural fear of consuming saturated or transfats and are unable to order normally in a restaurant. This behavior interferes with the most important coupling ritual of all: the dinner date. There is a published report of an individual whose girlfriend left him after he ordered steamed vegetables as an entrée at Smith & Wollensky. Another patient, on a first date at the Olive Garden, was thrown out by the restaurant manager after he set off the smoke detector while burning a sample of the Chicken Siena in a calorimeter.

Excerpts from
Richard's Poor Almanac

RICHARD THOMPSON

Spring Weeding Guide

Richard's Poor Almanac by Richard Thompson

NON-EUCLIDEAN CREEPER. Hard to remove. Ignores the geometry of the Space-Time Continuum common to most yards.

FALSE TEA ROSE. Looks & smells exactly like the lovely tea rose. But it's a weed! Soon your yard will be covered in it! Root it out! Tear it up! Kill it!

BAMZU. Combines the robust un-stoppability of kudzu with the hearty immortality of bamboo. It also attracts zebra mussels. Sell your house and get a condo.

DILATORY BULBVINE. Also known as YOUR LEFTOVER CHRISTMAS LIGHTS. Take them down already, it's Easter for crying out loud.

Richard's Poor ALMANAC — SKY HIGHLIGHTS FOR JUNE — by Richard THOMPSON

EARLY JUNE - Mercury, named for the god of Hyperactivity & Small Sweater Dogs, races in hectic random patterns across the evening sky, to everyone's extreme annoyance.

JUNE 12 - A newly discovered constellation appears in the west, near Thermidor, the Lobster. Scientists are divided as to whether it most resembles a lawn chair, a box of fried wontons or the head of Trent Lott.

ow ow ow hot hot hot ow ow

JUNE 20-22, SUMMER SOLSTICE - The Sun, a flaming ball of mostly hydrogen, loiters in the sky for 15 hours. It was once thought to be borne across the sky by Apollo, the god of Commuting, using big oven Mitts, but now we know better.

There's one!

Where?

Nope. I'm wrong

LATE JUNE - Jupiter, named for the god of Gassy Lethargy, heaves briefly into view then drops below the horizon with a wet squelchy sound. Stay indoors.

An over-hyped yet severely disappointing meteor shower is tentatively scheduled for the end of the month. It'll peak at 3:15 a.m. so don't miss it!

New Used Gibbous Bilious Sullen Boorish

Richard's Poor Almanac

Stargazing This Week
by Richard Thompson

Virago · Spot · Lacto the Milk Carton · Spirochete · Teleprompter · The Big Zigzag · Gary the CVS Assistant Manager · Speculum · Puddingcup · Rictus · Spinalzo · Jellomold

Hello Stargazers! Well, this week the night sky is a mess, an incoherent mishmash of mostly second-rate constellations. Frankly, I've done dot-to-dots on the Kids Menu at Bennigan's that were more compelling.

Phut

"Chapter One—the Infomercial"

Also, the planets are all clumped up in one corner, including some that don't even belong in our solar system. This seems unnecessary, wasteful even, and is best ignored.

Finally, the annual "Insipid" Meteor Shower promises fitful glimpses of random flaming space lint. Why bother? Go watch TV, or work on your novel, or both.

What the Hell Are You Looking At?

JEFF WARD

One of the many Gap stores near my apartment has a massive photo of a boy's face in the window. He's about 20 and windblown. I had passed him for about a week before realizing I always felt guilty in his presence. Glancing up at him vaguely wrecked my mornings, and I had begun to dread the encounter. One day, tempted to go out of my way to avoid him, I deliberately walked up to the giant face instead to see why it disturbed me so much.

Of course, any giant head can cause fear. But this wasn't the typical disquiet you'd get from seeing Nancy Reagan or the Bullwinkle balloon right up close. This guy had a look of *haunted distaste*, a reproachful glare that seemed rooted in some injury I had done him, and possibly his family, long ago.

What was he remembering? It seemed to be a physical assault of some kind, or perhaps a heinous act of negligence. Knowing me, I had probably gotten drunk when he was a kid, demanded he come along for a joyride in the Jeep, then thrown him from the moving vehicle, mistaking him for the empty Beefeater bottle in my left hand. The details are lost to history, but the point is I've returned all these years later, drawn by his fat modeling paychecks, exquisite collection of tropical-weight wools and amazing bone structure, and oafishly offered to "make friends." He can't believe my egotistical gall.

After this painful encounter with the giant bitter boy, I started seeing his expression on hundreds of smaller models. On bus stops, magazines and newspaper spreads, models used their gorgeous pusses to convey a single attitude: "Oh. So look who's back. My deadbeat dad."

Now, in the old days you'd be driving your Studebaker through the countryside and a buxom girl would beam at you from a billboard, exuberantly thrusting a Coca-Cola at you. Of course, this was largely drug-related. Cokes contained actual coke in those days, so some extra enthusiasm is understandable. But for the most part, models in the last century made some kind of effort to stimulate your pleasure center so that commercial intercourse might occur.

You can get pleasure from the demure type, too, used to sell upper-register perfumes and liquor. He or she is unapproachable, isolated in the gleaming onyx world of whatever brand of vermouth—but not irreconcilably offended by the viewer. Even Twiggy was fun to look at—blank, famished Twiggy, whose subtext was that if she kept standing for one more picture, maybe you'd give her a sandwich. But this is a fourth, profoundly mysterious category.

They don't want you to buy what they're wearing, but simply to abide by the terms of the restraining order.

They want you to stop looking at this damn ad right now. Haven't you done enough harm?

What do you keep coming around here for?

My own line of business is kosher lawn ornaments and bladder-control toothpaste. I don't know from advertising, but come on—is it really good to make the viewer feel like a hulking pervert? I usually don't even notice the brand they're selling, just my body odor.

Oh, I just remembered an especially harrowing example, from my optometrist's. On a poster for Ralph Lauren Children's Eyewear, there's a ten-year-old blonde kid in a school tie and sweater. Behind his spectacles, he wears an expression of wounded disgust, as if you not only molested him once but also just farted. Nor—and this is key—*could you redeem yourself in his eyes by buying his brand of glasses,* because let's face it, who are you kidding?

Kids in general do this expression as well as adults, or better. I started seeing it in pictures my sisters sent me of their kids. "Wendy," I asked, "are you giving your kids smack? Because, no offense, but they look like models." And last Thanksgiving in Louisville I took a photograph of three of them and I swear, before my eyes, their faces took on The Look—eyes crinkled with distant loathing, nostrils flaring at some nearby imagined bucket of scat. Of course, I know better than to demand that kids stop channeling the Zeitgeist; they're little mood rings and can't help it.

And God knows my parents must have looked at me and my peers, with our putty-colored spats, raccoon collars and freshly minted sardonic Dadaism, and thought, "Ye gods." Yes, we're all mere conduits, just scales on the chameleon. Today our models hold a sneering grudge against us; tomorrow it may be we who have the upper hand, staring appalled at their uncouth likenesses while they, like cannibal troglodytes, try to wipe the blood and gristle from their faces as they skulk away in hot, blistering shame.

Anything is possible. They may even learn to keep their lunches down back at the cave.

kosher lawn ornaments

ROD LOTT'S LISTS
13 ERNEST MOVIES THEY NEVER GOT TO MAKE

Ernest Goes to Compton
Ernest Saves Kwaanza
Ernest Scared Shitless
Bitch-Slap Ernest
Ernest Goes to Golden Corral on Sundays
Ernest Saves $2.99
Ernest in the Salvation Army
Ernest Goes to Pot
Wham-Bam Ernest
Ernest Goes to Hell
Ernest Scared All Children
Ernest Goes Postal
Drop Dead Ernest

It's All True

JEFF WARD

The HBO film *RKO 281* represents a new surge of interest in the writer, director and star of *Citizen Kane*—the greatest film of the sound era, and the most powerful influence on my own vision as a filmmaker (and my favorite movie!)—Orson Welles.

He has grown to encompass all of society. From dazzling new story techniques to false radio reports, his inventions have at last been embraced by the public who, long hostile, chased him into a tar pit in November 1949 and jeered at his blubbery form as he attempted to escape and reedit *The Magnificent Ambersons*. His ignoble death now seems the final striking image of a macabre *oeuvre* in the *Rashomon*-style *chiaroscuro* of the *nouvelle vague* canon.

In the era of his posthumous prestige, however, many have adopted Orson as a mascot without learning the basic facts of his career. About *Kane*, in particular, the public is heroically misinformed.

It was made on time and under budget; it was a commercial and critical success; it was not innovative; and starred the Three Stooges. It was not the first feature to exploit deep-focus techniques, nor the first to show Mothra in a filmy two-piece swimsuit.

Yet the misconceptions abound, as many continue to claim Orson as an influence without absorbing his creative essence. How many goateed *cinéastes*, so facile with a reference to *Touch of Evil*, would have fought to preserve it from studio butchery in 1942, when Orson was in Brazil shooting *Here Come the Nelsons*? How many of these name-dropping *auteurs*, discussing *Verfremdungseffekt* in *Kane* over *café noir*, have dismissed my films as "tedious"—unaware that *Kane* is one of the most boring movies ever made?

Despite the thicket of toadyism that surrounds his work, it retains its force and mystery. Unfortunately, the puzzle about Welles that most interests the public is, "What would you say is the most Orson Welles ever weighed? At one time, I mean?"

It is the showman in Welles/me that condescends to publish here some corpulent facts from Simon Callow's *Chives at Midnight*, due in March:

- Among U.S. cities ranked by square footage, Orson Welles would appear just behind Pluto.
- If Orson Welles were a satellite of Earth, he would circle the planet twenty-three times before his orbit decayed. Upon impact, he would create a crater 100,000 times wider than any other director. His left buttock alone would destroy Utah, and seriously damage other cracker states.
- Orson spent the last year of his life making a children's movie, which he finally admitted was just a ploy for luring children into a darkened room, where they could be buttered and eaten.
- Although he was grossly obese most of his life, Welles thought himself slender—"A stripling, a mere slip of a lad," he told doctors. He favored tube tops and Capri pants, and nauseated beachgoers with his brightly colored thong. He mocked other fat people, shouting, "Hey, flabby! You—chub! You sure ate your potatoes, didn't you!"
- Orson required the Heimlich maneuver at over forty Los Angeles restaurants. He died in October 1985 when the head of a hog he had eaten entered his aorta, causing blockage. Peter Bogdanovich and eight other diners joined to encircle the choking Welles, but were one person short. Ironically, Steven Spielberg, who had paid $425,000 for the "Rosebud" prop sled, sat eating nearby, oblivious to the cinematic disaster taking place.

New on DVD

JEFF WARD

Sense and Sensibility—Columbia/Tristar, 1995 (PG); Theatrical Trailer; $32.00

The Sussex of 1811, impressively recreated in Emma Thompson's film adaptation, is overwhelmingly *alive* on DVD. The rendering of the period's clothing and furniture is worthy of a time machine, and the countryside is so lush you'll smell the damp hay.

But the crispness of the format reveals a number of anachronisms—in a church cemetery, for instance, one can easily read "DIED 1915" on a tombstone. A niggling detail; but what of the vehicle that carries Col. Brandon so urgently to attend his ailing daughter in London? It is clearly a Pinto.

Careful viewing reveals distant power lines, contact lenses, a Timex watch, a Monkees poster—overall, a level of sloppiness not hinted at by the VHS.

The "enormous tome" sent to Elinor by the dashing Edward turns out to be *Yes I Can* by Sammy Davis Jr. Most flagrantly of all, in a medium shot of Marianne stuffing herself with JiffyPop and Tofutti by lava lamp, she sets down her bong and switches on *American Bandstand*, where Salt 'N' Pepa are doing their 1994 hit "Shoop"—nearly wrecking the believability of this otherwise masterful film. (*Bandstand* went off the air in 1989.)

Taxi Driver (Special Edition)—Columbia, 1976 (R); Widescreen, Dolby; $19.95

With its musical numbers removed, *Taxi Driver* became a grim urban drama instead of the delightfully tappy confection envisioned by Scorsese. Seeing them restored reminds us what a lithe, spruce dance team De Niro and Foster were.

The songs are pure champagne. Herrmann & Ebb's "When You're Pimpin'" and "Tippy-Tappin' Teen-Whore from Old Times Square" are the zenith of Columbia production numbers; and De Niro's specialty, "Bickle with a B," redefines the water ballet.

The Wizard of Oz—MGM, 1939 (G); $24.98

The big surprise is Kansas—the opening sequence is revealed as a series of Dorothea Lange tableaux, hardly less vivid in their evocative dustiness than Oz itself. Just as surprising is the original ending, unseen since Louis B. Mayer ordered it cut after a disastrous Pomona preview. After Dorothy's famous exclamation, "There's no place like home," Miss Gulch enters her bedroom and demands the return of the escaped Toto.

Uncle Henry and Aunt Em reread the order from the Sheriff and again hand the dog over to Gulch, who this time seals it into her basket with a thick bicycle chain and bears it outdoors to be shot. Dorothy, hysterical, pleads with the farmhands to rescue Toto using their brains, hearts and courage. "We're drifters, Dorothy," they explain, and exit to dig the dog a grave.

"Life is bleak, Dorothy," counsels Aunt Em. "All living things die. You'll be dead too, someday. Then there's an afterlife—but that's an open question, to say the least."

Professor Marvel opens a newspaper and announces the Nazi invasion of Poland. Everyone stares, numb with apprehension, as shots ring out in the yard and Dorothy, now irreversibly unhinged, screams uncontrollably. Fade to credits.

Commentary track by Sam Peckinpah and Lorna Luft.

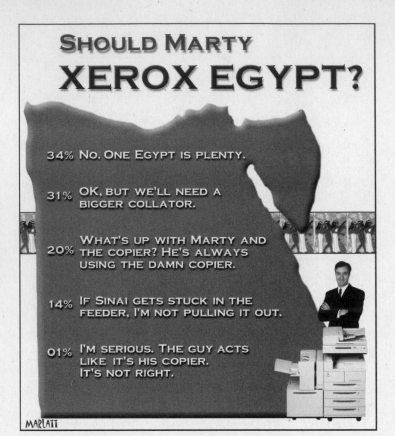

Obit Wan Kenobi

JEFF WARD

ALEC GUINNESS DIES

Sir Alec Guinness, the elegant and versatile actor known for roles in *The Bridge on the River Kwai* and *Star Wars*, died in England yesterday. In a tribute, critic Tom Shales called the actor a "sly genius" with a "chameleonlike face." That's because Sir Alec, more than other actors of his generation, had a laterally flattened head crested with spines, and bulging, independently rotating eyes.

Given his first break by John Gielgud, the young Alec won acclaim in a wide variety of stage roles. He became the toast of London for his Tybalt, then made a memorable Hamlet, in which he laid eggs onstage, then shed his skin and lay panting under a warm spotlight for the rest of the play. Unlike newts and salamanders, Sir Alec was knighted in the late '50s, after appearing as the prim, stodgy colonel in *The Bridge on the River Kwai*.

In one famous scene, he is shut up by the Japanese in a sweltering tin box, but survives by lapping from a nearby lagoon with his 35-foot tongue.

Younger fans were introduced to Sir Alec in 1977, when he appeared as the old Jedi Obi-Wan Kenobi in *Star Wars*. Although he didn't care for the film, he earned over $4 million from his percentage of the gross. True to form, he blew it on flies and small rodents, according to his costar Mark Hamill, who was then a 24-year-old Monitor lizard.

He is survived by the entire iguana family.

The *New York Times* Book Section Reviews My First High School Date

JOHN WARNER

In John Warner's first high school date, *Casual Dinner with Lori Victorson*, we are given (very) brief glimpses of wry, self-deprecating humor, and even some nascent signs of mid-adolescent charm. Unfortunately, these (very) mild pleasures are buried under an avalanche of bad planning, stammering, half-sensical attempts at conversation, and an omnipresent patina of rank gooniness.

While it strains credibility that the button-cute Ms. Victorson would ever accept Mr. Warner's invitation to "do something, sometime, umm . . . somewhere, you know," extending their relationship beyond Mr. Warner retrieving Ms. Victorson's dropped pencil in Biology lab, we are asked to suspend this disbelief as we enter *Casual Dinner*, a kind of loose sequel to Mr. Warner's ill-conceived eighth-grade effort, *Sadie Hawkins Dance with Karen Bach*.

By structuring *Casual Dinner* as a solo outing, Mr. Warner tries to avoid the pitfalls of the group date of *Sadie Hawkins*, where Mr. Warner's reticent nature was lost amongst the braying yet arresting pre-dance dinner high jinks of Todd Lobtarski, who employed his signature, "unscrewing the top *almost all the way off* the salt shaker so some unsuspecting diner dumps salt *all over* his food." This rough bravado led to an evening ending with Mr. Lobtarski whirling his blue blazer over his head while getting "funky" to Kool and the Gang, surrounded not only by his own date, but Ms. Bach as well. Meanwhile, Mr. Warner leaned against a nearby wall and counted the number of boards constituting the gymnasium floor.

As hard as it may be to believe, *Casual Dinner* is actually a step backward.

That said, *Casual Dinner* actually gets off to a fairly promising start. In greeting the father and older brothers Warner demonstrates solid eye contact, an engaging though braces-marred smile, and a firm, assured handshake, even when faced with oldest brother Thor Victorson's Viking-bred, meat-slab hand.

Sadly, *Casual Dinner* descends into madness when Mr. Warner fails to check the rearview mirror when exiting the Victorson family driveway. One would think that with the admonition of Driver's Education instructor Frank Lobedel "if you don't keep your goofy head on the road you're going to kill someone someday" still fresh in his ears, Mr. Warner would demonstrate more caution.

Alas, he does not.

Fortunately, the precious Pico (a Pekinese) survives mostly unharmed. What should have been an easygoing, breezy opening of light conversation about the vagaries of high school life instead turns into a formless hash of animal howls and desperate screaming from all corners.

The subsequent drive to the restaurant is mostly uneventful: Mr. Warner strangles the steering wheel as Ms. Victorson snuffles softly in the passenger seat. The attempts at dialog are pathetic. Mr. Warner inexplicably revisits the recent near tragedy, letting loose the groan-worthy, "Shouldn't a dog like that be kept inside?" One imagines that only through a supreme act of will did Ms. Victorson restrain herself from leaping free of the moving car, as an evening of tweezing road gravel and broken glass out of assorted cuts and abrasions would have been preferable to continuing this disastrous date with such a simpering boob.

As Mr. Warner and Ms. Victorson suffer a 45-minute wait for a table due to Mr. Warner's failure to make a reservation, we are "treated" to a kind of amateur improv that works a precarious balance between the mundane and the unexpected, the banal and the bizarre, the result of which is about as tasty as the underarm of a women's professional tennis player after a tough five-setter.

In truth, the less said about Mr. Warner's stab at chivalry while ordering dinner ("I'll have the veal and the lady will have the faffer . . . fallafer . . . feffer . . . bow tie pasta in cream sauce") the better.

Ditto for Mr. Warner's unfortunate encounter with his spinach salad ("Uhh . . . John, I think there's something in your teeth. No, to the left . . . the left. Nope, further, other one . . . left, left, left . . . Maybe you should just get a toothpick and go to the bathroom"). *Shudder.*

Six of the following seven words can be used to describe the interminable passage of the dinner conversation, the seventh can be used to describe the personality of a Staffordshire terrier: dolorous, crude, strained, hackneyed, sparkling, desperate, arrhythmic, bland.

At the culmination of this dreadful repast, Mr. Warner, at his panicky worst, blames a missing credit card (his mother's, natch) on "shallow pants pockets" of all things, and in a shocking breach of etiquette asks Ms. Victorson if she "has any cashola on her." That he places the varied (and frankly, disgusting) bits of effluvia (crumbs, matches, used Kleenex, and a "Smurfette" key chain) exhumed from the vinyl cushions of the restaurant booth *in front of* Ms. Victorson as he conducts his fruitless hunt for the missing card defies all possible logic. Ultimately, one does feel some sympathy for Mr. Warner when the waitperson (rather cruelly) informs him that "Mommy says you left the card on the kitchen table, and she's on her way to take care of things," but not much.

After the unmitigated disaster of dinner, Mr. Warner's hand on knee attempt during the silent drive home is as implausible as it is unwelcomed by Ms. Victorson. Perhaps Ms. Victorson goes overboard when, upon returning to school, she subsequently transfers into a different Biology class, so as to avoid further contact with Mr. Warner, but if one wishes to argue strenuously otherwise, they will not get strong disagreement from this reviewer.

At the last, we see Mr. Warner hunched into fetal form, rolling around his bed, moaning "why me" into his pillow over and over. Here, Mr. Warner makes a desperate plea for the evening to be chalked up to the frowning fates, but in the end, the best that can be said is that Mr. Warner falls a hair short of repulsive. For the sake of girlhood, this reviewer hopes that Mr. Warner's next foray into social relations with the opposite sex is titled *Brief Conversation at the Water Fountain*.

The Columbia Letters

KEVIN GUILFOILE AND JOHN WARNER

In March 2001, Three Rivers Press published the Modern Humorist book My First Presidentiary. *That summer, a college student contacted the authors and asked them for help with a class project. The following exchange was the sad result. Because she, understandably, no longer returns the authors' e-mails, the name of the student has been changed.*

To: Kevin Guilfoile and John Warner
From: Marcia Williams
Date: Wed, 11 Jul 2001

Dear Mssrs. Guilfoile and Warner,

As part of a book production workshop at the Columbia Publishing Program, a group of students and I are completing an assignment in which we pretend to launch a list of books at an imaginary publishing house. One of the six titles we came up with is a humor book about Jenna and Barbara Bush and their recent underage drinking digressions. It's entitled *Jenna and Barbara's Ultimate Party Guide* and features wacky things like "How to Make a Foolproof Fake ID," among other things. As part of this book launching assignment, the "editors" are supposed to contact people who could author these potential books to see if they think the idea is viable, etc. We thought your book was hilarious and thought you would do a good job with our "pretend book."

What do you think?

Many thanks,
Marcia Williams

To: Marcia Williams and John Warner
From: Kevin Guilfoile
Date: 7/13/01

Marcia,

My first impression is that a book like *Jenna and Barbara's Ultimate Party Guide* could be funny, but I'm not sure John and I would write it. Around the time we wrote our book, there were rumors the television program *That's My Bush!* was going to turn Jenna and Barbara into lesbian crime fighters, but we thought the kids should be considered out of bounds for our purposes.

Maybe this is my old age talking (I'm 32 and John will be 79 in September) but I feel a little sorry for Jenna and Barbara. When we were their age (1987 for me and 1939 for John) fake IDs were so accepted you didn't even have to have them printed and laminated. You'd just carry around the giant cardboard template and when you got to the bouncer you'd stick your head in the huge rectangular hole.

So you see, there's the hypocrisy issue.

Does that mean we'd say no? Of course not. You've talked about a pretend book, but you haven't mentioned pretend money. Our fake principles are for sale in exchange for an unprecedented fake advance.

If I were writing such a book, however (John, feel free to tell me I'm full of beans, using the vernacular of that "greatest generation" of yours), I might make it *Barbara and Jenna's Ultimate College Guide*. Then the humor wouldn't hinge entirely on one night when some cranky Chi-Chi's manager decided to narc them out to the local 5-0 (Those are policemen, John. You would call them "flatfeet" or "bobbies"). And you'd also have the state school vs. Ivy League thing which is always fun (I attended Notre Dame, incidentally, and John graduated from the Missouri College of Osteopaths).

I would also make them lesbian crime fighters.

Anyway, those are my thoughts. John has to take his glycerin pills so when his nurse wakes him up I'm sure he'll have something to say.

Best,
Kevin

To: Marcia Williams and Kevin Guilfoile
From: John Warner
Date: 7-14-01

Dear Marcia,

Frankly, I'm surprised that Kevin was able to get Internet access inside the "facility" and doubly surprised that he could type so fluidly with his hands straitjacketed behind his back.

In any event, ignore his mindless jibber-jabber as the hopeless ramblings of a desperate crank addict because that's exactly what he is, a desperate crank addict. Most of Kevin's time is usually spent "explaining" to his handlers how everyone should type in wingdings (confidential to Kevin: ♌︎✿◆♏︎ ○♏︎), instead of slandering me, but let me just clear up a couple of his most egregious trespasses into Kookyville.

One, my birthday is in April, and two, my alma mater is the College of Osteopathy at the University of Missouri at Cape Girardeau, the Battling Barnstormers as our intercollegiate sports organizations are known.

Kevin should also be ignored as to your question about whether or not "we" would be interested in writing your hypothetical *Jenna and Barbara's Ultimate Party Guide* because I am the one who does all the writing. Kevin does the drawing, which doubles as part of his state-mandated therapy.

I believe your project holds some hypothetical commercial promise, because, let's face it, that the President's daughters are a couple of teenage boozehounds is chuckle-worthy in and of itself. Not that it is so wrong for a couple of carefree young lasses to imbibe the demon alcohol in their carefree college years. Even in my day, at the weekend football set-to, we would let the attractive females (I believe your generation calls them "Bettys") nip from flasks of cognac we kept secreted in our furs.

Just for craps and titters, though, how much pretend money ("Bling Bling" in your vernacular) are we talking about, and is it possible that the money could be remunerated in the form of one of those oversized checks? (I have a collection which includes the very first winner's check received by Babe Didrikson Zaharias in the early days of the women's professional golf tour. We dated, you see.)

Best,

John Warner

To: Marcia Williams and John Warner
From: Kevin Guilfoile
Date: 7/14/01

Marcia,

My coauthor's claims regarding his contributions to *My First Presidentiary* are not just hyperbole, they are slander. Hyperslanboldery.

What John describes as "doing all the writing" consisted mostly of crying out from his wheelchair in the middle of some lesion-induced hallucination with an idea like, "Suppose the President is riding in a motor-car rumble seat with Lindbergh and Three-Finger Brown . . ." and in the middle of the non-sequitur-to-be he'd drift off to sleep, letting his glass of Bordeaux bleed onto the crease of his Sans-a-belts.

But let's get back to the real issue here, which is the viability of your Jenna and Barbara party concept. Valerie Harper's *Today I Am a Ma'am* aside, the purpose of publishing a humor book is to get as many people as possible to buy it. The Jenna and Barbara party book would likely be targeted to a pretty narrow audience: hip kids who know all the "lingo" and who wear their pants at Festus-on-*Gunsmoke* holster height.

This is usually the point in the conversation, by the way, where John lurches to his feet and yells "Jam banana time munster skip DIDDLE-FEE (gurgle-gargle) zhoooo-WIIIIING!!"

Also, there are the remaining questions of whether Jenna and Barbara are appropriate targets for the humorist and how we will be paid. My answers are "definitely not," and "wire transfer."

Best,
Kevin

To: Kevin Guilfoile and John Warner
From: Marcia Williams
Date: 7-15-01

Hi Kevin and John,
Thanks so much for your invaluable opinions on our book idea for what might seem a very vague assignment. As for the topic of the "advance negotiations."
Since you are the brilliant authors (or artists, as the case may be) of *My First Presidentiary*, you could probably name your sum. Any fictional amount can be wired anywhere. Swiss bank accounts, you name it.

Best,
Marcia

To: Marcia Williams and Kevin Guilfoile
From: John Warner
Date: 7-17-01

Marcia:
Regarding our hypothetical payment, I have dispatched my best carrier pigeon to your location with the details of my compensation demands in return for my services in pretending to write *Jenna and Barbara's Ultimate Party Guide*. While my monetary needs are large (trust that you have not seen this many zeros since Noodles Hahn first signed with the Cincinnati Red Stockings), you may have more difficulty acquiring the "extras," but fret not, they are illegal only in Hawaii and Alabama (and

only then if they are transported in improperly labeled containers). Kevin's payment, as per the standing court order, will be kept in a blind trust, with 85 cents released weekly for his personal use at the "facility" commissary. If he saves wisely, in nine short weeks he will be able to purchase the "naked lady" playing cards he seems to treasure so greatly.

Considering the colorful nature of Kevin's rap sheet, it's most surprising that he's blanching at the thought of making fun of the Bush offspring. Oh, how I remember the yellow-sheets that used to ruthlessly mock President Cleveland's avoirdupois! And ask yourself, is it worse to have Jay Leno imply that you are merely stupid on national television, or have the editorial cartoonist of the *Philadelphia Star-Register* portray you as a tiny baby, replete with diaper and pacifier, pounding a rattle against the Capitol dome when you make one, small complaint about the intransigence of a particularly surly Congress, as happened to Theo Roosevelt?

I trust the answer is obvious. Besides, as Kevin and I (meaning me) created a kind of George W. Bush "character" in *My First Presidentiary*, so may we do the same thing with Jenna and Barbara. I picture them as sassy, yet smart. Jenna carries one of those Pufferpuff Girls backpacks to class, while Barbara is highly skilled at cribbage.

When you have a chance, we should discuss the theoretical direction of our hypothetical project.

Best,
John

To: Marcia Williams and John Warner
From: Kevin Guilfoile
Date: 7-17-01

Marcia,

There are two things that motivate my partner: The first is a bitter rivalry with H. L. Mencken, which he refuses to let die (although he let Mencken himself expire 45 years ago when

John wordlessly fled a Baltimore hotel room as the famed columnist lurched about the parlor, pointing frantically at a peach pit lodged in his esophagus). The other is John's recent marriage to a freakishly bosomed Penthouse Pet, 60 years his junior, who would leave him for a wealthier, funnier man even nearer to death if she had any clue how much of his once vast fortune John has piddled away on ever-more-elaborate systems of morphine delivery.

Myself, I remain committed to the idea that the Bush girls should be off limits. I suppose I agree with the words of Pink Floyd who, on their classic album *The Wall*, implore us to "Leave those kids alone!" Of course, I also agree with Pink Floyd on the *Piper at the Gates of Dawn* disc when they sing, "Winding, finding places to go/And then one day—hooray!/Another way for gnomes to say/Hooooooooooray!/ Hoooooooooooooooooray!"

Nevertheless, I am certain the sum John's demanded will be adequate. I will require 51 percent of that figure in unmarked pesos and a small firearm to be concealed inside a concrete projectile of your own design. I will forward you a time at which this object is to be catapulted through the Plexiglas of our fourth-story exercise room. Following this, you are to leave the grounds immediately, throwing the hounds off your scent with liberal applications of Clamato to your hair, skin, and clothes. You will receive no further communication from me other than the completed pages of *Jenna and Barbara's Ultimate Party Guide*. You will agree to fake-publish our work exactly as you come to possess it, even if you find it to be illegible, nonsensical, or etched onto a pine board the size of a medieval drawbridge.

I look forward to pretend working with you.

Best,
Kevin

This Week on the *Law & Order* Network

JUSTIN WARNER

Monday, 8 p.m.—*Law & Order*
Parking Adjudication

A Manhattan shiatsu therapist receives a bogus $200 ticket. Fifteen consecutive written appeals are denied automatically by computer. He contemplates suicide on the Queensboro Bridge, where he receives another ticket for parking in a "loading zone."

Monday, 9 p.m.—*Law & Order:*
Suburban Township Board Meeting

(Part 5 of 12) Re-zoning the 4400 block of Fairfax Avenue for multi-unit non-commercial dwellings. As Himself: Rep. Jim Byer (at-large alternate delegate, Rappahannock County Council, VA).

Monday, 10 p.m.—*Law & Order:*
L.A. Police Brutality (Celebrity Edition)

Controversial white rapper Eminem fails to amortize the value of his Humvee on his state income tax return, and is mercilessly flagellated with a socket wrench. Officer O'Donnell: Rodney King.

Tuesday, 8 p.m.—*Law & Order:*
Orthodox Kosher

Talmudic scholars debate whether platypus may be served during Passover. Rabbi Judah Friedman: Martin Mull.

Tuesday, 9 p.m.—*Law & Order:*
Infield Fly Rule

Part One: An umpire defends a controversial call before a jury of agitated, nosebleed-seat Philadelphia fans. Part Two: Foreman Rich Leardi defends his verdict at a Camden, NJ, ESPN Zone before a jury consisting of his alcoholic Uncle Paul. Part Three: Uncle Paul defends himself in court against ESPN Zone, Inc., for unspecified damages to a foosball table. Uncle Paul: Billy Bob Thornton. Philadelphia: Baltimore.

Tuesday, 10 p.m.—*Law & Order:*
Advanced Dungeons & Dragons

A fifth-level Paladin half-elf (12 Strength, 14 Dexterity) attempts to lift the +3 mace in his right hand in order to strike the first of 42 marauding Orcs. ($6\frac{1}{2}$ hours)

Wednesday, 8 p.m.—*Law & Order:*
Catholic Girls' School Dress Code

Seniors at Notre Dame Academy in Worcester, MA, circumvent the 5" hemline rule with floor-length skirts made entirely of Saran Wrap.

Wednesday, 9 p.m.—*Law & Order: Your Mom's House*

You are grounded for flushing broccoli down the toilet, but your younger sister receives only mild reprobation for tie-dyeing the cat.

Wednesday, 10 p.m.—*Law & Order:*
Small Liberal Arts College

A freshman from the Midwest makes an offhand remark that a wealthy, white, heterosexual Protestant upperclassman perceives as prejudiced. The incident is exhaustively analyzed in 287 separate threads on the school's Internet newsgroup. The Rev. Al Sharpton: Don King. Don King: The Rev. Al Sharpton. Cornel West: Martin Mull.

Thursday, 8 p.m.—*Law & Order:*
Australian Parliament

Details of Aboriginal land grants in New South Wales are resolved through elocution and drunken fistfights. Prime Minister: Former Minnesota Gov. Jesse Ventura (18 Strength, 16 Dexterity, 8 Wisdom).

Thursday, 9 p.m.—*Law & Order:*
AFTRA Eligible

A man is shot in Grand Central Station, where 200 underemployed New York–area actors are given one-line walk-ons as witnesses. Corpse: Ted McGinley.

Thursday, 10 p.m.—*Law & Order:*
Occam's Razor

(4 minutes) A woman is found stabbed in an alley. Her ex-husband is caught running from the scene with a bloody knife. He is arrested and convicted. (Followed immediately by *Law & Order: 55 Minutes of Target Commercials*. Man Building Bookshelf/Street Mime/Komodo Dragon: Ben Vereen.)

Friday, 8 p.m.—*Law & Order:*
End-User License Agreement

(2-hour, back-to-back premiere) "Surprise" clauses are slipped into the licensing agreements for downloadable software, and then immediately enforced. Episode One: "The user agrees, in perpetuity throughout the known universe, to affect the physical likeness, manner, and vocal quality of the popular McDonaldland™ character Grimace®." Episode Two: "The user agrees, under penalty of immediate and irrevocable decapitation, never again to use words containing the letter 'S.' "

Friday, 10 p.m.—*Murphy's Law & Order*

The pilot should have been done by now, but it got held up by the directors' strike, and then there was a fire at the garage where they were shooting, and last night the editor's copy of FinalCut Pro crashed three times. *Three* freakin' times!

Saturday, 8 p.m.—*Law & Order: Second Thermodynamics Division*

(Time indeterminate.) At the top of the episode, the crime is solved, the perpetrator is behind bars, and justice is served. Eventually, all the lawyers, police officers, and suspects, along with the New York Superior Court and the entire island of Manhattan, have spontaneously disassociated into a homogeneous mixture of free-floating constituent atoms. Nitrogen gas: Barium gas. The Yawning Void of Infinite Chaos: Keanu Reeves. Shiatsu therapist: Martin Mull.

ROD LOTT'S LISTS
13 LEAST-BELOVED *LORD OF THE RINGS* CHARACTERS

Dildo	**Glando**
Frito	**Motrin**
Blotto	**Lotto**
Leadbelly	**Ralph**
Homo	**Dollop**
Ovaria	**Sean Astin**
Frugal	

New York Arcana

HOLLY WEBBER

Q. I've noticed that in lower Manhattan, just off Mulberry Street, there is a narrow, dead-end street marked by a sign that says Lingerie Lane. Can you tell me the history of this curious name?

A. Lingerie Lane harks back to the neighborhood's rough-and-tumble past as part of the notorious Five Points slum in the early nineteenth-century. The street was the territory of a gang known as the Filmy Lingerie Boys, whose trademark it was to wear corsets, bustiers, and lacy camisoles and to slit the throat of any man or boy who called them sissies. Many an incautious or jeering street tough met his end in the darkness of Lingerie Lane. Once a wayward newspaper lad caught sight of the gang's leader, Frilly Jack, having tea with his cronies, and called out, "Why, 'e looks like my sister Nancy" (the origin of the term *nancy boy*). He had little time to regret his thoughtless comment, for Frilly Jack instantly rose with a coarse oath and smothered the boy with a tea cozy, after which his body was wrapped in a lace tablecloth and dropped from a pier into the East River. The incident entered the argot of Five Points, where killing was known as "cozying" and death was often referred to as "teatime."

Q. On the corner of 39th Street and 7th Avenue, in the heart of the garment district, stands a giant needle and button. Is this sculpture intended as a memorial to the garment workers or just as a playful allusion to the business of the district?

A. Cast using 1.5 tons of steel and erected in 1995, the sculpture features a 31-foot needle as well as the world's largest button, locally known as "Irving Minsky's Button." It is intended as an homage to Irving Minsky, a folkloric figure of the garment district similar to Paul Bunyan. Like Bunyan, Minsky was said to be far above human size—"taller than a tenement"—but unlike Paul Bunyan he was not athletic, and he spent most of his time hunched over a worktable, sewing giant clothes. His long hours of sewing, and the extra studying he did at night, left him with very poor eyesight, and many "tall tales" recount Irving Minsky's mishaps on the Lower East Side, where he mistook a pickle barrel for a glass of tea and a rabbi for a hanky. He was always apologetic, and his cry of "Oy! What was I thinking!" would shake the windowpanes as far south as the Battery. He did not have a companion animal like Bunyan's blue ox, Babe, because he was allergic to pet hair; his asthma became proverbial, and on windy nights New Yorkers still remark, "Irving Minsky is wheezing."

Q. I've read that when the American Museum of Natural History was built in 1874, contractors had to divert an underground stream from the site. Is there any truth to the rumor that they constructed a lavish Roman bath in the basement of the museum, where taxidermists now frolic in their off hours?
A. The luxurious Roman-style baths in the basement of the Museum of Natural History are one of New York's best kept secrets. Lighted by torches and fed by an underground stream, the multi-chambered baths were originally intended for the private use of Phillip J. Vandermeek, the nineteenth-century ostrich-feather magnate who was the museum's largest donor, and his mistress, showgirl Nellie Soubrette. The elaborate mosaics that ornament the walls of the baths depict Mr. Vandermeek as a faun surrounded by woodland animals and Ms. Soubrette as a water nymph with a bevy of mink hanging fondly about her neck as if eager to form a stole. At one end of the main pool, water pours from the mouth of a marble wildebeest; overhead, a ceiling mural depicts ostriches racing across a pastoral landscape. Seldom used after Vandermeek's death in 1912, the baths gradually fell into disrepair. In 1974, however, they were painstakingly renovated, and they are now operated

as a spa for museum employees. "The health and pension benefits at the museum are not that good," said taxidermist Martin
Baumgartner, "but they treat their employees really well in
terms of small perks like free pelts and antlers and on-site
recreational facilities. I attribute a lot of the success of my sea-
otter piece to the hours I spent floating in the saltwater tank."

*Q. In Central Park there is a long path called, according to my map,
Literary Walk, and it features statues of William Shakespeare,
Robert Burns, Sir Walter Scott, and someone called Fitz Greene
Halleck. Who is this Fitz Greene Halleck?*
A. Fitz Greene Halleck was an old college friend of Jack
Waterford Dobbles, who served as mayor of New York from 1888
to 1892. In 1891 Halleck gave Dobbles a bundle of poems to
read, and when Dobbles told him that he liked the poems but had
a few criticisms, Halleck was deeply offended. Dobbles fell all
over himself asserting that they were very, very minor criticisms,
really not even worth mentioning, and that he had nothing but the
greatest admiration for Halleck's work, but Halleck was not mol-
lified until Dobbles, out of his own pocket, paid to have an enormous bronze statue of his high-strung friend erected on Literary
Walk. The outlay of cash nearly bankrupted Dobbles and is
thought to have led to his defeat in the 1892 election.

*Q. Is it true that the Bronx has its own official weather reporter,
even though the National Weather Service maintains a weather
station in Manhattan, only a few miles away?*
A. The position of official Weather Observer for the Bronx was
created in 1893, five years before the incorporation of Greater
New York, and it continues under an obscure and never-
repealed statute. The office was the brainchild of Horatio
Cadwallader, a Bronx legislator who believed that weathermen
would predict the weather more accurately if they experienced
it to the fullest by going aloft in it. Since 1963 the job has been
held by Mickey Santori, a frail, hollow-chested man who frequently lashes himself to a large box kite and leaps off the
Bronx Municipal Watertower, which is located on a windy hill-

side in the highest part of the borough. Clutching a thermometer in one hand and a windsock in the other, Mr. Santori allows himself to be buffeted by the elements for a good two hours before an assistant reels him back in to make his report. "Here in the Bronx we believe in observing the weather the old-fashioned way," said Mr. Santori, 61, in a voice hoarse from a lifetime of north-northeast winds blowing down his shirt collar. "At first I caught a lot of colds, but now I'm used to it." He enjoys his hours aloft, saying that he likes to be his own boss and to have "time to think." On days when the breeze isn't sufficient to lift his 137-pound frame, he addresses groups of confused elementary school children or simply runs down the hillside, making small leaps into the air.

Q. *During Fleet Week my wife and I were struck by the large number of clean-scrubbed young sailors we saw visiting Times Square. Can you tell us a little about the history of Fleet Week?*
A. Fleet Week was established in 1988 in an effort to give the members of the U.S. Navy a little R & R in a city famous for its accommodating barrooms and friendly population of prostitutes. It evolved, however, into a means of punishing enlisted men for various small infractions of navy rules such as falling asleep on watch, refusing to eat hardtack, short-sheeting hammocks, etc. The basic scheme is this: sailors in good standing are allowed to leave the ship wearing blue coats with epaulettes and flat, police-type caps, while those who have received demerits are forced to roam New York City in loose white pants, a white middy blouse with a blue kerchief, and a little round hat. On a recent day, as sailors walked down the gangway to the pier, a navy captain with a bad sunburn barked out, "If you behave like a child, you'll be treated like a child." Capt. L. J. Creevey, of Boca Raton, FL, says that if he gets any complaints, he usually shouts, "Oh, so you'd rather scrub out the head with a toothbrush? Stand at attention in the blazing sun until you get heat stroke? What about thirty lashes with the cat-o'-nine-tails?" Faced with these options, Capt. Creevey says, "Most guys choose the sailor suit."

Q. Was Coney Island ever an island?

A. Coney Island was indeed originally an island, separated from the rest of Long Island by a narrow stream. When a group of Dutch settlers first tried to visit the smaller island in 1674, they were met on the other side of the stream by a determined-looking group of coneys, or rabbits, who stood with elbows linked, seeking to bar their way. The doughty Dutchmen took off their boots, forded the stream, and clubbed the rabbits to death with their boot heels, thus giving Coney Island its name. Later, the stream was filled in, and the island became a place of pleasure and recreation for the people of New York City.

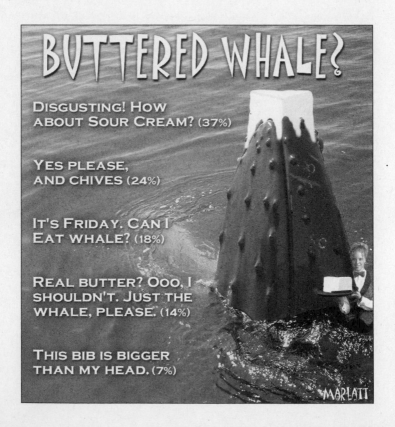

Vows of the *Times*

HOLLY WEBBER

Astrid Olinska is the kind of woman who can create a moment of vibrant poignancy by doing nothing more than casually building a pyramid of exotic fruit. She was stacking up quinces in the window of Balducci's on Sixth Avenue in the fall of 1997 when Roberto Castelo Branco, grand-nephew of the Italian furniture designer famous for his burnished stainless-steel nightstands, passed by and saw her like a Botticelli goddess. He tapped on the window, and she looked up and blushed laughingly when she saw that he was holding a camera. "You rival the quinces," he told her. "I want to take your picture." Ms. Olinska explained, "I didn't know him, but I immediately liked his tiny rectangular glasses."

Although both were married to other people at the time, they exchanged telephone numbers. "Roberto was my latte friend," said Ms. Olinska. "We would meet two or three times a week and Roberto would show me his black-and-white photographs of window displays, and the ones I didn't like he would tear up emotionally. Later, I found out he kept all the negatives."

Mr. Castelo Branco's marriage ended first, and he moved into a SoHo loft as vast and drafty as an ice skating rink. The only furniture was a pair of Eames chairs and a coffee table so small it seemed to be dwindling like a lozenge. "I hated going over there because there was nowhere to sit," said Sidney Estep, a glassware designer and a friend of the 47-year-old groom. "It was really clear that Roberto needed a woman in his life."

He bought a lushly upholstered ottoman and had the loft insulated, but it wasn't enough. By this time it was the spring of 1999, and Ms. Olinska was becoming single again. She moved into a tiny apartment in the West Village and decorated it with Christmas lights. She made fruit tarts and sold them at Balducci's, at first earning just enough to pay the rent and buy eight-pound bags of chow for her pet mongoose. But it soon became a profitable catering business, simply called Astrid. Ms. Olinska said she realized that Mr. Castelo Branco was right for her because he was the only one who understood why she had to leave off the apostrophe and the s.

Friends describe their courtship as quixotic. A three-star dinner at Le Flâneur on Spring Street might be followed by an impulsive game of bocci ball in Little Italy, with Mr. Castelo Branco playfully photographing the tiny old Italian men irritated by their intrusion onto the court. An expedition to choose the perfect mackerel at the Fulton Fish Market might end with a joyride on the Staten Island ferry. Cooking was important in their relationship. "Once we argued about fennel, and I refused to answer the telephone for an entire week," Ms. Olinska said. The argument ended when she rang Mr. Castelo Branco's doorbell at two in the morning with a mango flan. The couple traveled to London, Paris, and Tuscany, each time staying only twenty-one days, since Mr. Castelo Branco had acquired a five-foot Florida king snake, and none of his friends would agree to feed it. "The snake anchors us to the city," Mr. Castelo Branco explained. "It's like a natural clock, and we adjust ourselves to its rhythm."

On their final day in Tuscany last April, Mr. Castelo Branco hid a diamond-and-sapphire ring from Tiffany's inside an Italian rose that was just beginning to open. He handed the rose to Ms. Olinska and suggested that she play he loves me, he loves me not. "This is the best way of proposing," he said. "Unlike my first wife, Astrid didn't start crying and mess up her face." Instead, two perfect tears glistered on her lower lashes, like dew on the petals of the rose.

The couple approached their marriage with the same mixture of practicality and romanticism. The ceremony was held at Central Presbyterian Church on 64th Street and Park Avenue, where the altar was shrouded in billowing panels of white silk and heaped with exotic fruit, a reference to their first meeting. At the climax of the ceremony, Mr. Castelo Branco lobbed a pomegranate at Ms. Olinska, who caught it deftly. Later, it became the centerpiece of the bridal table.

"At first I didn't trust Roberto," Ms. Olinska's maid of honor, Bebe Saltsman, said. "I thought he was one of those artists manqué who pretend to earn a living by their work when they're actually paying the rent out of a fat trust fund. Then I realized the brilliance of his pictures lies in their shallowness—he really captures the emptiness you feel when you look at a window display."

"Roberto has two legs and two arms," Ms. Olinska's mother, Liv Olinska, added. "I just want to see Astrid married."

In a white silk sheath with elbow-length gloves, Ms. Olinska looked like a more grounded and muscular Grace Kelly. She catered her own wedding, making Navarin of Lamb and Artichokes Fontecchio for two hundred guests. Her hands shook slightly by the end of the evening, but her fixed smile never faded. "Astrid isn't just a business, it's a way of thinking," she said. Mr. Castelo Branco stroked her hair possessively as he steered her toward the bridal limousine.

"They've never really resolved the snake/mongoose thing, but I think that was deliberate," said Jute Simpleton, an old roommate of the bride's, as she tried to transfer hors d'oeuvres from a silver platter to her beaded purse without ruining the lining. "They both believe that marriage is about taking a blind leap into a wonderfully unpredictable life."

pet mongoose

. . . Naked anti-nudity protesters arrested, released . . . Shark that bit lottery winner struck by lightning . . . Just in: chicken first, then egg . . . Mimes with cell phones latest nuisance . . .

Astronaut Application

It is March 11, 2002. There is an astronaut application on my desk. I received it in the mail after filling out a simple form on NASA's Web site. Six months ago today, my choice to be a comedian suddenly seemed trivial, so I began researching alternative careers that might make me more useful to society. Astronaut seemed the most logical choice. At nine pages long, it is surprisingly concise, and consists mostly of ordinary questions that you would find on any job application. The only page that really stands out is the one labeled "Summary of Aeronautical Experience," in which the applicant is required to provide a detailed record of the number of hours they have spent piloting and/or copiloting various types of civilian and military aircraft. The application makes it clear that special consideration is given to those who have experience as test pilots. I had to leave that page blank. After reading further, I realized that my college degree was also unacceptable. NASA requires that you have at least a B.A. in a field related to engineering, biological or physical sciences. My degree is in English. At least that's what my diploma says. Please never ask me any actual questions about literature—my automatic response will probably be some flustered tirade about the wasted years of my life (1985–1997), followed by the sentence "Oh yeah, definitely Vonnegut, without a doubt." I will then eat. After thoroughly reading the entire application, I realized that the only minimum requirement I did meet was that of height. In order to be an astronaut, you have to be between 58.5 and 76 inches tall. I'm approximately 72.5 inches tall. 73 if I've just finished using the lat pulldown machine at the gym. I found it surprising that you could be so short and still be an astronaut, but what I found even more surprising is that one of the genetic attributes that allows so many great NBA players to soar high above the rim will forever prevent them from soaring high above the Earth. In a spaceship. If NASA ever establishes an elite team of basketball-playing astronauts (astrobasketnauts), it will have to be the smaller guards that lead the way. Mr. Iverson, set us down on that asteroid! Now bury the tre! BOOYAH! But I digress. I felt like I had hit a brick wall. I was having severe doubts about being a comedian, yet I was completely unfit to be an astronaut. I had run out of options. I fell into a deep depression, and abandoned my good friends Mr. Beer and Mr. Ice Cream for my arch-enemies Mr. Too Much Beer, Mr. Way Too Much Ice Cream, and Mr. What the Hell Are You Doing with That Suede Pillowcase Aw Man I Don't Need to See That for Crying Out Loud Andrés No. That was until yesterday, when I picked up the most recent issue of *Vicarious Astronaut Bi-Monthly* and came across an article by Buzz Aldrin entitled: "United We Laugh: Why Comedians Are This Country's Most Precious Non-Fuel or Military Related Resource." In compelling and sometimes even tender language, Buzz recounts how his career as an astronaut would not have been possible without some of the earlier Marx Brothers films. It's a very interesting article with some fascinating, serpentine leaps of logic, but in the end Buzz makes it crystal clear that the future of our space program is entirely dependent on the comedians of this great country. And on advances in Plasma and/or Fusion research. Immediately, I felt better. Validated. More committed to making people laugh than ever before. Except for maybe when I was eleven years old, and just would not shut the fuck up until people either laughed or hit me. I suggest all you comics out there pick up the article and read it yourselves. Though I doubt you will ever, ever find it. Even so, the knowledge that there is a man named Buzz, and that he has set foot on the moon, is reason enough to go on. Right?

—Andrés du Bouchet

PROOFREADERS' MARKS

OPERATIONAL SIGNS

○	Over-explaining
⌒	Irrational
◡	Unrealistic
@	Confrontational
N	Negatives
A	Attention-seeking
≡	Excess aggression
[	Insert objectivity
]	Insert subjectivity
ℓ	Let it go
][	Excess self-disclosure
fi	Flush irony
fs	Flush sincerity
‖	Ingratitude
×	Insensitivity
P/A	Passive-aggression
⊓	Insert pessimism
⊔	Insert optimism
□	Excess defensiveness
#	Insert compliment
¶	Insert politeness
tr	Insert truth

TYPOGRAPHIC SIGNS

imp	Reversal of an instinct into its opposite
del	Delusions of observation
scop	Scopophilia as an activity directed toward an extraneous object
sub	Sublimation
id	Id function
ex	Externalization of an internal process
UD	Unconscious desires
rep	Repression symptoms
p	Painful feelings connected with pleasurable feelings
sa	Superego activity
I	Complete object-love
∧	Primal libido
∨	Ego control
M	Delusional expectation of punishment

PUNCTUATION SIGNS

(|)	Insert feeling
|:	Insert empathy
oe	Over-emotional
+	Excess affectation
ed	Excess drama

—Stephanie Brooks

Mirth of a Mascot

A book without a mascot is like a platypus without a gallbladder. So we're looking for something to represent Mirth of a Nation. And we need some help. So pick up a pen, put on your thinking cap, and participate in our "Pick Our Mascot" Contest. Just be sure to follow the rules.

1. Entries will be accepted by mail only.
2. The entry may be in any language used to block a U.S. resolution at the United Nations.
3. All entries must have an essay of between 250 and 430 words expressing what a mascot means to you. Essay must be fastened to your entry form with Scotch tape, but not the really cheap kind that's kinda yellow and really stiff. The good stuff.
4. Entries may only be submitted in 26-point Hoefler Text.
5. Each entry must be accompanied by a videotape of the submitter actually coming up with the idea and writing it down on a small pad so we know you didn't steal the concept from someone else.
6. Entries with umlauts and tildes will be returned.
7. The mascot may *not* be the world's largest rodent, the capybara. The capybara cartel controls the Southern Hemisphere and is very protective of its beast. We would rather not start any trouble.
8. The mascot may not be a mythological creature, like a centaur or a unicorn. If you ardently believe that unicorns do exist, then this contest isn't for you.
9. Each entry must contain a type of mascot and a selected

name. Kooky names such as "Mrs. Ethel Mirth" may render you ineligible from all future HarperCollins contests.

10. Anyone who has ever been a mascot before, or has had a really elaborate Halloween costume that ultimately got him laid because for some reason some girl thought a guy dressed as a giant milk carton was sexy, is ineligible.

11. Banana daiquiris will not be accepted in lieu of a name unless also accompanied by at least two (2) other banana daiquiris.

12. The mascot may *not* be a former cast member of *Bosom Buddies*, such as Peter Scolari.

13. When physically constructing the mascot, his head should weigh no more than the combined weight of his upper limbs. An aerodynamic mascot is a dynamic mascot!

14. You may not have sex with the mascot.

15. Although he would ultimately make our book safer, John Ashcroft may not be considered for our mascot.

16. Please don't show up in our offices dressed as the mascot. There's barely enough coffee to go around as it is.

17. In the unlikely event that there is a winner, the grand prize of two (2) Hanes T-shirts (choice of V-neck or crew, medium only) must be picked up within seventeen hours of notification.

18. In the event of a tie, whoever supplies the most delicious recipe for eggplant parmesan will be declared the winner.

19. Each entry form must be accompanied by a processing fee of $3,000.

20. Entries must be sent in a clear, teal 9" × 16½" envelope. The color must be verified by a Notary and submitted along with a corresponding Sherwin-Williams paint chip.

21. Traveling to South America, the home of the capybara, to ask the natives what they think, will not be tolerated or accepted.

—**Brian Frazer**

Answers to Last Volume's Puzzle

ACROSS

1. Emotionally disturbed right-wing extremist who tried to assassinate Chirac
OVITZ

4. The *Nina*, the *Pinta* and the _____
ASTRODOME

7. How Ambrose spends his weekends
PLAGIARIZING

9. Shake, Rattle and _____
TAKEYOURPARKINSONS MEDICINE

10. From now on, the FAA will allow pilots to have these in cockpits
WHORES

11. Craig Kilborn is allergic to _____
FUNNY

16. Great Jaglom movie
AREYOUCRAZYTHEYALL SUCK

18. New Peruvian prime minister
NOT IMPORTANT

19. My stock portfolio's value
FORTY BUCKS

22. Voted best blender speed 1997–2002
PUREE

25. Monkey see, monkey _____
SMELL

29. '50s presidential slogan, "I Like _____"
CRAYONS

33. Generous tip on $4.95
THREEMILLIONDOLLARS

34. Best dodgeball player, Old Bethpage, New York
MARTYKUNOFF

36. Number of calories in half-gallon of Fudge Ripple ice cream, bad guess
FIVE

39. Third-millennium Lewis and Clark
WHOARELEWISAND CLARK?

47. Born in 1968
MYSISTER

48. Jeb Bush, abbr.
LIAR

50. What Mike Piazza might be
SAGITTARIUS

51. Wes Anderson's motto
QUIRKYBEATSTALENT

58. Where Arthur Andersen kept his money
UPHISASS

60. Best album of all time
THATSATOUGHIE

62. Where Walt Disney is right now
MAGGOTMOUNTAIN

64. Seventh wonder of the world
THISREALLYCOOLPEN IGOTATTHEMALL

DOWN

1. HBO's *Sex and the* _____
SHUTUP

2. Blue-book value of an '81 Accord with 153,000 miles
NINEFIFTY

3. City NE of Miami
BRUSSELS

4. Invented in 1989
AIRQUOTES

5. Largest coffee at Starbucks
SILO

6. Arafat overdid this with his lips
COLLAGEN

7. One-hit wonders
BEATLES

8. Boron and cobalt
YOUBETCHA

9. Star of *League of Extraordinary Gentlemen*
GUYNEXTTOMETHAT WOKEMEUPATTHEEND

10. Alan Greenspan has one
AUTOMOBILE

11. I wish the guy who drew *Garfield* was _____
DEAD

12. Samuel L. Jackson's bank PIN number
ONEONEFIVE

13. Turn off your cell phone!
SORRY

14. Jimmy Crack Corn and I _____.
COULDNTGIVEASHIT

15. Acronym for "acronym"
A

16. Wanna shoot some
hoops?
SURE

17. Has never won
Wimbledon
ALANALDA

18. Five day forecast,
rain forest
RAINRAINRAINRAINRAIN

19. Should have won the
1996 Oscar, abbr.
B

20. Polar bear, nickname
POLEY

21. Palindrome
PPPPPPPP

22. Nebraska capital
NOTIMPORTANTTOME

23. Lance Armstrong's won
five of these in a row
YAHTZEETOURNAMENTS

24. Best player on our soft-
ball team (by far!)
ME

25. General _____ chicken
SCHWARZKOPFS

26. Opposite of sans
NONSANS

27. Greek god of hot and
cold beverages
THERMOS

28. Jai _____
HOWAREYOU

29. Lakers probable starting
five
SHAQKARLGARYDE VEAN
ANDSOMEGUYTHAT'S
NOTAS GOODASKOBE

30. First Project Greenlight
winner
ORSONWELLES

31. Number of stamps you
need to mail a medium can-
taloupe from New York to
Denver
TWICEASMANYASTOSEND
APOMEGRANATETO
TULSA

32. "Judgment" incorrect
spelling
PRDUCSAWRQ

—Brian Frazer

Mirth of a Nation
Teacher's Companion

Compiled by the Greater Bristol, Connecticut, Grade School Teaching Professionals' Curriculum Enrichment Committee*
Lead Co-Facilitator: M. Sweeney Lawless

A Brief Guide to How to Use This Guide

This educational resource was developed as a pilot project by the Early Education Enrichment Committee, a group of teachers that believes the modern emphasis on skills and achievement in schools today has robbed the wonder from children in grades K[†] through 8.[‡] Test scores have taken the place of education until teaching is just another job and a teacher is just another employee to be held up to standards. Now that all of the outsiders have had their say—parents, academics, consultants, and special interest groups—it's time for teachers to put the richness back into education. We're on your side!

---

* The Greater Bristol, Connecticut, Grade School Teaching Professionals' Curriculum Enrichment Committee (GBCGSTPCEC) was founded in 1999 for the exchange of ideas, goals, and vision. Check out our Web site (currently under construction) for more exciting enrichment resources.

† Unless otherwise indicated, "K" will indicate "kindergarten" throughout the text except where it is used as shorthand for "thousand" or, in the science sections, where it is an abbreviation for "potassium" or, in those paragraphs with a legal context, where it will designate a "contract."

‡ Canadian schools are requested to extend the 6–8 category for use in Grade 9 to compensate for the additional year of post-secondary education. It is emphasized the authors do not wish to imply Canadian students are "smarter" than those in the United States—they are merely "more educated."

We hope this guide gives today's students the well-rounded skills they will need to remember and recite what they have learned. As an added feature, we have included suggestions from the Book Worm, the Computer Worm, and the Teaching Worm.

Unit I / Language and Writing Arts

Circle and Cross Out

"Blues for Advanced Beginners" by Judith Podell showed us the difference between good and bad blues songs. Look carefully at the choices and circle good topics for blues songs, cross out bad ones.

Paying dues	Paying Cub Scout dues
Paying your debt to society	Paying your babysitter
Paying a lot for that muffler	Doing time-motion studies
Doing time	Doing the Hokey Pokey
Doing hard time	Doing what comes naturally
Doing the crime if you can't do the time	Paying $\frac{1}{10}$ of your salary to a Hollywood religion

TEACHING TIP: HOWARD GARDNER CAN SAY ALL HE WANTS ABOUT "MULTIPLE INTELLIGENCES" BUT BE SURE YOUR STUDENTS KNOW THAT IT'S GETTING THE RIGHT ANSWER FIRST THAT MAKES YOU THE SMARTEST.

TEACHING TIP: REMIND STUDENTS WHO IS THE BOSS.

Vocabulary and Slang

Match the slang with the correct word or phrase:

Slang	Common Word or Phrase
Danish swamp corpse	peanut butter customer
a temp	neat, swell, or cool
velour donkey	a frustrating disappointment
600 square feet	a first husband or first wife
"Starlight Express" audition	hair in your nose
our damned senator	cold, weak, and bitter
the bee's vagina	an expensive Manhattan apartment
a guaranteed reservation from U-Haul	a politician
slap the claims adjustor	someone who is no fun at parties
old coffee	hockey game
choosy mother	talk about a tiresome subject
nose lashes	someone both attractive and annoying

Teach Your Class to Write an Original Story

Ask your class to choose a word from each column to create a story title.

For a thriller

For a mystery

The	[Lead Character's Name]	File
	[Former Cold War Nation]	[Species of Poisonous Plant or Dangerous Animal]
	Last	Sanction
	Day of the	Ordeal

For a romance

The	[Nursery Rhyme Character]	Victim
	[Historical Battle Site]	Homicide
	[Short-Lived Flower]	Killer
	[Unwieldy Farm Implement]	Murder

For a western

The	[Kind of Weather]	[Man's Occupation]
	[Passionate Emotion]	[European Capital City]
	[Kind of Spice]	[Type of Cosmetics]
	[Pretty Color]	Deborah

Still don't have a title yet? Consider using one of these:

The	Forlorn	Rodeo
	Lonesome	Paddock
	Abandoned	Homestead
	Lost	Mine

- a legal term
- a Latin legal term
- a type of crime
- a medical procedure
- a sports term

If you want to make your story more exciting, give your title an exclamation point:

Res Ipsa Loquitor!
Carjack!

DID YOU KNOW? CONFEDERATE PAPER MONEY WAS ONCE VALUABLE. PEOPLE USED IT IN THE SAME WAY WE USE MONEY TODAY.

Rhinoplasty!
Quarterback Sneak!

When you decide on a title, name the following characters:

Lead Character: _____
Love Interest: _____
Rival: _____

Now you're ready to write that story!

Title: _____

It was _____ [weather] in the _____ [place] and _____ [lead] had never been happier. The chance to realize a life-long dream, to _____ [opportunity] was at hand, at last. However, _____ [rival] also had dreams—evil dreams of thwarting the dreams of others—especially _____ [lead]'s dreams. Only _____ [love interest] understood and helped _____ [lead] defeat _____ [rival] to get _____ [opportunity]. The End.

Hint #1: Did you include enough acknowledgments? Mention as many names as you can of influential people you know or would like to know. If you owe anyone a favor, mention their name; now they owe you a favor.

Hint #2: Don't forget to add more details to your story in the second draft.

Letter-Writing Skills

*Read Ian Lendler's **"Live from Folsom Prison**: Liner Notes" to learn all about entertainment in the penal system.*

Did you know that many prisoners have pen pals? Here are some ways to have fun with prisoners:

Grades K–2 / Write a party invitation that looks like this:

> Dear _____ :
>
> We hope you can come to our class for a party. We will have these things to eat and drink _____ *[list food and drink]*. Please do not _____ *[specify negative behavior for which the prisoner is sentenced, if known]* while you are here. This behavior is not allowed in society or in our class.

Use a name instead of a number to make the invitation more personal, and review your work to be sure it will not make the prisoner angry. (If the prisoner has a long sentence, you may even get a reply!)

Grades 3–5 / Review the elements of an unfriendly letter:
- Date
- Salutation/opening salvo or "warning shot"
- Reiteration/description of your complaint in elaborate detail
- The body of the letter, also known as "the harangue"
- Conclusion/parting shot/threat
- Closing
- Signature/signed "a friend"

Grades 6–8 / Write a bread-and-butter note. How would your letter differ if you took home a few things you happened to find in the dresser or in the medicine cabinet where you stayed?

Unit II / Social Skills and Good Citizenship Arts

You're Never Too Young for Leadership!
Grades K–2 / Play Follow-the-Leader and take turns until everyone has been the leader. Sit in a circle and vote on who was the best leader and who was the worst.

Grades 3–5 / Read the definition of "democracy" to the class (repeat definition as often as necessary until everyone says they understand). Vote by show of hands on the following questions:

- What is your favorite ice cream flavor?
- What is your favorite color?
- What is your favorite animal?

(This exercise should closely resemble a real election, so be certain to limit choices.)

Grades 6–8 / Hold an anonymous election by paper ballot for "most popular student in the class." Hold a second election but this time, vote by show of hands. Did the votes change? Discuss.

Waiting Skills

Read Ian Lendler's **"Waiting Room Digest."** How good are you at waiting? Let's find out!
Grades K–2 / Wait for 5 minutes.
Grades 3–5 / Wait for 20 minutes.
Grades 6–8 / Wait without a time limit for the first half of the class, then wait with a time limit for the rest of the time available.

Unit III / Mathematics and Science

Subjects known as the "hard sciences" often discourage students from learning. Children are born with a natural sense of wonder, and it's important to sustain this quality as they get older; math and science are hard, but even mathematicians and scientists don't know why things happen. Make sure students know that it is just as important to wonder as it is to understand the subject:

Introduction to the Value of Money

Every day we hear parents complain, "My children don't know the value of money." This exercise can help. What if people were worth more or less money depending on how much you liked them? Ask your class to put a dollar value* on each of the following:

Rock Candy Demonstration and Discussion

_____ mother	_____ sister	_____ grandmother	_____ best friend
_____ father	_____ brother	_____ grandfather	_____ pet

1. Choose **any article** in this book.
2. Ask the class to boil **12 gallons of water,** slowly adding a **10-pound bag of sugar** into the liquid until it is entirely dissolved. Turn off the heat and pour the liquid into many, **many 4-ounce glasses.** For each glass, tie a short piece of **thread** to a **pencil** and let the thread dangle into the water until it touches the bottom of the glass; rest the pencil across the top of the glass (you may secure the pencil to the glass with rubber bands, more thread, cellophane tape, ordinary leather glue, rubber cement, epoxy, or mucilage).
3. As the mixture cools and the sugar crystallizes to form rock candy along the thread, form small groups and discuss the article you have chosen.

Unit IV / Timed Creativity Exercises†

Art, Art, Art

The way to make art come alive for students is to plan art-related activities:

---

*Remember: everyone is special, so no two people can be worth the same amount of money!

†A helpful note to teachers about occupying class time: any exercise may be extended to fill an entire class if you increase the amount of time students are allowed to complete them.

> *Ask the students to look at famous works of art and to draw the people they see in the painting. Use **Nude Descending a Staircase** and easier, messier art so students will feel encouraged that they can do art, too.*
>
> ---
>
> *Ask students to write a short television commercial that tells us what the people in the painting are feeling. When you know what kind of product they need, draw it in right next to them.*

Poems, Poems, and More Poems

> *Read "**Ars Gratia Artis?**" by Beth Teitell to find out all about creativity.*

Grades K–2 / Instruct the class to think of a short (two-line) poem about museum fatigue and ask each student to recite their poem. Remind them that it is better if the poem rhymes.

Grades 3–5 / Instruct the class to compose a haiku poem (five lines, seven lines, five lines) about lunch using these sample rhyming pairs: dromedary/urinary, parade/ spayed, water/slaughter.

Grades 6–8 / Ask your class to choose a partner and to write a poem about what makes another student different or about one of their personal experiences. Here's just one example of a personal student poem by Brian:

Poem About Philip

Lazy eye
Lazy eye
*You have a funny crazy eye.**

---

*Be sure to check out the GBCGSTPCEC Web site (under construction) for other creative student poems, such as "Clouds Can Cry Like Tommy Can," "Something's Missing on Sarah," and "Don't Go Home Through the Field."

Unit V / Text-Based Extracurriculars

Create a Fanciful Bulletin Board

1. Read *"Ten Increasingly Annoying Short Stories"* by Neil Pasricha. Cut out colorful construction paper shapes of toilets, mosquitoes, slums, bakeries, and France. Use newspaper clippings, fabric scraps, glitter, and glue for decoration.

2. Read *"More Sins of the Fathers"* by Bill Scheft. Cut several potatoes in half and carve the figures of priests and altar boys. Show pupils how to press them into poster paint and make exciting potato prints on a large sheet of butcher paper to make church really come to life!

3. Have students carefully trace quarters, nickels, dimes, and pennies onto gray and brown construction paper to make a gigantic pot of coins as a background for papers that receive A's or B's and are "On the Money."

4. For Spring, celebrate March with the bulletin board theme, In Like a Lamb, Out Like a Lion" or, if the weather is severe where you live, make a ferocious lion with a little lamb in its mouth to show "Winter Has Not Loosened Its Grip."

Diorama Fun

Read Jeff Ward's *"It's All True,"* and invite your students to make a diorama depicting the impact Orson Welles had on (1) on film and (2) on the Earth's surface if he had been launched by Marines. Use green soldiers and bits of green sponge from your kitchen sink at home to make a more realistic battle.

Unit VI / More Ideas for Teaching Learning

If you've reached the present section of your lesson plan, you and your students have studied enough *May Contain Nuts.*

INTERACTIVE LEARNING: LET YOUR STUDENTS TAKE TURNS TURNING OFF THE LIGHTS WHEN A QUESTION IS ANSWERED CORRECTLY.

The following activities fall into two categories: the syllabus-free kind that requires little or no planning on your part, and the kind that encourage students to become autonomous learners and provide for a bit of quiet time for the teacher (e.g., you don't need a roomful of chatty little voices first thing in the morning after a late night out.)*

Diversity Is Everywhere

Every one of us is a citizen of Earth, and we share this wonderful world with hundreds of other races, plants, lands, and waters. Animals are all around us and we hardly ever think of them. Even insects are animals although they might seem more like small robots than the nicer animals, like ponies or birds or dolphins. Bears and wolves often have beautiful eyes.

Invite the class to break up into small work groups to "walk a mile in someone else's shoes" and then ask each work group to give a presentation about the following imaginary situations:

If you were a DOG, what kind of dog would you be? Would you fetch and do tricks? Would you be a good dog?

If you were a COW, would you like to give milk? When you give meat, what kind would you like to give?

If you were a FOREIGNER (for example, from Canada or France or Italy—be creative!) what would you do all day? Would you have food and bathrooms? What would you do for the tourists who came to visit you?

Let's Get That Blood Moving in Grades K-5

Young children are full of energy. After a long day of sitting in their seats, many students appreciate a get-up-and-get-going activity to "wake up" the classroom. Ask the students

---

*See the GBCGSTPCEC Web site for ideas abut creating a "block of busy work" on days when teaching class is the last thing you need.

to draw a three-foot chalk outline by their desks. Take turns spinning around three times with their eyes closed and then trying to walk a straight line. Award prizes to students with the quickest "recovery time."

Let's Get That Blood to Stand Still in Grades 6-8

Adolescents are undergoing many hormonal, emotional, and social changes. Give each student a piece of string to wrap around his or her wrist or ankle, neck or finger. See who can go the longest without circulation.

Unit VII / Discussion Time

COMPUTER WORM SAYS: MAKE YOUR E-MAILS MORE ATTRACTIVE WITH DIFFERENT COLOR FONTS.

Last hours of the day? Day before a holiday? Behind on your lesson plans? These are perfect times for Discussion Time!

Human Dignity Discussion Time

Choose any entry in this book and discuss "human dignity" and whether everyone is really "equal."

Emotional Volcano Project Discussion Time

To illustrate lessons you could learn from science, why not pretend a volcano is human? Have the class build a papier-mâché volcano and paint it realistically. Show students a box of baking soda labeled "FEAR" and a glass of vinegar marked "LOYALTY" and pour them both into the volcano at once. Discuss until the end of the class period.

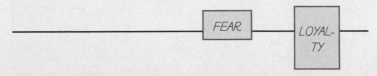

You Can't Find Good Ones: A Discussion

Not every person would make a good slave. Ask the students to write a brief essay about who in the class would make the best slave and why.

Unit VII / Activities to Spawn Imagination

Seeing Stars

Supplies you'll need: **black construction paper, white chalk, hair spray**

Tell the students to press their thumbs firmly against their eyelids for 30 seconds. When they open their eyes, tell them to draw a diagram of the flashing lights they see on the black paper and label them as a pretend constellation. Spray an even layer of hair spray (aerosol is best) to prevent the chalk from smudging.

Also to try: several pencil erasers (not the points!).

Also to try: pin the students' work against the ceiling to make your very own classroom planetarium!

Matching, Cross-Referencing and Rearranging

Read all selections in the text, then match the number for each item in Column A with the letter for the corresponding item in Column B:

	A		B
i.	Suzy Warner	O	Knicks uniform
ii.	Wormhole opening	N	Newspaper-vending machine
iii.	Julie Andrews and Robert Goulet	T	Dromedary
iv.	Dry cleaning bags	N	Bistro sandwiches
v.	Camel	A	Hungry, Hungry Hippos
vi.	EBay	S	Gummy bears
vii.	Ex-wife	T	Mother-in-law
viii.	Vagina	O	Realistic alien pseudo-pod
ix.	Fire hydrant	C	Hot
x.	Lunch money	N	Falling chunks of ceiling plaster
xi.	Incinerator	I	Beer bong

1. First write the results of your matches:

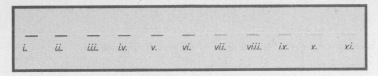

2. Then add the letters **P** and **E** . . .
3. Rearrange the letters to find another name for Istanbul:

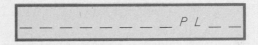

Unit VIII (or IIX) / Special Holiday Activities

Some schools are located in neighborhoods where parents may have opinions that are disruptive to the festive classroom activities you plan. "This land is your land, this land is my land," and unfortunately, some people in our land hide behind special privileges and interfere with traditions enjoyed by the majority. When holiday time comes around, these spoilers are on the lookout for an opportunity to question every activity: even one parent can ruin everybody's good time. Just because your students live in a chaotic neighborhood like this doesn't mean you can't put the fun back into your class. Here are some suggestions that won't offer these "spoilers" an excuse to take away your students' right to be merry:

Thanksgiving Turkeys[*]

For many generations, children have been making Thanksgiving turkeys. Although art is a creative activity, that doesn't mean it shouldn't be done the right way. Students should place their hand inside the outline of the Thanksgiving Tur-

---

[*]*Teacher's Note*: Don't let anyone tell you otherwise: Thanksgiving is a United States holiday, not a religious one. Stand your ground!

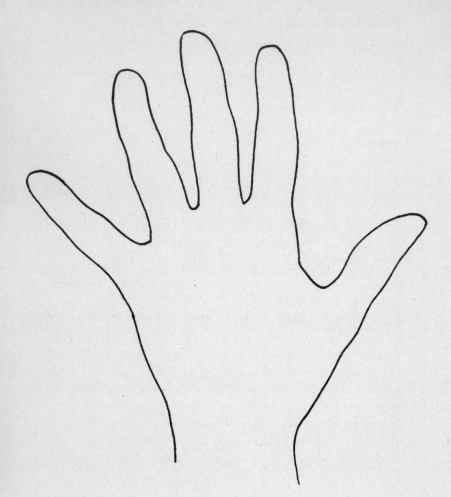

Thanksgiving Turkey—Figure 1

Students should place one hand in the outline and trace it slowly and carefully, then color within the lines for a perfect Thanksgiving!

key [See Thanksgiving Turkey—Figure 1] and carefully trace around it. Draw a face inside the outline for the thumb and color in the other fingers to look like feathers. Don't forget to remind your class to stay away from drugs.

Fun with Wars

To give your students a fun Flag Day activity or to reinforce lessons from U.S. history, ask your class to unscramble the names of the following wars and police actions:

YAVORELONIURY ARW
RWA OF 1182
CAMINEX RAW
LICIV WRA
SAPSNIH-RANIEMRAC RAW
LOWRD RAW I
ROWLD ARW II
DOLC RWA
ANFROK FLONCICT
TEVI MAN RAW
HET RIFST SERPANI FULG ARW

Grades K–2 / Have a race between the boys and the girls to see who can identify the most letters of the alphabet.

Grades 3–5 / Have a contest to see whether those born January through June can unscramble the words faster than those born July through December.

Grades 6–8 / Time each student and compare scores at the end of class to determine whether boys or girls are faster, and which religion is the best at unscrambling words.

Late October Vegetable Carving

Supplies you'll need: **newspapers, sharp carving knives, October vegetables**

1. Carefully supervise your students as they put down sheets of newspaper to catch the mess. Hollow out gourds, squash, or any late-ripening vegetables with their knives. They can choose any design they like, such as triangles, circles, squares, or even a face.
2. Place a candle or small battery-operated light inside to bring out the shapes of the carvings.

Macaroni Wreath for Any Holiday

This is a craft that can be used to enhance any home during December.

Supplies you'll need: **paper plates, green spray paint, glue, pastas in exciting shapes and sizes, glitter, ribbon**

1. Cut a circle out of the center of a paper plate. Glue pasta over the entire surface of the plate. Spray paint until the entire surface is covered. While the paint is drying, tie the ribbon into a bow.
2. Glue the bow to the wreath and hang on your front door for Christmas, Hanukkah, Kwanzaa, or Winter.

End-of-the-Year Stocking or Necktie Dispenser

Supplies you'll need: **one shoe box, several pairs of stockings OR several neckties, red and green construction paper, glue, scissors, glitter**

1. Cut a small hole in the side of the shoe box.
2. Decorate the shoe box with red and green construction paper and glitter.
3. While the shoe box is drying, tie the ends of the neckties or stockings together to form one long strand.

4. Place all the stockings or neckties into the shoe box. Make sure one end of the strand pokes out of the hole in the side so that someone can pull out the first stocking or necktie, untie it from the strand, and enjoy a new one each morning.
5. Give as an end-of-the-year gift.

Presidents Day Fun with Words

See who can find the most mistakes in this famous historical speech:

Good evening. This is the 37th time I have spoken to you from this office, where so many decisions have been made that shaped the history of this Nation. Each time I have done so to discuss with you some matter than I believe affected the national interest. In all the decisions I have made in my public life, I have always tried to do what was best for the Nation. Throughout the long and difficult period of Watergate, I have felt it was my duty to persevere, to make every possible effort to complete the term of office to which you elected me. In the past few days, however, it has become evident to me that I no longer have a strong enough political base in the Congress to justify continuing that effort. As long as there was such a base, I felt strongly that it was necessary to see the constitutional process through to its conclusion, that to do otherwise would be unfaithful to the spirit of that deliberately difficult process and a dangerously destabilizing precedent for the future. But with the disappearance of that base, I now believe that the constitutional purpose has been served, and there is no longer a need for the process to be prolonged. I would have preferred to carry through to the finish whatever the personal agony it would have involved, and my family unanimously urged me to do so. But the interest of the Nation must always come before any personal considerations. From the discussions I have had with Congressional and other leaders, I have concluded that because of the Watergate matter I might not have the support of the Congress that I would consider necessary to back the very difficult decisions and carry out the duties of this office in the way the interests of the Nation would require. I have never been a quitter. To leave office before my term is completed is abhorrent to every instinct in my body. But as President, I must put the interest of America first. America needs a full-time President and a full-time Congress, particularly at this time with problems we face at home and abroad. To continue to fight through the months ahead for my personal vindication would almost totally absorb the time and attention of both the President and the Congress in a period when our entire focus should be on the great issues of peace abroad and prosperity without inflation at home. Therefore, I shall resign the Presidency effective at noon tomorrow. Vice President Ford will be sworn in as President at that hour in this office. As I recall the high hopes for America with which we began this second term, I feel a great sadness that I will not be here in this office working on your behalf to achieve those hopes in the next 2½ years. But in turning over direction of the Government to Vice President Ford, I know, as I told the Nation when I nominated him for that office 10 months ago, that the leadership of America will be in good hands. In passing this office to the Vice President, I also do so with the profound sense of the weight of responsibility that will fall on his shoulders tomorrow and, therefore, of the understanding, the patience, the cooperation he will need from all Americans. As he assumes that responsibility, he will deserve the help and the support of all of us. As we look to the future, the first essential is to begin healing the wounds of this Nation, to put the bitterness and divisions of the recent past behind us, and to rediscover those shared ideals that lie at the heart of our strength and unity as a great and as a free people. By taking this action, I hope that I will have hastened the start of that process of healing which is so desperately needed in America. I regret deeply any injuries that may have been done in the course of the events that led to this decision. I would say only that if some of my judgments were wrong, and some were wrong, they were made in what I believed at the time to be the best interest of the Nation. To those who have stood with me during these past difficult months, to my family, my friends, to many others who joined in supporting my cause because they believed it was right, I will be eternally grateful for your support. And to those who have not felt able to give me your support, let me say I leave with no bitterness toward those who have opposed me, because all of us, in the final analysis, have been concerned with the good of the country, however our judgments might differ. So, let us all now join together in affirming that common commitment and in helping our new President succeed for the benefit of all Americans. I shall leave this office with regret at not completing my term, but with gratitude for the privilege of serving as your President for the past 5½ years. These years have been a momentous time in the history of our Nation and the world. They have been a time of achievement in which we can all be proud, achievements that represent the shared efforts of the Administration, the Congress, and the people. But the challenges ahead are equally great, and they, too, will require the support and the efforts of the Congress and the people working in cooperation with the new Administration. We have ended America's longest war, but in the work of securing a lasting peace in the world, the goals ahead are even more far-reaching and more difficult. We must complete a structure of peace so that it will be said of this generation, our generation of Americans, by the people of all nations, not only that we ended one war but that we prevented future wars. We have unlocked the doors that for a quarter of a century stood between the United States and the People's Republic of China. We must now ensure that the one quarter of the world's people who live in the People's Republic of China will be and remain not our enemies but our friends. In the Middle East, 100 million people in the Arab countries, many of whom have considered us their enemy for nearly 20 years, now look on us as their friends. We must continue to build on that friendship so that peace can settle at last over the Middle East and so that the cradle of civilization will not become its grave. Together with the Soviet Union we have made the crucial breakthroughs that have begun the process of limiting nuclear arms. But we must set as our goal not just limiting but reducing and finally destroying these terrible weapons so that they cannot destroy civilization and so that the threat of nuclear war will no longer hang over the world and the people. We have opened the new relation with the Soviet Union. We must continue to develop and expand that new relationship so that the two strongest nations of the world will live together in cooperation rather than confrontation. Around the world, in Asia, in Africa, in Latin America, in the Middle East, there are millions of people who live in terrible poverty, even starvation. We must keep as our goal turning away from production for war and expanding production for peace so that people everywhere on this earth can at last look forward in their children's time, if not in our own time, to having the necessities for a decent life. Here in America, we are fortunate that most of our people have not only the blessings of liberty but also the means to live full and good and, by the world's standards, even abundant lives. We must press on, however, toward a goal of not only more and better jobs but of full opportunity for every American and of what we are striving so hard right now to achieve, prosperity without inflation. For more than a quarter of a century in public life I have shared in the turbulent history of this era. I have fought for what I believed in. I have tried to the best of my ability to discharge those duties and meet those responsibilities that were entrusted to me. Sometimes I have succeeded and sometimes I have failed, but always I have taken heart from what Theodore Roosevelt once said about the man in the arena, "whose face is marred by dust and sweat and blood, who strives valiantly, who errs and comes short again and again because there is not effort without error and shortcoming, but who does actually strive to do the deed, who knows the great enthusiasms, the great devotions, who spends himself in a worthy cause, who at the best knows in the end the triumphs of high achievements and who at the worst, if he fails, at least fails while daring greatly." I pledge to you tonight that as long as I have a breath of life in my body, I shall continue in that spirit. I shall continue to work for the great causes to which I have been dedicated throughout my years as a Congressman, a Senator, a Vice President, and President, the cause of peace not just for America but among all nations, prosperity, justice, and opportunity for all of our people. There is one cause above all to which I have been devoted and to which I shall always be devoted for as long as I live. When I first took the oath of office as President 5½ years ago, I made this sacred commitment, to "consecrate my office, my energies, and all the wisdom I can summon to the cause of peace among nations." I have done my very best in all the days since to be true to that pledge. As a result of these efforts, I am confident that the world is a safer place today, not only for the people of America but for the people of all nations, and that all of our children have a better chance than before of living in peace rather than dying in war. This, more than anything, is what I hoped to achieve when I sought the Presidency. This, more than anything, is what I hope will be my legacy to you, to our country, as I leave the Presidency. To have served in this office is to have felt a very personal sense of kinship with each and every American. In leaving it, I do so with this prayer: May God's grace be with you in all the days ahead.

Unit X / Crafts 'n' Art 'n' Such

Activities for days when you
need an alternative to teaching . . .

Origami to Increase Learning Comprehension

Knowing what the teacher wants is important at any age. Ask
the class to fold the square they cut out from **Figure 2** into the
shape of a cricket or a dodecahedron. Read the instructions
aloud to see how well your students follow directions.

Directions for an Origami Cricket

Supplies you'll need: **one 8½ x 11" sheet of paper colored
green, brown, or another cricket color, OR cut out Figure 2.**

---

1. Place the piece of paper on a clean, smooth table surface.
2. Orient the paper with the short side of the paper on the top and the bottom and the long sides of the paper on the left and right.
3. Fold the upper-right-hand corner down to meet the left side and match the edges perfectly.
4. Unfold.
5. Fold the upper-left-hand corner down to meet the right side and match the edges perfectly.
6. Unfold.
7. Fold the upper-left and upper-right corners down behind the paper to meet the fold marks created in steps 3 and 5 on the lower sides of the paper.
8. Unfold.
9. Fold the upper-left and upper-right corners toward you, pushing the right and left creases toward each other until they meet beneath the flap.
10. Fold the left side over to meet the right side.
11. Unfold.

Figure 2

STUDENTS IN SOCIETY:
DID YOU KNOW THE STUDENT WITH A HAND IN THE
AIR FIRST MIGHT NOT HAVE THE ANSWER? IN FACT,
THEY HOPE YOU REMEMBER THEY VOLUNTEERED BUT
CALL ON SOMEONE ELSE. BE ON THE LOOK-OUT FOR
THESE "QUICK-DRAW MCGRAWS" WHO "FORGET
THE ANSWER" OR "NEED TO THINK ABOUT IT"
WHEN YOU CALL ON THEM. IF YOU CALL ON
THEM EVERY TIME YOU SEE THEIR HAND,
PRETTY SOON THEY WILL KEEP THE
SAFETY ON.

TEACHING WORM
SAYS:
IF THE CLASS TROUBLE-
MAKER GIVES YOU
A HARD TIME, WIN THE
ARGUMENT BY ENLIST-
ING SOME OF THE GOOD
STUDENTS
ON YOUR SIDE.

12. Fold the right edge over until it meets the center crease.

13. Fold the left edge over until it meets the center crease.

14. Fold the bottom up until the lower left and right points meet the new upper left and right points.

15. Fold the new top left and top right points down to meet the new bottom left and right points of the flap.

16. Unfold and adjust slightly until it looks like a cricket.

Now provide your own cricket noises and away you go!

Directions for a Simple Dodecahedron

1. Follow steps 1–16 above, but instead of following steps 15 and 16, unfold paper entirely, matching corners to diagonal points along lateral axes (measuring approximately ½ inch from each center point) until you have folded all the points in at right angles.

2. Unfold and adjust.

3. Now display your dodecahedron!

Kazoo-o-Phone

Supplies you'll need: **3 toilet paper tubes, 6 paper towel tubes, 2 combs (1 long, 1 short), 14 wax paper squares measuring 3 x 3 inches, a hot glue gun, rubber bands, paper clips (unbent), glitter**

1. Place all the tubes side by side and glue the row of tubes with a hot glue gun.

2. Secure a piece of wax paper to both ends of each tube with a rubber band.

3. Glue one comb on the near end of the outside tubes.

DID YOU KNOW?
THE UNITED STATES WAS
ONCE FILLED WITH IMMI-
GRANTS.

4. Glue wax paper to the near side of each comb.

5. Decorate with glitter.

6. Talk, sing, hum, or make noises into the uncovered opening of each tube or comb—the vibration will make the buzzing sound of a kazoo.

Unit XI / Let's Get Multi-Cultu!

Many countries have rituals and superstitions instead of religions. Celebrate other cultures with your class with these ideas:

1. Pretend you are in a primitive country and make up your own religion, houses, and food.

2. Make your own ritual (see Pet Kerchiefs and Make a Swap Meet Piñata, below).

Pet Kerchiefs

The class fish, mouse, hamster, or guinea pig has just died, but that doesn't mean everyone has to stay upset. Why not encourage students to take their mind off their loss by making a lasting souvenir to remember the little animal?

Supplies you'll need: **paper towels, clean white handkerchiefs from home, fabric paint, small paint roller, class pet**

1. Rinse the pet (for instance, a tropical fish) and carefully dry with paper towels.

2. Using the roller, apply an even layer of fabric paint to one side of the pet, then press it, paint side down, onto the handkerchief. Press gently, especially if you have a large class and everyone wants to make one. When you lift the pet, you will see its imprint on the handkerchief.

> 3. Carefully lay out the handkerchiefs to dry.

Discard used pet when everyone
has had a turn.

Make a Swap Meet Piñata!

Everyone has items around the home—small
tools, gadgets, and appliances, jewelry, toys,
and porcelain figurines—they no longer want
or need. Why not make a swap meet piñata
out of an empty cardboard box, inflated garbage bag, or any
large hollow plastic container? Fill your piñata with prizes,
seal it up, and decorate it with colorful crepe paper.
Suspend your piñata from the ceiling and let each student
have a turn being blindfolded and swinging a bat (gently!) to
try to break it open.*

TEACHING TIP:
EVERY FAMILY HAS ITS PROBLEMS
AND IT'S TOUGH TO KEEP
A SECRET AT SCHOOL. WHY NOT
GET IT ALL OUT INTO THE OPEN
WHEN YOU READ OR HEAR ABOUT
THAT ARREST, ASSAULT, OR
SENTENCING? AFTER ALL, THE
STUDENT PROBABLY WON'T ASK,
SO IT'S UP TO YOU TO GET THE
BALL ROLLING. IT WILL BE A
BREATH OF FRESH AIR WHEN THE
INCIDENT IS NO LONGER SUBJECT
TO SPECULATION.

*Publishing a text? The Greater Bristol, Connecticut, Grade School Teaching
Professionals' Curriculum Enrichment Committee is available on a consulting basis to enrich your book with activities, ideas, and vision. Please contact
the GBCGSTPCEC via our Web site (currently under construction).

Index

PROVIDED BY MARC JAFFE AND PETER
GAIDO FROM *GOO GOO GA GA: THE BABY
TALK DICTIONARY AND PHRASE BOOK*

99 Rules for Writing
by Elmore Leonard

*Editor's note: For this volume, in lieu of further submission guide-lines (either you've figured out what we've been up to in the last three volumes of Mirth of a Nation or you haven't), we are offering this bit of general literary counseling, compliments of **J. B. Miller.***

1. Steal from the masters—they're probably dead so they can't sue you.
2. Only use two-word titles.
3. Quick Monkey.
4. Trouser Snake.
5. Never use a Thesaurus.
6. Dinky Winky.
7. If you're gonna fake it, fake it *well*.
8. Gag Reflex.
9. Brush your teeth after every meal.
10. Never write on the same side of the page twice.
11. Don't pretend you don't read your reviews.
12. Take the money and run.
13. No anthrax.
14. For "he said," never write, "he expostulated."
15. Alwayz uze spelchek.
16. Never stick a fork in a toaster.
17. If you don't know something, make it up.
18. Write in English.
19. Never begin a book with the word "Vociferously."
20. No footnotes.
21. No prologue.
22. No index.

23. No pop-ups.
24. No nineteenth-century woodcuts by Boz.
25. No expensive, limited editions with fake fur covers.
26. No King of Pop.
27. No cats on the table.
28. Prepositions are your friends.
29. Adjectives are your enemy.
30. Posture, posture, posture.
31. Gut Feelings.
32. Skid Marks.
33. No baby talk.
34. No nookie between chapters.
35. Dunt tuse dia-lacht oonlass yer ken duit.
36. Never end a book with "and."
37. Or "but."
38. When typing, use as many fingers as possible.
39. When Shoreeen brings a sawed-off shotgun to the airport, it's likely the metal detectors will find it.
40. Or maybe not.
41. Never accept a blurb from a federal agent.
42. Or Bret Easton Ellis.
43. No waking up to find it was all just a dream. Or was it . . .
44. Hire a lot of researchers with a quick-response team.
45. Pay them in donuts.
46. Floss.
47. If asked to sign a breast, never use a pencil.
48. Or an eraser.
49. Try to keep it under a pack a day.
50. Order small, tip big.
51. Use a zip disk.
52. No children called "Rumor" or "Scout."
53. No haut couture.
54. No garage wines.
55. No novelle cuisine.
56. Nothing macrobiotic.
57. No Yoga.
58. No Author's Commentary.

59. No Director's Cut.
60. No meetings.
61. Try to keep it under a pint a day.
62. But try the Long Island Waffle Cone.
63. Always check your cholesterol.
64. Honey, disconnect the phone.
65. Get back to where you once belonged.
66. Never bet the Ace.
67. Beware the shill.
68. Look for the tell.
69. The lottery is for losers.
70. Don't forget to tip the super at Christmas.
71. Don't badmouth a cop who's stopped you for speeding.
72. If you've got it, show a little cleavage.
73. He who represents himself has a fool for a client.
74. Doctor Martens.
75. Eskimo Kiss.
76. Only a fool holds out for the top dollar.
77. If that's Quentin again, tell him I'm not home.
78. Don't take any wooden nickels.
79. Load the dice.
80. Load the bases.
81. Damn the torpedoes.
82. Cover your mouth when you cough.
83. Never ask Charlie Rose about his hair.
84. Recycle.
85. Soak.
86. Spit.
87. Never dive into a cold swimming pool right after you've eaten.
88. Risk Factored.
89. Fools Suffered Gladly.
90. Never lose your cool.
91. Don't lose the remote.
92. Rush Limbaugh is a big, fat idiot.
93. Always keep your car keys in the same place.
94. Never put a Q-Tip deep in your ear.

95. Keep the cigarette out of your author photo.
96. Always carry breath mints.
97. Wash behind your ears.
98. AOL sucks.
99. Clapton is God.

—J. B. Miller

Alumni Notes

'03 **Halcyon Malloy**, second tribute of **Bevish** (**'82**) and **Randall** (**'80**), married Lisa Slog on June 9 in a relatively civil ceremony at "The Hiccups." Also in attendance: big brother **Slalom** (**'98**), Aunt **Lola** (**'70**), Grandma **Snookers** (**'59**) and **Butch Cavanaugh** (**'83**), who promised to keep "in close touch" with the bride.

'02 **Ephram F. Eff**'s paper "To Punch a Duck" was Second Runner-Up at Phi Alpha Beta's Western Regional Haiku Kegger.

'01 **Parker Mlanghan** was recently spotted giving blood near a flophouse in downtown Butte. "The death-ray scheme didn't work out," he explained: "Damn Feds wouldn't fork over the last mill for research. Now I got a pistol that gives lab rats a toothache, some goon's trying to repossess the atomic accelerator and the Pinkville experiment turned everyone semi-visible. Still, Montana's had a great ski season!"

'98 Reaction to **Hilary Codweiler**'s series of children's books—*Kitty Williams: Junior Ontologist*—continues to grow; this fall will see the marketing of a line of Kitty Williams™ Morally-Accurate Syllogisms.

'97 **Laura Estherjill** is an Administrative Assistant on the Titling & Morony Line, a barge that carries Xerox paper to Administrative Assistants in the Portland School District. "I've learned so much about so much that I can't understand why everyone's so bored with so much about everything I've learned so much about . . ." her letter begins.

'94 **Frank O'Goldman** reports that Cheeseball's, his downtown D.C. eaterie, "pretty much runs itself." A recent customer was alumni **Butch Cavanaugh ('83)** from Virginia, accompanied by an unidentified lady "with a helluva built."

'93 We sadly note the passing of **Maura Plank**, struck by a runaway macro virus on the information superhighway. From *The Silicon Centinel* (a Web bi-minutely): "Ms. Plank, a Beta-tester for MindWear, the venerable Internet virtually like-new clothing store, was donning a turtleneck cyber-sweater when she was blindsided by an AI agent having cybersex with a teenager in a Rangoon chat-room." In lieu of flowers, her family requests forwarding three days of spam to Bill Gates.

'89 "Those of us active in the vitally crucial world of small-particle physics," writes **Lalo Montpar**, "deeply resent aspersions cast by the Neo-Communist, EU-dominated big-particle physics lobby. During the following year, I expect to bring my slide show 'Small-Particle: The American Molecular Physics' to Senior Citizens groups, the bedridden, and those generally unable to move."

'88 "Still enjoying what I like to call 'Our Nation's Capitol,'" writes **Archibald Kadish III** from Washington. He reports seeing **Butch Cavanaugh ('83)** recently: "I noticed him in the garden at dawn, crouching behind my dahlias while exchanging intimacies against a leather-clad woman with a helluva built."

'87 The Class of '87 had a mini-reunion in an unlikely place: the Valley Mount Psychiatric Ward. "Do we get extra credit for this?" quips **Helen Toledo**. "**Lyle Rasmuss**, **Benjamin Cord**, the **Saliva Twins**, Astrology Prof **Marimba Solipsus** and I all had severe emotional probs the same week!

But guess who's giving us electro-shock—(former lacrosse coach) **'Snuggles' Terrain**!"

'84   *A Mooing of Sofas*, **Sasha Hermosil**'s translation of the writings of fourteenth-century Italo-Nipponese poet Benvenuto Icagami, is now in its eighth printing. She anticipates sales moving into double figures if her parents purchase.

'82   **Barb** (Mrs. Doug Twart) **Klempsch** informs us that the sixties are finally over. "BARB'S CRASH PADS ('Realty—what a concept') has become U D-ZERVIT CONDOS ('Real Estate with a Vengeance'). Doug and I faced facts too and got a divorce. We're still friends, of course, and I'll be able to see the rubber plant on alternate weekends after I tell him where the Saturn's buried."

'80   **Randall Malloy** says "Not much excitement since Hal's wedding (see **'03**), although sometimes the mail's late. My dad, Harv, is still passed away. My faithful wife **Sonja** (**'83**) is spending a lot of time in Langley visiting sick people. Please tell alumni to stop by for a free speedometer-cable check."

'78   **Jon Drobelbush** has resigned from International Dynamics' Puppetry Division to protest the Spanish-American War.

'77   **Nellie Fox**'s hobby, time travel, has been causing some problems. "It's not enough that I spent most of last summer stuck in the eighth dimension," she writes. "Now I find that visiting the twelfth century two weeks ago somehow made my Blastercaster records disappear. I spent so much time (and money!) amassing a complete collection of the most popular rock group of the seventies and now, poof. Love to hear from any house-mates passing through Lynchburg."

'74   **Chester Bash** was recently named one of Seattle's Outstanding Young Black Women, a source of intense frustration and bewilderment to him.

'71   **Lola Malloy**, sister of **Randall ('80)**, is a "resingle" in Boston. "It just didn't work out with Sid but I'm looking forward to my work with Tangential Press as editor on the 'Fardwark the Aardvark' series. I also hope to assist Fardwark **(Lester Dunballs '70)** on his upcoming marimba album of children's sports poetry. P.S. to my old roomies: Saw **BC ('83)** in DC for AM SM in some alum's garden. What a hoot!"

'69   It's been a challenging few months for **Robert "Bob" Benoit**, who was locked in a broom closet by dissatisfied employees. "I can't get out," he writes, "and am hoping this letter is found before I suffocate."

'67   **Betsy Panacea** continues to be a wife and mother, show bulldogs, and play prominent parts in local theatrical productions, such as Third Guard in *Hamlet* (William Shakespeare), Offstage Voice in *The Skin of Our Teeth*, and the title role in *Waiting for Godot*.

'64   **Phillip Treacle** is teaching supply-side genetics at Cal Utah and finishing a book that explains how dramatic tax cuts will improve the gene pool. "Wish I could make the 40th get-together, but I can't."

'62   **Cecilia Styx** works at the Socio-Esthetic Pain Control Center, helping people who are uncomfortable in Laundromats. "All our training units are solar-powered!" she writes.

'61   **Farville N.** (Mrs. the late Harv) **"Bosoms" Malloy** was delighted to receive a "fun-packed" visit from **Butch Cavanaugh ('83)**, an old friend of the family, following which she was hospitalized for exhaustion.

'59   **Maureen Corona**, author of last year's *Feel My Tummy, Lord*, is active in "Pittsburgh Presbyterian Concerned Interaction," a quasi-denominational group that encourages self-expression by area Catholic, Jewish, Protestant and

African-American youth couples who can't pay their phone bills. "On our three-week retreats, we emphasize movement therapy, alpha training, spiritual massage and variable-rate loans to show that we truly care about helping youngsters avoid missing a chance not to learn about how to better get in touch with themselves or their society."

'58   "Anyone heard from **Daria Hummel ('59)**? She's still got my comb!" is the sad plaint of **Thalia St. Bill**, still consumed by irrelevant frippery with relish.

'56   From our Odyssey files, the recent trip of Carole and **Joe Flapling** deserves honors: "We started out in Genoa, Italy, and traveled north to North Genoa, where we sampled the table salt and bought postcards till dawn. Then we returned to Genoa and waited for the next boat north, which we discovered was manned by Venusians! We were brought to Venus, laughed at, and returned to . . . North Genoa!, where we found a postcard shop owner who believed our story then gave us a glass of water."

'55   **Fiona Brine** is a bit "off my feed" but otherwise doing great. She writes "Our sons and daughters have given us twenty-three grandchildren, most of whom we've given back."

'52   **Frieda (Mrs. Theodore Bowles '48) Phlegm**, a retired glass-eye blower from Fresno, has long been active in community affairs. She served as vice president of the Fresno Socialist Workers Party Teen Bowling Team Glee Club, was honored with a Promptness Citation by the Courtney Thorne-Smith/*According to Jim* Boosters (East Fresno Div.), and remains Tri-Fresno Phone Bank Resource Person for the U.S. Water Sports Safety Squad Civilian Review Board Pep Gals.

'49   "Darn my hat!" exclaims **Beverly Sornstra** of Pinkville, Montana. "Where *is* everyone? Whenever I go outside no one's there, and I'm not kidding! Nobody! I look and I look and sometimes I see these sort of half shapes moving around. What the heck is happening? If this is some kind of joke it's not very funny!"

'48   **Jock Cavanaugh**, living the life of Riley, has been served with a lawsuit by Riley, who wants his life back. "I won it fair and square in a poker game," declares Jock. "Let *him* take the flak for my bimbo son **('83)** with the floozies hangin' off him like flies on a old dried-up piece of goose-liver pâté— I *like* bein' an Admiral!"

'35   **Fred Kolodny** recently died and would like to hear from other dead alumni.

—**David Misch**

Contributor Notes

Henry Alford is the author of *Municipal Bondage, Out There,* and *Big Kiss: One Actor's Desperate Attempt to Claw His Way to the Middle,* which won the Thurber Prize for American Humor Honor Award.

Steve Altes is a former aerospace engineer turned humorist. He just wanted to follow in the footsteps of those other great comedians who began as rocket scientists: Dr. Wernher von Braun, Buzz Aldrin, and Pauly Shore. His first two books (*The Little Book of Bad Business Advice* and *If You Jam the Copier, Bolt*) mocked the heinousness of office life, but that freaking Scott Adams just seems to gobble up the entire office satire market. In 2003 he optioned a loosely autobiographical screenplay to a major Hollywood producer. So that was nice. His writing has appeared in places.

Ethan Anderson did not medal during the Winter Olympic Games in Lillehammer, Nagano, or Salt Lake City. He will also not medal in the 2006 Winter Olympic Games in Torino, Italy. He copes by being a writer in Berkeley, California, and staying mad at Sara Hughes, because "she knows what she did." What started as a small humor concern in a North Seattle garage has grown, ten years later, into a small humor concern in a North Seattle garage.

Sara Hope Anderson is like any other highly paid single professional male, except that she is an underpaid married mother of one. She lives in Boston. Or Chicago.

Larry Arnstein (Ironic Times Newscrawl) is the coauthor, with his son Zack, of *The Dog Ate My Résumé: Survival Tips for Life After College* (Santa Monica Press, April 2004).

Phil Austin, best known for his many years with the Firesign Theatre, is the creator of "Phil Austin's Blog of the Unknown," is Nick Danger, is married to Oona, is working on his gigantic novel called *Beaverteeth,* and hosts the TV show *Art of the Insane*. You can't get as confusing a life. You don't want to try, believe me.

Andrew Barlow has contributed humor pieces to *The New Yorker*. He is coauthor, with Kent Roberts, of *A Portrait of Yo Mama As a Young Man*, a humor book published by Crown.

Michael Ian Black is a celebrity (very famous). You have undoubtedly seen him on any number of obscure basic cable television programs including *The State* on MTV, *Viva Variety* on Comedy Central, and *I Love the '70s* and *I Love the '80s* on VH1. He starred on the NBC show *Ed*, and was also the voice and hirsute forearm of the once-ubiquitous (now deceased) Pets.com sock puppet. He is also one-third of the comedy trio Stella.

Roy Blount Jr.'s latest book is *Robert E. Lee*, a biography. In the offing are a cat book with photographer Valerie Shaff, a book about New Orleans, and a collection of essays about the South. He appears regularly on NPR's *Wait, Wait . . . Don't Tell Me*.

Joe Bob Briggs is a Texas satirist and TV personality who is best known as the world's foremost drive-in movie critic (also the world's only drive-in movie critic). His latest book is *Profoundly Disturbing: Shocking Movies That Changed History*. Among his proudest achievements is his commentary track for the Millennium Edition DVD of *I Spit on Your Grave*.

Stephanie Brooks is a conceptual artist living in Chicago. She has exhibited her work nationally and internationally since the Clinton administration, including exhibits in Chicago, Denmark, London, Los Angeles, New York, Vienna, and Phoenix. She is a part-time sculpture instructor at the School of the Art Institute of Chicago. Her artwork is available at Rhona Hoffman Gallery; Peter Blum Gallery, New York; Rocket Gallery, London; and online at www.stephaniebrooks.com.

Nancy Cohen lives in Los Angeles and has written for the TV shows *King of Queens, Blind Date,* and *Sabrina, the Teenage Witch*. She would really like to get a dog that will fit in a little pink bag but her husband won't let her.

David Colman writes about art, fashion design, and other symptoms of society for the *New York Times,* and other publications.

Jill A. Davis is the author of *Girls' Poker Night*. She was a writer for the *Late Show with David Letterman,* where she received five Emmy nominations. She lives in New York City with her husband and daughter.

D. Ellis Dickerson, underachieving wunderkind and former greeting card writer for Hallmark, is now based in Tallahassee, Florida. His work has appeared in *The Atlantic*—and *The New Yorker* and the *New York Times*, if the definition of "work" can be extended to include crossword puzzles. He proudly notes that his humor book, *The Potluck Hall of Fame and Other Bizarre Christian Lists,* written while he was still under the influence of conservative Christianity, made back its modest advance before tumbling out of print.

Andrés du Bouchet is a comedian based in New York City. He is the creator and host of the popular weekly variety show *Giant Tuesday Night of Amazing Inventions and Also There Is a Game* at the St. Marks Theater, and he is a frequent contributor to *Jest* magazine. He lives in Manhattan with his wonderful girlfriend Rebecca.

Brian Frazer is a former stand-up comic who writes for *Esquire* as well as a bevy of TV shows, most of which you probably haven't TiVo'd. He needs only two more stamps on his SubClub card to earn a free Turkey Melt.

Peter Gaido, a Chicago attorney, found he could understand Baby Language after being hit in the head with a foul ball at a Cubs game. Peter is one of the funniest attorneys at the firm of Gaido & Fintzen in Chicago, Illinois. Either that says something good about his sense of humor or something bad about his ability to practice law. Peter lives with his wife and three children (ages 5, 3, and 1) in St. Charles, Illinois, and, although he speaks their language, neither his sons nor his daughter listen to him.

David K. Gibson writes songs, recipes, short stories and things like the things that are included in this book, mostly from Colorado, but sometimes from Texas. He went to seventh grade with Parker Posey, back when she called herself "Missy." She probably wouldn't remember him, though.

Tom Gliatto is a playwright, humorist, and writer at *People* magazine.

Ben Greenman is an editor at *The New Yorker*, and the author of *Superbad*, a collection of fiction and humor. His work appeared in *More Mirth of a Nation*.

Kevin Guilfoile is the coauthor (with John Warner) of *My First Presidentiary: A Scrapbook by George W. Bush*. His work has appeared in the *New Republic, Salon, Business 2.0,* and *Maxim*. He is a contributing writer to themorningnews.org and, under the name Carlton Doby, author of the "Brain Exploder" column at www.McSweeneys.net.

Bob Hirshon has been a humor writer for nearly thirty years, in temperament and general inclination. He is now adding to that formidable record by actually writing things, the first of which appears in this volume. Hirshon hosts the daily radio feature *Science Update,* heard on finer radio stations coast to coast. He led a team that won the George Foster Peabody Award for a weekly science radio drama for kids, and how many people can say that? Hirshon is a singer and guitarist, and has composed and performed two songs for NPR. Along with Justin Warner (also in this volume), he works at the American Association for the Advancement of Science, the largest, oldest and now—who would argue?—funniest science association in the world.

Gregory Hischak is a playwright and performer. In addition to this mighty tome, his work has appeared in *More Mirth of a Nation*.

Marc's Accomplishments	Percentage of U.S. Population That Can Say the Same Thing
Graduated high-school *and* learned to drive by age 18	83%
Stand-up comedian	91%
A dozen TV appearances as a comedian	16%
Had great ideas for episodes of *Seinfeld*	94%
Was paid to write his ideas for *Seinfeld*	.05%
Average height, average build	50%
Author	33%
Two of his books are very funny and sold well	1%
One book, *Sleeping with Your Gynecologist,* is slated to become a sitcom	.0001%
Can blow air through his eye	.3%
Has written screenplays	66%
Had a screenplay optioned	65.8%
Seems to have recovered from rotator cuff surgery	1%
Right for your job	0%

The preceding chart should give an understanding of **Marc Jaffe**'s unique abilities and a sampling of his career path.

Renee A. James is a freelance writer. Her weekly opinion column appears online at www.mcall.com. She works at Rodale Books in Emmaus, Pennsylvania.

Merle Kessler is a writer and performer in San Francisco. His latest work is *Broke*, a live performance in his persona of Ian Shoales, concerning the state of being broke, and the wretched century so far.

Joe Lavin is a humorist from Somerville, Massachusetts. His work has appeared in the *Boston Globe, Salon, The Globe and Mail, Computeredge*, and several other publications. He also writes a weekly humor column at www.joelavin.com.

M. Sweeney Lawless, whose worked appeared in *More Mirth of a Nation*, is a writer, director, and performer living in New York City. Meg is a founding member of Young Survival Coalition (www.youngsurvival.org) and can hide up to five bees in her mouth.

Ian Lendler's first children's picture book, *An Undone Fairy Tale*, will be published by Simon & Schuster in Spring 2005. When not bringing laughter to the world, he lounges around his Manhattan apartment in silk pajamas, huffing glue.

Harmon Leon is a writer/comedian from San Francisco. He is the author of two books, *The Harmon Chronicles* and *Scam America* (ECW Press). Harmon has also written for NPR, *Salon, Details,* and the BBC. He has also performed comedy at the Edinburgh, Melbourne, and Montreal comedy festivals. Harmon is low in sodium and perfect for the elderly.

Danny Liebert is a humorist, dealer in used scholarly books, and Manhattan-based stand-up comedian who has been called one of the best joke writers in the country. He marches to the same goddam drummer everybody else does.

Rod Lott is the editor of *Hitch: The Journal of Pop Culture Absurdity* (www.hitchmagazine.com). The Oklahoma City–based freelance writer, graphic designer, and work-from-home dad has appeared in *More Mirth of a Nation*, *101 Damnations*, *The Book of Zines,* and national magazines you'd only know about if you are an old, crusty family physician.

Kurt Luchs (kurtluchs@aol.com) manages the American Comedy Network (www.americancomedynetwork.com), a radio syndicator. He contributes to the *Onion*, *The New Yorker*, McSweeney's Internet Tendency, and *The Late Late Show*, edits The Big Jewel (www.thebigjewel.com), writes screenplays and books, and also has a paper route.

Paul Maliszewski's writing has appeared in *Harper's, The Paris Review*, and the Pushcart Prize anthologies.

Mabel Maney is the author of *The Case of the Not-So-Nice Nurse, The Case of the Good-for-Nothing Girlfriend*, and *A Ghost in the Closet*, gay parodies of Nancy Drew and the Hardy Boys. Her new book, *The Girl with the Golden Bouffant*, is available in fine bookshops everywhere. She lives in San Francisco with two shelties. Hobbies include picking dog hair off her clothes, complaining about the Bush administration, and making new friends.

Andrew Marlatt is the author of *Economy of Errors*, the founder of SatireWire.com, and has contributed to numerous magazines, newspapers, and books of humor. Of all the contributors, he is the only one to win a Presidential Physical Fitness Award in sixth and seventh grade . . . well, at least he's the only one making a big deal out of it.

David Martin is an Ottawa attorney and contributor to *101 Damnations: The Humorists' Tour of Personal Hells*. His humor appears in the *Chicago Tribune, Los Angeles Times, Washington Post*, and the *New York Times*.

Michael Martone, author of *The Blue Guide to Indiana*, is publishing his memoirs entitled *Contributor Notes*, made up of contributors' notes published in the contributors' notes sections of magazines and literary journals often without any other contribution to the publication.

Michael Martone was born in Fort Wayne, Indiana, which is located on the confluence of three rivers—the St. Joseph, the St. Mary, and the Maumee. The city is situated on the summit of the eastern continental divide, giving it its nickname, the Summit City. The elevation, however, is only 765 feet above sea level, and the variation between the Atlantic and Mississippi basins is, in Fort Wayne, a matter of a few feet either way. Martone regards this unique topography as a contributing influence upon his aesthetic. The fact that the tributaries of the Maumee, flowing from the north and east, contribute to a river that then flows back the same way, north and east, astounds him. That and the fact that the river that issues from the confluence of the St. Joseph and St. Mary rivers was not named, for some reason, the Jesus.

Michael Martone was born in Fort Wayne, Indiana, where from an early age he entered contests and sweepstakes he found advertised on the side panels of cereal boxes or listed in his local newspaper. Often, he was required to collect and send box tops from specially marked packages or proof-of-purchase seals along with filled-in application forms. He would fill out pads of entry forms by hand to comply with the instruction in the fine print against photocopying or employing any means of mechanical reproduction. He wrote his name, address, and phone number over and over so that any time he picked up a pen or pencil he automatically began to print (the instructions always asked that he print) his contact information. His mother tracked his winnings. She kept a scrapbook she labeled "My

Achievements" where she taped in copies of coupons and receipts sent to Martone to redeem the prizes and awards, the congratulatory letters, and the original game rules. After all those blank entry blanks, Martone gravitated to the contests asking for a bit of his creative effort, a drawing or a brief essay as well as the completion of requisite entry form. The essays were his favorite since he couldn't draw to save his life. The rules always asked for the submission to be of a certain word length, 100 words or less or 250 words or less. That formulation of words in the guidelines always disturbed Martone's mother, who was an English teacher. She corrected the instructions, in red pencil no less, inserting "fewer" above the crossed-out "less." Martone liked the puzzle of the number of words, liked using every word allowed, liked to imagine that someone some-where actually read his little essays, counted the words as he or she did so, even though he suspected, quite early, that his efforts were simply more elaborate entry forms. The winners, runners-ups, and honorable mentions were all, no doubt, selected by the usual method of random drawing. Martone became adept at the form. His specialty was the use of words compounded by employing a hyphen such as "proof-of-purchase" or "runners-up." The grafting counted as one word instead of two or three. In high school he obsessively entered such essay contests sponsored by civic organizations and church groups, soliciting his thoughts on patriotic themes, good citizenship, personal health, and public sanitation. He often won contests and was invited to luncheon meetings of appreciative Rotarians, Lions, Zontas, and Veterans who appreciated the brevity of the winning essays. Years later, Martone is still entering contests, writing tiny paragraphs of prose. Now, oddly, these contests require that he pay to enter, more like a state lottery but with better odds. Martone likes using long titles. He figures those words don't count. Today, he writes on his computer. It has a word count feature. He pushes one button, and he automatically knows where he stands. His mother no longer has to count the words by hand, looking up at him at the end and whispering, "Fewer."

Four More Brief Contributor Notes by **Michael Martone**:

Michael Martone published his first book, *Big Words*, in graduate school. The children's book could only use thirty, age-appropriate words taken from the Dolch Word List. A kind of poetry.

Michael Martone grew up in Fort Wayne. Philo T. Farnsworth, inventor of electronic television, was his neighbor. Martone spied on Farnsworth. He watched the inventor watch the local stations sign off.

Michael Martone grew up in Fort Wayne. Each August, his mother took him downtown to shop for new underwear (briefs). Always August meant underwear. Later, married, Martone switched to boxers.

Michael Martone worked for the Fort Wayne newspapers where he wrote the obituaries and maintained the morgue. Every day he would add details to his own obit he kept on file.

Patty Marx writes TV scripts, screenplays, humor, and nonfiction for both children and adults. Her options abound. Recent work has appeared in *The New Yorker*.

Kim McCann grew up in Tecumseh, Michigan, lived in Colorado for a while, and now resides in Los Angeles. In her free time, she writes stuff. Her plays, *Yard Sale* and *Ockham's Raiser*, were produced by Trade City Productions in Santa Monica.

Writer and executive producer **Peter Mehlman** has been a writer for the *Washington Post*, a writer and producer for "SportsBeat" with Howard Cosell, and a freelancer for such national publications as the *New York Times* magazine, *GQ,* and *Elle*. In 1989 he moved to the city "where crazy dreams can come true, the place to come when you really want to change your life—Los Angeles," where he wrote for the first full season of *Seinfeld* as a program consultant (1991–92) and, over the next six years, worked his way up to co-executive producer. In 1997, Mehlman joined DreamWorks and created *"It's like, you know . . . ,"* a scathing and incisive look at life in the city of Los Angeles.

One of America's best known, funniest illustrators, **Rick Meyerowitz** has created thousands of illustrations for advertising agencies and magazines, including the once hilarious, now hilariously defunct *National Lampoon*. (Yes, he did that Mona Gorilla cover as well as the *Animal House* movie poster.) His publications include three *Nose Masks* books, *Dodosaurs: The Dinosaurs That Didn't Make It*, and *Elvis the Bulldozer*. Rick also adapted and illustrated two videos, *Paul Bunyan* and *Rip Van Winkle*. Rick and his friend **Maira Kalman**, who should be listed under the "K's," created the most talked-about *New Yorker* cover of 2001, "New Yorkistan," about which the *New York Times* wrote "when their cover came out, a dark cloud seemed to lift." Maira is the author and illustrator of several books, including the popular Max the Dog series.

Bryan J. Miller, author and former restaurant critic for the *New York Times*, writes about food and wine for various publications. He is currently a columnist for the *New York Observer*.

J. B. Miller is the author of *The Satanic Nurses and Other Literary Parodies* (St. Martin's Press) as well as an out-of-print novel, *My Life in Action Painting*. His plays, including *Bobby Supreme*, *White Lies*, and *Shirkers*, have been widely produced in New York City (and once, by mistake, in Canada). He regularly peppers the *New York Times* with inappropriate op-eds, and can often be seen ranting at local kids to get registered. He's seriously threatening to move to London, or maybe Sullivan Street.

After conquering the people of Rigel 3, **David Misch** decided to conquer Earth by publishing short humor pieces. He has also written and/or produced numerous TV series, including the Emmy Award–winning *Mork and Mindy* and the Emmy Award–losing *Duckman*. He is currently writing an autobiographical note for *May Contain Nuts*.

Jim Mullen writes the Hot Sheet for *Entertainment Weekly* and is the author of *It Takes a Village Idiot* about his experience buying a weekend house in the country. He is also the author of *Baby's First Tattoo* and its soon to be published sequel, *My First Wedding Planner*.

Matt Neuman (Ironic Times newscrawl) has written, produced, and watched numerous TV shows. His work has also appeared in the *New York Times*, the *Realist*, *Speak*, and *More Mirth of a Nation*. The rest of his oeuvre is available at www.mattneuman.com.

Mark O'Donnell won a Tony as coauthor of the Broadway musical *Hairspray*, and his recent comic novels include *Getting over Homer* and *Let Nothing You Dismay*, both short-listed, if not finalists, for the Thurber Prize in American Humor.

P. J. O'Rourke is a correspondent for *The Atlantic* and the author of ten books, the most recent of which is *The CEO of the Sofa*.

Ed Page is the copyeditor for the humor Web site the Big Jewel (www.thebigjewel.com). His writing has been published by *McSweeney's*, *ReadyMade*, and other fine magazines. He lives in Seattle.

Alysia Gray Painter lives in Los Angeles. Other work of hers has appeared in *101 Damnations*, *More Mirth of a Nation*, *Bark* magazine, PBS, McSweeney's Internet Tendency, and Modern Humorist.

Neil Pasricha is a freelance humor writer living in Toronto. In addition to founding www.thebigjewel.com, Neil has contributed to *Cosmopolitan*, Yahoo! Internet Life, *New York*, Modern Humorist, and McSweeney's Internet Tendency. He can be reached at neil@thebigjewel.com. Why not drop him a line? He's a real pleasure.

Humor pieces by **Louis Phillips** appeared in *More Mirth of a Nation* and his collection of short stories, The Bus to the Moon, published by Fort Schuyler Press. Livingston Press recently published his sequence of poems, *R.I.P.*, based on the legend of Rip Van Winkle. He lives in New York City and is definitely not a Republican.

Judith Podell's humor has appeared in the *Village Voice*, *Mademoiselle*, the *Washington Post*, and the *Journal of Employee Benefits and Compensation*. A collection of her short stories, *Blues for Beginners: Rants and Obsessions*, was published in 2002 by Argonne House Press. Her website is www.shoppinggoddess.com.

Neal Pollack is the author of *The Neal Pollack Anthology of American Literature*, *Poetry and Other Poems*, and *Never Mind the Pollacks: A Rock and Roll Novel*. He frequently records and performs his work.

Daniel Radosh (www.radosh.net) is a freelance writer and contributing editor at *The Week*. Like Jonathan Lethem, he lives and grew up in Brooklyn. Unlike Lethem, he never managed to cash in on it.

Laurie Rosenwald is the World's Most Commercial Artist and principal of www.rosenworld.com, an overfed, undertaxed, government-subsidized corporation with wholly owned subsidiaries in Gothenburg, Sweden, and TuCan, an up-and-coming New York neighborhood formerly known as "Too Close to Canal Street." Her illustrations appear regularly in *The New Yorker* and many other fine publications. Actually there is no studio, she usually works alone, and rosenworld doesn't exist. In spite of this, rosenworld.com was launched in 1995. Her hyper-illustrated, overdesigned guidebook, *New York Notebook* (Chronicle Books) includes the Haitian Cab Driver Cold Remedy and the address of Hervé Villechaise's tailor. For some reason, she was chosen to portray the arguably pivotal role of "woman" on the season-five opener of *The Sopranos*.

Jay Ruttenberg is a staff writer at *Time Out* (New York) and editor of the *Lowbrow Reader*, a fanzine about comedy.

Lane Sarasohn (Ironic Times newscrawl) is a comedy writer (*The Groove Tube, Not Necessarily the News*) and a Web designer (Ironic Times, Temple of Dreams). He first became interested in irony when a book by Sir Isaac Newton fell off a shelf in his high school library and struck him on the head.

Bill Scheft is a longtime writer for *Late Show with David Letterman*. He is the author of a novel, *The Ringer*, and contributed to the inaugural volume *Mirth of a Nation*.

Stephen Sherrill has written for *The New Yorker, New York Times, Esquire*, and the *Late Show with David Letterman*.

Matthew Summers-Sparks is a writer in Washington, D.C. His work has appeared in *More Mirth of a Nation, 101 Damnations, Mississippi Review, Gargoyle, Pindeldyboz, Washington City Paper*, and on the McSweeney's Internet Tendency and Creative Nonfiction Web sites.

Davis Sweet edits *The Bean Magazine* (www.beanmag.com), a political satire site. His writing, humorous and otherwise, has appeared in national publications, including the *Village Voice*, and he is the coauthor of the comic novel *Make Over*, with Rod Lott.

In addition to being a Gwyneth Paltrow look-alike and *Boston Herald* columnist, **Beth Teitell** is the author of the forthcoming *From Here to Maternity: The Education of a Rookie Mom*, which Broadway Books will publish in 2005. Her Web site is www.teitell.com. **Ken Mandl** is a pediatric emergency physician and medical researcher on the Harvard Medical School faculty. He is married to Beth Teitell.

Richard Thompson lives in Arlington, Virginia, with his wife and two daughters. His drawings (which are collected in his recent book, *Richard's Poor Almanac*) appear in the *Washington Post*, and in *The New Yorker*, *U.S. News & World Report*, etc. Since breaking his toe in a dancing accident, he's been forced to draw with his hands.

Vincent van Gogh is a Dutch-born Etch A Sketch artist and tumbler. His artwork has appeared in *Highlights*, *Cheese & Easels Online*, *State Route Monthly*, *Dutch-Born Artists Journal*, and *More Mirth of a Nation*.

Jeff Ward has written comedy for *Saturday Night Live*, NPR, and Modern Humorist, and songs for the musical *Cold Feet*. He lives in New York City and is currently understudying the role of Dream Laurie in the Broadway revival of *Oklahoma!*

John Warner is coauthor (with Kevin Guilfoile) of *My First Presidentiary: A Scrapbook by George W. Bush*. He is a contributing writer to www.themorningnews.org and editor of McSweeney's Internet Tendency. His work has appeared in *Book* magazine, *Salon*, and *Utne* among other places. He teaches in the Department of Communication at Virginia Tech University.

Justin Warner is a playwright, improviser, and science writer. He was an original member of Washington Improv Theater (WIT), D.C.'s leading improv comedy troupe. He lives with his wife, Courtney Birch, in New York City, where he is a member of the Ensemble Studio Theatre's CityLab and the BMI Musical Theater Workshop.

Holly Webber is an encyclopedia editor and playwright in New York City. Her sketches and monologues have been performed by the comedy group Rumble in the Red Room at PS-NBC and other venues.

Permissions

Also Edited by Michael J. Rosen

Mirth of a Nation: The Best Contemporary Humor

More Mirth of a Nation: The Best Contemporary Humor

The Dog Department: James Thurber on Hounds, Scotties, and Talking Poodles

BOOKS BY MICHAEL J. ROSEN

MIRTH OF A NATION
The Best Contemporary Humor
ISBN 0-06-095321-7 (paperback)
A premier showcase of great literary humorists
and masters of the journalistic jab, the social spoof,
the satire, the tirade, and the send-up.
Contributors include Rick Moranis, David Rakoff,
Michael Feldman, Mark O'Donnell, Paul Rudnick,
Gary Trudeau, and many others.

MORE MIRTH OF A NATION
The Best Contemporary Humor
ISBN 0-06-095322-5 (paperback)
Sixty-five writers deck the halls of hilarity with witty,
wise work including Ian Frazier, Merrill Markoe, Andy
Borowitz, Bruce McCall, Bobbie Ann Mason, Paul
Rudnick, Henry Alford, Tony Hendra, Will Durst,
Richard Bausch, and Susan McCarthy. Also featuring
the undiscovered Etch-a-Sketch drawings of Van Gogh
and much more.

MAY CONTAIN NUTS
A Very Loose Canon of American Humor
ISBN 0-06-051626-7 (paperback)
With 70 contributors and over 150 shots from the
loose cannon of American humor, this all-star edition
features *Ed*'s Michael Ian Black, *Seinfeld*'s Peter Mehlman,
Hairspray's Mark O'Donnell, the world's foremost drive-in
movie critic, Joe Bob Briggs, and many others.

(((LISTEN TO))) MIRTH OF A NATION • ISBN 0-06-051319-5 (audio cd)
The best of *Mirth of a Nation* and *More Mirth of a Nation*

Don't miss the next book by your favorite author.
Sign up for AuthorTracker by visiting *www.AuthorTracker.com*.

Available wherever books are sold, or call 1-800-331-3761 to order.